Issues in Mathematics Teachi

ARY

Issues in Mathematics Teaching brings together a number of key, and sometimes controversial, issues in mathematics education, which will be of concern to all those teaching the mathematics. It focuses in particular upon the social context of teaching mathematics and its impact upon teachers and pupils with diverse social and cultural backgrounds. The issues covered include:

- the role played by mathematics textbooks
- the national numeracy strategy
- incorporating ICT
- international comparisons of mathematical attainment
- the values adopted, implicitly and explicitly in mathematics teaching
- how to use—and not to use—classroom resources

All chapters benefit from being informed by current state-of-the-art research in mathematics education and each of the contributors has an international reputation in his or her field. Every chapter offers opportunities to reflect on the issues involved and directs the reader's attention and activity to the critical aspects of each issue. Written with new teachers in mind, *Issues in Mathematics Teaching* makes complex issues accessible without trivialisation and will be of interest to all those charged with teaching mathematics.

Peter Gates teaches at the University of Nottingham's School of Education and has previously taught at the Open University and the University of Bath. Prior to this he worked as a mathematics teacher for thirteen years, including four years as head of department at a Milton Keynes comprehensive and a spell in Moçambique. He has edited and written numerous books and articles on teaching mathematics and is currently interested in how practices in schools in general, and mathematics education in particular, contribute to social exclusion. Peter is a member of the International Committee of the International Group for the Psychology of Mathematics Education. Peter is a member of the International Committee of the International Group for the Psychology of Mathematics Education.

Issues in Subject Teaching Series
Edited by Susan Capel, Jon Davison,
James Arthur and John Moss

Other titles in the series:
Issues in Design and Technology
Issues in English Teaching
Issues in Geography Teaching
Issues in Physical Education Teaching
Issues in Modern Foreign Language Teaching
Issues in Music Teaching
Issues in Religious Education Teaching
Issues in Science Teaching
Issues in Teaching using ICT

Issues in Mathematics Teaching

Edited by Peter Gates

London and New York

First published 2001
by RoutledgeFalmer
11 New Fetter Lane, London EC4P 4EE

Simultaneously published in the USA and Canada
by RoutledgeFalmer
29 West 35th Street, New York, NY 10001

RoutledgeFalmer is an imprint of the Taylor & Francis Group

© 2001 Edited by Peter Gates

Typeset in Goudy by
Exe Valley Dataset Ltd, Exeter, Devon
Printed and bound in Great Britain by Biddles Ltd, Guildford and King's Lynn

British Library Cataloguing in Publication Data
A catalogue record for this book is available from the British Library

Library of Congress Cataloging in Publication Data
A library catalog for this book has been requested.

ISBN 0–415–23864–1 (hbk)
ISBN 0–415–23865–X (pbk)

Contents

Tables

Figures

Contributors

Janet Ainley is a senior lecturer in the Mathematics Education Research Centre, University of Warwick, and is also Deputy Director of the Warwick Institute of Education. Her main research interest is in the design of purposeful pedagogic settings that exploit the potential of computers in the learning and teaching of data handling and algebra. She is co-director of the Primary Laptop Project, based in a Warwickshire school, and has a national and international reputation in this field. She publishes regularly through international conferences and journals, and is the author of a popular book on the use of IT in primary mathematics.

Paul Andrews spent thirteen years teaching mathematics in three secondary comprehensive schools, the last five of which were as head of department. Since then he has spent ten years working in teacher education in both Manchester and Cambridge and has extensive experience of both pre-service and in-service award-bearing courses. His principal area of interest is in making mathematics accessible to all children – hence his exploration of the ways in which the subject is taught overseas – and sees equality of opportunity as a much compromised principle in British education, not least because of successive governments' obsessive drive towards differentiation with its systematic denial, for so many pupils, of access to the curriculum. He is also fascinated by teachers' understanding of, and beliefs about, mathematics and how they impact on classroom activity and, importantly, children's learning. He rejects unequivocally utilitarianism as a curricular justification for the subject.

Mike Askew is lecturer in mathematics education at King's College, University of London. A former primary school teacher for six years, he now researches, lectures and writes on teaching primary mathematics. He was a member of the advisory group to the National Numeracy Project and worked on both the content of the Project's Framework for teaching mathematics from Reception to Year 6 and the associated training materials. He was director of the Teacher Training Agency funded 'Effective Teachers of Numeracy in Primary Schools' and Nuffield Foundation funded 'Raising Attainment in Numeracy Project'. Both of these are now being followed up in the five-year Leverhulme Numeracy Research Programme, of which Mike is deputy director.

Alan Bishop is a professor in the Faculty of Education at Monash University in Melbourne, Australia where he has worked since 1992 after leaving Cambridge University and England. He has taught in different school situations and has been involved in teacher initial and in-service training all his working life. He was president of the Mathematical Association in 1991. His research has involved many aspects of classroom teaching and in particular he has researched the area of socio-cultural aspects of mathematics teaching for the last twenty-five years. He is now the director of two large government-funded research projects, one concerned with excellence in mathematics teaching, and the other with values in mathematics education.

Jo Boaler taught mathematics in secondary schools in Inner London and worked at the headquarters of the National Union of Teachers, developing equal opportunities policies. She worked for seven years as a lecturer and researcher at King's College London, and now lives and works in California, where she is an associate professor of mathematics education. Jo is the author of two books. *Experiencing School Mathematics*, was published by the Open University Press in 1997. It reports upon a study of two schools using different mathematics approaches and won a national book award for education in 1997. Jo's more recent book is *Multiple Perspectives on Mathematics Teaching and Learning*, published by Ablex in 2000. It is the first of an international series on mathematics education. Jo is the current president of the International Organization for Women and Mathematics Education.

Barry Cooper is currently Professor of Education, and Director of Research, in the School of Education, University of Durham. His research interests include the sociological study of the school curriculum and assessment, maths education, and Indian primary education. He has recently directed two projects investigating national curriculum testing in maths, both funded by the Economic and Social Research Council. His publications include *Renegotiating Secondary School Mathematics* (Falmer 1985) and *Assessing Children's Mathematical Knowledge: Social Class, Sex and Problem-Solving* (with Máiréad Dunne, Open University Press 2000). He was previously a Reader in Education at the University of Sussex.

Tony Cotton has taught in Sheffield, Leicester and Nottingham. He has worked as a mathematics teacher, an advisory teacher for anti-racist and multicultural education and an advisor to an educational publisher. He grew up in Liverpool and Manchester so is very much attached to northern industrial towns. His main claim to fame is having taught Jarvis Cocker and helping to put on Pulp's first ever gig in City School Hall, Sheffield. Apart from that he has written books on mathematics for pupils and books on teaching for teachers. He has also written several articles for *Mathematics Teaching*. He now works at the Nottingham Trent University in the Faculty of Education and would like to think he was asked to write this chapter because it is an area of work he has been committed to since starting teaching in 1981, rather than because of the fact he is a close colleague of the editor.

Kevin Delaney. After graduating with a degree in chemistry in 1969, Kevin Delaney took the obligatory year off to find himself and then found himself on a primary PGCE course at Southampton University. One of his tutors was Bill Brookes whose wild intellectual ways and intriguing ideas changed his life; he also introduced him to many kindred spirits who belonged to the Association of Teachers of Mathematics (ATM). He taught in 'normal' primary schools for five years in Southampton and Harrow before meeting John Dichmont at an ATM conference and joining him at Lynncroft Primary School in Nottingham in 1976. Here, under John's inspired guidance, his life changed for a second time and he discovered what working with primary age children could really be like when a creative and thoughtful staff dared each other to do useful and interesting things with children. Ten years later, after an M.Phil. with Bill Brookes exploring aspects of his own teaching, he joined Nottingham Trent University to teach on primary mathematics courses and is currently a senior lecturer there. In 1988 his life changed for a third time when he started a time-consuming second career as the father of Jack (11) and Alice (8); this and his first career seem to have taken up most of his waking hours since that time so he is particularly pleased to have found time to write a chapter on a subject close to his heart. From 1990 to 1998 he was consultant editor, with Adrian Pinel, for *Strategies*. He is excited by Islamic patterns and his own and other people's 'Aha!' moments during the teaching and learning of mathematics. He also remains open to the possibility of having his life changed a fourth time.

Paul Dowling is a sociologist. He taught mathematics in schools in and around London for fifteen years before joining the Institute of Education in 1987. He is currently a member of the Culture Communication and Societies academic group at the Institute. His research activities centrally concern the development of 'semiotic sociology' in and through the analysis of texts and practices associated with, amongst other areas: mathematics education; information and communications technologies; non-school pedagogic sites; the media; and the relationships between pedagogic practices and social and community structure. He has been involved with consultancies in the area of research methods in education around the world, particularly in South Africa. His Falmer Press publications include *The Sociology of Mathematics Education: Mathematical Myths, Pedagogic Texts*, *Doing Research/Reading Research: A Mode of Interrogation for Education* (co-authored with Andrew Brown), *Mathematics Versus the National Curriculum* (co-edited with Richard Noss).

Paul Ernest was born in New York but educated in England, where he became a school mathematics teacher in the 1970s. He studied mathematics, logic and philosophy at Sussex and London Universities where he obtained his B.Sc., M.Sc. and Ph.D. degrees. He has previously held lecturing positions in the Universities of Cambridge and the West Indies. Paul Ernest is currently Professor of the Philosophy of Mathematics Education at the University of Exeter, where he directs the masters and doctoral degree programmes in mathematics education. He edits the *Philosophy of Mathematics Education Journal* (web location: http://www.ex.ac.uk/~PErnest/). His main research interests concern fundamental questions about the nature of mathematics and how it relates to teaching, learning and society. His publications include: *The Philosophy of Mathematics Education*, Falmer 1991; *Social Constructivism as a Philosophy of Mathematics*, State University of New York Press, 1998; *Mathematics for Primary Teachers*, Routledge, 2000.

Peter Gates trained as a mathematics teacher in 1975 having successfully remained a student in Manchester for six years. He then taught in the East End of London where mere 11 year olds were so tough they had the capacity to turn his legs to jelly. From there he worked as a *'cooperante'* in the People's Republic of Moçambique, in the aftermath of independence. As a provincial mathematics advisor he worked in rural areas supporting teachers and children. It was the commitment and dedication of people who had so little that has helped him to retain his socialist inclinations ever since. After Moçambique, Peter worked as head of mathematics at Stantonbury Campus in Milton Keynes (with Anne Watson – see below). He considers himself immensely lucky in managing to work with other teachers so fully committed both to mathematics and to teaching for diversity, and held a commitment to teaching in all-attainment groups. Unlike Tony Cotton (see above) he has no major claim to fame – though he did once shake hands with the Duke of Edinburgh who is unlikely to remember the experience. He has so far edited two books – *Conceptualising Reflection in Education* (co-edited with James Calderhead and published by Falmer Press), and this one. He is currently a so-called academic at Nottingham University where he works with students on initial teacher education courses and with local mathematics teachers and children. With Tony Cotton, he established the first Mathematics Education and Society Conference, which is now an important international forum for discussion and dissemination of the social implications of teaching and learning mathematics. Peter got his Ph.D. as this book was going to print, with a thesis exploring the ideological orientations of mathematics teachers. He now spends much of his time trying to explain to his elderly relatives that even though he is a doctor he doesn't know how to cure their bunions or in-growing toenails. Peter has two children – Sophie (born 30th October 1994) and Megan (born 8th July 1998) who, in spite of all the trials and tribulations, make Peter's and his partner Jane's life worth living.

Derek Kassem entered teaching 'late' after a number of different jobs that includes capstan operator, tube guard/motorman and a welfare rights advisor in a law centre. Though he trained for middle schools he actually started teaching in the only all-boys school in Brixton – Tulse Hill. After a couple of years he switched to primary and has been a maths co-coordinator in schools in Tower Hamlets, Southwark and Lambeth. In the early '90s he became involved in providing Inset for a number of LEAs. Since 1996 he has been senior lecturer in mathematics education at Liverpool John Moores University. He has written teaching materials for the primary classroom and co-authored a number of conference papers on primary pupils' attitudes on a range of issues. He is currently researching for his Ph.D. on issues relating to ethnic minority attainment and the National Numeracy Strategy.

Candia Morgan taught mathematics for a number of years in secondary schools and at university level. She has also worked as an advisory teacher for mathematics. In her current position as senior lecturer in mathematics education at the Institute of Education of the University of London, she works with students in initial teacher education and with teachers undertaking further postgraduate study. Her current research interests include the role of language within mathematics education and teachers' assessment of pupils' mathematical activity. She is the author of *Writing Mathematically: The Discourse of Investigation* (Falmer 1998).

Mike Ollerton 'graduated' from the bottom stream (1960–3), leaving school with six O levels, gathered over four years. This experience was to have a profound effect upon his pedagogy for teaching mathematics. He started his teaching career in 1971 at Lowca, a small West Cumbrian primary school. In 1973 he began teaching at Wyndham, an 11–18 school in Egremont. Here he worked with Eric Love, a visionary and inspirational head of department. In 1986 Mike took up a head of department post at an 11–16 comprehensive in Telford, where he guided the department towards constructing mixed-ability teaching methods throughout the age range. He also taught mathematics without using textbooks, instead adopting problem-solving, equipment-based approaches. His work was supported by colleagues and members of the Association of Teachers of Mathematics; from 1986 until 1992 he was involved in the ATM/SEG pilot GCSE project, which at its inception, was based upon a 100 per cent coursework model. From 1990 until 1995 Mike worked part-time (at Keele and Manchester University) as a teacher trainer, continuing as a part-time head of department in Telford. Since 1995 Mike has worked full time at St Martin's College, Lancaster, with pre-service and in-service teachers, teaching undergraduate, postgraduate and Masters students. Mike gained his first degree at the age of 42, an Advanced Diploma at age 43 and completed his M.Phil. in 1997, aged 49. In this project he was strongly supported by Christine Shiu and Anne Watson. All of these qualifications were gained through the Open University, an institution to which he extends his heart-felt admiration. Mike frequently writes articles in *Mathematics Teaching* (the journal of the Association of Teachers of Mathematics); many of which focus on ways of teaching mathematics without needing to separate children into different supposed 'ability' groups. He has recently completed a book with Anne Watson (see below) about teaching mathematics in inclusive classrooms – *Inclusive Mathematics 11–18* (Cassell 2001).

Carrie Paechter is Director of the Centre for Curriculum and Teaching Studies in the Faculty of Education and Language Studies at the Open University. After a degree in Philosophy at Cambridge followed by a return to a further education college to take a second set of A levels, she trained as a primary school teacher and then went to work in a mathematics department in East London. After two more schools and a period as head of mathematics, she went to work as a researcher at King's College, London, looking at how teachers and students negotiated interdisciplinary coursework projects. This stimulated her emerging interest in power/knowledge, gender and curriculum negotiation, on which her research has been focused ever since. She lives in London with her partner, two sons and two stepdaughters, and is currently trying to work out how she can get other parents to take her ideas and concerns about gender and schooling seriously. Her publications include *Crossing Subject Boundaries* (HMSO 1995), *Educating the Other: Gender, Power and Schooling* (Falmer 1998) and *Changing School Subjects: Power, Gender and Curriculum* (Open University Press 2000).

Malcolm Swan taught for several years in a secondary school near Derby before being appointed as a lecturer at the University of Nottingham, where he has now been working for the past twenty years (gulp!). He is particularly interested in the design of teaching and assessment and has been involved in many curriculum, assessment and teacher education research and development projects. His particular interests include finding strategies for engaging people in reflection and discussion about mathematical ideas and approaches. At one time he was involved in creating and then being Chief Examiner at the NEAB (now AQA) for a GCSE called 'Mathematics Through Problem Solving' which, among other things, involved learning number through planning day trips and going on them, space and shape through designing 3-D pop-up cards and board games, and handling data through consumer testing. (This was just before the days when maths was cut up into tiny pieces in the National Curriculum; it all sadly came to an end when exam boards were forced to reduce the number of syllabuses.) He is currently working on balanced assessment of problem solving in mathematics for the Mathematics Assessment Resource Service (MARS) at Nottingham and in the US. (Maybe if it is assessed, teachers will be able to spend more time doing it.)

Anne Watson was a secondary mathematics teacher for many years, working in comprehensive schools. Subsequently she moved into teacher education, professional development and mathematics education research. Her doctoral research was into the informal assessment techniques used by teachers of mathematics and she also works on and writes about other aspects of mathematics classrooms, particularly those which improve achievement for all. Currently she is a lecturer in mathematics education at the University of Oxford, and she has also worked in Pakistan, South Africa and Jamaica. With Mike Ollerton (see above) she has written *Inclusive Mathematics 11–18* (Cassell 2001) which combines her twin passions for mathematics and social justice.

Dylan Wiliam. Despite pressure from his headteacher to introduce setting, Dylan Wiliam taught mathematics to mixed-ability classes in inner-city schools for seven years before joining King's College, London to work on developing innovative assessment materials for the Graded Assessment in Mathematics Project. Between 1989 and 1991 he co-ordinated the development of Key Stage 3 assessment tasks in English, mathematics, science and technology, where his efforts met with critical acclaim such as 'elaborate nonsense' (Kenneth Clarke, Secretary of State for Education) and 'getting children to do weird things in corners' (John Major, Prime Minister). He returned to King's where he is currently head of the School of Education and Professor of Educational Assessment and spends as much time as he can amassing information on the negative effects of ability grouping in mathematics.

Jan Winter is a lecturer in education at the University of Bristol. She taught in Bristol schools for eight years before working as an advisory teacher for Avon LEA. This experience provided her with a wealth of experiences of working with other teachers, through which she learned an enormous amount. For the last seven years she has worked at the University of Bristol on pre-service training courses for secondary mathematics teachers as well as masters degrees and other courses of in-service training. She has taken part in many research projects in the areas of assessment and of mathematics learning and continues to be fascinated by the learning process, both her own and that of pupils in school. She was chair of the General Council of the Association of Teachers of Mathematics for three years. She is currently starting work on a major research project on home–school links – improving the use of knowledge about learning between these two settings in which children learn.

Robyn Zevenbergen trained as a teacher at Deakin University in Australia in the 1980s. Robyn is a senior lecturer at Griffith University, Australia, where she works in (primary) mathematics education. Her research centres on issues of equity and social justice within a critical sociological framework. Currently, her work is exploring the role of language and its impact on learning and equity. She is also working on a project examining reforms in mathematics education and the barriers that these pose to learning and participation, with the intention of making explicit aspects of invisible pedagogy that hinder access to mathematics and success. While the main emphasis in her work is with students from working-class backgrounds, she has also been involved in projects with indigenous students and students with hearing difficulties – particularly in exploring the relationships between these groups.

Glossary

ALBSU	Adult Literacy and Basic Skills Unit
APU	Assessment and Performance Unit
ATM	Association of Teachers of Mathematics
BCME	British Congress of Mathematics Education
BSRLM	British Society for Research into Learning Mathematics
BSU	Basic Skills Unit
DFE	Department for Education
DfEE	Department for Education and Employment
EMTAG	Ethnic Minority and Traveller Achievement Grant
ESN	Educationally Sub-Normal
ESRC	Economic and Social Research Council
GAMMA	Gender and Mathematics Association
GCE	General Certificate of Education
GCSE	General Certificate of Secondary Education
GNVQ	General National Vocational Qualification
HMCI	Her Majesty's Chief Inspector of Schools
HMI	Her Majesty's Inspector
HMSO	Her Majesty's Stationery Office
ILEA	Inner London Education Authority
ITE	Initial Teacher Education
LEA	Local Education Authority
LMS	Local Management of Schools
NCC	National Curriculum Council
NFER	National Foundation for Educational Research
NNP	National Numeracy Pilot
NNS	National Numeracy Strategy
NQT	Newly Qualified Teacher
OFSTED	Office for Standards in Education
PSE	Personal and Social Education
QCA	Qualifications and Curriculum Authority
SATs	Standard Assessment Tests
SCAA	Schools Curriculum and Assessment Authority
SMP	Schools Mathematics Project
TES	*Times Education Supplement*
TGAT	Task Group on Assessment and Testing
THES	*Times Higher Educational Supplement*
TIMSS	Third International Mathematics and Science Study
TTA	Teacher Training Agency

Introduction

How to make the most of this book

Peter Gates

Who this book is for

This book has been specifically written with classroom teachers in mind, particularly new teachers. By 'new teachers', we mean student teachers on courses of initial teacher education (PGCE or B.Ed. courses or those on other routes into the profession, such as SCITT schemes, fast track programmes, modular courses etc.) as well as teachers in their first few years of teaching. We hope the book will be read by both teachers in primary schools who need to teach mathematics, and mathematics teachers in secondary schools. Most of the issues we address are issues that affect *both* primary and secondary phases – and we have avoided focusing this book exclusively on one phase or another because we feel there are issues of which all those who teach mathematics need to be aware. Due to the contextualisation of some of the issues, it might appear that some chapters are more appropriate for one phase rather than another. We would, however, urge all readers, whether working in the primary or secondary phase, to see that each chapter has something to offer once you have seen through that context into the wider issues. Hence, the *content* of the book and the issues raised in it will be of interest to all those responsible for teaching mathematics and mathematics education in all phases. The issues covered in the book are both contemporary and controversial, and are those currently under debate by the profession more generally. This audience has dictated also the *style and approach* of the writing used in the book. All contributors have attempted to make the issues as accessible as possible. This is not always easy given the complex nature of educational issues and at times, you might have to work hard. We make no apologies for that.

The book is likely also to be useful to teachers who are working as mentors to new teachers – either on ITE courses or NQT induction programmes. In addition it is likely to be of interest to higher education tutors of students on mathematics education courses, since it not only covers contemporary issues, but also offers reflective activities.

Because of the way in which current state-of-the-art research in mathematics education has been used by the contributors, (most of whom are currently active researchers in the area on which they write) this book is likely also to be of interest to those researching areas of mathematics education in order to foster a broader perspective on some complex issues.

How to read this book

With the exception of the first introductory chapter, which forms the overview and the backdrop to the book, all chapters have a common structure. The issue that each chapter addresses is briefly introduced and summarised in *Introducing the Issue*, to give you a feeling for what is about to come. This is not merely in order to follow a literary tradition, but is intended to mentally prepare you. These introductions, along with the *Key Questions* that follow, are intended to give you the opportunity to think ahead. Therefore, before you read each chapter, you might *read* the introduction, and then *ponder* over the key questions before fully engaging with the chapter.

Each chapter contains points where we think you might benefit by *Reflecting on the Issue*. . . . These opportunities have been designed to help you interact with and confront some of the essential ideas in each chapter. Naturally, we have no power over how or whether you undertake these activities – we are not going to put you through some assessment process! It is unlikely that you will always be in a position to stop reading and undertake some activity, since a number of the activities suggest you move away from the book to work with children or other teachers. However many of the *Reflecting on the Issue* . . . activities can be – and indeed need to be – worked on there and then because they require you to consider some important aspect before reading on. There will possibly be a tendency to just keep on reading because this is often the easiest way. (It's a bit like finding an excuse for not doing your homework isn't it?) Of course, how you want to use this book is up to you.

At the end of each chapter is a further *Invitation to Reflect*. This invites you to reconsider in some way, some of the arguments in the chapter and to relate what you have read to your own experience.

Finally, each chapter closes with *Further Suggested Readings*, which offer some ideas where you might usefully look if you want to learn more about the issues discussed in the chapter, and the *References* to material used or drawn on in the chapter. We have tried to make the suggested readings accessible and available.

My experience in working with teachers and pupils over many years leads me to suggest that you might find it helpful to keep a notebook – or use any blank pages at the back – to write down your responses to the key questions and the activities. You might write a response to the activity – or if this is less appropriate to your context (i.e. you might be a teacher educator, or researcher) then you might benefit from collecting your thoughts on the activities *as* activities? How might you use them? Why did the mathematics educators who wrote this book construct them as they did?

Naturally, we hope you enjoy engaging with this book, and that in some small way the world might become a slightly better place as a result.

Acknowledgements

The contributors to this book have agreed to donate all the royalties to the Save the Children Fund to contribute to their work with disadvantaged children throughout the world who in many cases do not even get the benefit of the largely imperfect education system critiqued throughout this book.

We would like to thank:

- Cambridge University Press, for permission to use the SMP 11–16 extracts in Chapter 12;
- The Metropolitan Police, for permission to use the photograph of the police also in Chapter 12;
- The Association of Teachers of Mathematics, for permission to adapt and enlarge Jan Winter's ATM Conference address, previously published in Mathematics Teaching 172, for Chapter 13.
- The Qualifications and Curriculum Authority, for permission to reproduce the SAT questions in Chapter 16.

Part I

Setting the scene; raising the issues

1 What is an/at issue in mathematics education?

Peter Gates

The introduction to the issues

Those of us with an interest in – and indeed a passion for – teaching mathematics learn pretty quickly not to divulge this information too readily in public places. One has to be careful responding to the apparently innocent 'and what do you do?' question for fear of throwing the hairdresser into a rant about how they never enjoyed maths, could never do it or understand all those letters. You then find that you are being looked at a bit askance in order to examine what other defects or peculiarities you might have. Hating mathematics is as much a national pastime as complaining about the weather and mathophobia is so acceptable that one can readily make light of it – as I just have, but of course, it is a very serious matter, that has serious implications for very many children. Mathematics is not just a complex collection of skills, concepts and ideas that we endeavour to pass on to the next generation. As many chapters in this book will go on to argue, mathematics serves as a 'badge of eligibility for the privileges of society' (Atweh, Bleicher and Cooper 1998: 63). Being successful at mathematics brings with it opportunities and riches; one stands a better chance of higher paid careers if one holds a higher qualification in mathematics. In addition, of course the converse is true. In order to keep certain sectors of the population away from such success, they have to be made to fail at mathematics. However, I am running away with myself here and need to develop this argument a little more.

Of course, many children enjoy mathematics – usually more so between the ages of 5 and 11 than 11 and 16 it has to be said, but there's another story! For many pupils, mathematics is a series of challenges and hurdles, which they face with passion and determination. For many others however, mathematics is a daily experience of continued failure and irrelevance. Mathematics education fails too many children; it fails children on the margins of society, it fails children from ethnic minorities, and it fails children from social and cultural backgrounds that are different from the majority of mathematics teachers.

In 1982, one submission to the Cockcroft Report into the teaching of mathematics in schools, *Mathematics Counts*, said 'Mathematics lessons in secondary schools are very often not about anything. You collect like terms, or learn the laws of indices, with no perception of why anyone needs to do such things' (Department for Education and Science 1982: para 462, p. 141). This seems to me to sum up what must be many children's experience of the subject. Mathematics is about all manner of things, but about nothing at all. It is about things that seem quite divorced from our everyday lives, interests or needs. Yet while this might reflect what goes on in many classrooms, it is a rather naïve description because it merely takes some of the surface features of the mathematics classroom and ignores the underlying complexity and the unintended outcomes of that complexity. Para-doxically, it is exactly because someone can say 'mathematics lessons are not about anything' that the situation is more worrying – showing how the processes of exclusion, rejection and de-motivation are hidden, obscured and misinterpreted.

Part of that complexity lies in the role that schools play in the construction of one's identity – forging how one compares oneself to others during some partic-ularly difficult times for young people – growing independence, the embarrassment of puberty and the frustrations of adolescence. So, in this gradual process of self-awareness and self-efficacy what are the issues for mathematics teachers? What do we need to think about? In a book titled *Issues in Mathematics Teaching*, one might naturally expect a bunch of mathematicians to begin with the definitions, and I'll not disappoint. '*Issues*' is the easy one, so I will start there. To be *an issue* means to be important and requiring of a decision; to be *at issue* implies something is under discussion due to disagreement; to *take issue* implies to disagree, whereas to *issue forth* means to expound. This book then is an opportunity for some writers to expound on matters about which there is likely to be some disagreement and which are under debate. As for defining '*mathematics*' and '*teaching*', little will be gained by opening that can of worms because the terms are so contentious and so slippery. I will 'leave it as an exercise for the reader' – as it used to say in my university mathematics books. Defining such terms is really only useful insofar as it engages you in discussion with others. Coming to understand and define what it means to teach mathematics requires a long-term professional commitment of critical engagement in debate, not a textbook definition.

The background to the issues

It can hardly be contested that we live in an uneven and unjust society where access to education and to justice depend on the capital one can appropriate and accumulate – particularly through the benefits the education system bestows on some individuals. There is ample evidence in the academic and research literature in education to support this contention such that it is hardly now contentious. Yet, unfairness, injustice and prejudice are not abstract concepts of some macro-social analysis of an internecine class war. They are felt through the disappointment, hopelessness and frustrations of ordinary people as they get though their everyday lives. They exist in the knots in the pit of the stomach and the tears in the eyes. Injustice exists in the disappointments many children face when they are not endowed with financial resources to have what other children have and take for granted. Injustice exists in the frustration, anger and self-depreciation when a pupil is placed in a low set for mathematics based on some assessment procedure over which they have no control and which they feel is unfair. Injustice is a process that goes on all around us, even when – and arguably *especially* when – we do not look for it or recognise it.

I have spent many years in a variety of classrooms as a mathematics teacher, and continue to do so in my current role as tutor to student teachers, and what I see often upsets me, and I guess it was this which, to some extent, encouraged me to put this book together. I feel uncomfortable when I see children labelled as 'less able' placed into 'bottom sets' and fed diets of at worst, tedium, or at best, irrelevant and uninteresting exercises. I feel uncomfortable when the majority of pupils I see in those bottom sets seem to have had very similar life experiences reflecting varying degrees of deprivation. I feel uncomfortable when I can see they realise that there really is no point in working hard to learn mathematics because the structure of the school means they cannot achieve high GCSE grades whatever they do. I feel frustrated when I see mathematics envisaged by pupils, parents and teachers as little more than a collection of techniques to be captured rather than an approach to understand and to tackle society's ills. Finally, (for now) I feel angry when I hear teachers criticise parents for not being interested enough in their children to come to parents' evenings when, of course, 'these are just the ones you want to see!'. Well that may be so, but they clearly don't want to see you very much – and that ought to be where we begin to ask questions.

However, this book is not about my feelings; this is about those children who give up on mathematics; because many of the children who give up on mathematics (or better, those whom mathematics gives up for sacrifice) give up on society. OK. You might think this is a bit extreme, but it is my contention that *mathematics* education in schools plays a *significant* role in organising the segregation of our society, and conversely as a mathematics teacher, you will play your part too.

Sue Willis is an Australian who works in mathematics education, and who in a book titled *Real Girls Don't do Maths* provocatively argued:

> Mathematics is not used as a selection device simply because it is useful, but rather the reverse.
>
> (Willis 1989: 35)

Hence she claims mathematics is not useful because it is useful; it is not useful because of what it helps you do. Mathematics is useful because it is organised and conceptualised in such a way that certain people can't do it. Now that is certainly a challenging and controversial claim – one you might take issue with or one you believe is right on. It certainly is an issue whichever way you look at it.

So, what makes something an *issue* in mathematics teaching? Let me give you one classic example – setting by ability. Why is setting an issue? Well, the answer to this will be obvious if you spend any time looking at the make-up of the different ability groups in any comprehensive school. Furthermore, setting is a mechanism for legitimising the very process of differential privileging of cultural background. We know from a great deal of international research that setting does not actually have an effect on raising overall standards – though the likelihood is that you will not accept my argument here. You might prefer the argument put to me by Alan Brown, a head of mathematics:

> I think it's probably only fair to say that I have a fairly high degree of scepticism about a lot of the qualitative and quantitative research. I think it tends to be done by people who, with the best will in the world, have an axe to grind. The people who've argued about mixed ability tend to be people who've moved out of the classroom.
>
> (Gates 2000: 299)

Which puts me firmly in my place (and as it happens all the other contributors to this book too). I don't intend here to argue the merits or demerits of this issue, because that type of controversy and disparity of perspective is in the nature of an issue – and because I don't expect any chapter in any book to radically alter deeply held beliefs on its own. What I hope this book does is to raise issues and expose the underlying values that need to be confronted. What is important is that you recognise the controversies, and enter into them with an awareness of what is at stake. When it comes down to it, it is a matter of whose side you are on and that is for you to decide by considering your own values. Of course, this book, like any other similar book, is deeply saturated with values. The difference here, that all contributors have striven to ensure, is that our values are somewhat more explicit and transparent than many others you might read. This does not make the book less useful, on the contrary. Because you will be able to ascertain from whence each writer is coming, you will be better placed to consider, evaluate and position yourself.

Actually, all the contributors to this book are qualified classroom teachers, trained and experienced either at primary or at secondary level, with decades of classroom experience between them, and they have something important to say about that experience. For half of the contributors in this book, the chapters they have written also derive directly from their own doctoral research studies.

About the issues in this book

Of course, any book represents someone's selection of material to include, and this book is no exception. We are not suggesting the issues we have written about are the only issues that are currently important in mathematics teaching, but they are the issues that engage the twenty-one of us who have contributed to the book. The importance of our selection is not only in its content, but is in the way that the politics of mathematics teaching is being made explicit throughout the book. We discuss a wide sweep of issues, and provide sources and resources for those wanting to know more. In an overview of many of the contemporary issues in mathematics education, Peter Bailey concludes that 'teachers of mathematics can play a crucial role in making the world a fairer place' (Bailey 1999: 84), and that is our starting point – which surely must be of interest to us all.

Our focus in this book is on teaching mathematics in schools, but no one interested in children's learning of mathematics can overlook the significant issue of the difference between doing mathematics in schools and being mathematical outside of school. This is a fast-growing area of study – and is something that teachers ought not ignore (though it will have to remain as the subject of another book). The number of studies of adults and children doing mathematics outside of school show that lack of competence in one context (usually school) is no indicator of lack of competence in the other. See for example the work of Mary Harris, (Harris 1991), Gelsa Knijnik (Knijnik 1996), Madelena Santos (Santos and Matos 1999), Jean Lave (Lave 1988) and Terezinha Nunes (Nunes, Schliemann and Carraher 1993). It is perhaps interesting that so many of these studies are carried out by female researchers in mathematics education. One small way of marking the contribution that women make to the academic literature is to identify gender through the use of first as well as second names. This is a practice utilised throughout this book.

The social context of mathematics education

The chapters forming **Part II – Issues in the Social Context of Mathematics Education**, really cover a broad sweep of contemporary issues at the heart of current debates about the teaching and learning of mathematics; social justice (**Chapter 2**), language, social class and social inclusion (**Chapter 3**), gender (**Chapter 4**) and ethnicity (**Chapter 5**) all have a central place in these debates, yet have not all had a central place in mainstream literature on mathematics education. However, in addition to these broad, macro-issues, there are chapters here that look more into the personal dimension of mathematics teaching – pupils' perspectives and emotions on their learning (**Chapter 6**), one's own values as a teacher (**Chapter 7**) and the ways in which one's values influence one's teaching style in the context of the current teaching of numeracy (**Chapter 8**).

In **Chapter 2**, 'Mathematics Teaching in the Real World', Tony Cotton discusses the relationship between mathematics education and social justice, an area in which Tony's work is well known. Tony's work – and his discussion of it in this chapter – is important because it helps us understand the nature of social exclusion and its manifestation in and through mathematics education. Furthermore, Tony offers some blueprints for strategies that we might incorporate into our teaching to try to make a difference. What comes across in Tony's chapter – and this issue is picked up at several other points in this book – is that pupils have a view, they have a right to a view, and a right to be listened to, and that no school, department or teacher can claim to be socially just without listening to and acting on those views. Of course, for this to be successful, effective channels of communication need to be established between the dominant voice of the teachers and the oft-suppressed voices of the pupils.

Robyn Zevenbergen problematises the idea that language is merely a means of communication. In **Chapter 3**, 'Language, social class and underachievement in school mathematics', she claims that the language forms and strategies we use in mathematics teaching differentially favour some social groups over others. What often passes as a lack of 'ability' in mathematics or a lack of understanding is more likely to be a result of differences in language use between the school and the home context. What makes this doubly complex is how the school acts as if it is the protector of appropriate behaviour and communication rather than just one arbitrary context.

Carrie Paechter's writing is often challenging but inspiring, and in **Chapter 4**, 'Gender, Reason and Emotion in Secondary Mathematics Classrooms' she looks beyond the issue of differential mathematics attainment between genders. This has been a rather unhelpful diversion in recent years, something that is now becoming clearer as girls begin to race ahead in the achievement stakes. For while girls are showing a tendency to be more successful they show little interest in studying mathematics (or indeed the sciences) beyond school. To understand this issue more fully, we need to adopt concepts and perspectives that get below the surface features. Carrie does this by looking back over the development of rational thought, and suggests that, empirically, girls and boys approach mathematics, and therefore rationality, rather differently; boys seem to have a predilection for decontextualised rationality while girls seem to be more comfortable basing their decisions on emotional morality. Now we need to be clear about what is being claimed here. What is not being argued is that there is something 'essentially' rational about the male, and something 'essentially' emotive about the female. Such a position is usually called *essentialism* – or 'the belief that individuals have a unique essence that transcends historical and cultural boundaries' (Gale and Densmore 2000: 128). For example this would include the belief that women have an inherent capacity as carers and nurturers, thus being subjected to a 'stereotyping upheld by the fact that in practice women do more actual caring and feeding of children than men do' (Gale and Densmore 2000: 128). So rather than accepting stereotypical roles as essences of gender, we have instead the social construction of identity, with the result that some groups or sections of society are forced, encouraged or constrained to adopt preferred ways of behaving, interacting and responding to challenges that go on to be undervalued by the education system. Hence, the issue of gender becomes not merely who does best, but how, as teachers of mathematics, we influence and constrain some pupils more than others through our classroom practices and our curriculum.

In **Chapter 5**, 'Ethnicity and Mathematics Education' Derek Kassem describes how pupils' ethnic background places them at a disadvantage when success at mathematics is being distributed and he pulls no punches. He reminds us that while, in discussions about the mathematics curriculum over recent years, the issue of ethnicity might not have had the same high profile as gender, we are equally culpable here of some subtle discriminatory practices. An issue that Derek raises – which again permeates this book – is the importance of pupils' cultural inheritance to their attainment, especially since mathematics educational practices tend to favour one cultural tradition over others.

Jo Boaler and Dylan Wiliam explore the highly disputed issue of ability grouping from the pupils' point of view in **Chapter 6**. '"We've still got to learn!" Students' perspectives on ability grouping and mathematics achievement'. This is a story that needs to be heard, and heard more widely because it lays a most significant dimension onto the usually polarised debate on setting or target grouping in mathematics teaching. There is currently considerable research underway in the UK into the efficacy of the practice of segregation by 'ability' – a practice that is not common elsewhere in the world (as we see later in

Chapter 18). Jo and Dylan identify the considerable disadvantages that such segregation brings and which beg us all at least to reconsider the practice.

Research evidence suggesting there are disadvantages in grouping pupils by ability for mathematics teaching contradicts the widely held perception that ability discrimination enhances attainment. Indeed, it is this perception that leads to the almost universal application of ability grouping in mathematics at secondary level in the UK. The widely held professional logic is that in 'ability groups' teachers can better match work to the ability levels of pupils since the spread of ability is more narrow than would otherwise be the case in all attainment groups. One argument which may explain findings that setting restricts attainment can be found in the paradoxical claim that when teaching in setted groups, teachers actually respond less to pupils individual needs than they do when teaching all attainment classes. The significance of this draws Jo and Dylan to conclude that 'the traditional British concern with ensuring that some of the ablest students reach the highest possible standards appears to have resulted in a situation in which the vast majority of students achieve well below their potential'.

Grouping by ability or attainment (setting) has not been part of the culture of primary schools in the UK for a long time, however it has recently been reported that 'nearly two-thirds of primary schools appear to be adopting ability grouping in response to government pressure for higher educational standards' (TES 1999b). The assumption here is that educational standards may be raised by utilising some form of grouping of pupils by ability – becoming termed 'target grouping' when used in primary schools. However, Anita Straker, Director of the National Numeracy Strategy, speaking at the annual conference of the Association of Teachers of Mathematics in 1999, advised caution, telling schools not to put pupils in ability groups due to the inconclusive nature of the evidence (TES 1999a).

A review of the literature on grouping by ability across all school subjects, carried out by NFER has suggested that 'it is possible to identify a general trend which suggests that setting, compared with mixed ability teaching, has no significant effect on pupil achievement' (Sukhnanden 1999: 6–7). There are some interesting findings from the research. In comparison to pupils in high ability streams, those in low ability streams are provided with a lower quality of instruction and with teachers who are less experienced and less qualified. Furthermore, placement in low ability groups reinforces differences relating to social class, gender and ethnicity by lowering self-concepts and attitudes (Sukhnandan and Lee 1998: 11). In terms of pupil achievement, research indicates that grouping by ability has no effect on average achievement. What Jo and Dylan illustrate here, and in their work elsewhere, is that there are some very clear disadvantages for pupils across the school in the adoption of forms of ability segregation. The real question here is, can a school rightly claim to be providing an education that helps each child achieve their best while adopting some form of ability segregation? Jo and Dylan seem to be suggesting the only answer to this question is 'no!'. My argument here is that teachers do not actually know setting 'works', but can actually not conceive of doing it another way. (All is not lost, however, because Mike Ollerton discusses some strategies for inclusive teaching of mathematics in **Chapter 16.**) However, the practice of ability (or target) grouping in schools rests not on some systematic analysis of efficacy or effectiveness, but actually on the underlying beliefs and values of teachers – something discussed in the next chapter.

In **Chapter 7**, 'What values do you teach when you teach mathematics?', Alan Bishop opens up the issue of what constitutes a 'value' and further explores how values are both explicitly and implicitly conveyed in our teaching of mathematics. He offers us some examples of where we have opportunities to make decisions about the way in which our values can be incorporated into our teaching through different types of classroom activity and teacher–pupil relationships.

Arguably, one of the most significant developments in the mathematics curriculum in recent years has been the introduction of the National Numeracy Strategy (NNS) and in **Chapter 8**, 'Policy, practices and principles in teaching numeracy: What makes a difference?' Mike Askew looks into the history and the chronology of the NNS. He explores the roots of the current pedagogical imperatives and locates some of these in the international comparative studies of mathematical attainment. Mike identifies that such comparisons are not always to be taken at face value and that we need to be vigilant in order not to lose sight of what might lie behind classroom strategies that could be obscured by simplistic comparisons focused on superficial forms of classroom organisations. He draws on a research study which indicates that what seems to make teachers effective in the teaching of numeracy is being able to help pupils construct a rich interconnecting web of mathematical ideas. Nothing really surprising here perhaps, but it does suggest than many of the teaching strategies which result in fragmentation of mathematics might be rather less effective than their widespread use might suggest.

Teaching and learning mathematics

Part III – Issues in the teaching and learning of mathematics, moves on to consider some of the issues in the practical day-to-day work of teachers. Kevin Delaney looks into the thorny issue of the use of resources in **Chapter 9**, 'Teaching mathematics resourcefully'. The struggle to find the right language here illustrates perhaps some of the complexity in the issue. The terms: teaching aids, learning aids, apparatus, equipment, practical equipment, manipulatives, etc. all seem to be widely used, yet how, why and when they are used perhaps received less attention. Perhaps the most correct term – 'physical embodiment' hardly rolls off the tongue, yet does suggest that some form of representation of some mathematics can rest in or be embodied in some physical entity, albeit temporarily. Kevin opens up this issue and illustrates where the real issues lie by looking first at the processes of learning in the classroom and secondly at the practice of teaching by considering the proposals in the National Numeracy Strategy – which Kevin suggests need to be carefully scrutinised and critiqued.

Teachers of mathematics might learn a great deal about this issue by looking at how adults, children and babies learn *outside* the classroom. Babies seem to do most of their learning before they even get to school. Dave Hewitt gives a very passionate description of his own baby girl learning mathematics in 'The first two years' (Hewitt, 2000) which suggests what active learners very young children are and how objects are used to learn then cast aside when they have no further utility. I have to say my own experience with my own children has made me realise how impotent the 'teacher' often is when real learning is taking place – and how they seem to be absent too with learning coming as the result of creative synergy between learner and object.

'Dealing with misconceptions in mathematics' is the topic Malcolm Swan addresses in **Chapter 10**. He makes a clear distinction between mistakes and errors on the one hand, and misconceptions and alternative conceptions on the other. Malcolm stresses how the widespread nature of misconceptions across both space and time ought to underline for us all the *conceptual* roots of *misconceptions*. He locates his discussion of the issue in the process of coming to understand mathematics and draws on Vygotskian ideas. As one comes to expect from Malcolm, the discussion becomes very practical by looking at the implications for classroom strategies and offers some activities that help teachers and pupils to *confront* and *address* misconceptions. The use of this language is important. Malcolm cautions against the dangerous over-simplification in 'official' govern-ment statements, which require new teachers to be taught how to prevent misconceptions arising. Assuming that misconceptions can be simply remedied or avoided has to be a misconception in itself.

No discussion of issues in mathematics teaching can justifiably overlook the impact of new technology and Janet Ainley looks at how computers need to influence teaching styles in **Chapter 11**, 'Adjusting to the newcomer: Roles for the computer in mathematics classrooms'. A major consideration for Janet is not just how computers can be used, or what software or hardware there is available, but how one *interacts* with a computer both as a learner and as a teacher. She offers three different roles a computer can play in the classroom – each of which have their own rationales, objectives and patterns of interaction. A greater clarity in the diversity between these roles can only help the classroom teacher more effectively utilise the potential that computer technology can bring. One aspect that Janet touches on is the way in which pupils' differential access to computer technology can influence their engagement and eventual success in the classroom. There is a clear issue of social exclusion here that needs confronting unless we are to unwittingly privilege those children from families where access to computers is as accepted as access to microwaves, digital camcorders and DVD players at the expense of children from less advantaged backgrounds – large families, small overcrowded properties or even bed and breakfast accommodation.

While for teachers the computer might be the newcomer, the mathematics textbook has been around for decades. More's the pity some would say, and Paul Dowling offers a fresh perspective on them in **Chapter 12**, 'Reading mathematics texts'. There are some difficult ideas in this chapter – and it might be easy to consider that Paul 'doth protest too much'. However, the real issue here is looking at the everyday, ordinary, taken-for-granted and reading it differently. Looking at things differently has been, of course, one major way in which mathematics itself has developed over the centuries. What Paul's work helps me to do is to see more clearly why many children can't see the point in much of the mathematics we give them to do in textbooks. While much of it *is* pretty daft and pointless, this is because the real purpose is hidden, obscured and unrecognised. The purpose, as agued by Paul, seems to be to position pupils differentially within the social hierarchy.

One dimension of children's educational experience that seems to be largely overlooked in teaching mathematics is addressed by Jan Winter in **Chapter 13,** 'Personal, spiritual, moral, social and cultural issues in teaching mathematics'. Jan discusses each of these five elements in terms of what they might mean in the context of teaching mathematics, and offers some suggestions and strategies for the classroom. This is a very important chapter inasmuch as it places mathematics teaching more closely at the centre of children's spiritual, moral, social, cultural and personal education than it currently lies.

Assessing mathematics

In **Part IV – Issues in the assessment of mathematics,** three contributors look into some of the more controversial aspects of assessing pupils' level of attainment. Anne Watson writes about 'Making Judgements about Pupils' Mathematics' in **Chapter 14**. Anne is particularly interested in the nature of the judgements that teachers make about their pupils' mathematics. These judgements are important because they can greatly influence much of what goes on in the classroom, and furthermore can influence significant key decisions made on behalf of the pupil – such as examination entry and ability group allocation for example. This chapter then needs to be read in the context of a number of the chapters in **Part 2**. Anne's concern is over the way there might be a tendency for decisions to be made about pupils based not just on evidence, but also on teachers' expectations and assumptions about what a particular child ought to be able to do. There are some very good reasons for valuing and utilising teacher assessments of pupil capability – and Anne lists six, yet there are a number of reasons to be cautious. Teacher assessment has to be based on evidence, gleaned from what pupils say, write or do, yet none of these are unproblematic since each depends to some extent on communication between participants who may have differing cultural backgrounds.

One of these controversial areas forms the central plank of Candia Morgan's issue in **Chapter 15**, 'The place of pupil writing in learning, teaching and assessing mathematics'. Candia describes the ways in which writing contributes to and potentially enhances learning. Yet this is not without some disadvantages and conflicts especially in the social class differences in the incorporation of writing into communicative strategies. Unlike speaking, where children become largely fluent around the age of three, children do not just pick up the skill of writing and it takes many years to hone one's writing capability. Writing leaves a permanent record that can be held up for scrutiny and analysis; the interactive dynamic is stripped away, leaving the result heavily dependent on conventions and acceptable styles of grammar, syntax and semantics. The task of the teacher of mathematics then is to balance the positive and negative aspects of writing to learn.

The final issue in assessment of pupils' mathematical ability looks at the official Standard Assessment Tests (SATs) and Barry Cooper looks at the underlying bias inherent in such tests in **Chapter 16**, 'Social class and 'real-life' mathematics assessments'. The main issue in Barry's chapter is the role of *context* in the framing and interpretation of mathematical test questions. For many years it has been assumed that mathematical tasks and problems become more meaningful for the learner, and by implication more easily internalised, if they are placed in some 'real-life' context. Now, many of us know that most of these contexts are contrived and largely meaningless, and assume that this state of affairs is basically harmless – even though it loses opportunities for making mathematics really meaningful. What Barry's work highlights is that this process of fabrication of context is far from harmless – but has the effect of further disadvantaging those pupils from more disadvantaged social groups, and Barry shows us in some detail how this comes about.

Now, there is a game being played here. We claim most strongly that mathematics is a real-world discipline and that it is useful to solve real-world problems; we construct real-world problems for pupils to solve in the comfort of the classroom, away from the real realities of everyday life. Yet in the problems we offer, pupils are only supposed – or better, only allowed – to take the reality so far. This is the goldilocks principle of the reality behind mathematical problems – not too much, not too little – just enough. You have to learn your place and your role, whether you are a teacher or a pupil. Pupils have to learn to be a learner, but more than this, they have to learn the limitation of what they have to learn. In achieving this, children learn the rules of social order – what Basil Bernstein called 'hierarchical rules'. Basil Bernstein argued that the way in which school practices organise the educational experiences for different children separates the *local* from the *less-local*. The children who tend to fall through this net are often those children from lower working class families who become constrained into local, context-dependent skills.

The culture of teaching mathematics

Making mathematics more real gets taken up in the next section, **Part V – Issues in the Culture of Mathematics Teaching**. Mike Ollerton opens with **Chapter 17** on 'Inclusion, learning and teaching mathematics: Beliefs and values'. Here Mike returns to the issue raised earlier by Jo and Dylan, but offers strategies for teaching in a way that is inclusive rather than exclusive. Mike is one of several contributors to this book who have actually taught mathematics throughout the secondary phase in all attainment groups, and who therefore know how to make it work. Of course it's not easy – but then again it's not hard either. Mike's argument is that the persistence of exclusive teaching (that is grouping pupils by ability) depends on what you believe in and what you value. Conversely, teaching inclusively demands a determination and a commitment to put inclusive strategies into practice.

The importance of one's belief systems gets taken up again by Paul Ernest in **Chapter 18**, 'Critical mathematics education'. Paul begins by discussing the nature of mathematics – or more accurately the natures of different mathematics – and shows that while these might rest upon different philosophical traditions, they also reflect different ideological positions. A fundamental issue here is whether one conceives of mathematics as a set of absolute truths or rather as some set of growing and adapting human practices and Paul offers a couple of examples of how mathematics is far from absolute.

There is possibly another example, which relates more closely to the developments in the mathematics curriculum and to the classroom practices of teachers: how can we quickly multiply by ten?, e.g. $3 \times 10 = ?$ Well, this is easy, just put a zero on the end. This system works perfectly well for some numbers (well, an infinite number, of numbers actually) and for some children at an early developmental level. Indeed it might well be taught in many classrooms as a 'rule of thumb' and as long as we only have natural numbers all is well. Once we introduce fractions, life is not so easy. $\frac{1}{2} \times 10 = ?$ Where do we put the zero now? Why is it so different? Fractions have a stormy history and the development of a suitable notion has gone through many changes, reformulations really because at different historical periods people needed to do things with non-integer numbers (see Ifrah 1998 for much more on this). Well, let us leave vulgar fractions, and move on up to decimal fraction notation. Here how do we multiply by ten? OK, a new rule of thumb – move the decimal point one place to the right – or more accurately (and more consistently with our previous rule) move the numbers all along one place to the left. Then someone comes along needing complex numbers – or our pupil moves into year 11. Waiting in the wings are matrices, vectors, tensors – and life gets ever more complex. Someone who believes that mathematics is an absolute unchanging set of principles might easily dismiss this, of course, by pointing out that actually all the earlier rules are not really 'rules' at all. What this argument overlooks is, first, the mathematics from the point of view of the learner, and second, it misses the historical development of mathematics as a growing response to real problems. This is often seen as the 'ontogeny versus phylogeny' problem – does the historical development of mathematics mirror the cognitive development of the child.

Paul offers us a way of distinguishing between different ideological positions on mathematics and mathematics education and moves on to look at how these not only influence one's view of the nature of mathematics, but they also influence one's position on the purposes of mathematics on how mathematics needs to be used in schools. Paul describes a critical approach to mathematics, where the aim is the empowerment of learners as critical and mathematically literate citizens in society. He exemplifies this argument theoretically, and practically by offering some ideas that may be used in the classroom.

Finally, having looked in detail at our own system of mathematics education, Paul Andrews looks further afield and examines the comparative data provided in the Third International Mathematics and Science Study (TIMSS). In **Chapter 19,** 'Comparing international practice in the teaching of mathematics', Paul takes a critical look at the claims that somehow pupils in the UK seem to be doing worse than certain other countries. (We ought to acknowledge here that embedded in such concerns is often a form of incipient racism or colonialism.) He finds a rather pic'n'mix approach that seems more designed to introduce changes to UK mathematics practices that fit a new-right agenda, rather than to place all of our practices under the spotlight. If we are to learn from international comparisons we need to do at least two things. We need to consider the importance of context and culture in the deeply rooted educational practices that take place in classrooms in different countries, and also we need to be prepared to place our own practices similarly in a cultural tradition.

One last issue . . .

I started this book by describing how we had written it with new-ish teachers in mind. Naturally, we want to inform and educate – but I want more than that; I want to change things too. I would like children to enjoy their mathematics, and for it to empower them to make better choices in life. However, I suspect that there needs to be changes too, changes in the way mathematics is taught, conceptualised, assessed and utilised. A challenge for those of us in teacher education, especially those of us committed to social justice, is to understand why teachers find it so difficult to change and internalise new ideas. You may find some new ideas in this book, you may engage with some of our reflective activities: whether it makes a difference will, in the end, depend on you.

We have not been able to present the totality of contemporary issues facing teachers of mathematics but if we have left you wanting to know more then you could consider contacting and involving yourself in some of the following.

Association of Teachers of Mathematics (ATM)

The ATM is a professional association for those teaching mathematics. The ATM holds a conference each year and local branches hold regular local meetings. The ATM produces two journals – *Mathematics Teaching* and *Micromath*. *www.atm.org.uk*

British Society for Research into the Learning of Mathematics (BSRLM)

BSRLM holds regular day conferences where current research is reported and discussed. Classroom teachers regularly attend conferences. BSRLM produces reports of its day conferences and an annual collection of research papers. *www.warwick.ac.uk/BSRLM/*

British Congress of Mathematics Education (BCME)

BCME is a regular biennial conference for all people interested in mathematics education including those who teach mathematics from pre-school to further and higher education, as well as researchers, advisers and teacher educators. *www.bcme.org.uk*

Further suggested readings

Walter Secada, Elizabeth Fennema and Lisa Adajian (eds) (1995) *New Directions in Equity in Mathematics Education*, Cambridge: Cambridge University Press. This is a collection of readings covering contemporary issues of international interest and importance all of which have a concern for equity and social justice as a common theme.

Pat Rogers and Gabriele Kaiser (eds) (1995) *Equity in Mathematics Education. Influences of feminism and culture*, London: Falmer Press. This collection also offers new perspectives, this time with a focus on the relationship between gender and participation in mathematics education.

Leone Burton (ed.) (1999) *Learning Mathematics. From hierarchies to networks*, London: Falmer Press. This book brings together a collection of contributions exploring current developments in our understanding of the learning of mathematics.

References

Atweh, B., Bleicher, R. and Cooper, T. (1998) 'The Construction of Social Context of Mathematics Classrooms: A Sociolinguistic Analysis', *Journal for Research in Mathematics Education* 2(1), 63–82.

Bailey, P. (1999) 'Mathematics', in Hill, D. and Cole, M. (eds), *Promoting Equality in Secondary Schools*, London: Cassell, pp. 57–90.

Department for Education and Science (DES) (1982) *Mathematics Counts. Report of the Committee of Inquiry into the Teaching of Mathematics in Schools, chaired by W.H. Cockcroft (the Cockcroft Report)*, London: HMSO.

Gale, T. and Densmore, K. (2000) *Just Schooling. Explorations in the Cultural Politics of Teaching*, Buckingham: Open University Press.

Gates, P. (2000) 'A study of the structure of the professional orientation of two teachers of mathematics: a sociological approach', unpublished Ph.D. thesis, University of Nottingham.

Harris, M. (ed.) (1991) *School, Mathematics and Work*, London: Falmer Press.

Hewitt, D. (2000) 'The first two years', *Mathematics Teaching* 173, 4–17.

Ifrah, G. (1998) *The Universal History of Numbers. From Prehistory to the Invention of the Computer*, London: Harvill Press.

Knijnik, G. (1996) Exclusão e Resistência. Educação Matemática e Legitimidade Cultural, Porto Alegre, Brasil: Artes Médicas.

Lave, J. (1988) *Cognition in Practice: Mind, Mathematics and Culture in Everyday Life*, Cambridge: Cambridge University Press.

Nunes, T., Schliemann, A. and Carraher, D. (1993) *Street Mathematics and School Mathematics*, Cambridge: Cambridge University Press.

Santos, M. and Matos, J. (1999) 'Learning about learning with ardinas at Cabo Verde' in Gates, P. and Cotton, T. (eds), *Mathematics Education and Society. Proceedings of the First International Conference (MEAS1) (Second edition)*, Nottingham: Centre for the Study of Mathematics Education, pp. 394–400.

Sukhnandan, L. (1999) 'Sorting, sifting and setting. Does grouping pupils according to ability affect attainment?', *NFER News*, Spring 1999, Slough: NFER, pp. 6–7.

Sukhnandan, L. and Lee, B. (1998) *Streaming, Setting and Grouping by Ability. A Review of the Literature*, Slough: National Foundation for Educational Research.

Times Educational Supplement (1999a) 'Maths Sets are bad for infants says advisor', *Times Educational Supplement*, 16 April 1999, London, p. 2.

Times Educational Supplement (1999b) 'Set to see a rise in standards' *Times Educational Supplement*, 23 July 1999, London, p. 19.

Willis, S. (1989) *Real Girls Don't do Maths. Gender and the Construction of Privilege*, Geelong, Australia: Deakin University Press.

Part II

Issues in the social context of mathematics education

2 Mathematics teaching in the real world

Tony Cotton

Introducing the issue

People become teachers of mathematics for many reasons. Some because they were inspired by their own teachers of mathematics, some because they enjoy mathematics and wish to share this enjoyment with others and some because they believe that education in general and mathematics education in particular is the only route through which we can create a more socially just society. Unfortunately my experience in many schools suggests that, at present, much of what I see within education reflects the injustice within our society. I visit schools and work with teachers teaching what they would term 'bottom sets'. Often these groups contain an over-representation of those pupils who make up minority ethnic groups within the school. I look at patterns within the examination results and the best predictor of mathematics grade seems to be the area in which the student lives. In this chapter I reflect on how we, as teachers of mathematics, may unwittingly contribute to this injustice and, more importantly, I suggest what we may do about it.

In the opening section, I explore the ways in which mathematics contributes to injustice before I explain in more detail what I mean by the term social justice. It is important to define terms, especially those which have become a common part of political discourse and which are often used with an assumption that we share an understanding of what the words mean. In the next section I ask the question: how can we explore social justice in our schools? Here I move from the theoretical to the practical. Having explored ways in which we can notice what is happening within our classrooms, in the final part of the chapter I look towards teaching strategies and a mathematics curriculum that would support mathematics teachers working for social justice. So the key questions addressed by the chapter are as follows . . .

Key questions

- How does mathematics contribute to injustice?
- What is social justice?
- How can I explore social justice in my classroom and my working practices?
- What can I change within my working context?

I look at these in turn as the chapter develops.

How does mathematics contribute to injustice?

As a mathematician, I am of the view that mathematics is a powerful tool in explaining and interpreting the world in which we live. I also believe that mathematics both explains and constructs reality within our society. We constantly use mathematics when we present and interpret data offered us through the media in our homes and workplaces. Many people take it for granted that this offers us a kind of truth. This is the 'Well it must be right, it was in the newspaper' attitude. Even if we are more critical and question the interpretations we are offered, we may not often question the motives underpinning the selection and representation of the data. Why has the newspaper editor chosen to highlight this particular issue in this particular way? Why has the manager chosen this time to present the budget forecasts? Who decided how we are to measure the unemployment statistics? These are the mathematical decisions that construct reality. It is not *true* that unemployment stands at a particular figure every month. What this figure tells us is based on a mathematical model devised by a civil servant; yet, another civil servant who wanted to present a *different* image of unemployment could have come up with a very different mathematical model. However, the unemployment figure is treated as a truth along with inflation statistics and other economic indicators. In turn, these indicators influence both government policy and the money markets, both of which impinge directly on our lives – in some instances tragically as workers are made redundant, building societies and banks foreclose on mortgages and children have to go without. In these very stark ways mathematics *constructs* the world in which we live. As teachers of mathematics perhaps we should ask: Whose interests are being served by these statistics and might there be alternative interpretations that would serve alternative interests?

If mathematics outside school constructs a reality over which individuals may feel powerless, then mathematics within school also helps to construct individuals through feelings of belonging and exclusion. A feeling of belonging to the community of mathematicians can empower individuals and groups of individuals to make interpretations of reality and to construct alternative models of reality. This can support us in challenging injustice within our everyday lives. Alternatively a feeling of exclusion from the community of mathematicians can lead to individuals feeling powerless and unable to challenge future injustices.

Another important factor is that mathematics qualifications have a significant effect on the viability of individual life plans. Put simply, we are more likely to earn a higher salary later on in life if we are successful in school mathematics than if we fail in mathematics at school. All of this suggests that mathematics education and issues of social justice are closely bound together.

What is social justice?

We all have our own definitions of justice and injustice – we all have different limits on what we will tolerate both on our own behalf and on the behalf of others. For me, social justice is linked directly to issues of power and control. It is connected to the ways in which individuals can feel powerful or be made to feel powerless. It is to do with individuals feeling in control of decisions that affect the way they live their lives. We feel as though an injustice has been done when someone takes a decision that affects us personally or emotionally and with which we disagree but against which we have no power to argue. Social justice is also linked with individual rights: rights to education, rights to individual life choices without being denied access to certain chances through discriminatory practices, and the right to fight practices we perceive as unjust.

Let me offer a personal anecdote as a metaphor for the way in which issues of mathematics teaching and social justice are linked. As a child of 11 I was taught in the top group in my primary school. On Fridays we had a mental arithmetic test. The child who scored highest in the test sat in desk 1 (next to the teacher) for the following week, the child coming second sat in the next desk and so on. After a week or two I realised that by getting two or three questions wrong I would be about fifth in the test and get to sit by the door – and consequently get to go out before the rest of the class. I could engineer this result, as I was confident that I knew all the correct answers and so could deliberately make my two or three errors. I offer this as a metaphor for how confidence and skill in mathematics carries with it power over life choices. A teacher on a course brought this memory back to me when she told of a similar experience she had although her experience had left her feeling powerless and out of control. She felt she could not do mathematics. Fridays brought with them anxiety and panic. She knew she would do badly in the test, would be made to sit in a lower desk and, worst of all, that her mother would see she had failed when she collected her after school. I also note the gender of the tellers of the two stories (and the connection with Carrie Paechter's arguments in her chapter).

Jerome Bruner suggests, 'we all know by now that many scientific and mathematical hypotheses start their lives as little stories or metaphors' (Bruner 1986: 12). It is in this spirit that I share these memories of mine and memories of others as illustrations of early experiences that can affect the way we view mathematics and mathematics learning throughout our lives. The story of the Friday morning test offers a metaphor for both the physical injustice (forcing individuals into places or situations against their will) which certain practices in mathematics education can be responsible for, and also an image of mathematics as a rigid hierarchy within which we position ourselves as learners at an early age. As a consequence, we, all too often, blame *ourselves* for personal failings within mathematics rather than blaming our teachers or institutions. As a mathematics teacher, I have heard adults and children tell me, too many times, that they are 'no good at maths'. This all too common statement is ultimately personally disempowering and harmful to individual self-esteem.

Reflecting on the issue . . .
Consider the learners in the mathematics classrooms in which you work. To whose benefit are administrative arrangements and resourcing arrangements made? Which pupils or which groups of pupils may be seen to hold the 'power' within the classroom or the school? Is there a focus on GCSE grade borderlines, or SATs borderlines? If you were to carry out an audit of examination results in your school, what would be the result of auditing by ethnicity, or by postcode? What does this suggest to you?

In what follows I outline my views of social justice and the part which mathematics education has to play in supporting the development of institutions within a society in which social justice is seen as a basic tenet. An important approach that helps me in forming a working definition of social justice is John Rawls's book, A *Theory of Justice*. Working with John Rawls's ideas allows me to look at some of the ways in which schools can be examined and critiqued in order to move over to more just ways of working thereby opening up possibilities for change.

John Rawls uses the metaphor of *halving an apple* to explain the basis of his theory. If two people are sharing an apple, one person cuts the apple and the other has the choice of which half they want. The theory being that the first person will be as fair as possible in cutting the apple in order to ensure they receive a fair share. Similarly to build a just society, we should create a society as if our enemy would choose the position in which we are placed in the social order within that society. John Rawls also argues that inequalities in distribution within institutions or societies are only just if they benefit the least well-off within that institution or society.

This approach offers us ways to critically examine our institutions and our classrooms by applying his tests of justice. Do the organisational and pedagogical decisions we make about our educational practices always benefit the worst-off, the least advantaged amongst our learners? Would we feel comfortable if we thought that our enemies could decide where to place us, or our own children, in order for us to learn mathematics within our schools? If the answer to either of these questions is no, in what ways would we alter what we teach, or the way that we teach it to accord to Rawlsian justice?

I am reminded of a conversation I had with a group of 11 and 12-year-olds just starting at secondary school. I had worked with them extensively at their primary school and was visiting them to talk about how useful they had found the mathematics we explored in the primary school now they were at secondary school. I happened to arrive on the day in which they had been placed in sets 'according to ability'. The pupils were unclear how such *ability* was defined, although it had been measured by a whole school test. The school definition of *ability* also seemed to them to ignore many talents they had such as the *ability* to speak three languages, or the *ability* to work efficiently as a group.

Two of the pupils were adamant that the new school wasn't *fair*. They had been placed in the 'bottom set' and complained bitterly that the mathematics was repetitive and too easy. A social justice perspective would suggest the school should look carefully at this process, as it is clearly not seen by all pupils to be to their best advantage. A social justice view only allows unfairness within an institution if the 'unfairness' benefits the worst off within that institution. Again this is not the case in the system adopted by the school above. Yet how often do we see this situation replicated in our schools? Soberingly, it is no longer only secondary schools that discriminate in this way.

Reflecting on the issue . . .
Think of a learner whom you would define as '*able*' in mathematics. List all the qualities they exhibit which make you see them as 'able'. Now think of a student you would describe as '*less able*'. Again list the behaviours that label them as 'less able'. Compare the two lists and ask yourself: how do I work with pupils in mathematics lessons to develop those traits I may label as 'less able' into traits I would wish to see in 'able' pupils?

This view of social justice raises many questions concerning the mathematical education we offer in our schools. In what ways has the curriculum and its pedagogy addressed the skills and ideas mathematics learners in our classrooms will find useful in order to become fully functioning members of a democratic society? Have we begun to address the idea of 'mathemacy' as Ole Skovsmose (1994) calls it? The idea of mathemacy is that we demand not only a skills base, but more than that, a knowledge of how we may employ these mathematical skills, and a reflective knowledge which allows us to understand how our mathematical choices affect the ways in which we view and create our worlds through the results of our mathematising. This view of mathemacy 'enables people to participate in the understanding and transformation of their society' (Skovsmose 1994: 27). Ole Skovsmose suggests that this view of mathemacy envisages the possibility of constructing a learning of mathematics that supports learners in their development as reflective adults capable of using their mathematics to critique and challenge structures within society.

It would seem to me that these ideas are entirely compatible with the desire that mathematics classrooms should be places where we educate both for mathematics and for a society based on ideas of social justice. However, we cannot move towards a mathematics for justice without questioning our notions of the nature of mathematics and the nature of mathematical knowledge. Indeed by exploring the social perspectives of mathematics education we begin to question many of the unjust practices present in our schools today and so the search for alternatives begins.

The approaches to social justice I have explored so far are, in the main, products of the deliberations of groups of men. Although offering useful models they tend to see the values of justice and autonomy as moral issues detached from everyday human behaviour. Carol Gilligan challenged this narrow view of social justice, asserting that for many women, the notion of *care* is a key to the way that moral decisions are made (Gilligan 1982). The push for autonomy within a society leads to a detached view of an individual, living within a hierarchically ordered society, whereas the values of care and attachment create a world of individuals within an attached network of relationships.

This view suggests we should not strive simply to produce autonomous, independent human beings, ready to play an aggressive role in pushing forward the domestic economy, or individually self-confident to take their place fighting for a place in a new job market, but must also look towards pedagogies in mathematics which encourage values of sharing, co-operation, joint labour and skill sharing.

Most importantly we should consider the existence of multiple and differing perspectives when viewing actions and interactions in our classrooms; we should acknowledge difference rather than foster homogeneity. This might not lead to a straightforward compartmentalised curriculum but it may guide the way to a more socially just curriculum or even a curriculum whose effect can be felt outside the mathematics classroom.

The idea that we can achieve equality in mathematics education by developing a curriculum that is identical for all actually goes against the idea of social justice. A social justice model would be based on the assumption that people are alike in some ways yet different in other ways. In fact somewhat paradoxically, for me the concept of social justice represents a shift in thinking *away from* equality in classrooms. 'Equality' can suggest a norm towards which we should strive. It does not easily accept and value difference, although attempts have been made to address this issue through slogans such as 'equal but different'. Maybe a social justice perspective can be seen as the beginning of a theory around this slogan:

> People should be treated identically in ways they are alike and differently in ways they are not alike. Relevant differences are respected and treated fairly, and justice is achieved.
>
> (Bennison 1984: 3)

How can we examine social justice in our schools?

In order to look at in more detail at how we can develop a social justice perspective on and in mathematics education, I need to make a strong claim. I claim that injustice is prevalent in mathematics classrooms and is perpetuated through:

- the mathematics curriculum;
- the mathematics pedagogy practised in classrooms;
- the assessment methods through which we organise and sort our pupils;
- the social and cultural environment within which we learn and teach mathematics.

Much of this injustice goes unseen, unrecognised and unchallenged of course, and you may already be disagreeing with my fundamental premises, yet before you put the book back on the shelf, stay with my argument a little longer. To think about the way we need to operate as teachers of mathematics, I think we can look at three key areas. These three areas overlap of course but in doing so they inform each other. If we effect change in one area, we influence the others. However, by breaking down the way we think about our work, we may find it easier to make sense of what we do and consider practical possibilities for change. My three key areas are:

1. The curriculum: What counts as knowledge, from what perspective does the teaching take place? What images are used in teaching? What material is selected?

2. The pedagogy: How do we actually teach? What expectations are there underpinning teacher/pupil relationships?
3. The social and cultural environment of the school: How are individuals and their community heritages and practices valued in the school and in our classrooms? To what extent do the school and the classroom reflect the communities in which we live and the democratic practices we espouse?

As a teacher interested in exploring issues of justice in mathematics classrooms through looking at injustices presently built into our practices, I need to turn this list into a set of questions I can use to explore teaching and learning in the classroom.

- What do we teach?
- How do we teach it?
- What do we value as knowledge and ability in the subject?
- How do we, and the learners in our care, feel about our practices and our institutions?

Reflecting on the issue . . .
Explore the four questions above from a range of viewpoints. How would the following people in your institution answer them?
> the headteacher
> the head of mathematics
> an NQT in the mathematics department
> a pupil leaving attaining A* at mathematics GCSE
> a pupil leaving having failed mathematics GCSE
> a pupil excluded from mathematics lessons through their challenging behaviour
> the parents of the above three pupils

Cameron McCarthy (McCarthy 1990) engaged himself on a similar set of questions, and through observations within classrooms he came to the conclusion that injustices are played out through relationships of competition, domination, exploitation and cultural selection. I have found that working with these ideas offers me alternative ways of viewing my classroom and my school. This alternative viewpoint allows me to question institutional and personal practices from a standpoint of social justice. Let me try to develop the ideas a little further.

Competition becomes a problem for teachers and their learners when it leads to individuals or groups becoming isolated from mathematics and from mathematics learning. This can lead to individuals or groups of individuals becoming isolated from each other both within the classroom and between teaching groups. Such competition can be seen as a competition for access to education, who gets entrance to 'the best' schools; a competition for credentials from education, who gets the 'best' grades; as well as the competition for the scarcity of resources and teacher time, who gets the most highly qualified teachers.

Exploitation and domination are closely linked and can be seen as the over-representation of one group over another in the classroom, of one teaching style over another within mathematics teaching, of the focus of teacher time on a single aspect of mathematics, or on a single group of mathematics learners, and an unrepresentative selection of resources. Such relationships of domination clearly take us back to the exploration of power relations.

The idea of cultural selection has been described earlier when I suggested schools audit examination results against pupil background. There are also echoes of Pierre Bourdieu's ideas of cultural capital in here. (See Robyn Zevenbergen's chapter for more on this.)

I do not wish to seem as though I am a prophet of doom. On the contrary, I would suggest that there is much we can do to challenge injustice by examining the mathematics curriculum, by being critical about the practices adopted in classrooms and by being aware of the social and political context in which we operate. I will develop these ideas a little further and will do so by posing – and then addressing – four questions which relate to the first of my initial key questions and my underlying assumption that injustice is perpetuated through the social and cultural environments in which we learn and teach mathematics. My questions are:

- How do we and how do our learners feel about our practices and institutions?
- How does the competition for access to educational rewards and resources manifest itself?
- To what extent does a particular view of mathematics dominate in classrooms?
- Is there evidence that mathematics education prepares individuals for particular life choices rather than rational life choices, or do schools make it appear as though we are behaving rationally?

I will offer a personal response to these questions in the next five sections. In doing so, I draw on my own experience in three cities and across all phases of education as a mathematics teacher, as an observer of mathematics classrooms and as a researcher engaged in doctoral work within mathematics classrooms (you can see this in Cotton 1998). This should be read as a personal reflection on these questions and as an invitation for your own reflection rather than simply a model to be followed.

How do we and how do our learners feel about our practices and institutions?

Many pupils I come into contact with do not *feel* anything about the practices within the institutions they attended. They do not seem to think there is any other way it could be. This is not to say that they are not capable of critical engagement with important and complex issues – rather that they see such critical engagement in terms of mathematics teaching as rather pointless. This suggests to me that before we can establish a classroom environment in which critical engagement with the practice of learning and teaching is the norm we have other practical questions to work on:

- How can mathematics teachers help to develop an ethos of mutual respect?
- How can we support the development of mathematics teachers as good role models?
- How can children's views of learning and their expectations of mathematics be valued?
- How can we enable pupils to be more involved in the decisions we take over their learning?

I have found two ways of working that help me towards answers to these questions. The first is the use of learning journals that focus on issues of teaching and learning. These journals are the focus of critical conversations between teachers and their pupils around issues both teachers and pupils see as important. Similarly, working with focus groups of pupils consisting of representatives from all the groups taught by an individual teacher, or the formation of a mathematics pupil council who will meet half-termly to discuss issues that are being raised across all teaching groups, offers critical space for engagement between teachers and pupils. In this way, pupils' voices can be heard, a basic condition for social justice, but which also helps both teachers and pupils begin to see the possibilities for change.

Another way to allow for possibilities for change to be explored is to ask pupils to act as observers of lessons rather than as pupils in lessons. Such pupils can be trained through the use of video and adapted OFSTED inspection criteria. These observations will be reported back to the whole group – together with suggestions for ways the lesson could be conducted differently. To develop this idea, pupils and teachers could develop their own set of criteria for conditions for effective learning and then act as auditors for these criteria.

How does the competition for access to educational rewards and resources manifest itself?

The impact of this competition can be seen in the way it is more often the case that it is individuals who blame themselves for lack of success. We can also see the competition at work in groups of pupils who feel excluded, or are literally excluded, from success at mathematics. One way to challenge the results of this competition is to expose the results of the competition as unjust. Pupils can begin to see how societal influences work within schooling by using and critically examining data on exam results in terms of gender, ethnicity and class with pupils, as well as data on staffing issues such as the recruitment of teachers from minority ethnic communities.

How can we support the development of mathematics teachers as good role models?

Another manifestation of the competition within education is in the staffing crisis in schools. More flexibility seems to be one way in which the pressures can be eased on those teachers remaining in the system. This may serve to help answer the question. An exploration of ways in which individual teachers can develop such flexibility may be one way forward. Team teaching and partnership teaching with double groups, working with teachers from other subjects to enhance skills, as well as creative and imaginative (whilst not exploitative) use of student teachers would also benefit pupils. Intensive use of large groups of teacher training students with those who have missed out on parts of their mathematics education, the use of students in community numeracy projects involving both learners and their parents would be two examples of this in practice.

To what extent does a particular view of mathematics dominate in classrooms?

My own research suggests that a utilitarian view of mathematics is dominant both within and outside classrooms. This is most dangerous when it is not recognised that such an ideology is present. One way to explore the view of mathematics that dominates our classrooms is to ask colleagues to observe lessons, noting down any asides and informal messages about the nature of mathematics and how it is learnt. The results of this discussion can be used to explore beliefs with teaching groups. This way of working can also include pupils through such things as journals and focus groups mentioned above. Another process which can expose practices that we take as common sense that are more deeply ideological is twinning activities with schools which differ radically from the school the pupils usually operate in. The results of these visits can be used to explore our own beliefs and values.

Is there evidence that mathematics education prepares individuals for particular life choices rather than rational life choices, or do schools make it appear as though we are behaving rationally?

Schools can be seen as places in which life choices are legitimated. I would suggest it is important to be critical rather than idealistic. We do not live in a meritocracy; pupils need the skills that will enable them to engage critically with the world outside school. These skills may be very different from the ones we are offering them through mathematics in school at the moment. At present the only choice we offer many pupils is to remove themselves from their own 'culture' in order to make the transition into the culture of mathematics learning. Rather than try to change the pupils, we should work at changing the mathematics education we offer. This involves a reassessment of the aims of mathematics education and a reappraisal of the view of mathematics that permeates the current curriculum.

Towards a pedagogy for social justice

Clearly a pedagogy for social justice should satisfy the demands of the model of social justice we see as appropriate. Fundamentally it seems that such a pedagogy would be anti-competitive, would work against the domination of mathematics classrooms by particularly advantaged groups of learners or communities, would be non-exploitative of both learners and teachers and would not lead to cultural selection or cultural imperialism. Within such a pedagogy individuals would feel empowered as learners and as individuals, would feel secure in their environment, an active member of their communities within the classroom and an equal partner

Table 2.1   A Pedagogy for Social Justice

Theme	Teaching strategies	Contribution to social justice
Acknowledge and build on learners' heritage, valuing and emphasising cultural practices and knowledges.	Brainstorming, pair work, student choices, different entry points within activities.	Culture creating, challenges domination. Emphasises connections.
Move from informal to formal languages of mathematics to develop oral, formal and informal traditions.	Whole group dialogue, two-way pedagogies including learner presentations, discussions, journals and learning logs, debriefings, interviews and conferences.	Culture-creating, anti-competitive.
Promote collaborative and mutually supportive ways of working.	Working pairs, collaborative activity, development of connected relationships within which learners feel valued.	Anti-competitive, challenges domination, builds security in the learning environment.
Encourage learners to become active in both interpreting and changing their worlds, develop critical consciousness through mathematics activity.	Reading exercises, projects and performances that use the methods of a field study and represent a whole piece of work within that field, mathematical studies of political and social issues.	Empowerment through mathematics.
Moving towards learner autonomy, emphasis on power with not power over.	Learner board work, problem posing, self-evaluation, scaffolding a process of successive conversations, learning experiences that take learners from different starting points to proficient performance.	Challenges domination, culture creating, anti-competitive.

in the building of a culture of learning. I would suggest such a pedagogy would contain the following themes (Table 2.1).

The teaching strategies here are taken from Linda Darling-Hammond (1996) who suggests that the strategies mentioned here are used by teachers who:

> seem to succeed at developing real understanding of challenging subjects – and who seem able to do so for an array of students who include some traditionally thought to be at risk.
>
> (Darling-Hammond 1996: 15)

I hope that this checklist offers a view of pedagogy rather than a list of teaching styles. My aim is that it should give suggestions for teaching styles together with the validation for using this style. Remember, pedagogy is both the teaching style and the political/educational aim for working in this way. Thus for example, brainstorming is not just a pedagogy for social justice – it is a strategy that is a means of validating and valuing cultural knowledge.

Toward a mathematics curriculum for social justice

What do I mean by curriculum? One response could be – 'well it's everything we teach really isn't it?' This is not a definition that I have personally found very useful. Roland Meighan playfully listed several other definitions (Meighan 1986: 68):

- an elaborate device for filling the time available;
- a rough and ready bargain between what some people are prepared to teach and others are prepared to learn;
- a mechanism for separating the children into good learners and poor ones;
- a social construction in which the selection and organisation of knowledge into the timetable of the school is the result of choice from possible alternatives;
- a course of study.

In this chapter, however, curriculum is seen as how 'society classifies . . . the educational knowledge it considers to be public' (Bernstein 1975: 85). Basil Bernstein saw this form of curriculum as a reflection of both the distribution of power within society and as a form of social control. For Basil Bernstein, curriculum defines what counts as valid knowledge in schools, pedagogy what was seen as acceptable ways of transmitting this knowledge and evaluation or assessment as the way in which this knowledge could be tested. So for me a mathematics curriculum is that which describes the mathematical knowledge that is to be taught to the children in our schools, and the ways in which this knowledge is ordered as it is presented to pupils in school. Clearly at the moment in England this curriculum takes the form of the National Curriculum (or the Framework for Teaching Mathematics as enshrined in the National Numeracy Strategy – DfEE, 1999a and b) – and resources chosen by teachers to reflect this prescribed body of knowledge.

The initial documents emanating from the National Curriculum Council in the United Kingdom described a scheme of work as 'the essential working document of classroom practice' (National Curriculum Council 1989: B7). This document is designed to outline the mathematical knowledge and skills to be covered by a cohort of children as well as the processes through which these are to be taught. The scheme of work is also expected to reflect broad principles of whole school policy, thus a scheme of work gives guidance about both the content and the pedagogy. This description offers me a way of translating my issue in this chapter into some form of practical document. The non-statutory guidance offers me a set of guidelines that should be taken into account by all those preparing a scheme of work. They are (National Curriculum Council 1989: B7–B11):

- Activities should bring together different areas of mathematics.
- The order of activities should be flexible.

- Activities should be balanced between those which develop knowledge, skills and understanding and those which develop the ability to tackle practical problems.
- Activities should be balanced between applications of mathematics and ideas which are purely mathematical.
- Activities should be balanced between those which are short in duration and those which have scope for development over an extended period.
- Activities should use pupils' own interests as starting points.
- Activities should involve both independent and group work.
- Tasks should be both of the kind which have an exact result and those which have many possible outcomes.
- Activities should be balanced between different modes of learning: doing, observing, talking and listening, discussing with other pupils, reflecting, drafting, reading and writing.
- Activities should encourage pupils to use mental arithmetic, and become confident in the use of a range of mathematical tools.
- Activities should enable pupils to communicate their mathematics.
- Activities should enable pupils to develop their personal qualities.
- Activities should enable pupils to develop a positive attitude to mathematics.

It might be worth pausing to wonder why this set of guidelines has failed to permeate the planning of many teachers in mathematics classrooms. In conclusion, however, let us remind ourselves of the propositions from a social justice perspective which also need to inform a scheme of work. These would be:

- the use of learning journals to engage in critical conversations with learners about learning and teaching;
- the use of a focus group to raise issues about learning and teaching in my mathematics lessons;
- the use of pupil observers to critically engage in debate about learning and teaching;
- the use of examination data for critical analysis;
- the use of flexible staffing including paired and partnership teaching;
- the use of colleagues to observe and critique lessons;
- twinning with other schools to enable pupils to engage with educational issues and explore personal values and beliefs;
- activities which acknowledge and build on learners' cultural heritage, valuing and emphasising cultural practices and knowledges;
- activities which allow learners to move from informal to formal languages of mathematics and to develop oral, formal and informal traditions;
- activities which promote collaborative and mutually supportive ways of working;
- activities which encourage learners to become active in interpreting and changing their worlds, activities which allow learners to move towards autonomy;
- activities which involve authentic modes of assessment;
- critical analysis with learners of the content of the curriculum;
- activities which offer an overview of the curriculum as a whole and how it will be developed in the classroom;

- activities which include as a matter of course new and relevant technologies;
- activities which both acknowledge individual cultures and introduce new cultures and connections in an affirmative way.

I hope that the two sections above have offered two things. First, I hope my personal response illustrates what drives my teaching, both of learners of mathematics and of beginning teachers of mathematics. What can I do to work towards a more just society through my work? However, perhaps more importantly I hope that I have offered alternative ways in which you as an individual teacher of mathematics may operate in your classroom. Do not read the chapter as a prescription or as an alternative curriculum, but rather as a vision of the way things might be and a set of strategies through which we may begin to construct such a vision.

Invitation to reflect

I hope this chapter invites you to reflect on the fundamental questions that face us as educators. What do we teach mathematics for? How will we measure our success as a mathematics teacher? Clearly examination results are not a sufficient measure. We must also reflect on the question 'what is this thing called mathematics that we teach?'; it is not simply bound by the constraints of the content of the curriculum (as many other chapters here illustrate, in particular Alan Bishop's chapter on values in the teaching of mathematics). I hope these questions have been raised for you through reading the chapter, I also hope that you finish the chapter feeling a little confused; it is through such confusion that we challenge our common sense assumptions and begin the exciting search for alternatives.

In a more structured way, you may care to consider that final set of bullet points. Which will you begin to adopt and work on, say, next week? What or who might actually (i.e. really) stop you working on the others?

Further suggested reading

Boaler, J. (1997) *Experiencing School Mathematics*, Buckingham: Open University Press. This book describes the results of a three-year research project that Jo was involved with in two secondary schools. It is a book that challenges the common sense notion that 'setting by ability' is the most efficient way of learning and teaching mathematics. Indeed Jo shows that working in all attainment groups actually raises 'standards' whilst questioning what such 'standards' might be.

Richardson, R. (1990) *Daring to be a Teacher*, Stoke on Trent: Trentham Books. Robin Richardson comes from a background of multicultural and anti-racist education. This book is a collection of essays and reflections on teaching for social justice with an emphasis on anti-racist practice.

Rudduck, J., Chaplain, R. and Wallace, G. (eds) (1996) *School Improvement: What Can Pupils Tell Us?* London: David Fulton Publishers. This is a book that draws on pupils' own views of schooling to critique and develop arguments for what effective schools should aspire to.

Skovsmose, O. (1994) *Towards a Philosophy of Critical Mathematics Education*, Dordrecht: Kluwer. In this book, Ole Skovsmose explores critical mathematics education from both a philosophical and a practical point of view. The middle section of the book contains examples of projects carried out in Danish schools committed to ideas of critical mathematics education.

References

Bennison, A. (1984) 'Equity or equality: What shall it be?' In Fennema, E. and Jane-Ayer, M. (eds) *Women and Education*, Berkeley: McCutchan Publishing Corporation, pp. 1–19.

Bernstein, B. (1975) *Class, Codes and Control: Volume 3 – Towards a Theory of Educational Transmissions*, London: Routledge and Kegan Paul.

Bruner, J. (1986) *Actual Minds, Possible Worlds*, London: Harvard University Press.

Cotton, T. (1998) *Toward a mathematics curriculum for social justice*, unpublished Ph.D thesis, the University of Nottingham.

Darling-Hammond, L. (1996) 'The right to learn and the advancement of teaching: Research, policy, and practice for democratic education', *Educational Researcher* 25(6), 5–17.

DfEE (1999a) *The National Numeracy Strategy: Framework for teaching mathematics from Reception to Year 6*, London: Department for Education and Employment.

DfEE (1999b) *The National Numeracy Strategy: Framework for teaching mathematics: Year 7*, London: Department for Education and Employment.

Gilligan, C. (1982) *In a Different Voice*, London: Harvard University Press.

McCarthy, C. (1990) *Race and Curriculum: Social Inequality and the Theories and Politics of Difference in Contemporary Research on Schooling*, Basingstoke: The Falmer Press.

Meighan, R. (1986) *A Sociology of Educating*, London: Cassell Press.

National Curriculum Council (1989) *The Mathematics National Curriculum: The Non Statutory Guidance*, London: NCC.

Rawls, J. (1971) *A Theory of Justice*, Oxford: Oxford University Press

Skovsmose, O. (1994) *Towards a Philosophy of Critical Mathematics Education*, Dordrecht: Kluwer Press.

3 Language, social class and underachievement in school mathematics

Robyn Zevenbergen

Introduction to the issue

Studies have shown consistently that one's social and cultural backgrounds are deeply influential in determining whether or not anyone is likely to perform well in mathematics (Lamb 1997; Marjoribanks 1987; Secada 1992). Such findings have remained relatively consistent over the past 30 or 40 years and have been replicated across diverse countries.

In some people's minds, such findings represented the 'natural order' of social life, that is, that some groups of people are naturally inferior to others. This type of argument is very evident in conservative politics and has been advocated in controversial texts such as *The Bell Curve* (Herrnstein and Murray 1994). In contrast, other researchers, teachers, administrators and politicians have tried to develop intervention policies and practices to redress these outcomes, recognising that the practices in schools can contribute to the unequal outcomes of schooling.

In the case of gender equity programmes, there have been considerable changes and successes – though we need to treat any such 'successes' with some degree of caution (see Carrie Paechter's chapter). However, there has been less success in the area of social disadvantage, geographical disadvantage (that is, students living in rural and/or remote communities) and cultural disadvantage where the students' culture is very different from that of schools (particularly indigenous, or 'first nation', people). Walter Secada, an American who has worked for years in the area of equity and mathematics education, puts it this way,

> Frankly the literature does not bristle with the same sense of outrage that the poor do not do as well as their middle-class peers as it does with similar findings among other such groups. We should ask why.
>
> (Secada 1992: 640)

In this chapter, I explore why students from disadvantaged backgrounds are less successful than they could be when assessed by traditional measures of school mathematics and I consider what teachers can do to address this problem. My central focus is the role of language in learning mathematics and I argue that it is the *language* of mathematics that causes marginalisation by systematically favouring some students while disadvantaging others. In developing this argument,

I take social class as my focus. This is important because students who are marginalised or disadvantaged by their social class are often not perceived as being disadvantaged by their language because they are native speakers. Hence, the usual argument that lack of familiarity with the language is a hurdle to learning is not seen to apply. It is my contention that this is actually not the case. I contend that the English used to teach mathematics and the form of English used in mathematics itself is a very particularised form that is some distance away from the forms of English used by students from working-class backgrounds.

Key questions

The key question I want to pose in this chapter is: What aspects of language can be problematic for students when learning mathematics? In particular, I focus on problems likely to be encountered by students in relation to their social background. In other words, this chapter seeks to identify areas of difficulty for students when they come to learn the highly specific language of mathematics particularly where the form of the language spoken at home is different from that spoken within the formal school context. In adopting such an approach it becomes possible to analyse critically various aspects of mathematical language in order to understand the processes through which social and educational exclusion can occur almost unnoticed through the adoption of certain language conventions, forms and styles. Consequently, we might be in a better position to develop effective strategies for improving learning outcomes for those students who have been frequently excluded from participation and success.

Mathematics and language

For some time, mathematics was thought to be largely symbolic and educators believed that students who experienced language difficulties could still succeed in mathematics. It was (and often still is) common folklore that mathematics is not affected by the language that is used to talk about and describe it; that two plus two will always equal four, the world over.

With these views being so commonly held, it is often assumed that mathematics is socially and culturally neutral. However, more recently, there has been an increasing awareness of language and its impact on mathematics learning (Ellerton and Clements 1991; Orton 1996; Pimm 1991). Much of this attention adopts either a psychological focus – where the emphasis is on the individual, or a mathematical focus – where the emphasis is on the mathematics and aspects of language related to it. Within this framework the main focus is directed at how the language of mathematics should be a significant component of classroom practice but *without* recognising that biases inherent in the language determine to a large extent who is included and who is excluded.

What is less well documented is the political aspect of language; how language factors represent particular forms of culture and in so doing, exclude some students from effective participation in mathematics. In this light, I want to explore some aspects of language as it is used in mathematics in order to understand how some groups of students are marginalised and consequently excluded from education. I will draw upon Basil Bernstein's (1990) notion of 'elaborated' and 'restricted' codes and extend his theoretical underpinnings in order to understand the communication mechanisms of social class reproduction in mathematics. I argue that students from socially disadvantaged backgrounds use different forms of language from that valued within the mathematics and indeed school contexts. I want to suggest that the language used by some students positions them as marginal within the context of contemporary mathematics classrooms. From this perspective, it becomes possible to see that the language background of the students becomes an important factor in their subsequent positioning within school mathematics. Hence, rather than seeing some students as deficient, it is important to recognise that the mathematics curriculum is acting as a social filter. Through the practices embedded within mathematics teaching, some students are being constructed as effective 'successful' learners of mathematics while others are being constructed as 'failures'. Consequently, underachievement by the group of students labeled as 'failures' can be seen as a result of the mismatch between the language of the student and the language of the school, rather than as an individual lack of ability or facility with mathematics. This perspective allows teachers to recognise the critical aspects of language that contribute to educational and mathematical marginalisation and in so doing develop effective strategies for overcoming this aspect of mathematical learning. Such a perspective also challenges other more deterministic suggestions that there is a biological basis to mathematical success such as some inherent or genetic ability.

Reflecting on the issue . . .

It would be useful at this stage for you to get some idea of the possible range and diversity in the language experience of pupils you might teach. You could do this in the following ways. Select several small groups of pupils from a year group who have been identified as having different levels of mathematical ability. Show them a photograph and ask then to tell you about it. Make a note of, or possibly record on tape their responses and listen to the types of language they use. Focus on:

(a) their use of grammar and syntax;
(b) their use of imagination compared to direct description;
(c) the extent to which they talk about their own everyday experience.

Make notes of any differences and diversity you notice and compare notes with either one of your contemporaries, or an experienced teacher.

Families, schools and mathematics

Numerous studies show that the links between the school and the home tend to be stronger with middle-class families than for working-class families. This has been shown across a number of countries (Connell, Ashendon, Kessler and Dowsett 1982; Willis 1977). Such studies indicate that there are substantial differences in the values held by working-class families when compared to middle-class families – particularly over such matters as the importance of schooling for example. For me, this is reinforced when I spend time with new student teachers in their first weeks of teaching. As I spend time in their classrooms, in schools with a wide range of socio-economic backgrounds, it is clear that in the schools where there was a predominantly working-class population, parents often comment that they were no good at mathematics, so they couldn't expect their own children to be otherwise. Other comments are very gendered, where mothers would say 'I could never do maths so can't help him/her, but his/her Dad is OK with maths so he will have to help him with that.' Such comments are not as common in the schools where there were predominantly middle-class families. Comments were more of the kind, 'We will have to work on that tonight' so there was little indication of whether or not the parent/s could do the mathematics or whether there tends to be a gendered division of help. Such comments indicated a more collaborative approach to helping the children in more affluent homes. In both cases, there was an indication of willingness to support their children, but it would appear that the working-class families might not be able to be as supportive due to their own feelings of inadequacy towards mathematics either through lack of ability or gender stereotyping. In contrast, in the middle-class families there appears to be a stronger collaborative commitment to working with their children.

Aside from a commitment to supporting their children, families can offer other forms of support for learning. One's level of prosperity (called 'economic capital') plays a significant role in how well families are able to support their children's learning. In many middle-class families, the resources provided to the children are likely to exceed that which can be offered to the working-class children. Computers and other forms of technology are an excellent example of this difference. However, there are aspects of the resource issue that are more mundane. For example, many working-class families are likely to be financially restricted and unable to offer the funds for essential learning equipment at the start of the new school year. Consider how long it takes for all students to be properly equipped with the expected tools – books, rulers, pencils and so forth.

On a more systemic level, one only has to consider the resources across various schools. In my position as a teacher educator, I am continually confronted by the contrasts between students working in schools where there is no mathematics equipment and others where pupils have access to high technology in every classroom. More often than not, the differences correspond quite starkly with the social background of the school community. Frequently, the resources in schools are a direct result of a very active parent group, which takes on fund-raising for aspects of school projects. Most often, these schools (and parent groups) are based in middle-class neighbourhoods where the parents have the skills, knowledge and ethos towards school improvement and learning.

Aside from economic capital, the notion of cultural capital (Bourdieu 1983) is also critical. This refers, among other things, to the attitudes and dispositions held towards schooling and mathematics and are evident in the values parents hold. For example, in spite of not having the economic capital to provide resources, such as books, for their children, parents may recognise the importance of exposing their children to literature and ensure that they are active borrowers at the local library. Such parents recognise the importance of being educated and seek ways to ensure that their children gain access to all possibilities. Similarly, they recognise that reading the classics is more valued than reading comics. In these examples, the parents may not have the economic capital or financial resources to provide books, but they have the cultural capital to recognise the importance of books in education, and that some books are better than others in this respect than others. However, the provision of cultural capital is usually quite directly coupled with the accumulation of economic capital. That is to say, while the provision of cultural capital (going to museums, libraries etc.) does not always require money, such activities are less prevalent amongst less affluent families.

Another form of cultural capital is in the language spoken by the students. As teachers would quickly recognise, students who do not 'speak well', will have their language corrected so that it is of the 'proper' form. Correction of expression is a common practice in teaching. What is less commonly recognised is that the language spoken by students is often the form of language used in the home context. Basil Bernstein (1990) has developed a complex theory on the differences of linguistic form between social classes. It is also less well recognised that the linguistic form used, and hence that most valued, within the formal school context is that of the middle classes (Bernstein 1990). This means that the language that students learn from their homes is likely to position them more or less favourably depending on the accord between the home and school languages. As such, language becomes a form of capital that can be used and exchanged within the school context and within the context of mathematics. (We could call this linguistic capital, but it is intimately linked to culture and therefore cultural capital.) Where students are able to speak, use and understand the language of the school, they are more likely to unpack the messages and content being conveyed by the teacher than students who are less familiar with the language and hence unable to 'crack the code' of school English.

Diversity in home and school language

A number of studies have highlighted these differences in language use between the home and school, particularly for students whose culture is different from that of the school setting (Heath 1982, 1983; Walkerdine and Lucey 1989). Basil Bernstein's work with different linguistic codes gives a theory around which it becomes possible to discuss the differences between the forms of language used by different social classes and their links with the language used in the school context. For example, Basil Bernstein's notion of an 'elaborated code' identifies the preponderance of embellished language commonly used within middle-class families. For example, when parents ask their children to locate items, they are more likely to use rich positional language – 'your red jumper is on the top left hand shelf' whereas the 'restricted code' of the working class is more likely to be devoid of contextual cues. Not only does the elaborated language help the student locate the jumper more effectively, but it also prepares the student for the instructions that they will hear in the classroom as well as the language they will hear, and be expected to use, in mathematics. The parents are not explicitly teaching positional language to the students, but rather it is embedded in the interaction of everyday life. In this way, the child progressively learns the richness of the language but also the mode of communication so that such modes of talk are seen as natural. In contrast, the interactions between working-class parents is somewhat restrictive in both content and prose so that when the children enter the school contexts, their experiences are very different from their middle-class peers. Not only do they have to learn new words and their meanings, but also the mode of communication is substantially different. Working-class language is far more contextual and students take significantly more cues from other aspects of the interaction. (This issue is discussed in the context of pupil assessment in Barry Cooper's chapter.)

An extreme example of the highly contextual features of language became apparent when I was working with indigenous students on a remote island community in Australia. I needed directions to the local high school and asked a group of 12-year-olds. Their response was 'Over there miss' with a flick of the head in a very general direction. When I asked for more help, they repeated their instructions. Direction and distance were not of any consequence and hence not necessary in the interaction: I needed to take my cues from other aspects of the interaction.

The rich language of middle-class parents prepares children for the language they will encounter in school mathematics. Conversely, working-class children encounter forms of language in the home environment different from that which they encounter in the school. Hence, it is not valid to assume that problems in the levels of attainment of working-class students arise solely from any deficiency in their mathematical ability. Within this perspective, it becomes important to recognise the difference in home–school languages and to build bridges in order that students can access the mathematical language and hence, mathematical knowledge.

There are specific examples of language causing a barrier to the access some children have to learning mathematics. Valerie Walkerdine (1988) has shown that the use of comparative terms – such as 'more' and 'less' – are used differently according to social background. She found that working-class families are less likely to use the term 'less' in their everyday language so that when their children enter the mathematics classroom, the language and concept for 'less' is not as accessible as would be commonly expected by possibly middle-class teachers. Rather than use both 'more' and 'less' to describe quantities, the term 'more' is used, as in: 'I will have more ice-cream' or 'I will have no more ice-cream'. Very early mathematics lessons use the terms 'more' and 'less' very frequently, for example in lessons where numbers are being compared and ordered. Teachers use both terms when comparing numbers and do so unproblematically. Yet, the work from Valerie Walkerdine suggests that many of the working-class students may not have the language, and hence concepts, to comprehend clearly and unambiguously what is being meant. Simple ordering tasks rely heavily on the use of more and less – which is more, 3 or 5; which is less 3 or 6; what number is 2 less than 8. Similar examples can be found when undertaking operations – namely addition and subtraction – where 'more' is more frequently associated with addition and 'less' associated with subtraction, although the work undertaken with word problems indicates that this is not always the case (De Corte and Verschaffel 1991). For example, the most common use of 'more' is in the types of questions such as: I had

4 marbles and then I got 3 more marbles, how many have I got altogether? Similarly, I have 5 marbles, and Simon has 2 less than me, how many marbles does Simon have? Particularly in the early years of school, students for whom there is less contact with the formal language of school mathematics have a greatly reduced chance of making sense of teacher talk.

The language of the student has been shaped by their familial contexts and clearly some enter the school context with greater control over, and familiarity with, the language of mathematics. Where students have had rich experiences – linguistic and otherwise – they will be better positioned to deconstruct teacher talk. The language of mathematics is very specific and students need to be able to identify the correct meanings of words if they are to be able to communicate effectively and to construct appropriate meanings. For example, one only needs to consider the vast number of words that are used in mathematics that have different meanings in other contexts, or in other parts of mathematics. Words such as 'whole' and 'hole' sound the same to students and when used in the classroom can cause them to misunderstand and attempt to construct meaning from the teacher or student talk based on a set of incorrect assumptions. One only needs to consider the effect of teaching fractions where '½ plus ½ equals a whole' is spoken by the teacher which the students (mis)interpret to be '½ plus ½ equals a hole'. The culture of many classrooms – and indeed the culture of schooling more generally – is that the teacher is the conveyor of truths, so the student is left to try and make sense of how two halves make a hole. Similar examples can occur with the use of 'base', 'volume', 'face', all of which have a specific mathematical meaning as well as it having another meaning outside the mathematics classroom. If students identify with the wrong meaning, then making 'accurate' meaning (in the sense of accepted meaning) is again difficult. (Candia Morgan in her chapter discusses similar issues in the context of valuing student writing in mathematics.) Where students enter the mathematics classroom with rich prior experiences in language, they are more likely to be able to make sense of, and hence construct more appropriate forms of mathematical meaning than their peers who have not had the same rich prior experiences in language. The potential for achievement is greatly enhanced.

Reflecting on the issue . . .

At this point, it would be useful trying to identify lists of words or phrases that have both a technical mathematical meaning, and a more common everyday meaning which pupils might encounter outside the classroom. There are probably many more than you realise.

Additionally you might like to talk to some teachers about things pupils have said in mathematics, which on the surface might appear amusing, but actually mask deeper issues of understanding and mental representation. Sometimes these are rather patronisingly called 'howlers'. Try to identify the source of the mistranslation. Consider for instance the following example in which Sophie is actually quite correct:

Teacher: Sophie, how many times can you take 2 from 8?
Sophie: Every time I do it Miss, I get 6!

The mistake Sophie is actually making is to misinterpret the meaning behind the teacher's question. Her response could well be interpreted by a teacher as inappropriate.

Classroom interactions and styles of language

Another area in which disjunction occurs between home and school language is in the implicit rules through which classroom management is achieved. At the beginning of a year, a common practice within classrooms is the establishment of a list of classroom rules. This is often undertaken through a process of 'negotiation' with the students so that there is a perceived ownership of the rules, and hence accountability to the rules. However, within these explicitly negotiated rules is another set of rules that govern classroom behaviour. Such rules are not usually actually negotiated, but are rather a set of culturally accepted and expected norms that are a hidden aspect of classroom culture and are almost universal in Western-style classrooms. One only has to consider going into the classroom of another teacher; another school; another region, county, state or even country and there is a strong sense of familiarity. These are the unspoken aspects of classroom culture.

In the intergenerational interactions between parents and child or teacher and student, the styles of interacting are quite different depending on the social background of the participants. Shirley Brice Heath (1982) has shown that the styles of requesting for working-class families are more likely to be of a declarative form – 'Go and do the dishes'. Alternatively, middle-class families still expect the child to do the task, but are more likely to pose the task as a question such as 'Would you like to do the dishes?'. The consequences of the interactions are the same – the child must do the dishes – but the request is posed quite differently by the parents.

Within the classroom, the implications of this research is that students who do not recognise the pseudo-question 'Would you like to . . .' as merely a request or demand for a particular action, are more likely to misinterpret the teacher's intentions and offer inappropriate responses – such as 'No thanks!'. While good advice to intending teachers suggests that the use of questions such as 'Could you open your maths books up?' is not ideal, even the inclusion of 'please' at the end of a declarative statement is construed frequently as an indication to working-class students that they may have an option. What is apparent in these situations is a difference between the home and school rather than as something inherently wrong with the students as is often thought to be the case. Hence, rather than interpret the behaviour of some students *as* deviant or con-frontational, the teacher might recognise the root cause lies in the differential patterns of interaction at home and school. In Shirley Brice Heath's work, she found that some parents were aware of the different sets of rules operating in schools and classrooms – something that was evident in the comment offered by one mother: 'My kid, he too scared to talk, 'cause nobody play by the rules he know. At home, I cain't shut him up' (cited in Heath 1982: 107). While this child was being silenced by the rules for interaction, other students may be seen to be flaunting school rules. An alternative interpretation is they may not appreciate the subtlety and difference between the interactional rules of the school and of the home.

Reflecting on the issue . . .

Try to observe, or reconstruct some classroom incidents where it appeared that a pupil was being deviant in some way. Given what you have read above, try to revisit the incident from the pupils' perspective as a clash of cultures.

Talk to some pupils who have been identified by teachers in the school as difficult, deviant or disruptive. Try to get the picture from their point of view. What alternative explanations can you uncover?

Now try to relate that task to mathematics teaching. Find some pupils who seem to be alienated or switched off by mathematics. What's their perspective?

Language and context

Perhaps one of the more powerful movements in mathematics education has been the attempt to make mathematics more 'real' by embedding tasks into contexts that are supposed to represent real-life situations. One of the main reasons for this approach to mathematics education is that it seeks to demonstrate to students the relevance and application of mathematics to real-life situations outside of the school. (Paul Dowling discusses this issue in his chapter.) It is often argued that this is to provide students with the means to think mathematically. Yet, this approach itself raises further problems. Often the context within which the mathematics has been embedded contains particular assumptions that are limited and limiting and hence do not reflect the real world. For example, a commonly used example is the purchase of a car, the associated running costs, and the development of a savings plan through which the student will be able to purchase the car. The teachers or writers of the textbooks have attempted to embed the mathematics in a task with which the students may have some familiarity. However, within these problems there are also set parameters and assumptions built into the tasks. In the car-purchasing example, assumptions of deposits, purchasing schedules, maintenance schedules are based around particular economic and value systems that may or may not resonate with the students' life circumstances. Eugene Maier (1991) argues that the difficulties students encounter with these types of problems is that they actually have very little to do with their real world; the problems are 'school problems, coated with a thin veneer of 'real world' associations' (Maier 1991: 63). There are of course other questions we could ask that might for example relate the price of different cars compared to the average wage of a school cleaner. (Paul Ernest discusses issues related to this in his chapter.)

However, embedding mathematical tasks within word problems – and providing a context for a problem means it has to be embedded in a word problem – raises another set of issues for disadvantaged students. Within the literature examining performance on tests, Barry Cooper and Mairéad Dunne (1999) have found that working-class students perform equally as well as their middle-class peers on tasks that are decontextualised, but when tasks are embedded into contexts, the performance of working-class students declines. (See also Barry Cooper's chapter in this book.) This research is significant in that it alerts educators to the potential difficulties faced by working-class students when mathematics is embedded in some context. This will be startling for many educators who have assumed that working-class students are often more concrete thinkers and that the embedding of mathematics into concrete situations will enhance their understandings of the task. Barry Cooper and Mairéad Dunne's research indicates that considerable care must be taken with such assumptions about learning and learners. Similar caution should be taken with other cultural groups as well.

The impact of Barry Cooper and Mairéad Dunne's work is that it indicates the role of language in the mathematical tasks. Embedding school mathematics into some context demands a higher level of language saturation. For example, the equation $3+4=?$ is simple, but to put it into even a simple task such as 'I bought 3 oranges and then went to another shop to buy another 4 oranges, how many did I have altogether' requires substantially more reading and language-based learning. Furthermore, Basil Bernstein (1990) has shown that the approaches used in many mathematics classrooms have what he called 'strong framing', where the mathematics is heavily controlled by teachers, and more importantly but less directly the nature of educational discourse, so that the all-important context acts as a frame around the mathematics which must be interpreted by the learner. When the task is embedded in a word problem and other contextual cues are provided, then there is greater chance for misinterpretations – or perhaps we should say alternative interpretations – of the task, and hence greater chance of error for students not familiar with unpacking the meaning embedded in the tasks.

Conclusion

In the preceding sections, I have attempted to draw attention to potential areas of difficulty for some students in our mathematics classrooms. The approach that I have taken is one where I have argued that it is important to recognise that students from different social backgrounds come into our classrooms with very different life experiences and a very different language background based on these experiences. The French sociologist Pierre Bourdieu (Bourdieu and Passeron 1977) argues that this is because some students come into mathematics classrooms *predisposed* to learn mathematics. This predisposition, however, is not due to their innate ability but rather due to the experiences – linguistic and otherwise – that they have had in their familial settings. For such students, the language and styles of interacting with others which they are used to is similar to that of the formal mathematics classrooms, so they are better able to crack the code of the culture represented in these classrooms. In having this cultural knowledge and linguistic experience, such students are better able to position themselves more favourably in the eyes of their teachers. The converse is also true, so that for those students whose experiences are different from that of the mathematics classrooms, success is more evasive than for their middle-class peers. In understanding success within this framework it becomes possible to see the language experiences of the students as forms of capital that can be exchanged for success – those who have the capital recognised by the school setting are more likely to trade that capital for successes in mathematics, and subsequently obtain qualifications they can use in the future.

In the past, mathematics has been seen to be a discipline that is devoid of language, yet it is now clear that it is very language-based. For students whose out-of-school experiences position them favourably with the practices and language of in-school mathematics, the chances of success are greater than when the converse is true. What this means is that for working-class students, and indeed other students for whom language is different from that used within the formal school setting, the chances of success are reduced. Rather than view the child as deficit in their learning of mathematics, it may be more productive to recognise the language differences and seek ways to redress these differences.

Invitation to reflect

There are a number of very useful strategies for developing an awareness of the importance of language in mathematics.

On page 44, you looked at the vast array of words that are used in mathematics and which are commonly occurring words in out-of-school contexts (for example, volume, square, root, multiply). In addition, mathematics has a vast specific technical vocabulary consisting of difficult mathematical terms (for example, integer, tessellation). You could create two lists of words (common and specific) for a particular topic by going through the textbooks used in your school and identifying the words that are used. It is surprising how many words appear in these lists! Individual teachers or school schemes of work may use such lists as triggers that need to be carefully watched when introducing or teaching concepts as they can create stumbling blocks or misconceptions for the students. Consider the potential difficulties that students may encounter when they hear these words used, then try to consider teaching strategies for using, clarifying or explicitly teaching these words. Creating awareness in students of the complex array of words is the first step in addressing the issue.

A more personally challenging strategy is to tape one of your lessons – either using videotape or audiotape. My experience with teachers (and with myself) with this strategy is that they are initially surprised by poor pronunciation or other aspects of their own delivery. However, it is important to move beyond this aspect of delivery and consider other aspects of the language being used – such as those indicted in the various sections of this chapter. Consider for example:

- the ways in which there is potential slippage in terminology for students that results in misconceptions;
- student misbehaviour as a misinterpretation of the unspoken classroom rules for interaction rather than just 'calling out';
- the complexity of embedding mathematics into 'concrete' problems as hiding the mathematics from the students.

By reconsidering teaching within this framework, different potential for under-standing learning and teaching emerge – particularly for teachers' understanding of the complexity of the mathematics classroom.

Further suggested readings

Dirkin, K. and Shire, B. (1995) *Language in Mathematical Education: Research and practice*, Buckingham: Open University Press. This book contains a range of chapters that open up a number of issues connecting mathematics education and language. In various chapters you will find discussions of research on how children's language capabilities influence their learning of mathematics and vice versa.

Heath, S. B. (1983) *Ways with Words: Language, Life and Work in Communities and Classrooms*, Cambridge: Cambridge University Press. This book is a fascinating study of how children's social background plays a central role in helping – or hindering – their access to the formal education provided in their local schools. Shirley Brice Heath reports on an in-depth study that she undertook in some contrasting American communities. It is in many ways a classic text in this area.

Zevenbergen, R. (2000) 'Mathematics, social class and linguistic capital: An analysis of a mathematics classroom', in Atweh, B. and Forgasz, H. (eds), *Socio-cultural Aspects of Mathematics Education: An International Perspective*, Mahwah, NJ: Lawrence Erlbaum, pp. 201–215. In this chapter, I try to develop some of the ideas I have presented here much further and more deeply.

References

Bernstein, B. (1990) *The Structuring of Pedagogic Discourse: Vol 4. Class, codes and control*, London: Routledge.

Bourdieu, P. (1983) 'The forms of capital', in Richardson, J. G. (ed.), *Handbook of Theory and Research for the Sociology of Education*, New York: Greenwood Press.

Bourdieu, P. and Passeron, J.-C. (1977) *Reproduction in Education, Society and Culture*, (translated in 1990 by Richard Nice), London: Sage.

Connell, R. W., Ashendon, D. J., Kessler, S. and Dowsett, G. W. (1982) *Making the Difference: Schools, Families and Social Division*, Sydney: George Allen and Unwin.

Cooper, B. and Dunne, M. (1999) *Assessing Children's Mathematical Knowledge: Social Class, Sex and Problem Solving*, London: Open University Press.

de Corte, E. and Verschffell, L. (1991) 'Some factors influencing the solution of addition and subtraction word problems' in Durkin, K. and Shire, B. (eds.) *Language in Mathematical Education: Research and Practice*, Milton Keynes: Open University Press, pp. 117–30.

Ellerton, N. F. and Clements, M. A. (1991) *The Mathematics of Language: A Review of Language Factors in School Mathematics*, Geelong: Deakin University Press.

Heath, S. B. (1982) 'Questioning at home and at school: A comparative study', in Spindler G. D. (ed.), *Doing the Ethnography of Schooling*, New York: Holt, Rinehart and Winston, pp. 102–31.

Heath, S. B. (1983) *Ways with Words: Language, Life and Work in Communities and Classrooms* (1989 edition), Cambridge: Cambridge University Press.

Herrnstein, R. J. and Murray, C. (1994) *The Bell Curve: Intelligence and Class Structure in American Life*, New York: Free Press.

Lamb, S. (1997) *Completing School in Australia: Trends in the 1990s*, Melbourne: Australian Council for Educational Research.

Maier, E. (1991) 'Folk Mathematics', in Harris, M. (ed.), *Schools, Mathematics and Work*, London: Falmer Press, pp. 62–66.

Marjoribanks, K. (1987) 'Individual–environment correlates of children's mathematical achievement', *Educational Studies* 13(2), 115–23.

Orton, A. (1996) *Learning Mathematics: Issues, Theory and Classroom Practice* (2nd edition), London: Cassell.

Pimm, D. (1991) 'Communicating mathematically', in Durkin, K. and Shire, B. (eds), *Language in Mathematical Education: Research and Practice*, Philadelphia: Open University Press, pp. 17–24.

Secada, W. G. (1992) 'Race, ethnicity, social class, language and achievement in mathematics', in Grouws D. A. (ed.), *Handbook of Research on Mathematics Teaching and Learning: A Project of the National Council of Teachers of Mathematics*, New York: Macmillan Publishing Company, pp. 623–60.

Walkerdine, V. (1988) *The Mastery of Reason: Cognitive Development and the Production of Rationality*, London: Routledge.

Walkerdine, V. and Lucey, H. (1989) *Democracy in the Kitchen: Regulating Mothers and Socialising Daughters*, London: Virago.

Willis, P. (1977) *Learning to labour: How Working Class Kids Get Working Class Jobs*, Aldershot: Gower.

4 Gender, reason and emotion in secondary mathematics classrooms

Carrie Paechter

Introducing the issue

There has been a long history of concern about differential performance of boys and girls in mathematics. Until the last decade of the twentieth century, this focused around the comparative underachievement of girls. In 1980, for example, the Assessment of Performance Unit (APU) found that:

> the average scores for boys at age 15 were higher than those for girls in all fifteen topics tested (significantly so in 12 of them). However, at the higher attainment ranges, the discrepancy was even more marked. In the top 10 per cent of pupils, the boys outnumbered the girls three to two.
>
> (Askew and Wiliam 1995: 32)

Due at least in part to considerable efforts on the part of individuals and organisations with a particular interest in eradicating this differential attainment (such as the Gender and MatheMatics Association – GAMMA), by the end of the century the situation had changed completely. In 1999, 48 per cent of 15 year old boys compared with 49 per cent of girls achieved grades A*–C in the GCSE examination, and the numbers gaining GCSE at any grade were equal at 96 per cent of the overall cohort. Even allowing for the differences in aims and procedures between the APU tests and GCSE this is a very significant and welcome change. This equalisation of broad achievement is retained at GCE A level, with success rates for those taking A levels at ages 16–18 being 86.7 per cent for males and 89.8 per cent for females in 1999 (DfEE 1999). However, there is some evidence from earlier years that despite having a slightly higher GCE A level pass rate for mathematics than do males, female pupils are gaining proportionally fewer of the very top grades (DfEE 1996; Elwood 1999).

Given that female pupils do seem broadly to be performing as well as males in mathematics at both GCSE and GCE A level, why do we still need to concern ourselves with issues of gender and mathematics? The answer to this question is that it has increasingly become apparent that performance is not the only issue with which we should be concerned when looking at the relationship between gender and mathematics at the school level. Girls' enjoyment of and engagement with mathematics does not seem to have increased with increased success. While boys and girls are gaining roughly equivalent numbers of A*–C passes at GCSE, this is not translating into equal numbers of GCE A level entries. In 1999, for example, the female entry among 16–18 year olds was only 57.6 per cent of the male entry. This translates into GCE A level passes for 31,065 male pupils as against 18,512 for females in this age group. We have to treat such statistics with care, as all entries for GCE A level mathematics are grouped together in the statistical tables and some students (predominantly males) take two mathematics A levels and are therefore counted twice (Kitchen 1999). However, this group is small and declining and so is unlikely to affect the larger picture of widely discrepant male and female entry. This discrepancy matters. It matters for girls because by not opting to take GCE A level they are closing doors to high status careers in mathematics, science and engineering. It matters for the country because it is significantly reducing the numbers of those who might go on to work in the wealth-producing fields of science and technology.

Key questions

This leads us to the key question for this chapter: Why do so many girls give up mathematics as soon as they are allowed to? I am going to look at this question through four lenses. First I will examine the nature of mathematics, considering how and why this has rendered the subject relatively off-putting to girls. Then I will go on to look at a related issue: the decontextualised nature of school mathematics and the implications of this for girls' choices regarding the subject. Third, I look at anxiety and emotions and how these affect how girls perceive their mathematical ability. Finally, I consider some of the structural barriers to greater take-up of GCE A level by girls, and how these may be overcome.

Gender and the nature of mathematics

Reflecting on the issue . . .
You might like at this point to take a look at the statistics on A level take-up in your own school. Does the take-up of mathematics at A level reflect the performance of girls at GCSE?

You could also interview some of the male and female pupils in years 7, 9 and 11 about their feelings and experiences in mathematics lessons, and about their aspirations to study mathematics (or not) in the future.

- How do pupils perceive mathematics? How do they see it as the same as or different to other subjects?
- Are there any differences between male and female pupils' perceptions of mathematics? If there are, are these the same across all the year groups?
- Do the pupils' feelings, experiences and aspirations differ between year groups?

From the Enlightenment period of the eighteenth century, reason and ration-ality have been seen as forming the basis of Western philosophical thought. Enlightenment thinkers conceptualised human beings as autonomous moral agents who should take decisions, particularly moral decisions, based on abstract, rational principles – that is, principles that are seen as separate from and independent of the circumstances in which those decisions are taken. These philosophical ideas gradually came to underpin the thinking not just of philosophers but also of most people in the West. The dominance of decontextualised reason as a basis for judgement has now become so embedded in the way we think that we more or less take it for granted; to say someone is irrational is not a value-free comment but suggests that their opinions are less worthy of consideration than those of other people. However, the origins of the dominance of reason over emotion are gendered. Enlightenment thinkers saw reason as the province of males, emotion as female territory (Paechter 1998). The perceived failure of women to deploy reason in taking decisions lay behind the failure to recognise women as full citizens (able to own property in their own right even when married, able to vote, etc.) until relatively recently; citizenship was and remains seen as something that is exercised by rational beings. Although we now recognise that women and girls are as capable of rational thought as are men and boys, it remains the case that females are more likely to use alternative methods of making decisions. Girls and women are more likely to argue that strictly reasoned conclusions are not always an appropriate way to approach certain situations; in this they could be described as using emotional, rather than logical intelligence (Goleman 1996). Carol Gilligan and her collaborators (Gilligan 1982; Gilligan and Attanucci 1988), for example, have found that when it comes to moral decision-making, males have a tendency to use strictly rational criteria for moral choice, focusing in particular on moral rules. They tend to see moral choices as being founded on general ethical principles that are followed whatever the circumstances. Females, on the other hand, tend to focus on the particular situation in which the moral decision is being made. Although each gender can take the other perspective when prompted, each has a tendency to concentrate on one as the decision-making method of first choice; males are more likely to use the rationalistic, 'justice' perspective that emphasises moral principles, females to take a non-rationalistic, 'caring' approach that focuses on the support and preservation of human relationships. Thus the association of masculinity with reason, and femininity with alternative approaches, is both traditional and stereotypical and at the same time has a basis in actual behaviour (which may of course arise because of these traditional associations).

The perceived differences between males and females in the ways in which they approach moral decision-making may also have effects in terms of their feeling comfortable in relation to mathematical thinking. If males generally give precedence to reason as a way of making decisions, they are more likely to be comfortable with mathematical procedures and the elicitation of one single right answer. One of Carol Gilligan's young male subjects described moral dilemmas as 'sort of like a math problem with humans' (Gilligan 1982: 26). This close relation-ship between two powerful ways of thinking about the world, moral reason and mathematics, is likely to be mutually reinforcing; young men are likely to be relatively comfortable with mathematics because it resembles other ways in which they approach important questions in their lives. Girls, on the other hand, are more likely to find that the single correct answer required by mathematics is something unique to that subject. In other areas success can derive from finding a variety of solutions as depending on a multiplicity of variable factors. Thus in order to succeed in the mathematics classroom, as opposed to many other curriculum areas, they will have to change their dominant mode of thinking, and they may find this shift difficult or uncongenial.

Not only is reason stereotypically and traditionally associated with masculinity, mathematics is also perceived as the ultimately rational subject. Valerie Walkerdine argues that:

> Success at Mathematics is taken to be an indication of success at reasoning. Mathematics is seen as a *development* of the reasoned and logical mind.
> (Walkerdine and The Girls and Mathematics Unit 1989: 25)

When considering mathematics as a potential path, girls are in effect considering whether they are going to study a subject that is associated with the masculine gender, both in terms of its image as reason, and in terms of its congruence with their preferred thinking styles.

This is borne out by a number of studies on school subject choice. When selecting school subjects, adolescents tend to split on gender lines. While this has become masked in England and Wales in recent years because the national curriculum gives very little choice before 16, it remains the case that where choice is permitted, male pupils are more likely to choose subjects marked as masculine, female as feminine. Prior to age 16 this is mainly expressed in the choice of design and technology options, where girls tend to choose food and compliant materials (textiles), boys resistant materials (wood and metal), and in GNVQ level 1, where the entry is predominantly male, except in the case of health and social care, which is overwhelmingly female. It is only after age 16, however, that gendered choices are given free rein, and it is at this point that girls overwhelmingly reject mathematics in favour of arts and humanities subjects.

It is likely that this bias in academic and vocational choice is particularly strong at adolescence, which unfortunately is when pupils have to make some of the most important decisions about future careers. Adolescence is a time at which individuals are particularly focused on working out who they are; in a world in which so much is organised around gender boundaries, an important part of this concerns what it is like to be a man or a woman. Adolescent gender identity can be very precarious and vulnerable to challenge, and young people may feel the need to assert their gender identities by the overt display of gender role behaviour. Thus, for example, teenage girls tend to assert femininity by rejecting physical education, which has strong masculine connotations, while boys at this age are often very reluctant to take part in dance activities. Girls also, because of its masculine connotations, often reject mathematics.

John Archer (1992) found that 'masculine' subjects, like mathematics and science, are seen as 'difficult' by girls but 'interesting' by boys. Thus girls, even if they are interested in mathematics, may have reservations because they perceive the subject as being difficult. Sheila Riddell (1992) also found that both genders actively reinforced gender boundaries through their perceptions of certain subjects as being male or female. Both girls and boys used each other as a negative reference group in the maintenance of gender boundaries; for example, girls saw doing stereotypically masculine subjects such as physics as a threat to their feminine identity.

The association of mathematics with reason and hence masculinity may thus have several effects on the degree of comfort that adolescent girls feel in mathematics classrooms. Success and enjoyment of the subject conflict with stereotypical images of femininity. Girls who are seen to enjoy mathematics are visibly not conforming to feminine models; this may result not only in teasing but in a questioning or undermining of some aspects of identity. It is therefore the case that for a girl to choose to study mathematics she will need to have already developed a strong sense of personal, including gender, identity (Head 1997); those girls whose femininity remains precarious (as may well be the case at age 16) are likely to leave it unthreatened and select stereotypically feminine subjects.

Reflecting on the issue . . .
You might at this point like to interview some pupils in your own classes about their attitudes to different school subjects.

- Are there any differences between girls and boys in their attitudes to particular subjects?

- Are there some subjects that are perceived as being 'girls' subjects ' or 'boys' subjects'?

- How do these perceptions compare with the options girls and boys actually choose for GCSE and A level?

Context and decontextualisation in school mathematics

Related to the identification of mathematics with reason is the decontextualised nature of school mathematics and the relative importance that males and females give to contextual matters when considering options and making decisions. There has been a considerable amount of research conducted into issues of gender and context, though most of it has not been carried out in the mathematical domain.

Deborah Tannen's (1991) work on differences in language styles between men and women suggests that women are both more comfortable with dealing with the complexities of context and less focused than are men on finding solutions to problems. When discussing personal difficulties, for example, women are more likely to want to talk around and explore the problem with friends; this mutual support in adversity is more important to them than is finding a solution. Males, on the other hand, are more solution-focused; their discussion of personal problems prioritises working out what to do. This is reflected in research carried out by Jo Boaler (1997), which suggests that teenage boys are more interested in completing mathematics exercises than in understanding the techniques being practised. Girls, on the other hand, are more concerned with gaining understanding than with rapid completion of the work. It is likely that this focus on coming to a solution as rapidly as possible underlies the differences between male and female pupils in their approach to contextualised problems.

Carol Gilligan, in her work on moral development, found that females tended to see the context of a moral dilemma as important, and took this explicitly into account when making ethical decisions; males, on the other hand, sought decontextualised solutions that would apply universally. Similar differences have been found in the ways in which boys and girls approach school science investigations. School science problems are often framed in real-life contexts, but the pupils are expected to 'extract' the scientific work from the story told around it. Patricia Murphy (1990) found, however, that girls carrying out science experiments focused very explicitly on contextual features, while boys looked for the 'scientific problem' buried within the context and concentrated on solving it. The girls' approach could lead to conflicts with teachers' aims and expectations; taking all the contextual factors into account can lead to girls being penalised by teachers and assessors. In one example,

> Students were investigating a load that a model boat would support but in the context of a supposed trip round the world. More girls than boys decided to investigate the stability of the boat in different conditions i.e. monsoons, whirlpools and gales. The girls' actions involving watering cans, spoons and hairdryers were interpreted as a lack of understanding of the task rather than evidence of an alternative task.
>
> (Murphy 1990: 6)

Boys, on the other hand, are more likely to ignore the context and focus on the abstracted science investigation (Gipps and Murphy 1994). This allows them to come to a solution much more easily and reflects their greater comfort in working decontextually.

All of this has a number of implications for mathematics education. Mathematics problems are often framed in a very similar way to those found in science, with a contextualising story that has to be ignored at an early stage. Focusing on this context is likely to lead to girls spending time on aspects of the situation seen as 'non-mathematical' by teachers, with consequent loss of time to fully complete and understand the 'mathematical' aspects. Given the high value placed by girls on understanding their work (Boaler 1997) this is likely to lead to girls feeling frustrated by mathematics lessons.

Carol Gilligan's research suggests that girls and women reject the assumption of single decontextualised solutions that underlies the presentation of moral issues as dilemmas. This idea has been developed in mathematics education by Stephen Brown and Marion Walter (Brown 1986; Brown and Walter 1983; Walter 1987a; Walter 1987b; Walter and Brown 1977). They suggest that in focusing on the contextual issues surrounding a presented problem, women and girls are 'de-posing' the problem and replacing it with a 're-posed' alternative. Problem posing, they argue, is an essential precursor to problem solving. The number and kinds of solution to a problem depend at least in part on the way that it is posed. If you accept the problem as presented you are more likely to be able to come to a rapid solution, but this can be unnecessarily limiting and may in some cases even inhibit solutions. They suggest that mathematical questions should be 'de-posed' by moving from the question to the situation that prompted it. A fertile approach to a problem, they argue, is to look at the assumptions behind its formulation and to consider what would be the case if they were false. Stephen Brown and Marion Walter (Brown and Walter 1983) suggest that it is these assumptions that often prevent creative thinking and successful solutions of longstanding problems in mathematics:

> For a very long time, people tried to *prove* Euclid's fifth postulate:
>
> > Through a given external point, there is exactly one line parallel to a given line.
>
> It was only in the past century that we began to realize that the difficulty in answering the question lay in the assumptions behind the question itself. The implicit question was:
>
> > How can you prove the parallel postulate from the other postulates or axioms?
>
> It took hundreds of years to appreciate that the 'how' was an unrecognized monster. If you delete the 'how' the question is answerable (in the negative it turns out); if you do not do so, the question destroys itself by its excess baggage.
>
> (Brown and Walter 1983: 4)

Stephen Brown (1986) argues that concentrating more on posing, de-posing and re-posing problems is a useful way of making mathematics more interesting to girls as it capitalises on their interest in exploring the contextual underpinnings of presented problems. Given that the evidence from science education suggests that girls may be put off by the gap between the context of problems as presented and the underlying mathematics required by the teacher, it may indeed be a fertile way forward in encouraging girls to retain their places in mathematics classrooms beyond age 16.

Reflecting on the issue . . .
Try giving a group you teach some mathematical problems embedded in a range of contexts.

- How do the pupils react to the contexts?
- Do boys and girls react in similar ways to similar contexts? What differences are there?

Anxiety and emotions

Anxiety inhibits learning. Many pupils find the mathematics classroom an anxiety-provoking place, with consequences for their ability to learn there. Laurie Buxton (1981) suggests that much mathematics anxiety is related to time pressure; the need to come to the one correct answer quickly can induce panic. Jo Boaler (1997) suggests that mathematics anxiety remains widespread and argues that it is a particular issue for pupils in top sets, where time pressure is especially acute throughout the lesson. This is echoed by work carried out by Nikki Landau (1994), who investigated why so many high-achieving girls did not continue with their mathematical studies after GCSE. She found that being in the top set frequently had a negative effect on girls' self-confidence; they felt unable to keep up with the pace and that they did not really belong in this group. The anxiety and lack of confidence induced by the use of express sets was a particularly salient factor in the decisions of these high-achieving girls not to pursue mathematics further:

> The practice of having an 'express group', which sat GCSE mathematics at the end of year 10, seemed quite damaging for these young women. Four students had been in express groups and achieved the top grade, but their self-confidence had not benefited. Incredibly, all of them felt that they were weak mathematics students, commenting, 'I was like the bottom of the set the whole time', 'maths was always my hard subject that I couldn't do' and 'they were really clever, like genius clever. I didn't think I was very good at it'. They had also suffered the pressure imposed by the pace, and having achieved the accolade of being included in such a group, they felt obliged to keep up in a very competitive and pressurized atmosphere.
>
> (Landau 1994: 44)

Even those who achieved the top grade (Grade A at the time the research was carried out) a year earlier than normal, came out of this experience lacking in confidence and perceiving mathematics as difficult. Furthermore, as well as causing tremendous pressure to those in the express set, the practice of having such groups also caused those in the next group down, who 'only' got their A grades at the end of year 11, to believe that they were not very good at the subject, a situation reinforced in some cases by the attitudes of teachers who argued that only those from the express set should study mathematics to GCE A level.

The levels of anxiety in high mathematics sets, fuelled by the fast pace of the work, is further exacerbated for girls by the priority they give to attaining understanding, over completing a set amount of work in a specified time. Where the pace is particularly fast, exercise completion may come to take precedence over understanding, and this may lead girls to become disaffected in relation to mathematics (Boaler 1997). The competitive environment fostered by many teachers of high mathematics sets is also likely to discourage girls from taking the subject further; John Head (1996) suggests that girls prefer learning environments that are co-operative and supportive, while boys work better in those that are competitive and pressurised. The atmosphere of these sets thus explicitly favours the learning styles of boys.

This solution-focused, fast-paced approach to mathematics learning can also be inimical to the development, in all pupils, of the exploratory attitude required at higher levels in the subject. Carol Dweck (1986) distinguishes between 'adaptive' and 'maladaptive' motivational patterns in learners.

> The adaptive ('mastery-oriented') pattern is characterized by challenge seeking and high, effective persistence in the face of obstacles. Children displaying this pattern appear to enjoy exerting effort in the pursuit of task mastery. In contrast, the maladaptive ('helpless') pattern is characterized by challenge avoidance and low persistence in the face of difficulty. Children displaying this pattern tend to evidence negative affect (such as anxiety) and negative self-cognitions when they confront obstacles.
>
> (Dweck 1986: 1040)

Jo Boaler (1997) argues that in traditional mathematics classrooms students are rewarded for having 'maladaptive' motivational patterns. She suggests that the organisation of mathematics lessons, particularly those for high attainers, encourages students to approach the subject in ways that actually work against their long-term learning:

> I would question whether such tendencies can really be described as 'maladaptive' in many of the mathematics classrooms in which girls are learning. [In traditional mathematics classrooms] students are rewarded for the number of correct answers they get, not for the acquisition of understanding. In such classrooms it seems unreasonable to expect students to seek difficult and demanding situations which may not lead to correct answers, particularly when correct answers, in a mathematics classroom, have always been the only route to success.
>
> (Boaler 1997: 117)

She goes on to point out that, given that the situations in which they are learning actively encourage such 'maladaptive' approaches, it is hardly fair to cite these approaches as reasons for girls' underachievement:

> Dweck's suggestion that bright girls underachieve because of *maladaptive* tendencies may be seen as an example of blaming the victim.
>
> (Boaler 1997: 117)

Although the negative emotional responses described here are mainly connected with the ways in which mathematics is taught, it is not surprising that this anxiety carries over to affect the pupil's relationship with mathematics itself. Girls whose experience of learning mathematics is characterised by a pacing too fast to allow for understanding, a competitive environment and an emphasis on single, correct answers, are unlikely to want to continue the subject further.

Reflecting on the issue . . .
At this point you may find it useful to observe some mathematics lessons. If your school divides pupils into ability groups, try to observe groups of different ability levels, including a top set.
- What evidence can you see for the arguments put forward by Jo Boaler and Nikki Landau that the way 'top set' lessons are structured inhibits girls' learning?
- How could these lessons be changed to support greater pupil understanding?

Structural issues

The discussion so far assumes that the question we are addressing simply concerns girls' decisions whether or not to continue their studies of mathematics to GCE A level and beyond. This is not, however, the only issue. There are structural reasons why girls are studying GCE A level mathematics in much fewer numbers than their male peers.

Not all pupils who choose to do so are permitted to study for GCE A level mathematics. Ann Kitchen (1999) points out that very few students take the subject if they have only gained a grade C in GCSE. Furthermore, tiered entry to GCSE mathematics examinations means that even those with a grade B will not usually be allowed onto an A level mathematics course if this was attained through entry at the intermediate tier; even successful students at this level would not have covered the necessary content prerequisite for starting a GCE A level course. She argues that this may result in fewer students of both sexes being permitted to progress to A level, as some 11–16 schools abandon the highest tier and enter all their students at the intermediate level in order not to risk their total number of A*–C grades.

Other evidence, however, suggests that girls are more likely than boys to be excluded from GCE A level courses as a result of tiered entry. Because teachers read girls' concern about fully understanding their work as an indication that they lack confidence, they tend to enter girls for the intermediate tier even if they are performing at similar levels to boys entered for the higher tier (Walkerdine and The Girls and Mathematics Unit 1989). Jannette Elwood (1999) notes, for example, that in 1994 nearly 59 per cent of the female entry in GCSE mathematics was entered for the middle tier as opposed to 54 per cent of the male entry and that this 5 per cent difference accounts for nearly 21,000 candidates. This means that even if they achieve a grade B at GCSE (the highest grade permitted at this level of entry) these girls are unlikely to be allowed to progress to A level mathematics courses.

Reflecting on the issue . . .
Look at the policies on GCSE entry that are followed in your school. Trace how the policy works out in practice with one cohort of pupils.

Does the entry policy make it more likely that there will be differences in the numbers of male and female pupils eligible to study GCE A level mathematics?

Conclusion

As we have seen, a number of factors combine to conspire against girls continuing with their studies in mathematics after GCSE. It has a masculine image and its association with reason is off-putting to students wanting to assert femininity at a time when their personal and gender identity may feel precarious. Its association with reason not only supports this masculine marking but also makes its processes and procedures less than congruent with the ways many females prefer to approach problems. At the same time, many of the ways in which the subject is taught seem to be explicitly designed to discourage girls. While girls are giving emphasis to working collectively and conceptual understanding, teachers in traditional mathematics classrooms are prioritising speed and individualised competition. Finally, this lack of congruence leads to teacher perceptions of girls as lacking the confidence to tackle the highest level of examination entry, with the consequence that they are inadequately prepared for GCE A level studies. It is really hardly surprising that comparatively few girls are taking A level mathematics.

This problem is not confined to mathematics; it applies to other subjects that have become labeled as masculine. Unfortunately, these all tend to be those which not only confer prestige (and in some cases high future earnings) on those who study them, but also those in which we need more recruits if we are to retain our national prosperity and competitiveness. The total female entry for GCE A level physics, for example, was less than 30 per cent of the male entry in 1999 (DfEE 1999). However, it is reasonable to speculate that many of the same issues lie behind these figures. If we are to allow girls and young women to fulfil their potential in mathematics and allied subjects, we need to think hard about the image of mathematics, how we teach it, and how we ensure that all students are given a fair chance of being entered for high levels of assessment.

Invitation to reflect

1. Should we be concerned that girls tend to give up mathematics after age 16? Should we accept that girls and boys might want to follow different paths? Who is losing out as a consequence of girls' distaste for mathematics?
2. What can you do, as an individual teacher, to encourage girls to take mathematics at GCE A level? You might want to think about this in terms of classroom, departmental and whole-school strategies.
3. How might you use the strategies of problem posing, de-posing and re-posing in your own classroom? You might want to try and write some materials around a specific mathematical topic and try them out with a group of students.
4. How might you alter your own classroom practices to promote adaptive rather than maladaptive motivational patterns?
5. 'It's all very well to argue that the fast pace of top sets puts girls off. But we have to live in the real world – and we have a syllabus to get through.' How might you counter such a remark?

Further suggested readings

Boaler, J. (1997) *Experiencing School Mathematics: Teaching Styles, Sex and Setting*, Buckingham: Open University Press. This book looks in detail at the differential effects on boys and girls of two contrasting approaches to the teaching of secondary mathematics

Murphy, P. and Gipps, C. (eds) (1996) *Equity in the Classroom: Towards Effective Pedagogy for Girls and Boys*, London: Falmer Press/UNESCO Publishing. This is a useful source of readings on equity issues in schooling that includes discussion of possible ways in which teachers can work for change.

Walkerdine, V. and the Girls and Mathematics Unit (1989) *Counting Girls Out*, London: Virago. This influential book looks at the experiences of girls learning mathematics from nursery to secondary school. Based on a series of empirical studies, it traces the ways in which girls end up excluded from mathematics learning.

References

Archer, J. (1992) 'Gender stereotyping of school subjects', *The Psychologist: Bulletin of the British Psychological Society* 5, 66–9.

Askew, M. and Wiliam, D. (1995) *Recent Research in Mathematics Education 5–16*, London: HMSO.

Boaler, J. (1997) *Experiencing School Mathematics*, Buckingham: Open University Press.

Brown, S. I. (1986) 'The logic of problem generation: from morality and solving to de-posing and rebellion', in Burton, L. (ed.), *Girls into Maths Can Go*, Eastbourne: Holt, Rinehart and Winston, pp. 196–222.

Brown, S. I. and Walter, M. (1983) *The Art of Problem Posing*, New Jersey: Lawrence Erlbaum Associates.

Buxton, L. (1981) *Do You Panic About Maths? Coping with Maths Anxiety*, London: Heinemann.

DfEE (Department for Education and Employment) (1996) *Statistics of Education: Public Examinations in GCSE and GCE in England 1995*, London: HMSO.

DfEE (1999) *DFEE Statistical First Release: GCSE/GNVQ and GCE A/AS/Advanced GNVQ Results for Young People in England, 1998/99 (Early Statistics)*, London: Department for Education and Employment.

Dweck, C. (1986) 'Motivational processes affecting learning', *American Psychologist* 41(10), 1040–8.

Elwood, J. (1999) 'Who is underachieving – boys or girls? The case of GCSE mathematics', *International Organization for Women in Mathematics Education Newsletter* 12, 14–19.

Gilligan, C. (1982) *In a Different Voice: Psychological Theory and Women's Development*, Cambridge, Mass.: Harvard University Press.

Gilligan, C. and Attanucci, J. (1988) 'Two moral orientations: gender differences and similarities', *Merrill-Palmer Quarterly* 34, 223–227.

Gipps, C. and Murphy, P. (1994) *A Fair Test? Assessment, Achievement and Equity*, Buckingham: Open University Press.

Goleman, D. (1996) *Emotional Intelligence: Why it Can Matter More than IQ*, London: Bloomsbury.

Head, J. O. (1996) 'Gender identity and cognitive style', in Murphy, P. and Gipps, C. (eds) *Equity in the Classroom: Towards an Effective Pedagogy for Girls and Boys*, London: Falmer Press/UNESCO Publishing, pp. 59–69.

Head, J. O. (1997) *Working With Adolescents: Constructing Identity*, London: Falmer Press.

Kitchen, A. (1999) 'The changing profile of entrants to mathematics at A level and to mathematical subjects in higher education', *British Educational Research Journal* 25(1), 57–74.

Landau, N. R. (1994) *'Love, hate and mathematics'*, unpublished M.A. dissertation, King's College, London.

Murphy, P. (1990) 'Gender difference: implications for assessment and curriculum planning', paper presented at British Educational Research Association Annual Conference, London, September.

Paechter, C. F. (1998) *Educating the Other: Gender, Power and Schooling*, London: Falmer Press.

Riddell, S. (1992) *Gender and the Politics of the Curriculum*, London: Routledge.

Tannen, D. (1991) *You Just Don't Understand: Women and Men in Conversation*, London: Virago Press.

Walkerdine, V. and The Girls and Mathematics Unit (1989) *Counting Girls Out*, London: Virago.

Walter, M. (1987a) 'Generating problems from almost anything, Part 1', *Mathematics Teaching* 120, 2–6.

Walter, M. (1987b) 'Generating problems from almost anything, Part 2', *Mathematics Teaching* 121, 3–7.

Walter, M. and Brown, S. (1977) 'Problem posing and problem solving: an illustration of their interdependence', *Mathematics Teacher*, January 1977, 4–13.

5 Ethnicity and mathematics education

Derek Kassem

Introducing the issue

> Who Says Britain is Racist?
> 67% of whites
> 79% of blacks
> 56% of Asians
>   (Runnymede Trust 1992)

The attainment of pupils from ethnic minority backgrounds has been a concern of the education system for the last thirty years or more. Over this period there has been a variety of initiatives ranging from immigrant education in the 1950s through multiracial, multiethnic, multicultural and anti-racist education. However, in the plethora of reforms from the late 1980s, including the introduction of the National Curriculum (NC), Local Management of Schools (LMS), the introduction of league tables and most recently the National Numeracy Strategy (NNS), specific approaches to ethnic minority pupils have not been prioritised at a national level. Indeed a 'colour-blind' approach – seeing the issue as raising standards for 'all' by a single method – has returned.

It was just at the start of the present period of reform that the last major review of the attainment of ethnic minority pupils took place. The Swann Committee, set up by the Thatcher government, reported in 1985, and attempted to extend the notion of multicultural education to all schools. This was a significant development because the approaches taken to the education of minority ethnic pupils up to that point could be characterised by two attitudes, first, viewing the black pupil as a problem with special needs and second, that any form of multicultural education was totally irrelevant to all-white schools. The issues relating to racism in schools and the attainment of minority ethnic pupils have not gone away. African-Caribbean boys remain over-represented in exclusion figures from school, 'some black children are nine to thirteen times more likely to be excluded than white pupils' (TES 9/7/99). As a result of pressure from groups such as the Commission for Racial Equality, both OFSTED and the Teacher Training Agency (TTA) have responded to concerns, particularly around minority ethnic attainment. They have released a range of publications (OFSTED 1996; DfEE 2000; TTA 2000) along with a new web site entitled 'Removing the Barriers' aimed at raising the attainment levels of ethnic minority pupils.

In this chapter I focus on ethnicity, mathematics education and the strategies that have been used to challenge racism and the identified underachievement of minority ethnic pupils within the context of multicultural and anti-racist education.

Key questions

In writing this chapter I have decided to respond to the following key questions:

- What is the evidence for underachievement of minority ethnic pupils?
- What responses have been made to the evident cultural diversity?
- What are governmental responses to underachievement?
- How does the current curriculum and classroom practice contribute to this problem?
- What alternatives can take us forward?

You might care to consider your own response to these questions in the light of your own experience before reading into the chapter.

What is the evidence for underachievement of minority ethnic pupils?

We are presented with some difficulties in answering this question, as there is a lack of data. Nationally there is no systematic gathering of data from the Key Stage 1, 2 and 3 Standard Attainment Tasks (SATs) or General Certificate of Secondary Education (GCSE) results by ethnic group, as there is for gender. All LEAs have been requested to collect data on the attainment of ethnic minority pupils by the DfEE though it is not a legal requirement and consequently few do. The small number that do collect the information often use categories that are too crude (e.g. 'Asian'), to be of use to gain a clear picture of what is happening to ethnic minority pupils (OFSTED 1999).

However, OFSTED has recently published a damning report by David Gillborn and Heidi Mirza titled *Educational Inequality: Mapping Race, Class and Gender* (Gillborn and Mirza 2000) which provides a clearer picture of the ways in which pupils from ethnic minority groups fall behind in relation to their white peers. To get the data for this study, the researchers needed to extract data from the Youth Cohort Study of England and Wales and from the data submitted by LEAs in support of their bids for ethnic minority and traveller achieving grants (EMTAG). *The Guardian* newspaper reported the publication of the report in the following way.

Schools fail ethnic minority pupils

Black and ethnic minority youngsters are disadvantaged in the classroom by an education system which perpetuates existing inequalities. ... Despite the government's commitment to tackling racism, the report says that black children failed to share in the dramatic rise in attainment at GCSE, which took place in the 1990s, to the same degree as their white peers.

(*The Guardian* 27/10/00, p. 15)

How does this relate to mathematics? The report itself goes on to illustrate one way this disadvantage becomes institutionalised through the allocation of pupils to different groups preparing for the different tiers at GCSE:

> Black pupils were significantly less likely to be placed in the higher tier, but more likely to be entered in the lowest tier. This situation was most pronounced in mathematics where a *majority* of Black pupils were entered for the Foundation Tier, where a higher grade pass (of C or above) is not available to candidates regardless of how well they perform in the exam.
>
> (Gillborn and Mirza 2000: 17)

This practice of allocating pupils to different teaching groups is now almost universal in mathematics teaching in the UK and while it might be claimed that it is carried out on the basis of objective (and thereby supposedly 'fair') tests or criteria, it is becoming clear that the allocation carries with it long-term implications. Pupils from ethnic minorities are disproportionately placed in 'lower ability groups' very early on in their school careers, and this results subsequently in their being unable to achieve high grades at GCSE at 16. The issue here has to be how it is that such pupils become identified as having limited ability or low attainment.

The OFSTED report discussed the difficulty researching in this area because of the paucity of data. What appears difficult to assemble is longitudinal data broken down by ethnic origins for different school subjects. One of the earliest studies to include ethnic minority performance was the 'Junior School Project', a longitudinal study carried out by the Inner London Education Authority (ILEA) (Mortimer *et al.* 1988). Although the data is somewhat dated it does provide an insight into some of the issues. The study identified a difference in attainment between ethnic minority groups on entry to the school system and the 'gap in mathematics attainment remained marked throughout the junior years for children of different ethnic background' (Mortimer *et al.* 1988: 153). A study of the effectiveness of secondary schools (Smith and Tomlinson 1989) found that Bengali, Pakistan and Afro-Caribbean pupils all scored below average in reading and mathematics, with the Bengali and Pakistani pupils performing at a lower level than Afro-Caribbean pupils. On an LEA level the picture is similar, 'Birmingham's 1994 GCSE results show only 12% of African/Caribbean boys achieving five or more A–C grades, as opposed to nearly twice that figure for Asian boys and 33% for white boys. In all categories, girls did appreciably better' (TES 26/5/1995). A slightly different picture is drawn when looking at the figures from Brent, a North West London borough, which has the highest proportion of pupils from an ethnic minority background. Asian pupils are the most academically successful, showing a major improvement between 1991 and 1993 compared with whites and the lowest performing Afro-Caribbean pupils (TES 6/9/1996). The recent interim evaluation of the National Numeracy Strategy also identifies Afro-Caribbean pupils as underperforming relative to whites, while Chinese pupils 'significantly out-performed those from all other ethnic groups' (OFSTED 2000).

While there is clear evidence of underachievement by ethnic minority groups the picture is far from simple. The tendency of various bodies to group different ethnic communities under single headings obscures the reality. There is evidence that those pupils from an Indian background do better than other ethnic groups and this has been used to argue, by those on the right of the political spectrum, that there is no problem (Tooley 1990). It might be noted at this point that the patterns of immigration of different ethnic minority groups differ a great deal; for instance, those who arrived from East Africa in the 1970s were very much the displaced Asian middle class of countries such as Uganda, whose attainment is higher than a lot of groups. In contrast, those who arrived from the Caribbean were frequently skilled, semi-skilled or unskilled workers, like those who came from the agrarian-based economy of the Sylheti region in Bangladesh, under-achieve as compared with other groups. This suggests that class as well as ethnicity plays a role in the levels of attainment of ethnic minority pupils.

Reflecting on the issue . . .

Given the difficulty of getting data, try to collect data in your school on academic achievement as measured by GCSEs and the ethnic background of pupils. Does the school in which you work monitor both achievement and positions in teaching groups by ethnicity? Is there evidence either of differing rates of achievement or of over-representation of minority groups in 'bottom sets'. Look into the different 'ability' groups and ask whether pupils from ethnic minority groups appear to be over-represented in some groups and under-represented in others. How does mathematics compare to the school picture as a whole? You might need to look at any baseline data the school collects on pupils.

If you can't get data, it might be useful to ask why this data is not routinely kept and analysed to check on the progress of different groups of pupils.

Responses to cultural diversity

The view that the school system treats the ethnic minority pupil as a 'problem' is clearly demonstrated by the initial response to mass immigration from the New Commonwealth and Pakistan in the 1950s. The needs of Afro-Caribbean children were ignored and the support given to pupils of Asian descent was for English language tuition only, frequently on separate sites, the idea being 'teach them English and assimilate as quickly as possible'. At the same time, in some areas, for example Ealing, quotas were applied on the number of ethnic minority pupils that any one school could enrol. To support the quota system pupils (but only the black pupils) were bussed around to different schools. This approach to the needs of ethnic minority pupils lasted to the 1960s. It is worth noting at this stage that concern over the curriculum and specifically mathematics was not an issue.

Racial tension in parts of the country (racist attacks took place in the Notting Hill area of London and copycatted in other towns in 1959) linked to black immigration and race relations generally forced a change in government policy towards the minority ethnic community to one of restricting immigration and 'banning' overt racism. Education policy moved from assimilation to 'integration', an approach that is best described as 'unity through cultural diversity'. As a consequence:

> Dispersal was officially abandoned, concern expressed about West Indian children in ESN (Educational Sub-Normal) schools, and an increasing amount of money was being spent on the special needs of such children.
>
> (Street-Porter 1978, cited in Mullard 1982)

This approach of 'cultural diversity' has been described as, the three S's of multiethnic education, 'Saris, Somosas and Steel bands'. The policy essentially viewed racism and the problems faced by black pupils as a moral issue (MacDonald *et al.* 1989) confounded by cultural misunderstandings. It is at this point that curriculum resources drawn from other cultures began to appear; in mathematics for example we see the use of Rangoli patterns to teach symmetry (Cockcroft 1982: para. 224, p. 66). Yet we need to be aware of the tendency to trivialise certain cultural practices by presenting such cultural devices as Rangoli patterns as if they, of themselves, only had some existence and significance outside of the cultures within which they are found. Presenting Rangoli patterns to pupils as an example of geometrical symmetry, without delving into the wider Hindu culture (When are Rangoli patterns used? Why? How? etc.) would perhaps be similar to using snowflakes as an expression of the meaning of Christmas. The same is true of course for Islamic tessellations, which have an important cultural and historical significance not only in the reality of Islam, but also in the history of Islamic art, architecture and mathematics. Far from diverting attention from 'the mathematics' (i.e. the attainment targets and learning objectives in curriculum documents) such broadening and embedding gives mathematics more significance, meaning and importance to our cultural and social life.

Reflecting on the issue . . .
You might find it useful here to explore the wider cultural significance of some of the multicultural manifestations of mathematics. You could look through some textbooks for common examples and contexts, and from there explore resources that would present a wider picture. Bear in mind that potentially one of the more useful 'resources' you might use are the pupils (and their families) in the classes you teach.

The start of the 1980s saw widespread social disturbances in areas such as Brixton, Moss Side, St Paul's in Bristol and Toxteth in Liverpool. The causes of the riots are complex, with a variety of competing factors such as poverty, unemployment, bad housing and police relationships with black youth. However, education came out as a major concern for the ethnic minority community in the inquiry (Scarman 1981) that followed the events of 1981. These events reinforced a growing change of perspective by policy makers, for instance, two of the major concerns of Afro-Caribbean parents, the level of attainment of their children in the mainstream schools and the disproportionate number of children of Afro-Caribbean origin in special schools were the subject of formal inquiries (Rampton

1981; Warnock 1978). The Warnock inquiry while not specifically addressing the needs of ethnic minority children resulted in the Code of Practice for the identification of special needs that prevented ethnic minority pupils being 'dumped' in ESN schools without due process for unspecified reasons. Rampton (1981) was quickly followed by Swann (1985), and raised the issue of racism, challenging the prevailing attitudes to ethnic minority pupils and condemning the approaches taken in the past:

> We regard both the assimilationist and integrationist education responses to the need of ethnic minority pupils as, in retrospect, misguided and ill founded.
> (Swann 1985: 198)

Swann criticised the approach put forward by many who argued for a 'colour-blind' attitude. This can best be characterised by the statement: 'I don't see black, brown, white or yellow children, only children.' The report castigated this stance stating:

> We regard 'colour-blindness' . . . as potentially just as negative as a straight-forward rejection of people with a different skin colour since both types of attitude seek to deny the validity of an important aspect of a person's identity.
> (Swann 1985: 26–7)

For all the good intentions of the Swann Report the net effect was limited, for the multicultural approach suggested by Swann is at best an exchange of cultures or at worst a 'pick 'n' mix' of aspects of ethnic minority culture as an added extra to the mainstream curriculum. Though Swann stated multiculturalism was appropriate to all schools, it was, for the most part, taken up only in those inner city schools with ethnic minority children. For many teachers it is seen to be relevant only to the black child.

In some areas, mainly areas containing a multiethnic population, the mathematics curriculum developed to include Islamic patterns, games from around the world, different methods of calculation such as Vedic mathematics, greater use of statistics about poverty and exploitation of third world countries and number symbols from around the world (e.g. Shan and Bailey 1991). This approach attempted to give due recognition and value to the distinctive cultural traditions of ethnic minority pupils in the school system, though the actual mathematics curriculum was not challenged or broadened in any way. The issue of the level of attainment of ethnic minority pupils was not effectively addressed and parents became increasingly disillusioned with the education system. This can be evidenced by the increasing significance of the 'Saturday school' movement which, organised by the community, sought to address the needs of ethnic minority pupils outside the formal school structure. It is in this context that some professionals argued for an anti-racist approach to education; they specifically attempted to address issues of race as well as gender and class. Unlike all the earlier approaches, anti-racism did not seek to locate the 'problem' in the individual, but viewed racism and the low levels of attainment to be a question of power that functions on an institutional level. However, class as an issue was rarely dealt with, rather it was race and gender that took the leading role, and for all the rhetoric, again it was only a few schools with high numbers of ethnic minority pupils that sought to implement an anti-racist approach. From this point on, with the introduction of the reforms initiated by the Conservative government, the issue of ethnic minority performance, multicultural education or for that matter anti-racist education effectively disappeared from nearly all teachers' agendas, and it might also be added multiculturalism also disappeared from most Initial Teacher Education courses (Jones 1999). Even government quangos seemed rather confused about the nature of multicultural education until relatively recently:

> No, I've not heard of multicultural education. I am not aware it is a particular requirement of the National Curriculum. I can see why it may be more appropriate in multicultural areas or you might find it linked to things like education about drugs.
>
> (TTA representative, 10.6.96, cited in Jones 1999: 108)

This brief review of the approach the education system has taken to the presence of the black child, shows that the concerns expressed by the ethnic minority communities through the Scarman Report on the riots of the early 1980s – concern for the curriculum, levels of achievement, exclusion rates – are almost identical to the concerns about education found in the MacPherson Report (1999), nearly twenty years later, on the murder of Stephen Lawrence:

> That consideration be given to amendment of the National Curriculum aimed at valuing cultural diversity and preventing racism, in order better to reflect the needs of a diverse society...that Local Education Authorities and school Governors have the duty to create and implement strategies in their schools to prevent and address racism.
>
> (MacPherson 1999: 334)

Moreover, twenty years ago it was claimed

> [There is a] lack of understanding by teachers of the cultural background of black pupils and failure of the curriculum sufficiently to recognise the value of the distinctive cultural traditions of the various ethnic minorities.
>
> (Scarman 1981: 164)

It should also be remembered that when the National Curriculum was in the process of being drawn up in the late 1980s, consideration of the multicultural dimension was considered then rejected by the (Conservative) government of the day.

The Mathematics National Curriculum and attainment of minority ethnic groups.

From its inception, the NC has rejected any attempt at incorporating a strategy that met the needs of the different ethnic minority communities:

Many of those who argue for a multi-cultural approach to the mathematics curriculum do so on the basis that such an approach is necessary to raise the self-esteem of ethnic minority cultures and to improve mutual understanding and respect between races. We believe that this attitude is misconceived and patronising.

(DES 1988: para 10.22, p. 87)

The report also states that:

It is sometimes suggested that the multi-cultural complexion of society demands a 'multi-cultural' approach to mathematics, with children being introduced to different number systems, foreign currencies and non-European measuring and counting devices. We are concerned that undue emphasis on multi-cultural mathematics, in these terms, could confuse young children. Whilst it is right to make clear to children that mathematics is the product of a diversity of cultures, priority must be given to ensuring that they have the knowledge, understanding and skills that they will need for adult life and employment in Britain in the twenty-first century. We believe that most ethnic minority parents would share this view. We have not therefore included any 'multi-cultural' aspects in any of our attainment targets.

(DES 1988: para 10.20, p. 87)

The discussion stopped there; for the next ten or more years there has been no real discussion about giving the NC a multicultural dimension. The new National Curriculum effectively states that mathematics 'transcends cultural boundaries' (DfEE/QCA 1999: 14). In its favour it does remind us that 'different cultures have contributed to the development and application of mathematics' (DfEE/QCA 1999: 14) yet it fails to give this a socially or historically critical qualification. Presumably, this is referring to the contributions made to the development of mathematics by the Greeks, Hindus and Arabs – without whom mathematics would probably not be where it is today. Yet this focus on the historical dimension of the contribution of culture to the advancement of mathematics fails to cover the more recent dimension of the failure of mathematics to offer much in the way of advancement for pupils from ethnic minority backgrounds.

Slightly more chilling is the superficially attractive pronouncement that learning mathematics can promote pupils' cultural development. But, whose culture and whose development? We read:

Mathematics provides opportunities to promote *cultural development*, through helping pupils appreciate that mathematical thought contributes to the development of our culture and is becoming increasingly central to our highly technological future.

(DfEE/QCA 1999: 8)

Whose culture? Whose highly technological future? As Peter Gates points out:

There is certainly no mention here of how mathematics also contributes to the defence industry, to the eradication of other cultures through the destruction of the rainforests, to the poverty and starvation of children in developing countries due to the mathematics of interest payments on third world debt. It is surely not *mathematics* that contributes to the development (or destruction) of culture, but *those who use* the mathematics. We might have hoped to have seen some mention of how useful mathematics is in helping us explore the extent and roots of poverty and injustice, or to ask critically searching questions about the world in which we live – which includes those countries and cultures with which many pupils from ethnic minority backgrounds share some history.

(Gates 2000: 5)

(Paul Ernest explores this issue in his chapter.)

In addition to the failings of the National Curriculum, a multicultural dimension is clearly absent also in the National Numeracy Strategy, though they do at least use names drawn from a range of different cultures (DfEE 1999).

Challenging some myths

The factors that contribute to the differences in attainment between ethnic minority pupils vary from one group to another and include issues relating to poverty, discrimination or racism, cultural background, social class, neighbourhood and peer pressure as well as the quality of teaching. While many of these issues are touched on in some aspect of government policy, the only area that is not really up for discussion is the nature and form of the curriculum, as indicated above. Yet, it is the curriculum that parents from the ethnic minority community have consistently indicated excludes them, they are invisible as far as the curriculum is concerned: in history this is obvious but in mathematics there is still the deep-seated notion that the subject is value-free, independent of society, and an exemplification of absolute truth.

The reality is, mathematics is not value-free, it is a product of the range of cultures as well as socio-economic systems. What counts as mathematics and who does mathematics is fairly contentious though. From America, George Stanic points out that the question of 'whose mathematics?' is fairly clear.

All current statistics indicate that those who study advanced mathematics are most often white males.

(Stanic 1989: 58)

This poses the central question of how it is that this comes about; what contribution does the content of the actual mathematics curriculum make to this and what influence do mathematics classroom practices have?

No matter which area of the curriculum is under debate the different stances on multicultural education are deeply rooted:

- in one's response to primary immigration of non-Europeans from the New Commonwealth and Pakistan, which for the most part has located this to be the source of a 'problem';
- in how one positions the black child (Carby 1982). While racism might be recognised and rejected, it has been viewed as inevitably an individual problem, or as moral issue (MacDonald *et al.* 1989).

The conclusions that Rampton (1981) and Swann (1985) draw, along with most multiculturalists, is the need for a cultural pluralism. Ian MacDonald, Reena Bhavnani, Lily Khan and Gus John (1989) describe the main thesis of multicultural education in terms of

> A central tenet . . . and one of the theories under-pinning it, is that racism and racial conflict in Britain are caused by some sort of cultural misunderstanding. If only people understood each other's cultures, then racial conflict would be unnecessary and would wither away. Thus in the Swann Report great emphasis is placed on the need to understand the cultures of Britain's Immigrant population and to teach these in schools. In this scheme of things, nothing need be said about such disturbing and controversial things as power relations as they have to do with sex, race or class.
>
> (MacDonald *et al.* 1989: 345)

In a large number of schools this has manifested itself in the celebration of cultural and religious festivals coming from the ethnic minority community. As a cross-curricula resource Rangoli patterns and Islamic art (as recommended in Cockcroft, 1982 and Shuard 1986) are used when teaching mathematics. At no point have those who argue for a multicultural element with mathematics teaching attempted to examine the nature of the mathematics curriculum or mathematical pedagogy. At best their approach may be described in real terms as a demand for a multi-cultural adjunct to the main mathematical curriculum: this is clearly demonstrated by Hilary Shuard (1986) who suggests, that the bias of British primary school mathematics texts might be less obvious to us than to those from other countries,

> but it still reflects the values of twenty years ago, presenting a view of the world that is largely Euro-centric, male and middle class. In present-day Britain, the social context of school mathematics needs to respect and accept cultural diversity.
>
> (Shuard 1986: 39)

The anti-racists do, however, attempt to link the issues of class, gender and race in the process of questioning the mathematical curriculum and the traditional mathematical pedagogy. An example of their approach is to be found in the Association for Curriculum Change In Mathematics guidelines for 'good practice', which emphasises the historical development of mathematics as an explicit part of the curriculum. Here mathematics is described as in global terms. Second, mathematics may be set in a real world context to enable students to understand and interpret physical and social reality using mathematics. An important part of this world context allows students to use mathematics to challenge racist myths and stereotypes, sexist ideas and other oppressive structures. Mathematics should enable students to gain a fuller understanding of local and global economic relationships and enhance the student's ability to unpick reliable and distorted information (see Singh 1985: 23). This indicates the nature of an anti-racist mathematical pedagogy which contextualises mathematics as well as making links with issues such as gender and class. In that sense the anti-racist perspective is clearly different from the multiculturalist approach as described above. This perspective was developed by Tony Cotton (1990) who suggested the following as facets of anti-racist mathematics:

- a mathematics which recognises and builds on pupils' cultural heritage;
- a mathematics which draws on pupils' lived experiences;
- a mathematics which develops anti-racist attitudes in its learners;
- a mathematics which develops pupils' understanding of cultures other than their own;
- a mathematics which counters bias in materials and teaching styles;
- a mathematics which employs a range of teaching strategies including experiential learning and collaborative learning.

> *Reflecting on the issue . . .*
> Audit the mathematics that is offered to the learners in your school. Can you think of activities that meet the suggestions in the bullet points above?

Invitation to reflect

The issues in this chapter invite a reflection on those values of which we may not be aware. What are our beliefs about mathematics and about the way it should be taught? My suggestion in the chapter is that beliefs which see mathematics as simply a tool to be applied in other areas of curriculum or as a problem solving tool-kit may be a facet of institutional racism, that is that these views militate against the success of certain groups in our schools. A view that believes that a single approach to the teaching of mathematics for all, regardless of context, needs to be challenged in the same way. This is not to accuse individuals of racism, rather to point out that the historical and social development of schooling and mathematics within schools has ignored large groups of its population. However, this challenge should not be seen as a personal indictment on mathematics teachers, rather a challenge. If mathematics teachers and mathematics teaching is a part of the problem the solution also rests in our hands. There are suggestions in this chapter of ways in which individuals and departments within schools may work for change. This begins with an audit of current practice through ethnic monitoring within the school if we are fortunate enough to work in a multiethnic school, or an audit of pupil attitudes if we work in a predominantly white school. Once we have an understanding of the current position we can then ask questions of our administrative arrangements for teaching. Is our allocation to sets based on a 'just' system? Does it discriminate against certain groups? Where can we seek support for change? Similarly we can explore ways to develop the curriculum to support all our learners to succeed and more importantly to equip all our learners for life in the multiethnic community that is Great Britain. As a way of reflecting more deeply on the issue behind this chapter, you might like to consider these questions in the context of your own school.

Recommended further reading

Gaine, C. (1985) *No Problem Here: A Practical Approach to Education and 'Race' in White Schools*, London: Hutchinson Education.

Gaine, C. (1995) *Still No Problem Here*, Stoke-on-Trent: Trentham Books.

These two books are the perfect starting point for teachers working in schools where the issue of ethnicity is seen as unimportant due to the make-up of the school. I still hear teachers tell me that they do not have to think about racism in education, as '*we don't have any of them here*'! These books blow that myth.

Richardson, R. and Woodman, A. (1999) *Inclusive Schools, Inclusive Society: Race and Identity on the Agenda*, Stoke-on-Trent: Trentham Books, produced by Race On The Agenda in partnership with Association of London Government and Save the Children. *Inclusive Schools, Inclusive Society* sets out practical steps that schools can take to make themselves more inclusive and to help build a more inclusive society. The book discusses key ideas and principles relating to identity, 'race' and racism, and outlines ways of improving curriculum content, teaching methodology, and ethos and relationships. It offers practical suggestions for using the Ethnic Minority and Travellers Achievement Grant to maximum effect, and for qualitative evaluation. Based on surveys of good practice and the findings of recent research, this book shows how schools can improve the experience and attainment of all pupils and particularly those from ethnic minority backgrounds.

Shan, S. and Bailey, P. (1991) *Multiple Factors: Classroom Mathematics for Equality and Justice*, Stoke-on-Trent: Trentham Books. This book illustrates how current teaching methodology and school management and the bias in existing textbooks can and often does disadvantage black, working-class and female students, and how this might often be changed. The authors have gathered their mathematics from sources across the world and from a multiplicity of disciplines: from the Vedas, from global statistics, from architectural principles and from art forms.

References

Carby, H. V. (1982) 'Schooling in Babylon', in The Centre for Contemporary Cultural Studies (1982) *The Empire Strikes Back: Race and Racism in 70s Britain*, London: Hutchinson, pp. 183–211.

Cockcroft, W. (1982) *Mathematics Counts. Report of the Committee of Inquiry into the Teaching of Mathematics in Schools*, London, HMSO.

Cotton, T. (1990) 'Anti-racist mathematics teaching and the National Curriculum', *Mathematics Teaching* 132, 22–6.

D.E.S. (1988) *Mathematics for Ages 5 to 16. National Curriculum Working Party Final Report*, London: Department of Education and Science.

DfEE (1999) *National Numeracy Strategy, Framework for Teaching Mathematics from Reception to Year 6*, London: Department for Education and Employment.

DfEE/QCA (1999) *Mathematics. The National Curriculum for England. Key Stages 1–4*, London: Department for Education and Employment and the Qualifications and Curriculum Authority.

DfEE (2000) *Removing the Barriers, Raising Achievement Levels for Minority Ethnic Pupils*, London: Department for Education and Employment.

Gates, P. (2000) 'The social and political responsibilities of the mathematics teacher', paper presented to *Profmat2000 – Conferência da Associação de Professores da Matemática de Portugal*, 8th–11th November, Funchal: Universidade da Madeira.

Gilborn, D. and Gipps, C. (1996) *OFSTED Reviews of Research. Recent Research on the Achievements of Ethnic Minority Pupils*, London: OFSTED.

Gilborn, D. and Mirza, H. (2000) *Educational Inequality: Mapping Race, Class and Gender*, London: OFSTED.

The Guardian (27/10/00) 'Schools fail ethnic minority pupils', London: *The Guardian*, p. 15.

HMI (1985) *Mathematics from 5 to 16*, Curriculum Matters 3, London: HMSO.

Jones, R. (1999) *Teaching Racism or Tackling it?* Stoke-on-Trent: Trentham Books.

MacDonald, I., Bhavnani, R., Khan, L. and John, G. (1989) *Murder in the Playground, The Report of the Macdonald Inquiry into Racism and Racial Violence in Manchester Schools*, London: Longsight Press.

MacPherson, W. (1999) *The Stephen Lawrence Inquiry*, London: HMSO.

Mortimer, P., Sammons, P., Stoll, L., Lewis, D. and Ecob, R. (1988) *School Matters: The Junior Years*, Wells: Open Books.

Mullard, C. (1982) 'Multiracial education in Britain: From assimilation to cultural pluralism' in Tierney, J. (ed.), *Race Immigration and Schooling*, London: Holt Education, 120–33.

OFSTED (Office for Standards in Education) (2000) *The National Numeracy Strategy: An Interim Evaluation by HMI*, London: OFSTED.

OFSTED (Office for Standards in Education) (1999) *Raising the Attainment of Minority Ethnic Pupils, School and LEA Responses*, London: OFSTED.

Rampton, A. (1981) *West Indian Children in Our Schools*, London: HMSO.

Runnymede Trust (1992) 'Race and Immigration: Runnymede Trust Bulletin' cited in Gillborn, D. (1995) *Racism and Antiracism in Real Schools: Theory, Policy, Practice*, Buckingham: Open University Press.

Scarman (1981) *The Scarman Report: The Brixton Disorders 10–12 April 1981*, London: HMSO.

Shan, S. and Bailey, P. (1991) *Multiple Factors. Classroom Mathematics for Equality and Justice*, Stoke-on-Trent: Trentham Books.

Shuard, H. (1986) *Primary Mathematics Today and Tomorrow*, London: Longman.

Singh, E. (1989) 'The Secondary Years: Mathematics and Science', in Cole, M. (ed.), *Education and Equality*, London: Routledge, pp. 139–61.

Smith, D. and Tomlinson, S. (1989) *The School Effect: A Study of Multi-Racial Comprehensives*, London: Policy Studies Institute.

Stanic, G. (1989) 'Social inequality, cultural discontinuity, and equity in school mathematics', *Peabody Journal of Education* 66(1), 57–71.

Swann (1985) *Education For All*, London, HMSO.

Teacher Training Agency (2000) *Raising the Attainment of Minority Ethnic Pupils, Guidance and Resource Materials for Providers of Initial Teacher Training*, London: TTA.

TES (26/05/95) 'Myth and reality of the race factor', London: *Times Educational Supplement*.

TES (9/7/99) 'Exclusion still highest in minority groups,' London: *Times Educational Supplement*.

Tooley, J. (1990) 'Multicultural mathematics, underachievement and the National Curriculum', *Mathematics in School* 19(2), 10–11.

Warnock, M. (1978) *Special Educational Needs. Report of the Committee of Enquiry into the Education of Handicapped Children and Young People*, London: HMSO.

6 'We've still got to learn!' Students' perspectives on ability grouping and mathematics achievement

Jo Boaler and Dylan Wiliam

Introduction to the issue

In the UK there is a long tradition of grouping students by 'ability', particularly in mathematics. This practice is founded upon a widespread and deeply held belief that ability grouping raises attainment. However, the research that has been conducted on the relationship between ability grouping and achievement suggests that this is not the case. Studies have tended to fall within three areas, suggesting the following findings.

1 High attaining students are not significantly advantaged by their placement in high groups, but the attainment of students in low groups is significantly reduced by their placement in such groups (Slavin 1990).
2 The placement of students into ability groups is critical to their future level of attainment. Two students whose levels of attainment are judged to be on either side of a borderline for group placement may go on to be placed into different groups – one preparing for an 'intermediate' examination paper, the other for a less demanding 'foundation' paper. This placement decision will significantly affect the students' future achievement, with the student in the higher group being given greater opportunity to learn mathematics at a higher level, even though their levels of attainment were virtually the same and differences in their future potential were indeterminable. This aspect of ability grouping reveals both its arbitrary and its inequitable nature.
3 Ability groups can serve to enhance educational inequalities. When grouping decisions are made, it is common for students from working-class homes and ethnic and cultural minority groups to be over-represented in the lower groups, even after prior attainment is taken into account (Boaler 1997a). (Some of the reasons for this are discussed in Robyn Zevenbergen's chapter.)

Despite the negative research findings, many people still believe that ability grouping (or 'setting') is necessary for effective teaching, and that ability grouping raises levels of achievement. In this chapter, we will present an alternative perspective on ability grouping that has emerged from five years of research in mathematics classrooms.

Key questions

In this chapter we will address three key questions:

- What are students' experiences of, and beliefs about ability grouping?
- What effects does ability grouping have upon students' progress and attainment?
- How does ability grouping serve to disadvantage many students?

One of the main points we would like to make in this chapter is that insufficient attention has been given to the negative outcomes of ability grouping in the UK and that we need to explore alternatives.

Setting the scene

Ability grouping in mathematics appears to be more prevalent in the UK than in any other country of the world. Indeed, many of the Pacific Rim countries do not organise student grouping along ability criteria, yet student attainment far exceeds that of students in the UK on international tests. This is a challenging fact – but one that is not often raised by those voices who argue that we need to adopt many of the classroom practices (for example interactive whole-class teaching) of those countries. (More information on this issue can be found in Paul Andrews's chapter.)

Reflecting on the issue . . .
Before you go any further, spend some time considering your own position on ability grouping in mathematics. Is it necessary? Is it helpful? For whom? Why? List three positive aspects of ability grouping, and three negative aspects.

In this chapter, we discuss some students' reactions to ability grouping. In preparation for that, arrange to talk to some small groups of students who have been placed in high, middle and lower sets. As well as this – or alternatively if meeting is difficult – give the students an anonymous questionnaire. Do they believe that they are being well served by setting? Are they involved in making the decisions as to which set they will go into? Are parents involved? What other questions might you want to ask them?

One of us (Jo Boaler) is currently living and working in the USA, where students are allowed to choose courses in mathematics. When schools do employ 'tracking' (which is the nearest equivalent to setting in the UK), it is generally to sort students into one of two, or very unusually, three groups at the age of 14 or higher. Colleagues in the USA are shocked by the British traditions of: placing students into ability groups at a young age; of sorting students into large numbers of groups, as many as eight or more in some schools; and of using group placement as the basis for determining the mathematics that students can learn and the examination grades that will be accessible to them.

Hence, although placing students into ability groups seems both natural and essential to many practitioners in the UK, it is probably more appropriate to see it as a cultural practice, rather than an essential way of organising students for the effective teaching of a curriculum. There are many countries in the world where setting is *not* an established practice; countries where suggestions that students be placed in ability groups would be considered as ridiculous as the suggestion in the UK that all mathematics teaching should be in mixed-ability classes. Consider for example the case of Denmark. Here, there is no streaming or grouping by ability; all students remain in the same group. Nevertheless, the Curricular Guidelines in mathematics for schools (1st to 10th grade) invite not a differentiation *of students*, but a differentiation *in teaching*, which means that teachers have to make an effort to meet all students' needs wherever they are and give them work according to their development, but not with any explicit streaming or ability grouping. One thing that is important to note in the Danish system is the lack of any national tests, marks and exams. This means that even the informal differentiation does not have any public recognition among students because there is no public stratification. (Further examples of such situations are discussed in Paul Andrews's chapter.)

Finding alternatives to ability grouping is not a simple task, and we cannot expect schools and teachers to change grouping methods overnight without curriculum materials and methods of teaching that have been developed to support this task. Governmental support is vital, yet our current (Labour) government has turned its back on the idea of exploring or improving ability grouping practices. Along with other researchers who have been examining ability grouping practices, we recently met Department for Education and Employment (DfEE) officials. All the invited researchers communicated the same message – we do not have evidence that ability grouping works but we have a lot of evidence that it lowers achievement. Despite these meetings, the Labour Government has continued to exert pressure on schools to employ ability grouping, even during the primary school years. The implications of such a government policy are profound and need to be examined in detail.

One of us (Jo Boaler) recently undertook a three-year, longitudinal study of approximately 300 students who were learning mathematics in two schools in England (Boaler 1997a, b, c). Although ability grouping was not an initial focus of that research study, it emerged as a significant factor for the students, one that influenced their ideas, their responses to mathematics, and their eventual achievement. We would like now to give you some sense of the students' views – views that are often marginalised or ignored. You can find a full report of this research in Jo Boaler's book: *Experiencing School Mathematics: Teaching Styles, Sex and Setting* (see the further suggested readings at the end of this chapter). The intention is that you consider the situations we describe, and compare them with your own experiences and context.

Reflecting on the issue . . .
We shall be reporting on research in several schools in this chapter, but what will be important is for you to use the research findings to look into your own context. How are students organised for their mathematics lessons? Are they grouped by ability? How are such decisions made? When are such decisions made? What evidence is used? Who makes the decisions? Are placement decisions flexible? How often do students move between groups?

Who benefits and who suffers from setting?

One of the schools studied in the research project taught mathematics in mixed-ability groups, the other in setted ability groups. A combination of lesson observations, questionnaires, interviews and assessments – including the GCSE examination – revealed that students in the setted school were significantly disadvantaged by their placement in ability groups. A complete cohort of students in each school (approximately 300 students in all) was monitored over a three-year period from when they entered year 9 until they came to the end of year 11 (ages 13–16). The disadvantages of ability grouping affected students from across the ability range and were not restricted to students in low groups. The results relating to ability grouping in that study may be summarised as follows:

- Approximately one-third of the students taught in the highest ability groups were disadvantaged by their placement in these groups because of high expectations, fast-paced lessons and pressure to succeed. This particularly affected the most able girls.
- Students from a range of groups were severely disaffected by the limits placed upon their attainment. Students reported that they gave up on mathematics when they discovered their teachers had been preparing them for examinations that gave access to only the lowest grades.
- Students' social class had influenced setting decisions, resulting in disproportionate numbers of working-class students being allocated to low sets (even after their prior attainment was taken into account).
- Significant numbers of students experienced difficulties working at the pace of the particular set in which they were placed. For some students the pace was too slow, resulting in disaffection, while for others it was too fast, resulting in anxiety. For both higher and lower attaining students, levels of achievement were lower than would have been expected, given the students' attainment on entry to the school.

A range of evidence in that study linked setting to under-achievement, both for students in low *and high* sets, despite the widely held public, media and government perception that setting increases achievement. It is possible that you will find some of the results given in this chapter unexpected or challenging. This would not be surprising as ability grouping in mathematics is deeply embedded into school practices and British traditions. Very few teachers have considered it important to look for alternatives, and of those who have, many have faced opposition from colleagues, school management or parents. As a result we have only a small number of examples of successful alternatives and we face a critical need for research and dissemination of good practice, as well as support from local and national policy makers.

Reflecting on the issue . . .
Having read that, why do you think that the practice of setting continues to be the prevailing means of organising students in mathematics in the UK? You might want to offer your own opinion, that of your tutor/mentor or other teachers in the school.

Extending the evidence base

We considered the evidence for the negative effects of setting was sufficiently broad-ranging and pronounced in that first study to prompt further research in a wider range of schools. We therefore decided, with two colleagues – Margaret Brown and Hannah Bartholomew – to conduct further research in six other schools that varied in their grouping practices. We chose six schools in London that provided a range of learning environments and contexts. All the schools were regarded as providing a satisfactory or good standard of education and all were partner schools with Higher Education Institutions for initial teacher training. The schools were located in five different local education authorities. Some of the school populations were mainly white, others mainly Asian, while others included students from a wide range of ethnic and cultural backgrounds. The GCSE performance of the schools ranges from the upper quartile to the lower quartile of the national distribution, and the social class of the school populations ranges from some that were mainly working-class, through schools with nationally representative distributions of social class, to schools that were strongly middle-class. One of the schools is an all-girls school and the other five are mixed.

All six schools teach mathematics in mixed-ability groups when students are in year 7 (age 11). One of the schools allocates students to setted ability groups for mathematics at the beginning of year 8 (age 12), three others set the students into ability groups at the beginning of year 9 (age 13), and the other two schools continue teaching in mixed ability groups. At the time of writing this chapter, the cohort of students in our study had completed the end of year 9, which meant a change from mixed ability to setted teaching for three of the school cohorts. There are approximately 1,000 students in the study. The research methods we used have included approximately 120 hours of lesson observations, during years 8 and 9, questionnaires given to students in the cohort in the six schools (943 for year 8 and 977 for year 9, with matched questionnaires for both years from 843 students) and in-depth interviews with 72 of the year 9 students. This included four students each from a high, middle and low set in the setted schools and students from a comparable range of attainment in the mixed ability schools. We have described the context of the research project in some detail in o   r to illustrate that the findings that are emerging are not due to particularly unusual settings and are likely to be widespread. There are still a number of very profound questions hanging over the general practice of ability grouping. We hope in this chapter to raise a number of questions about that practice and to challenge a number of preconceptions.

The relationship between ability grouping and teaching and learning

When students moved from year 8 to year 9 in our study, it became clear from questionnaires, lesson observations and interview data that many students began to face negative repercussions as a result of the change from mixed-ability to setted grouping. Forty of the forty-eight students interviewed from setted groups wanted either to return to mixed-ability teaching or to change sets. The students reported that teaching practices emanating from setting had negatively affected both their learning of mathematics and their attitudes towards mathematics. Three major issues that were raised by students were: (1) the high expectations and high pressure in high sets; (2) the limited opportunities and low expectations in low sets; and (3) the restricted pedagogy and pace in all setted groups. We will consider each of these briefly. As you read the rest of this chapter, consider how the voices of the students might be pertinent to the school(s) with which you are familiar, or in which you are working.

Issue 1 – High sets, high expectations, high pressure

In the previous study (Boaler 1997b), at least one-third of the students taught in the highest set were disadvantaged by their placement in this group, because they could not cope with the fast pace of lessons and the pressure to work at a high level. The students that were most disaffected were able girls, apparently because able girls, more than any others, wanted to understand what they were doing – in depth – but the environment of set 1 classes did not allow them to do this. (You might care to consider what connections there may be here with some of the arguments in Carrie Paechter's chapter.)

We decided to observe lessons and interview students in the highest groups in this study to determine whether the environment of set 1 lessons in other schools was similar to those in the previous study and whether students were disadvantaged in similar ways. Early evidence suggested that this was the case. Each of the girls interviewed from set 1 wanted to move down into set 2 or lower. Six out of eight of the boys in set 1 were also extremely unhappy, but they did not want to move into lower groups, presumably because they were more confident (although no more able) than the girls, and because they knew that being in a top set was important. Observations of set 1 lessons make such reactions easy to understand. In a range of top set classes the teachers moved through examples on the board very quickly, often interjecting their speech with phrases such as 'Come on we haven't got much time' and 'Just do this quickly'. Set 1 lessons were also more procedural than others – with teachers giving quick demonstrations of method without explanation, and without giving the students the opportunity to find out about the meaning of different methods or the situations in which they might be used. Some of the teachers also reprimanded students who said that they didn't understand, adding comments such as 'You should be able to, you're in the top set'. The following are descriptions of 'top-set' lessons, from students in the four setted schools. As you read these excerpts, do bear in mind that they were made by *real* students. It is important for teachers to consider the challenges in the students' point of view and how they might differ from that we might expect from the teacher.

School A: Mainly white, middle- and working-class school with average attainment

Ayla: Sometimes they work too fast for me and I can't keep up with the rest of the class.

Josie:	And all your other friends are in different groups so you can't really ask them for help, because you're the top set and you're supposed to know it all.
Simon:	Most of the difference is with the teachers, the way they treat you. They expect us to be like, just doing it straight away.
Mitch:	Like we're robots.

School C: Mainly white, middle-class school with very high attainment:

Lena:	This year I find it really hard and I haven't been doing as well as I wanted to be.
Intvwr.:	Did you enjoy it more last year in mixed-ability groups?
Lena:	Yeah definitely, because it's a whole different process, you're doing different books, you're able to be taught more, you just feel that you're not being rushed all the time.
Andrea:	I used to enjoy maths, but I don't enjoy it any more because I don't understand it. I don't understand what I'm doing. So if I was to move down I probably would enjoy it. I think I am working at a pace that is just too fast for me.

School E: Mainly white, working-class school with low attainment

Graham:	If we can't answer the question or something, he'll say 'Oh yeah, you're not going to be in set 1 next year—you are the set 1 class you shouldn't be doing this, you should be doing this. (...) He wants to turn up a number 1 set – but he's going too fast, you know, a bit over the top.
Paul:	He explains it as if we're maths teachers. He explains it like really complex kind of thing, and I don't get most of the stuff.
Molly:	I want to get a good mark, but I don't want to be put in the top set again, it's too hard and I won't learn anything.

School F: Mainly Asian, middle- and working-class school with average attainment

Lena:	The teacher says 'You'd better do this, by like 5 minutes time' then you start to rush and just write anything.
Nareen:	You don't even get time to think in the maths lessons.
Aisha:	I want to go down because they can do the same work but just at a slower pace, so they understand it better, but we just have to get it into our head the first time and that's it.

These are just a small selection of the many complaints raised by students in top sets, who characterised their mathematical experiences as fast, pressured and procedural. It was interesting and important that the students' perceptions of set 1 lessons were similar in each of the schools. In the earlier study (Boaler 1997b), it was found that teachers change their normal practices when they are given top-set classes to teach, appearing to believe that 'top-set' students are profoundly different from other students, rather than simply being in the highest-attaining range of students in the school.

Many teachers in our follow-up study also seemed to think that top-set children did not need detailed help, time to think, or the space to make mistakes. Rather they seemed to believe they could be taught quickly and procedurally because they were clever enough to draw their own meaning from the procedures they were shown. In questionnaires, students in the six schools were asked 'Do you enjoy maths lessons?'. Set 1 students were the most negative in the entire sample, choosing 'never' or 'not very often', more frequently than students in other sets or students in mixed-ability classes. Students were also asked whether it was more important 'to remember work done before or think hard?' when answering mathematics questions. The set 1 classes had the highest proportion of students who thought remembering was more important than thinking. Thus, our results suggested that the experience of working in high sets caused many students to become disaffected and to view mathematics as a system of rules to be memorised.

Evidence from both of the studies suggests that the fast, procedural and competitive nature of set 1 classes particularly disadvantages girls and that the nature of high-set classes contributes to the disparity in attainment of girls and boys at the highest levels. Despite media claims that girls are now overtaking boys in all subjects (Epstein *et al.* 1998), boys still outnumber girls in attaining A or A* grades in mathematics GCSE by five to four. It seems likely that the under-achievement and non-representation of girls at the highest levels is linked to the environments generated within top-set classrooms.

Reflecting on the issue . . .
It would be useful for you to explore the views of high-set students in your school, perhaps through an anonymous questionnaire. How do students feel about the learning environment of the top set? What do they feel about students in lower sets? How do they think about the work and the pace? In addition, talk to some of the teachers about the difficulties they perceive in teaching top sets. What constraints are there, what limitations on their work?

Issue 2 – Low sets, low expectations and limited opportunities

The second issue that seemed to concern students was the low expectations placed upon those students who were allocated to lower sets. Students in low sets at the four schools appeared to be experiencing the reverse of the students in high sets, with repercussions that were more severe and damaging. Indeed, the most worrying reports of the implications of the setting process for students in our sample came from students in lower groups. These students reported a wide range of negative experiences, substantiated by observations of lessons. These included a frequent change of teachers (in one school the 'bottom' set had been taught by three different teachers in the first nine months), the allocation of non-mathematics teachers to low sets and a continuous diet of low-level work that the students found too easy. Here is what some students said to us.

Lynne: It's just our group who keeps changing teachers.
Intvwr.: Why?
Lynne: Cause they don't think they have to bother with us. I know that sounds really mean and unrealistic, but they just think they don't have to bother with us, 'cause we're group 5. They get say a teacher who knows nothing about maths, and they'll give them us, a PE teacher or something. They think they can send anyone down to us, they always do that, they think they can give us anybody.

(School E, set 5)

Ramesh: We come in and sir tells us to be quiet and gives us some work and then he does them on the board and then that's basically it.
Jack: Even though we're second from bottom group, I think it would be much better if we didn't have the help with it.
Ramesh: Because he thinks we're really low.
Jack: Really stupid or something.

(School A, set 6)

Students were particularly concerned about the low level of their work and talked at length about teachers ignoring their pleas for more difficult work. In some lower-set lessons students reported not being given any mathematics questions to answer – only worked solutions to copy off the board.

Lee: We come in, sit down, and there's like work on the board and he just says copy it. I think it's all too easy.
Ray: It's far too easy.
Intvwr.: What happens if it's too easy? Do they make it any harder?
Lee: No we just have to carry on. We just have to do it. If you refuse to do it he'll just give you a detention. It's just so easy.
Ray: Last year it was harder. Much harder.

(School E, set 5)

Carol: He just writes down the answers for us from the board, and we say to him, we say we can do it, but he just writes them down anyway.
Intvwr.: So what are you meant to do?
Carol: Just have to copy them down. That's what we say to him, 'cause a lot of people get frustrated from just copying off the board all the time.

(School A, set 6)

Lynn: We do baby work off the board.
Nelly: Yeah it's just like what we already know, you know 1 add 1.
Lynne: Say it's three times something equals nine.
Nelly: It's easy and it's boring.

(School E, set 5)

Students in lower groups were upset and annoyed about the low level of the work they were given; in addition to finding lessons boring, they knew that their opportunities for learning were being minimised, as three girls in set 6 at one of the schools told us:

> Sir treats us like we're babies, puts us down, makes us copy stuff off the board, puts up all the answers like we don't know anything.
> And we're not going to learn from that, 'cause we've got to think for ourselves. Once or twice someone has said something and he's shouted at us, he's said, 'Well you're the bottom group, you've got to learn it', but you're not going to learn from copying off the board.

(School A, set 6)

The students sound extremely critical of teachers, but their reflections were, unfortunately, consistent with our observations of low-set lessons, in which students were given answers to exercises a few minutes after starting them or required to copy work off the board for the majority or all of lessons. In response to the questionnaire item 'how long would you be prepared to spend on a maths question before giving up?' 32 per cent of students in the lower sets chose the lowest option – 'less than 2 minutes' compared with 7 per cent of students in sets in the top half and 22 per cent of students in mixed ability groups. The polarisation in the students' perceptions about mathematics questions in the setted schools probably reflects the polarisation in their experiences of mathematics. The students were convinced that teachers simply regarded students in low sets as limited:

Imran: Sir used to normally say, 'You're the bottom group, you're not going to learn anything'.
Intvwr.: He says that to you?
Imran: Yeah.
Intvwr.: Why?
Imran: I don't know, I don't think he's got – maybe you'd call it faith in us, or whatever, he doesn't believe we can do it.

(School A, set 6)

Teachers in all four schools that used ability grouping told us that the system was flexible and that students could change groups if they were inappropriately placed, but the students in low groups believed there to be little hope of moving to higher groups. They believed that they were trapped within a vicious circle – to move up they needed good end of year test results, comparable with students in higher groups, but they could not attain good results because they were not taught the work that was assessed in the tests.

Ray: In our class it was very easy and as soon as we got into the SATS, it was just like we hadn't done it.
Lee: I want to be brainy, I want to go up, but I won't go up if this work is too easy.

(School E, set 5)

In the same way as the 'top-set' teachers had fixed ideas about the high level and pace of work students should have been able to do, the teachers of the lower sets had fixed ideas about the low level of work appropriate for 'bottom-set' students. The students reported that teachers continued with these ideas, even when students asked them for work that was more difficult.

Nelly: I say 'Oh, I've done this before already'.
Lynn: And he says 'Well you can do it again'. He's nothing like 'Oh, I'll set you with some harder work or nothing'.
(School R, set 5)

The students clearly felt disadvantaged by the diet of low-level numeracy work that they were given. This problem seemed to derive partly from the students' belief that teachers had a low opinion of the level of work appropriate for low-set students but also from an idea that is intrinsic to setting policies and which will be discussed in the final section – that students in setted groups have the same mathematical capabilities and learning styles as each other and may be taught in exactly the same way.

We have not said much about the teachers' views, and it might be considered that the presentation of the students' view without some response from teachers presents only part of the picture. Nevertheless, it is an important part of the picture, one that has implications for students' progress, and motivation to learn mathematics.

Issue 3 – Restricted pedagogy and pace

The final issue that appears to be a central concern for students is the restrictions placed upon their pace of work. In interviews students talked at length about the need to work at the same speed as each other. If they worked slower than others, they would often miss out on work as teachers moved the class on before they were finished.

David: People who are slow they don't never get the chance to finish because she starts correcting them on the board already.
Scott: You don't finish the module.
(School A, set 4)

On the other hand, if they worked too quickly they were disadvantaged as teachers made them wait for the rest of the class.

David: Now we are sort of, people can be really far behind and people can be in front. Because it is sort of set, and we have these questions, say 'C', we have to all start.
Intvwr.: So you all start at the same, you all start at C?
Scott: Yeah but then the people who work fast have to wait for the people at the end to catch up.

David: Because I finished, nearly before half the class and I had a lesson to do nothing.

(School A, set 4)

Students also described the ways in which teachers used a small proportion of the class as reference points for the speed of the whole class (Dahllöf 1971), and the detrimental effect this could have on their learning.

Aisha: Sometimes you can do it fast, and at the end, you don't really know it.

Lena: But if she knows some people have finished, then she tells the class, 'OK you've got even less time to do the work'. She's like, 'Look at these 5 people, they have finished, hurry up!'

(School F, set 1)

The students linked these restrictions to the norms generated within setted groups.

Craig: Last year it was OK but when we finished our work or anything miss would give us harder work to do. But in this year when you finish it you just got to sit there and do nothing.

Liam: Yeah because in sets you all have to stay at one stage.

(School W, set 3)

Such problems were not caused by teachers simply imposing an inappropriate pace upon their groups – some students found lessons too fast whilst other students in the same groups found the same lessons too slow. The two boys in school F, quoted above, described the problem well – in mixed-ability classes students would be given work that was chosen for them, if they finished the work teachers would give them harder work, whereas in setted lessons 'you all have to stay at the same stage'. Being able to teach the whole class as a single unit is the main reason that teachers put students into 'ability' groups, and it was also one of the main sources of the students' disaffection. The students also described an interesting phenomenon – that some teachers seemed to hold ideas about the pace at which a class should work that were independent of the capabilities of the students who were in that set. For example:

David: If you're slow she's a bit harsh really, I don't think she really can understand the fact that some people aren't as fast as others. Because if you say that I don't understand the work – she'll just say something like 'You're in the middle set, you had to get here somehow, so you've got to do middle set work'.

(School A, set 4)

The teachers of the top sets also exemplified this phenomenon with the frequent remarks they made to students in the vein of:

Peter: He says, 'You are the set 1 class, you shouldn't be finding this difficult'.

(School E, set 1)

It seems that the placing of students into 'ability' groups creates a set of expectations for teachers that overrides their awareness of individual capabilities. This is a particularly interesting finding, given that the main argument that the current Prime Minister, Tony Blair, and other government ministers have given for supporting setting is that children need work that is at an appropriate pace and level for their particular 'ability'.

However, the process of ability grouping did not only appear to place restrictions on the pace and level of work available to students, it also impacted upon the teacher's choice of pedagogy. Teachers in the four schools in our study that used ability grouping responded to the move to setted teaching by adopting a more prescriptive pedagogy and the same teachers who offered worksheets, investigations and practical activities to students in mixed-ability groups concentrated upon blackboard teaching and textbook work when teaching groups with a narrower range of attainment. This is not surprising given that one of the main reasons mathematics teachers support setting is that it allows them to 'class teach' to their classes, but it has important implications for the learning of students. When students were asked in their questionnaires to 'describe their maths lessons', the forms of pedagogy that appeared to be favoured by teachers in the schools using ability grouping were clearly quite different from those in the schools using mixed-ability teaching. Twelve per cent of students from setted groups described their lessons as 'working through books', compared with 2 per cent of students in mixed-ability groups whilst 8 per cent of setted students volunteered that 'the teacher talks at the board', compared with 1 per cent of mixed-ability students. Twelve per cent of responses from students in setted groups reflected a lack of involvement, compared with 4 per cent of responses from students in mixed-ability groups. Only 15 per cent of students in setted groups described their mathematics lessons as 'OK', 'fun', 'good' or 'enjoyable' compared with 34 per cent of mixed-ability students. In a separate open question, students were asked how maths lessons could be improved. This also produced differences between the students, with 19 per cent of students taught in sets saying that there should be more open work, more variety, more group work, maths games or opportunity to think, compared to 9 per cent of mixed-ability students.

The influence of ability grouping upon teachers' pedagogy also emerged from the students' comments in interview. The following comments came from students across the spectrum of setted groups:

Intvwr.: What are maths lessons like?
Jenat: Rubbish – we just do work out of a book.
Intvwr.: How does that compare with other lessons in years 7 and 8?
Molly: They were better. We did more fun work.
(*School E, set 1*)

Intvwr.: What would be your ideal maths lesson?
Lynn: I would like work that is more different. Also when you can work through a chapter, but more fun.
Nelly: It would have to be a bit more different.

Lynn: Could do a chapter for 2 weeks, then the next 2 weeks do something
            else, an investigation or something – the kind of stuff we used to do.
(School E, set 5)

Ray: Last year it was better, 'cause of the work. It was harder. In year 8 we did
            wall charts, bar charts etc, but we don't do anything like that. It's just
            from the board.
Lee: I really liked it in year 7, because we used to like do it from the books.
            Like at the end of the year we used to play games. But like this year it's
            just been like work from the board.
(School E, set 5)

David: In year 8, sir did a lot more investigations, now you just copy off the
            board so you don't have to be that clever.
Scott: Before, we did investigations, like Mystic Rose, it was different to
            bookwork, 'cause books is just really short questions but those were ones
            sir set for himself, or posters and that, that didn't give you the answers.
(School A, set 4)

Carol   In year 7 maths was good. We done much more stuff, like cutting out
            stuff, sticking in, worksheets and all stuff like that. Now, every day is
            copying off the board and just doing the next page, then the next page
            and it gets really boring.
(School A, set 6)

The change in teaching approaches that appeared to be initiated by organising
students into ability groups could simply reflect the increase in students' age and
progression towards GCSE, but similar changes did not take place in the mixed-
ability schools. The implications of such changes for students' learning of
mathematics are quite significant. The students in the schools that used ability
grouping created an image of mathematics lessons that reflected disaffection and
polarisation, which was broadly substantiated by our observations of lessons and by
questionnaire data. It seems that when students were taught in mixed-ability
groups, their mathematics teachers gave them work that was at an appropriate
level and pace. When the students were divided into ability groups, students in
high sets came to be regarded as 'mini-mathematicians' who could work through
high-level work at a sustained fast pace, whereas students in low sets came to be
regarded as failures who could cope only with low-level work or, worse, copying off
the board. This suggests that students are *constructed* as successes or failures by the
set in which they are placed as well as the extent to which they conform to the
expectations the teachers have of their set. This is quite a controversial suggestion
– that was nevertheless supported by evidence – but how might it come about?

In mixed-ability classes, teachers have to cater for a range of students whose
previous attainment varies considerably. Most teachers respond to this challenge
by providing work that is differentiated either by providing different tasks for
different students within the same class ('differentiation by task'), or by giving all

students a task that can be attempted in a variety of ways and at a variety of different levels ('differentiation by outcome'). Teachers in the first study used this latter option – giving students a range of open work, which produced excellent examination grades (Boaler 1997a). Teachers often let students work 'at their own pace' through differentiated books or worksheets. In setted classes, students are brought together because they are believed to be of similar 'ability'. Yet setted lessons are often conducted as though students are not only similar, but *identical* – in terms of ability, preferred learning style and pace of working. In the setted lessons, students have been given identical work, whether or not they have found it easy or difficult and they have all been required to complete it at the same speed. This aspect of setted lessons has distinguished them from the mixed-ability lessons. The restrictions on pace and level of work that are imposed in setted lessons have also been a considerable source of disaffection, both for students who find the pace of lessons too fast and for those who find it too slow.

In the first study, the teachers only communicated the meaning of being in a low set a few weeks before students were entered for the GCSE examination. At that time they told some students that the highest grade they could get was a D. The students were devastated by that news, revealing one of the ironies of ability grouping. The students had been placed in a low set and taught easier work – and they had gone through three years of secondary school being extremely successful, or so they thought. They had got most of their questions correct in class, without realising that they were being given easier work, and they always assumed they were doing well, even those who knew they were in a low set. The impact of knowing they were being entered for a foundation examination was extremely negative. We are not suggesting that teachers should spell that out for students at the earliest stage, rather that they should try and avoid making such pre-determined decisions. The school initially studied in depth for three years that employed mixed-ability grouping and gave students open work that they could do at multiple levels, attained extremely high examination grades from students. When some students entered that school, they had been attaining at a low level, and would have been placed in the lowest set in another school. Nevertheless, they worked hard and attained a GCSE grade B in the examination. It seems salient that the students would have probably attained a D if the school had used ability grouping and even if that is true for a small proportion of students, the impact is so great for those students, it should give pause for thought.

A final challenging but sobering thought – the extent of curriculum polaris-ation, and diminution of opportunity to learn that we have found, if replicated across the country, could be the single most important cause of the low levels of achievement in mathematics in Great Britain. The traditional British concern with ensuring that *some* of the ablest students reach the highest possible standards appears to have resulted in a situation in which the vast majority of students achieve well below their potential. As one student poignantly remarked:

Lynn: Obviously we're not the cleverest, we're group 5, but still – it's still maths, we're still in year 9, we've still got to learn.
(*School E, set 5*)

Invitation to reflect

For any teacher reading this chapter we would offer two sources of reflection:

- First, to consider the alternatives to ability grouping. It is extremely important that teachers remain open to the idea that mixed-ability teaching may be more productive and equitable and support exploration of ways in which it could work. This is a difficult task as it is not being supported by government, but teachers now have the responsibility to consider ways in which mixed-ability teaching may be supported in their schools.
- Second, for those who are teaching students in setted groups – we would suggest exploring the students' experiences of mathematics teaching. For example, give students the opportunity to write anonymously about their experiences – are they being given work at an appropriate level? How would they change lessons if they could? Do they believe they should be in a different group? In addition, we would ask students to say what examination grade they are aiming for.

Further suggested readings

Boaler, J. (1997c) *Experiencing School Mathematics: Teaching Styles, Sex and Setting*, Buckingham: Open University Press. This book tells the story of two schools that taught mathematics in totally different ways. The book is the first of its kind to provide longitudinal evidence of students' beliefs and understandings as they developed over three years – and the ways that these were affected by the students' experiences in setted and mixed-ability teaching groups.

Harlen, W. and Malcolm, H. (1999) *Setting and Streaming. A Research Review*, Edinburgh: Scottish Council for Research in Education. This short (72 pages) readable book reviews a range of studies on the advantages and disadvantages of setting and mixed-ability grouping at primary and secondary levels that have been undertaken over the past forty years. It concludes that the research provides no strong clear-cut evidence that achievement is raised by setting or streaming.

References

Boaler, J. (1997a) 'Setting, social class and survival of the quickest', *British Educational Research Journal* 23(5), 575–95.

Boaler, J. (1997b) 'When even the winners are losers: evaluating the experiences of 'top set' students', *Journal of Curriculum Studies* 29(2), 165–82.

Boaler, J. (1997c) *Experiencing School Mathematics: Teaching Styles, Sex and Setting*, Buckingham: Open University Press.

Dahllöf, U. (1971) *Ability Grouping, Content Validity and Curriculum Process Analysis*, New York, NY: Teachers College Press.

Epstein, D., Maw, J., Elwood, J. and Hey, V. (1998) Guest editorial, *Journal of Inclusive Education* 2(2), 91–4.

Slavin, R. E. (1990) 'Achievement effects of ability grouping in secondary schools: a best evidence synthesis', *Review of Educational Research* 60(3), 471–99.

7 What values do *you* teach when you teach mathematics?

Alan Bishop

Introducing the issue

At first sight this seems a very strange question. Of course, if you are a teacher, you know that you teach values, but have you ever thought about the values that you teach – albeit implicitly – in mathematics? On the other hand, what opportunities are there for explicitly teaching values through the teaching of mathematics? This area is fundamental to initial teacher education, since it helps us to enlarge our understanding of why mathematics teachers teach in the way they do. It helps us consider more carefully how we are to educate our future citizens, and furthermore, it helps us to decide on what are desirable and feasible goals for mathematics education in democratic societies. In this chapter, I raise the issue of values in the context of mathematics education and argue that a focus on education for democracy inevitably involves educating about values.

> We know that pupils *do* develop certain values toward mathematics, that adults *do* have views about the relevance and importance of mathematics, that choices *are* made by pupils when comparing mathematics to other subjects and that teachers *do* have individual ideas about the importance and aims of studying mathematics. These values-related aspects of mathematics *are* learnt, and they are probably learnt implicitly and unintentionally. They are therefore likely to be influential to an extent not always recognised and this may not necessarily be beneficial to pupils' mathematical education.
>
> (Bishop 1991: 195)

Key questions

In addressing that issue of the values we teach through our mathematics, I have the following questions in mind:

- How do you teach values when teaching mathematics?
- What mathematical values do you teach?
- Perhaps more importantly, what mathematical values are your students learning from you?

Before you read further you might care to consider how you personally might respond to these questions.

The present context

If you've not thought about this issue very much, you may wonder why it is important. Well, one reason is that we know that all teachers teach values but it seems from research that most teaching and learning of values in mathematics classes happens implicitly. There seems to be very little explicit values teaching, and somehow teaching values isn't like teaching fractions. There are no right answers for one thing; you may be an expert on fractions, but can you be an expert on values?

Understanding more about values is in my view the key to generating more possibilities for mathematics teaching. Sadly we know little about the values that mathematics teachers think they are imparting, or how successful they are in imparting them. There is plenty of research on values education generally (Tomlinson and Quinton 1986), but we know much less about what currently happens with values teaching in mathematics classrooms. It appears relatively easy to identify the teaching of values in the teaching of humanities and art subjects, but this is not so in mathematics teaching. Many mathematics teachers would not even consider that they are teaching any values when they teach mathematics – and changing that perception may prove to be one of the biggest hurdles to overcome.

There seem to be several important questions that are worth considering here:

- What is the current situation regarding teaching values in mathematics classrooms?
- What values do mathematics teachers think they are teaching?
- What values are being learnt by students?
- Can teachers gain sufficient control over their values teaching to teach other values besides those which they currently teach?

Before looking into these questions, however, it is necessary to clarify what we mean when we talk about values in mathematics education.

What *are* values?

Values in mathematics education are the deep affective qualities that education fosters through the school subject of mathematics. They appear to survive longer in people's memories than does conceptual and procedural knowledge, which unless it is regularly used tends to fade. Research suggests that the negative features of these values lead subsequently to a dislike of mathematics in adulthood and hence to negative parental influences (Cockcroft 1982). Hence attention to values in mathematics teaching has deep-seated and long-lasting implications.

For example, in some of the original writing in this area, David Krathwohl, Benjamin Bloom and Bertram Masia (Krathwohl *et al.* 1964) in their taxonomy of educational objectives, put *values* and *valuing* clearly within the affective domain, and pointed also to their deep-seated nature.

Behaviour classified at this level is sufficiently consistent and stable to have taken on the characteristics of a belief or an attitude. The learner displays this behaviour with sufficient consistency in appropriate situations that he comes to be perceived as holding a value.

(Krathwohl 1964: 180)

Louis Raths, Merrill Harmin and Sidney Simon (1987) describe seven criteria for calling something a value. They say 'unless something satisfies all seven of the criteria, we do not call it a value, but rather a "belief" or "attitude" or something other than a value' (Raths *et al.* 1987: 199). Their criteria are:

1　choosing freely;
2　choosing from alternatives;
3　choosing after thoughtful consideration of the consequences of each alternative;
4　prizing and cherishing;
5　affirming;
6　acting upon choices;
7　repeating.

They add 'those processes collectively define valuing. Results of this valuing process are called values' (Raths *et al.* 1987: 201). Generally, the research literature on values in education indicates that values education should involve the existence of alternatives, choices and choosing, preferences, and consistency.

In my experience there are some teachers who know very little about the values they are teaching in mathematics classes. I am not of course saying that they think that the mathematics they teach has no value for their students. But I am saying that most values teaching in mathematics seems to happen implicitly, and what is more, your values teaching *will* depend on your own sets of values as a person and as a teacher.

For example, imagine that you have to deal with this incident: it's the first day back after the Christmas holiday, and you are chatting with your year 7 class before getting down to work. You ask if anyone had any mathematical presents. One boy says that he had been given a 'maths game from my uncle's country'. He says 'It's very interesting and has lots of variations. Can I show you how we play it?'.

What would *you* do? Would you let him go ahead and see what develops? Would you say something like: 'Well that would be nice, but we don't have time now to do it, maybe later' or maybe 'that's excellent, show me after the class, and I'll decide then if we can play it'. Are mathematical games a part of your own curriculum ideas?

You would make your choice in the way that you normally do, and perhaps not think much more about it. But the fact remains that you must make a choice, and that choice depends on your values.

What about this one? This happened to me many years ago, and I remember it well: you are working on fractions with a lively year 5 class, and you ask them to suggest a fraction that lies between one half and three-quarters. One of the sharper students in the class offers the answer 'Two-thirds'. When you ask how she knows that it lies between the other two fractions, she answers: 'Well you can see that on the top the numbers go 1, 2, 3 and on the bottom they go 2, 3, 4. The 2 is between the 1 and the 3, and on the bottom the 3 lies between the 2 and the 4, so therefore two-thirds must be between the other two fractions.'

It is certainly an interesting answer but what would your decision be? Would you say: 'No, that's not the right reason.' Or: 'Yes, very interesting but I don't think that'll work for any two fractions.' Or: 'Very interesting. Let's see whether that will be true for any two fractions.' Or . . . what else might you say? Once again your decision will depend on your values, and through the choices you make you are implicitly shaping the values of your students.

Reflecting on the issue . . .
So, how might you respond in such a situation? What does your response (to both the pupil and to this task) suggest about your own values?

Try this one:

Teacher: I want you to think, for tomorrow, of a mathematical problem or situation that can be linked with this photograph (a picture of a woman selling produce at a rural market).

Miguel: (the next day) This was a trick! There is no mathematics problem, the woman has never been to school. She does not know any mathematics.

How would you react to Miguel? And what would you do if all the class agreed with Miguel? Or suppose only the boys in the class agreed with him, what would you do? Once more your choice will depend on your values, and your choice will influence your students' values.

Research on mathematics teacher beliefs, particularly in relation to teachers' actions in the classroom, seems to demonstrate that teachers' actions frequently bear no relation to their professed beliefs about mathematics and mathematics teaching (Thompson 1992). Other research has shown striking inconsistencies between different belief statements given by the same teachers (Sosniak, Ethington and Varelas 1991). This discrepancy is precisely why I believe it is necessary to focus on values rather than beliefs, in order to determine the deeper affective qualities that are likely to underpin teachers' preferred decisions and actions.

Your values influence your teaching all the time. As well as making *in situ* teaching decisions like those above, all the following teacher activities also involve your values.

Planning your curriculum for the year

Should I emphasise breadth or depth in the topics? What out-of-school visits should I include? How should my mathematics curriculum link with those in science, language, art, etc.? What big ideas should I focus on this year? What curriculum choices should I offer my students?

Choosing textbooks/electronic teaching aids

What do I expect from a good textbook? What extra materials should I prepare? How much calculator use would be desirable for my class? How should I tap into the maths resources on the Internet? (Textbooks can also be considered to be carriers and shapers of values. They are in effect 'text-teachers' and are certainly written by people interested in developing certain values.)

Planning lessons

How much choice of activities should I give my students? How much routine practice is important for them? How much group work do I want to build in? How detailed should my planning be?

Planning and setting assessment tasks, mark schemes

How many multi-digit multiplication problems are sufficient? Should I allow calculator use? Should students mark their own work?

Setting homework

Is my homework always 'after the lesson' type rather than 'before the lesson'? Should I encourage parents to help as much as possible? Should I let my students co-operate with their homework assignments?

Grouping students in class

Should I encourage friendship groupings by letting my students work with their friends? Should I mix the non-English speakers with the first-language English speakers?

Socio-cultural values in mathematics teaching

Of course the important practical question is however: 'what do we mean by values in mathematics education?' I believe that it is essential to consider them within the whole socio-cultural framework of education and schooling. Culture has been defined as 'an organised system of values which are transmitted to its members both formally and informally' (McConatha and Schnell 1995: 81). Mathematics education as cultural induction has been well researched over the last twenty years (see for example, Bishop 1988; Gerdes 1996), and it is clear from this research that values are an integral part of any mathematics teaching and a range of levels.

At the individual level learners have their own preferences and abilities that predispose them to value certain activities more than others.

In the classroom there are values inherent in the negotiation of meanings between teacher and students, and between the students themselves.

At the institutional level we enter the small political world of any organisation in which issues, both deep and superficial, engage everyone in value arguments about priorities in determining local curricula, schedules, teaching approaches etc.

The large political scene is at the societal level, where the powerful institutions of any society with their own values determine national and state priorities in terms of the mathematics curriculum, teacher preparation requirements etc.

Finally, at the cultural level, the very sources of knowledge, beliefs, and language, influence our values in mathematics education. Further, different cultures will influence values in different ways. Cultures don't share all the same values.

A socio-cultural perspective on values is crucial to understanding their role in mathematics education because valuing is done by *people*. The symbols, practices and products of mathematical activity don't have any values in or of themselves. It is people, and the institutions of which they are a part, who place value on them. The research and writing on socio-cultural aspects of mathematics education (e.g. Ernest 1995; Joseph 1991; Wilson 1986) makes this abundantly clear.

Fostering values in mathematics

Initial analyses reveal that there are two main kinds of values which teachers seek to convey: the general and the mathematical. For example, when a teacher admonishes a student for cheating in an examination, the values of 'honesty' and 'good behaviour' derive from the general socialising demands of society. In this case, the values are not especially concerned with, or particularly fostered by, the teaching of mathematics.

However, when we think about the three incidents above we very soon get into mathematical values. So let's think about those. In two other articles I have written on this subject, (Bishop 1988; 1991) I argued that the values associated with what can be called Western mathematics could be described as three sets of complementary pairs – rationalism vs objectism, control vs progress and openness vs mystery – as follows:

The main value that people think about with mathematics I call rationalism. An important aspect of that set of values is that it is not the concrete world that is logical; it is the explanations that are. It involves ideas such as logical and hypothetical reasoning, and, if you value this idea, then for example in the fractions incident above you would want the class to explore the generality of the student's conjecture.

Mathematics involves ideas such as symbolising, and concretising, and I refer to this value as objectism. This represents the fact that Western culture's worldview is dominated by the idea of 'object'. Mathematicians throughout its history have created symbols and other forms of representation, and have then treated those symbols as the source for the next level of abstraction. Through its symbols (letters, numerals, figures) people have been enabled to deal with abstract entities *as if they were* objects. Encouraging your students to search for different ways to symbolise and represent ideas, and then to compare their symbols for conciseness and efficiency, is a good way to encourage this value.

The value of being in control is another one that most people are very conscious of. It involves valuing the existence and security that mathematics offers. It involves aspects such as having rules, being able to predict, and being able to apply the ideas to situations in the environment. Mathematics, through science and technology has given Western culture strong feelings of security in knowledge. We feel we are in control of phenomena when we can describe them mathematically. It is one of the main reasons that people like mathematics. It has right answers that can always be checked. The woman selling in the street market in the incident above will value the control she can exert over her profit and the quantities of her goods.

The complementary value to control is one that I call progress. Because mathematics can feel like such secure knowledge, mathematicians feel able to explore and develop ideas. Mathematical progress is about change and alternatives; the unknown can become known. This value is involved in ideas such as abstracting and generalising, which is how mathematics grows. Mathematical progress is achieved by seeking out situations where generalisations do not hold. The search for counter-example, the extreme case and the logical inconsistencies lead to new problems that must be mastered. Questions like: 'Can you make up another problem that uses the same information but is more complicated?' or 'Can you suggest a generalisation that is true for all those examples?' are good for encouraging that value.

Another familiar value I call openness because mathematicians believe in the public verification of their ideas by proofs and demonstrations. This is to do with the quality that mathematical truths are open to examination by all – provided of course that one has the necessary prerequisite knowledge, it is theoretically and practically possible for anyone and everyone to verify and examine the truth of any proposition. While opinions may be held by people, Western mathematical knowledge is valued because it represents what people like to think of as 'facts'. Asking students to explain their ideas to the whole class is good practice for developing the openness value.

Finally there is the value I call mystery. Despite the apparent openness, there is nevertheless a mysterious quality about mathematical ideas. Anyone who has ever explored a mathematical problem or investigated a puzzle knows how mystifying, wonderful, and surprising mathematics can be. For example, I am still amazed by this result: If you take any Pythagorean triple like 3,4,5 or 5,12,13 and multiply the three numbers together, the result is always a multiple of 60! Now isn't that surprising? And why should it be 60 since 90 might in some way seem to be a more logical answer!

So these are the values I believe have been fostered by Western mathematicians over the last centuries, and it is these values that you are probably promoting when you teach mathematics. Of course you may promote some more than others, so maybe you could think about promoting all of them. Then you would be encouraging your students to be thoroughly mathematical.

Reflecting on the issue . . .
Have a look back over that set of six values I have presented above. Where do you place yourself in each one? Now, think about your own preferred way of working in the classroom. How does this fit in with the six value positions? Is there any conflict between these two espoused and lived values?

The mathematics teacher and values education

In relation to values, the teacher is both a value carrier and a value mediator. She is a value carrier because of her own mathematical education through which she would have developed certain attitudes, beliefs and values. She is a value mediator because of her role in helping the pupils share and develop their mathematical ideas.

As a value carrier the teacher is therefore acting as some sort of model. The values she has assimilated are likely to affect all aspects of her work – for example her choice of topics, her emphasis toward certain kinds of mathematical activities, her preferred teaching style and the support of criticism which she gives to her pupils' efforts in class.

Only rarely does one find explicit values teaching going on in mathematics classrooms, the reason being the widespread (though mistaken) belief that mathematics is a values-free subject. Indeed many politicians and parents might initially be concerned about explicit values teaching in mathematics. What parents and others should be concerned about is that values teaching and learning does go on in mathematics classrooms, and because most of this appears to be done implicitly, there is only a limited understanding at present of what values are being transmitted and how effectively they are being transmitted.

Several questions come to mind here. Are values *explicitly* expounded, discussed or raised as teaching content? Since they do not appear in detailed syllabus descriptions (and do not appear in the UK National Curriculum for Mathematics) but only, if at all, in the aims statements of curriculum documents, it is unlikely that they will be considered as content to be explicitly taught or addressed. The assumption is undoubtedly that they will be addressed *through* the mathematical content or process topics.

More pupils come into contact with mathematics in schools through textbooks than through any other source – so we might expect these to be a significant resource for addressing values. Do textbooks have explicit values-focused exercises or activities? A look at several textbooks will most likely fail to reveal any activities of this nature. Yet what values do textbooks convey and legitimate? (This issue is further explored by Paul Dowling in his chapter.)

Reflecting on the issue . . .

Have a look through as many mathematics textbook series you can find. If (as I suspect) you can find no explicit activities focusing pupils on values, what *implicit* values are there in the way the books are organised? Concentrate on the way the book is structured? What language is used? What pictures or graphics are used? What sorts of questions are asked? How are they asked? What implicit values are hidden in the way the different books are written for pupils of different ages and capabilities?

You might find it useful here to have a look at just how such values-explicit activities might be formulated. One of the best sources for such activities is Sharanjeet Shan and Peter Bailey's book: Multiple Factors: Classroom Mathematics for Equality and Justice.

Ole Skovsmose is a Danish mathematics educator who has written extensively around the issue of the teaching of certain values through mathematics. He argues that

> Critical mathematics education is concerned with the development of citizens who are able to take part in discussions and are able to make their own decisions. We therefore have to take into consideration the fact that students will also want and should be given the opportunity to 'evaluate' what happens in the classroom.
>
> (Skovsmose 1996: 1267)

This comment echoes the idea that for values education to develop, it is necessary to ensure that the mathematics classroom is a place of choices and of choosing for the pupils. Teachers could, and in my view should, be presenting pupils with activities that encourage them to make choices; for example, about the selection of problems to be solved; about the approaches to solutions to be taken; about the criteria for judging the worth of solutions; and about the wider appropriateness of the mathematical models being taught It could be a natural part of a teacher's repertoire to present activities which require choices to be made: for example, a task such as 'describe and compare three different proofs of the Pythagorean theorem' would inevitably engage pupils in discussing the values associated with proving. Even the simple act of presenting different problem-solving solutions to be compared and contrasted by the pupils stimulates the ideas of choice, criteria and values. Indeed a general teaching strategy would be always to take time, following some problem-solving activity, to discuss what happened, why, and what has been learnt which could help next time. This is not a natural thing for pupils to do, nor is it at present a typical thing for teachers to do, but I firmly believe that class or group reflection following an activity offers an excellent context for dealing specifically with values. This is where mathematics teachers need to initiate some kinds of mathematical activities that focus pupils' direct attention on:

- the awareness of values;
- the clarification of values;
- the conflict between different values, and
- the criticism of values.

The teacher's task here would be to expose criteria and values, to make pupils more aware of the range of values, to contrast different views and to show there are other aspects of mathematics which are important besides merely technical aspects. What Ole Skovsmose's focus on students' interests does is to remind us that, rather than thinking of mathematics teaching as just teaching mathematics to students, we are also teaching pupils through mathematics. They *are* learning values through how they are being taught.

In addition to such discussion-generating activities, other types of activities that are useful in generating a greater awareness of values are small group work, projects and investigations. Small groups are excellent contexts for generating multiple approaches to problems and to other tasks. These clearly relate to the values of alternativism and progress, but once again these will lie dormant, though they may be learnt implicitly of course, until exposed by the teacher's intervention and reflected upon. In fact I believe that the absence of small group work in most mathematics classrooms undoubtedly contributes to the general lack of understanding and belief in the value of alternativism and progress in mathematics.

Projects are I believe excellent activities for the consideration of relationships between mathematics and society and of the values concerned with those relationships. There are historical projects that can concern the social history of mathematical ideas and which can demonstrate the growth of ideas and the development of values. Second, there are projects concerning present-day society, which can demonstrate the roles mathematical ideas and values play in the present society. Third, there are projects on society in the future in which potential solutions to environmental problems for example can be explored.

Mathematical investigations are an activity where the pupil does creative, exploratory work on a mathematical idea. In a good investigation, the pupil must define some terms, symbolise some variables, explore and describe some relationships and demonstrate the truth or otherwise of those relationships. A great deal of creative mathematical activity can be done and the pupil thereby experiences the decision-making, the criteria and the values of the practising mathematician.

Thus I maintain that by using discussions, small group work, mathematical projects and investigations, the teacher can create a variety of learning contexts in which the education of mathematical values can happen. Note that I say 'can' because it still demands the intention on the part of the teacher to focus the pupils' attention on mathematical values, and it requires an appreciation of the asymmetrical aspect of the teaching process to ensure that the pupils don't just assimilate the teacher's personal view. Only then will the teaching of values contribute positively to the pupils' mathematical education rather than detract negatively from it, as I believe it does at present.

However, one last word of caution . . .

I said above that culture is a strong determinant of mathematical values, and research shows us that not all cultures share the same values. So if you are teaching a class of students where some of them have a very different cultural background to the mainstream culture, be very sensitive and careful about your values teaching. Those students may feel a bit uncomfortable and, for example, they may not want to explain their ideas to everybody else in the class. For example approaching some aspects of probability through gambling games might cause difficulties for pupils whose cultural background and values reject such practices. (Derek Kassem in his chapter also touches on the values we might implicitly place upon other cultures through tokenist practices that reduce or trivialise them.)

An invitation to reflect

You might like to explore some of these values ideas further, and one way to do this would be to look at your teaching and your textbooks in terms of the six mathematical values described above. You could audio or videotape some of your own lessons and analyse them, or work with a colleague to analyse each other's teaching. You could also discuss these ideas, or your findings, with the parents of your students to help them understand more about mathematical ideas.

Here are some questions to help you do the analysis, and perhaps also they might enable you to teach these values more explicitly:

1 *Rationalism*
   Do you encourage your students to argue in your classes? Do you have debates? Do you emphasise mathematical proving? Could you show the students examples of proofs from history (for example, different proofs of Pythagoras' theorem)?

2 *Objectism*
   Do you encourage your students to invent their own symbols and terminology before showing them the 'official' ones? Do you use geometric diagrams to illustrate algebraic relationships? Could you show them different numerals used by different cultural groups in history? Could you discuss the need for simplicity and conciseness in choosing symbols, and why that helps with further abstractions?

3 *Control*
   Do you emphasise not just 'right' answers, but also the checking of answers, and the reasons for other answers not being 'right'? Do you encourage the analysis and understanding of why routine calculations and algorithms 'work'? Could you emphasise more the bases of these algorithms? Do you always show examples of how the mathematical ideas you are teaching are used in society?

4 *Progress*
   Do you emphasise alternative, and non-routine, solution strategies together with their reasons? Do you encourage students to extend and generalise ideas from particular examples? Could you stimulate them with stories of mathematical developments in history?

5 *Openness*
   Do you encourage your students to defend and justify their answers publicly to the class? Do you encourage the creation of posters so that the students can display their ideas? Could you create a student mathematics newsletter, or a web page, where they could present their ideas?

6 *Mystery*
   Do you tell them any stories about mathematical puzzles in the past, about for example the 'search' for negative numbers, or for zero? Do you stimulate their mathematical imagination with pictures, artworks, images of infinity etc.?

Finally, to what extent do (could) you discuss these values explicitly in your classes? Would it help your students to understand why mathematics is so important today?

Further suggested readings

Davis, P. J. and Hersh, R. (1986) *Descartes' Dream*, New York: Penguin.
Davis, P. J. and Hersh, R. (1981) *The Mathematical Experience*, New York: Penguin.

These two books add ideas about the values in Western mathematical culture. *Descartes' Dream* is more of a historical piece and emphasises the 'mathematised world'. *The Mathematical Experience* explains what it is like to be a mathematician today although it too contains some historical references.

Tomlinson, P. and Quinton, M. (eds) (1986) *Values Across the Curriculum*, Lewes: Falmer Press. This is a book that would be useful to anyone particularly interested in reading more about values across the curriculum .

Note

With a number of colleagues, I am involved in a research project on Values in Mathematics and this chapter has built on various ideas that have developed through that project. Other colleagues involved in that project are Gail FitzSimons and Wee Tiong Seah from Monash University, Melbourne, Australia and Phil Clarkson from the Australian Catholic University. More information about the project is available on the web-site http://www.education.monash.edu.au/projects/vamp.

References

Bishop, A. J. (1988) *Mathematical Enculturation: A Cultural Perspective on Mathematics Education*, Dordrecht: Kluwer.

Bishop, A. J. (1991) 'Mathematical values in the teaching process', in Bishop, A. J., Mellin-Olsen, S. and van Dormolen, J. (eds), *Mathematical Knowledge: Its Growth through Teaching*, Dordrecht: Kluwer, pp. 195–214.

Cockcroft, W. H. (1982) *Mathematics Counts. Report of the Committee of Inquiry into the Teaching of Mathematics in Schools*, London: HMSO.

Ernest, P. (1995) 'Values, gender and images of mathematics: A philosophical perspective', *International Journal of Mathematical Education in Science and Technology* 26, 449–62.

Gerdes, P. (1995) *Ethnomathematics and Education in Africa*, Sweden: Stockholm University.

Joseph, G. G. (1991) *The Crest of the Peacock*, London: I. B. Tauris.

Krathwohl, D. R., Bloom, B. S. and Masia, B. B. (1964). *Taxonomy of Educational Objectives, the Classification of Educational Goals: Handbook 2: Affective Domain*, New York: Longmans.

McConatha, J. T. and Schnell, F. (1995) 'The confluence of values: Implications for educational research and policy', *Educational Practice and Theory* 17(2), 79–83.

Raths, L. E., Harmin, M. and Simon, S. B. (1987) 'Selections from values and teaching', in Carbone, P. F. (ed.), *Value Theory and Education*, Malabar, USA: Krieger, pp. 198–214.

Shan, S. and Bailey, P. (1991) *Multiple Factors: Classroom Mathematics for Equality and Justice*, Stoke-on-Trent: Trentham Books.

Skovsmose, O. (1996) 'Critical mathematics education', in Bishop, A. J., Clements, K., Keitel, C., Kilpatrick, J. and Laborde, C. (eds), *International Handbook of Mathematics Education*, Dordrecht: Kluwer, pp. 1257–88.

Sosniak, L. A., Ethington, C. A. and Varelas, M. (1991) 'Teaching mathematics without a coherent point of view. Findings from the IEA Second International Mathematics Study', *Journal of Curriculum Studies* 23(2), 119–31.

Thompson, A. (1992) 'Teachers' beliefs and conceptions. A synthesis of the research', in Grouws, D. (ed.), *Handbook of Research on Mathematics Teaching and Learning*, New York: McGraw-Hill, pp. 127–46.

Tomlinson, P. and Quinton, M. (eds.) (1986) *Values Across the Curriculum*, Lewes: Falmer Press.

Wilson, B. J. (1986) 'Values in mathematics education', in Tomlinson, P. and Quinton, M. (eds), *Values Across the Curriculum*, Lewes: Falmer Press, pp. 94–108.

8 Policy, practices and principles in teaching numeracy

What makes a difference?

Mike Askew

Introducing the issue

At the time we were writing this book, there were unprecedented changes in the form and content of teaching mathematics (or numeracy) in English primary schools – and similar changes were also being introduced in secondary schools. While nothing may ever match the level of state intervention in education of the introduction of the National Curriculum (NC) for England and Wales, the arrival of the National Numeracy Strategy (NNS) into English primary schools could possibly have a greater influence. Unlike the National Curriculum, the NNS is not mandatory, yet its impact has been widespread and early evidence suggests that the Strategy's recommendations have been taken up by the vast majority of schools. If this and associated initiatives such as booster classes and summer schools achieve the Secretary of State for Education's vision of future generations of primary school pupils all reaching a minimum level of attainment and eradicating the need for grammar schools then the effects will indeed be dramatic. *The Independent* newspaper reported that David Blunkett, the Secretary of State for Education and Employment, in response to a question about the continuing existence of selective grammar schools, stated his expectation by 2010 of all pupils 'being on a par with each other in terms of the basic grasp of English, maths and science' leading to the result that the babies of today would prove selection was an 'anachronism' (*The Independent* 14/7/2000).

Over and above influencing the teaching of primary mathematics, the NNS also looks set to affect teaching in secondary schools, both indirectly and directly. It will affect it indirectly through raising the levels of attainment and changing the understandings of pupils entering secondary schools. It will change it directly through the introduction of a pilot year 7 numeracy project which is being extended into year 8 and year 9. It seems likely that this will be developed into an extension of the NNS into secondary schools and further change the landscape of mathematics teaching.

In this chapter I want to examine some of the possible relationships between the policy of the NNS and the classroom practices that might arise as a result of the policy and the mediating effect of teachers' principles and beliefs in bridging between policy and practice.

Key questions

The key questions that I address in this chapter are:

- How do we define numeracy?
- What are the policy recommendations for teaching numeracy?
- What is the evidence for the practices of teaching that make a difference?
- What makes a difference?

Whatever sector of education you are in, these questions are likely to have relevance.

How do we define numeracy?

> *Reflecting on the issue . . .*
> Jot down any content of the mathematics curriculum that you think would *not* be included in a numeracy curriculum.

Why did we not originally have a National Mathematics Strategy? The term 'numeracy' came to be used partly, no doubt, to mirror government attention to literacy and partly because of its potential association with arithmetic ('numeracy' sounds very number-based) and consequent appeal to the advocates of a 'back to basics' movement. This is mirrored in the Secretary of State's claim in the White Paper *Excellence in Schools* that the primary function of the education service is 'to ensure that every child is taught to read, write and add up' (DfEE 1997).

Historically, the term numeracy was first coined in the Crowther Report (DES 1959) and was meant to mean something like 'scientific literacy'. While Michael Girling's (1997) suggestion that being numerate consists of 'sensible use of a 4-function calculator' might seem appropriate for the new millennium, in recent research at King's College we adopted a functional definition:

> . . . the ability to process, communicate, and interpret numerical information in a variety of contexts.
>
> (Askew *et al.* 1997)

This definition is similar to the sense in which numeracy is used in some other parts of the world, notably New Zealand, and also to the way the term 'number sense' is used in the US (McIntosh *et al.* 1992). The definition proposed by the NNS shares something of the functionality of this definition, with a focus on 'proficiency' (and an anthropomorphising of numeracy in that it 'demands' understanding) (DfEE 1999a).

> Numeracy is a proficiency which involves confidence and competence with numbers and measures. It requires an understanding of the number system, a repertoire of computational skills and an inclination and ability to solve number problems in a variety of contexts. Numeracy also demands practical

understanding of the ways in which information is gathered by counting and measuring, and is presented in graphs, diagrams, charts and tables.

(DfEE 1999a: 4)

However, the statutory content of the Mathematics National Curriculum could not be set aside with the introduction of the National Numeracy Strategy, and there is now a blurring of the distinction between numeracy and mathematics. The summary of recommendations in the preliminary report of the Numeracy Task Force sets out the recommendations they have for a National Numeracy Strategy that we believe will improve standards and expectations in primary mathematics (DfEE 1998: 2), and includes recommendations for a 'daily mathematics lesson' and training to ensure that the daily lesson 'will allow pupils to reach a high standard of numeracy', with 'a high proportion of these lessons spent on numeracy'. The final curriculum content document of the NNS includes teaching objectives for shape and space and rather than being the framework for teaching numeracy, it is called the 'Framework for Teaching Mathematics' (DfEE 1999a). Thus it seems that, within NNS policy, numeracy and mathematics are easily interchangeable.

Richard Noss (1997) emphasises the danger of equating mathematics with numeracy, as it may turn out that the mathematics curriculum is reduced merely to the elements of mathematics that are most easily learnable. I want to suggest that one of the dangers is that the curriculum gets reduced to those parts that are teachable. In order to examine this, I want to look at the metaphors for describing learning that are currently around.

As Anna Sfard (1998) points out, theories of learning can broadly be divided along the lines of whether they rest upon the metaphor of 'learning as acquisition' or 'learning as participation'. Learning as acquisition theories can be regarded broadly as mentalist in their orientation, with the emphasis on the individual building up cognitive structures (see Alexander 1991; Baroody and Ginsburg 1990; Carpenter *et al.* 1982; Kieran 1990; Peterson *et al.* 1984). In contrast, learning as participation theories attend to the socio-cultural contexts within which learners can take part (see for example Brown *et al.* 1989; Lave and Wenger 1991; Rogoff 1990). I do not suggest that either of these metaphors is the correct one to work with, each has its strengths and weaknesses. But I do suggest that in considering the sort of classroom experiences that we offer children, whether one starts with 'acquisition' or 'participation' does make a difference.

The NNS framework for teaching mathematics can be read as setting out the mathematics that children are expected to acquire through the detailed examples of what children are able to do at the end of each year. While we might broadly agree with the thrust of these examples, the sort of experiences that children participate in also need to be taken into account. For example, the child who only learns multiplication facts through the rote memorisation of tables will have a different understanding of the nature of multiplication from the child who learns multiplication facts through participating in a range of activities that link multiplication to problem solving and highlight the relationship with division.

Attending to what children participate in leads to acknowledging numeracy as a social practice (Baker 1999) rather than as a set of commodities (in the form of skills, concepts or procedures) that can be passed on (and thus 'acquired'). The question then shifts from 'how do we define numeracy?' in terms of what needs to be passed on to 'what are the policy recommendations for teaching practices?'

What are the policy recommendations for teaching numeracy?

David Robitaille and Michael Dirks (1982) argue that there are three aspects of any curriculum that each needs to be addressed:

- the intended curriculum: what it is expected that pupils should be taught;
- the implemented curriculum: the curriculum that is actually enacted in classrooms;
- the attained curriculum: what children actually learn.

At the time of writing, it is early days in the implementation of the NNS and there is not yet clear evidence of the impact on pupils' learning (although national test results are indeed steadily rising). I shall examine therefore the policy recommendations of the NNS in terms of the effect on the intended and implemented curriculum.

Policy recommendations and the intended curriculum

While the policy of the NC marked a great change in the content and culture of teaching mathematics, the approach to policy recommendations in the NNS moves in the opposite direction to policy developments in the NC. The first National Curriculum for mathematics had two 'profile components' with fourteen 'attainment targets' and level descriptors. To clarify the levels of attainment expected, examples of the sorts of questions pupils were expected to be able to answer were included in the orders (the legal and mandatory part of the curriculum).

However, once the NC was in place, feedback from teachers indicated that it was perceived as over-detailed and over-prescriptive. The long list of examples appeared to be leading to a 'tick-list' attitude towards learning: if children could be 'ticked-off' as having succeeded on such items then learning must have been brought about. In the light of this, curriculum revisions were speedily put in place. The two revisions to the National Curriculum have both resulted in a reduced level of detail prescribed by the programmes of study (PoS).

In contrast, the NNS National Framework for Teaching Mathematics from Reception to Year 6 (DfEE 1999a) and Year 7 Framework (DfEE 1999b) both provide a breakdown of the curriculum in terms of teaching objectives and learning outcomes that are far more detailed than the statements contained in the first National Curriculum for mathematics. But rather perceiving it in the same way as the first NC as over-prescriptive, teachers seem, if not to have actively welcomed the framework, then at least not to have actively objected to it.

One possible reason why the NNS may be being well received is that the content specified not only sets out what children should be able to do, but also hints at how they might be taught to do it. I shall examine this in more detail later.

Another possible reason is that the content, on the surface, appears close to what many people might regard as a 'traditional' mathematics, or arithmetic curriculum. While the sort of 'mental mathematics' envisaged by the Strategy is far removed from the mental arithmetic tests of years ago, the later emphasis on paper and pencil methods is close to what many teachers would themselves have been taught at school. One has to pay close attention to the way that the NNS links mental and written methods to appreciate that there are some very subtle distinctions expected.

Reflecting on the issue . . .
Jot down what you think are the key elements influencing whether to carry out a calculation using a mental method or paper and pencil.

Traditionally the relationship between mental and written methods was largely based on the size of the numbers involved: small numbers could be worked with mentally, greater numbers needed paper and pencil. The NNS promotes a rather different view. In deciding which method to use, not only must the size of the numbers be taken into account, but also the relationship between the numbers needs to be considered. For example, a child may need to use paper and pencil to calculate $237 - 188$ but be confident to choose to calculate $3002 - 1998$ mentally.

The five-year longitudinal Leverhulme Numeracy Research Programme at King's College is looking at children's progress in learning mathematics by following two cohorts of children – each of some 1,500 reception and year 4 children – over five years of schooling. As part of this programme we interviewed a small group of teachers about their understandings of the expectations of the NNS at the end of the first year of the implementation of the strategy. Part of the interview involves providing the teachers with 'vignettes' of classroom events and asking them how typical they think each of these is in terms of being in the spirit of the NNS. One of the vignettes is:

A year 5 pupil is working out the difference between 5001 and 4997 using decomposition.

The majority of the teachers are quite happy that this is in line with policy recommendations, even though the numbers chosen are clearly identified in the numeracy framework as the type of calculation that a numerate pupil should choose to carry out mentally. In some previous research it was found that implementation of the National Curriculum was affected by the way in which teachers tended to interpret what they were expected to do rather than merely adopting the new curriculum guidelines. Generally these interpretations tended to fit closely the classroom practices that teachers were presently operating rather than requiring them to adopt alternative classroom practices that challenged them to teach in new ways (Brown *et al.* 2000). The same thing may well happen with the NNS if teachers are not encouraged to look closely at the detail of the framework and to work together on reaching common understandings of what is really expected.

Policy recommendations and the implemented curriculum

Over and above the detailed specification of the curriculum content, the NNS goes on to make explicit prescriptions for how the curriculum should be taught in a way that the National Curriculum did not. Although the original 'Non-Statutory Guidance' that accompanied the National Curriculum explored teaching issues, it was far less prescriptive. In part, the recommendations for teaching methods are set out in the introduction to the framework with the setting out of what the 'three part daily mathematics lesson' should look like. Advice is also provided on general aspects of teaching such as pupil grouping, layout of room, use of resources and so forth. Such aspects of teaching, which are largely independent of the specific content to be taught, might be described as the 'pedagogical' aspects of teaching.

Complementing 'pedagogy' is 'didactics': the moment-to-moment processes of actually teaching a particular topic. This includes decisions about the content and nature of specific tasks set; aspects of the topic chosen to attend to (for example concentrating on fractions as parts of a whole or as parts of sets): specific questions asked and teachers' responses to these. I will look at each of these in turn.

NNS and pedagogy

The NNS is quite clear in its recommendations for the style of teaching advocated:

> . . . a structured daily mathematics lesson of 45 minutes to one hour for all pupils of primary age. Teachers will teach the whole class together for a high proportion of the time, and oral and mental work will feature strongly in each lesson.

> (DfEE 1999a: 2)

One of the consistent findings from international comparisons of attainment in mathematics is that 'opportunity to learn' is a good predictor of pupil outcomes. Two aspects of this recommendation would seem to lean towards increasing opportunity to learn: the entitlement to a daily mathematics lesson and more whole-class teaching. Is there research evidence to support this?

With respect to the requirement for a daily mathematics lesson (interestingly the only part of the NNS to be enshrined in the law), the data from the Third International Mathematics and Science Study (TIMSS) suggest that English pupils in years 4 and 5 in 1994 already spent on average between 55 and 60 minutes daily on mathematics (Mullis *et al.* 1997). So it would appear that concerns over whether or not children were receiving sufficient mathematics teaching may not be well founded and that the key issue is the type of teaching they receive.

In contrast to the TIMSS finding on the amount of teaching pupils receive, data from the same study suggest a smaller proportion of English teachers of year 5 pupils (11 per cent) use whole-class teaching in most mathematics lessons than that of teachers in almost any other country (Mullis *et al.* 1997). So, will more whole-class teaching raise standards? (The TIMSS study is further discussed in Paul Andrews's chapter.)

While one can find evidence in support of an association between whole class teaching and standards of attainment, the findings are not unequivocal. For example, in reviewing generic Dutch studies, Bert Creemers (1997) noted that the proportion of whole-class teaching appeared to have a significant positive association with attainment in only three out of the twenty-nine studies. Penelope Peterson and Terence Janicki (1979), in a review of mathematical learning studies, found that with the more direct approaches of traditional whole-class teaching, pupils tended to perform slightly better on achievement tests. However, they performed worse on tests of more abstract thinking, such as creativity and problem-solving.

In line with this, early signs from HMI monitoring of the NNS suggest that the format of the daily mathematics lesson has been taken up by teachers and that certain areas of mathematical knowledge, although not all, appear to be improving, notably pupils' ability to solve non-routine problems (OFSTED 2000). In addition, the team of Canadian researchers evaluating the NNS in their first-year report also note that the Strategy may not be the most effective way of teaching higher order thinking (Earl *et al.* 2000).

In other large-scale statistical studies there has been a positive correlation between whole-class teaching and attainment (Galton *et al.* 1980; Galton and Simon 1980; Good *et al.* 1983). However, noting that in individual cases particularly poor results have also been associated with whole-class styles, investigators have cited evidence for the quality of teacher–pupil interaction being a much more important factor than class organisation (Good and Grouws 1979; Good and Biddle 1988; Galton 1995). These studies suggest that a whole-class format may make better use of high quality teaching, but may equally increase the negative effect of lower quality interaction.

The suggestion that the quality of teacher–pupil interaction may be more important than the style of organisation is also supported by recent work in the Teacher Training Agency funded study of 'Effective Teachers of Numeracy' at King's College (Askew *et al.* 1997). In this study of ninety teachers, classes of pupils were assessed on a specially designed test of numeracy in the autumn and summer terms of one year of schooling. The changes in results on these tests were used to calculate mean average class gain scores on the tests, which were then used to put the classes in order of mean gains.

Examining the style of lesson organisation that the teachers in the study used, we could find no association between whole-class, group or individualised work and pupil gains. Teachers of classes with high mean gains did not necessarily work with whole classes; many used group work or even an individualised approach.

Equally, the teachers of classes with low mean gains displayed styles of lesson organisation that spanned whole-class, group or individualised work. Early findings from the Leverhulme Numeracy Research Programme further support this finding with no association being found between teachers' reported time on whole-class teaching and pupil gains.

NNS and didactics

The NNS framework for teaching mathematics, while setting out detailed teaching objectives, does not explicitly tell the reader what sort of teaching acts need to be used to bring these about. However, suggestions for teaching methods can be discerned through the examples of the sort of methods that pupils are expected to display at the end of each year of teaching. For example, the use of the empty number line was developed in the Netherlands as a teaching tool: by specifying that pupils should be able to use one as a learning outcome, teachers are directed towards a particular teaching approach. The empty number line is simply a blank line that the pupil puts their own choice of numbers on. For example, if they were adding 26 and 13 they might put 26 at one end of the line, make a jump of 10 and write 36, make a jump of 3 and write down 39.

I want to take as an example the didactics of teaching mental and written calculation methods. When I run courses for teachers, I find many are concerned to clarify the distinction between a written and a mental calculation method. I want to suggest that a more helpful distinction is between a strategic and a procedural method. Table 8.1 below summarises the key differences between these.

Table 8.1   Strategic vs procedural calculation methods

Strategic	Procedural
• Method of calculation is in part determined by the numbers involved. For example, 2657–1778 may be calculated differently from 2003–1998.	• Method of calculation is the same, irrespective of the numbers. For example, decomposition would be an acceptable method for each of 2657–1778 and 2003 – 1998.
• Small differences in the numbers involved may provoke different strategies. For example 99×25 and 97×23 may be calculated by different methods.	• Small differences in the numbers make no difference to the method of calculation.
• Different numbers may provoke different calculation strategies. For example, 102−98 may provoke a counting-on strategy, while 102−13 a counting back strategy.	• Differences in the numbers makes no difference to the method of calculation.
• Paper and pencil supports mental calculations, often through 'jottings'.	• Mental recall of number facts supports paper and pencil working.

Looked at in terms of 'strategic' or 'procedural' these can be seen to involve two distinct sets of skills. The 'procedural' skills, that many adults would prefer to use, would be to reach for a calculator, but for political rather than educational reasons paper and pencil procedures still have a central place in our curriculum. But whether the procedure is paper and pencil-based or calculator-based, it is distinct from choosing a strategy. When choosing how to do a calculation, the question pupils need to be encouraged to ask themselves, is: Do I have a strategy for this calculation or do I have to use a procedure? The didactic advice provided in the Framework for teaching mathematics suggests that procedures can somehow emerge out of strategies, a process that may not be quite that simple.

Reflecting on the issue . . .
Jot down, say, five calculations that you think an average seven-year-old could carry out strategically and five that you think they would need to use a procedure for. What would similar calculations look like for an 11 year old?

What makes a difference to learning outcomes?

In the section on pedagogy I noted that research suggests that it may be the quality of teacher–pupil interactions that makes a difference to pupil learning outcomes. In this final section I want to discuss how it might be that teachers' beliefs about the nature of the relationship between teaching and learning is the key to understanding differences in the ways they interact with pupils.

As I mentioned earlier, in the 'Effective Teachers of Numeracy' study the ninety teachers in the study could not be distinguished as effective in terms of pupil gains on a test of numeracy when measures such as amount of whole-class teaching, pupil grouping or qualifications were considered. However, through analysis of case studies of eighteen of the teachers, three clusters of beliefs – three 'orientations', namely connectionist, transmission and discovery – characterising beliefs and understandings of the relationship between teaching and learning – were derived. And, as I shall demonstrate below, the extent to which a teacher identified with one or other of these orientations did appear to be associated with pupil learning gains. I will look at each of these orientations briefly by looking at the way they characterise views on the nature of the relationship between teacher and learner and between learner and mathematics.

A connectionist orientation towards teaching numeracy

From our analysis, what seemed to distinguish some highly effective teachers from the others was a consistent and coherent set of beliefs about how best to teach mathematics whilst taking into account children's learning. In particular, the theme of 'connections' was one that particularly stood out. Several of the highly effective teachers (as measured by pupil test gains) in the study paid attention to:

- *connections between different aspects of mathematics*: for example, addition and subtraction or fractions, decimals and percentages;
- *connections between different representations of mathematics*: moving between symbols, words, diagrams and objects;
- *connections with children's methods*: valuing these and being interested in children's thinking but also sharing their methods.

We came to refer to such teachers having a *connectionist orientation* to teaching and learning numeracy.

This connectionist orientation includes the belief that being numerate involves being both efficient and effective. For example, while 2016 −1999 can be effectively calculated using a paper and pencil algorithm, it is more efficient to work it out mentally. Being numerate, for the connectionist-orientated teacher, requires an awareness of different methods of calculation and the ability to choose an appropriate method.

Further to this is the belief that children come to lessons already in possession of mental strategies for calculating but that the teacher had responsibility for intervening, working with the children on becoming more efficient. Misunderstandings that children may display are seen as important parts of lessons, needing to be explicitly identified and worked with in order to improve understanding.

As indicated, a connectionist orientation means emphasising the links between different aspects of the mathematics curriculum. The application of number to new situations is important to the connectionist orientation with children drawing on their mathematical understandings to solve realistic problems. The connectionist orientation also places a strong emphasis on developing reasoning and justification, leading to the proof aspects of using and applying mathematics.

Associated with the connectionist orientation is a belief that most children are able to learn mathematics given appropriate teaching that explicitly introduces the links between different aspects of mathematics. As one of the teachers put it:

> I have the same expectations for the children, I always think about it as not so much what the children are doing as what they have the potential to do. So even if I have children like Mary in the classroom who are tremendously able, I am really just as excited with the children who are having that nice slow start, because, who knows, tomorrow they may fly – you just don't know.

Finally, within a connectionist orientation, a primary belief is that teaching mathematics is based on dialogue between teacher and children, so that teachers better understand the children's thinking and children gain access to the teachers' mathematical knowledge. (Kevin Delaney discusses connectivist teaching approaches in his chapter.)

Discovery and transmission orientations towards teaching numeracy

Two other orientations were also identified: one where the teacher's beliefs were more focused upon the role of the teacher (a *transmission* orientation) and one where beliefs focused upon the children learning mathematics independently (*discovery* orientation).

The transmission orientation means placing more emphasis on teaching than learning. This entails a belief in the importance of a collection of procedures or routines, particularly about paper and pencil methods, one for doing each particular type of calculation regardless of whether or not a different method would be more efficient in a particular case. This emphasis on a set of routines and methods to be learned leads to the presentation of mathematics in discrete packages, for example, fractions taught separately from division. In a transmission orientation, teaching is believed to be most effective when it consists of clear verbal explanations of routines. Interactions between teachers and children tend to be question and answer exchanges in order to check whether or not children can reproduce the routine or method being introduced to them. What children already know is of less importance, unless it forms part of a new procedure.

For the transmission-orientated teacher, children are believed to vary in their ability to become numerate. If the teacher has explained a method clearly and logically, then any failure to learn must be the result of the children's inability rather than a consequence of the teaching. Any misunderstandings that children may display are seen as the result of the children's failure to 'grasp' what was being taught; misunderstandings are remedied by further reinforcement of the 'correct' method and more practice to help children remember.

In the discovery orientation, learning takes precedence over teaching and the pace of learning is largely determined by the children. Children's own strategies are the most important: understanding is based on working things out for themselves. Children are seen as needing to be 'ready' before they can learn certain mathematical ideas. This results in a view that children vary in their ability to become numerate. Children's misunderstandings are the result of pupils not being 'ready' to learn the ideas. In this orientation, teaching children requires extensive use of practical experiences that are seen as embodying mathematical ideas so that they discover methods for themselves. Learning about mathematical concepts precedes the ability to apply these concepts and application is introduced through practical problems.

The discovery-orientated teacher tends to treat all methods of calculation as equally acceptable. As long as an answer is obtained, whether or not the method is particularly effective or efficient is not perceived as important. Children's creation of their own methods is a valued process, and is based upon building up their confidence and ability in practical methods. Calculation methods are selected primarily on the basis of practically representing the operation. The mathematics curriculum is seen as being made up of mostly separate elements.

The orientations of connectionist, transmission and discovery are what we might call 'ideal types'. This means that no single teacher is likely to hold a set of beliefs that precisely matches those set out within each orientation. However, analysis of the data we obtained revealed that some teachers were more pre-disposed to talk and behave in ways that fitted with one orientation over the others. The connection between these three orientations and the classification of the teachers into having relatively high, medium or low mean class gain scores suggests that there may be a relationship between pupil learning outcomes and teacher orientations.

Reflecting on the issue . . .

For each set of three statements below, decide which one of the three statements you most closely agree with. Try asking some teachers and parents. Do they share the same views?

1a   Learning mathematics involves building up a network of ideas through being challenged and struggling to overcome difficulties.

1b   Teaching the connections between mathematical ideas can confuse children, so they should be taught separately.

1c   Pupils need to be ready before they can learn certain mathematical ideas.

2a   Children learn mathematical ideas separately and make their own connections later.

2b   Pupils need to be taught mathematics step by step and be secure in their knowledge before moving on.

2c   Working on the connections between mathematical ideas strengthens children's understandings.

Where does this leave us?

These beliefs would seem to link back to the metaphors for learning that I discussed earlier. Both the transmission and discovery orientations can fit well with a view of learning as acquisition. For the transmission-orientated teacher, it is simply a matter of 'delivering' the curriculum, while for the discovery-orientated teacher it is the responsibility of the pupil to find mathematics in the activities presented.

Within the connectionist orientation there is more emphasis on pupil participation. The roles of teacher and pupil are seen as complementing each other, both taking an active part in the lesson and each having some responsibility for the learning outcomes. This means seeing teaching in ways that go beyond simply the implementation of the three-part lesson and examining practices that maximise the opportunity for all pupils to take part in lessons.

As well as these different orientations having an effect on teaching and learning, the research findings indicated that the amount of time a school spent on discussing approaches to mathematics teaching also had an impact. While the NNS has required schools to devote several days to professional development in mathematics, it would seem likely that changes in teachers' practice arise from the interplay of looking at what they do in classrooms together with examining their beliefs for why they do it. With a National Strategy there is bound to be a certain amount of striving for conformity but without changes in beliefs, changes in teachers' practices may be short-lived. Teachers and schools need to make sure they have time to discuss and debate their responses to the policy recommendations as well as simply considering whether or not they are in place.

Invitation to reflect

Look back over recent mathematics lessons that you have taught or look at a textbook for pupils. To what extent does the content:

- encourage pupils to choose between using strategic and procedural methods?
- encourage them to make connections between different aspects of mathematics?

You might like to discuss and investigate these questions with colleagues.

Further suggested readings

Askew, M., Brown, M., Rhodes, V., Wiliam, D. and Johnson, D. (1997) *Effective Teachers of Numeracy: Report of a Study carried out for the Teacher Training Agency*, London: King's College, University of London. This is a detailed account of the large-scale longitudinal study on what might make effective teachers effective. In particular it identifies the beliefs and practices of a sample of primary teachers who seem to be achieving higher than average gains in pupil understanding.

Thompson, I. (ed.) (1999) *Issues in Teaching Numeracy in Primary Schools*, London: Open University. This book focuses on numeracy and presents a readable account of current research findings in the area. Ian Thompson brings together various authors who look at: family numeracy, the use of calculators, IT, and mental calculations. There are also chapters on international research in numeracy teaching and a discussion of the genesis of the national numeracy strategy.

Thompson, I. (ed.) (1997) *Teaching and Learning Early Number*, Buckingham: Open University Press. This book looks at much current research into the teaching and the learning of early number concepts and asks whether it is not time to question some of the traditional approaches. Of particular interest is the book's emphasis upon the beliefs and understanding of pupils at nursery and reception levels.

Hughes, M., Desforges, C. and Mitchell, C. (with Carré, C.) (2000) *Numeracy and Beyond. Applying Mathematics in the Primary School*, Buckingham: Open University Press. This book is based on the findings of another research project where teachers integrated both the using and applying of mathematics throughout the mathematics curriculum. There is a chapter on numeracy teaching in Japan, which gives a useful insight into some alternative sets of practices.

References

Alexander, P. A. (1991) 'A cognitive perspective on mathematics: Issues of perception, instruction and assessment', in *Proceedings of NATO Advanced Research Workshop: Information Technologies and Mathematical Problem Solving Research conference*, Oporto, Portugal.

Askew, M., Brown, M., Rhodes, V., Wiliam, D. and Johnson, D. (1997) *Effective Teachers of Numeracy: Report of a Study carried out for the Teacher Training Agency*, London: King's College, University of London.

Baker, D. (1999) 'What does it mean to understand maths as social?', Paper presented to the British Congress of Mathematics Education Conference, 15–17 July 1999 University College Northampton.

Baroody, A. J. and Ginsburg, H. P. (1990) 'Children's mathematical learning: A cognitive view', in Davis, R. B., Maher, C. A. and Noddings, N. (eds), *Constructivist Views on the Teaching and Learning of Mathematics,* Reston, VA: NCTM, pp. 51–64.

Brown, J. S., Collins, A. and Duguid, P. (1989) 'Situated cognition and the culture of learning', *Educational Researcher* **18**(1), 32–42.

Brown, M., Denvir, H., Rhodes, V., Askew, M., Wiliam, D. and Ranson, E. (2000) 'The effect of some classroom factors on Grade 3 pupil gains in the Leverhulme Numeracy Research Programme', in Nakahara, T. and Koyama, M. (eds), *Proceedings of the 24th Conference of the International Group for the Psychology of Mathematics Education*, Vol 2, 121–8, Japan: Hiroshima University.

Carpenter, T. P., Moser, J. M. and Romberg, T. A. (1982) *Addition and Subtraction: A Cognitive Perspective*, Hillsdale, NJ: Lawrence Erlbaum Associates.

Creemers, B. (1997) *Effective Schools and Effective Teachers: an International Perspective*, Warwick: Centre for Research in Elementary and Primary Education.

DfEE (1997) *Excellence in Schools*, London: Her Majesty's Stationery Office.

DfEE (1998) *Numeracy Matters: The Preliminary Report of the Numeracy Task Force*, London: Department for Education and Employment.

DfEE (1999a) *The National Numeracy Strategy: Framework for Teaching Mathematics from Reception to Year 6*, London: Department for Education and Employment.

DfEE (1999b) *The National Numeracy Strategy: Framework for Teaching Mathematics: Year 7*. London: Department for Education and Employment.

DES (Department of Education and Science) Central Advisory Council for Education (1959) *15–18: A report (The Crowther Report)*, London: Her Majesty's Stationery Office.

Earl, L., Fullan, M., Leithwood, K., Watson, N., with Jantzi, D., Levin, B. and Torrance, N. (2000) 'Watching and learning', OISE/UT evaluation of the Implementation of the National Literacy and Numeracy Strategies. First Annual Report, Toronto: OISE/ University of Toronto.

Galton, M. (1995) *Crisis in the Primary School*, London: Routledge.

Galton, M. and Simon, B. (eds.) (1980) *Progress and Performance in the Primary Classroom*, London: Routledge.

Galton, M., Simon, B. and Croll, P. (eds) (1980) *Inside the Primary Classroom*, London: Routledge.

Girling, M. (1997) 'Towards a definition of basic numeracy', *Mathematics Teaching* **81**(4), 1–4.

Good, T. L. and Biddle, B. J. (1988) 'Research and the improvement of mathematics instruction: the need for observational resources', in Grouws, D. A. and Cooney, T. J. (eds), *Perspectives on Research on Effective Mathematics Teaching*, Reston, Va: NCTM/ Lawrence Erlbaum, pp. 114–142.

Good, T. L. and Grouws, D. A. (1979) 'The Missouri Mathematics Effectiveness Project: An experimental study in fourth-grade classrooms', *Journal of Educational Psychology*, 71 (3), 355–362.

Good, T. L., Grouws, D. A. and Ebmeier, H. (1983) *Active Mathematics Teaching*, New York: Longman.

Kieran, C. (1990) 'Cognitive processes involved in learning school algebra', in Nesher, P. and Kilpatrick, J. (eds), *Mathematics and Cognition: A Research Synthesis by the International Group for the Psychology of Mathematics Education (ICMI Study Series)* Cambridge: Cambridge University Press, pp. 96–112.

Lave, J. and Wenger, E. (1991) *Situated Learning: Legitimate Peripheral Participation*, Cambridge: Cambridge University Press.

McIntosh, A., Reys, B. J. and Reys, R. E. (1992) 'A proposed framework for examining basic number sense', *For the Learning of Mathematics* 12(3), 2–8.

Mullis, I. V. S., Martin, M. O., Beaton, A. E., Gonzalez, E. J., Kelly, D. L. and Smith, T. A. (1997) *Mathematics Achievement in the Primary School Years: IEA's Third Mathematics and Science Study*, Chestnut Hill, Massachusetts: Boston College.

Noss, R. (1997) *New Cultures, New Literacies*. London: Institute of Education.

Office for Standards in Education (OFSTED) (2000) *National Numeracy Strategy: An Interim Evaluation by HMI*, London: Her Majesty's Stationery Office.

Peterson, P. L. and Janicki, T. C. (1979) 'Individual characteristics and children's learning in large-group and small-group approaches', *Journal of Educational Psychology*, 71(5), 677–687.

Peterson, P. L., Swing, S. R., Stark, K. D. and Waas, G. A. (1984) 'Students' cognitions and time on task during mathematics instruction', *American Educational Research Journal* **21**(3), 487–515.

Robitaille, D. and Dirks, M. (1982) 'Models for the mathematics curriculum', *For the Learning of Mathematics* **2**(3), 3–21.

Rogoff, B. (1990) *Apprenticeship in Thinking: Cognitive Development in Social Context*. New York: Oxford University Press.

Sfard, A. (1998) 'On two metaphors for learning and the dangers of choosing just one', *Educational Researcher* 27(2), 4–13.

Part III

Issues in the teaching and learning of mathematics

9 Teaching mathematics resourcefully

Kevin Delaney

Introducing the issue

Throughout history, the abstract nature of mathematics has inevitably led teachers to make use of resources or teaching aids of various kinds to help pupils understand mathematical ideas and the underlying principles of numerical calculations. 'Resources' is, of course, a very broad term that has been used to include everything from everyday objects like photographs, timetables and dolls to structural apparatus such as base-10 blocks. For many years, pupils have been helped by resources such as:

- manipulative materials with varying amounts of structure, ranging from natural objects like stones to manufactured materials like counters, Unifix cubes or Cuisenaire rods;
- rather more abstract images such as number lines, 100 squares and place value cards;
- computer graphics or graphic calculators;
- their own bodies as they, for example, use fingers to count or jump along a large number line.

Within this chapter I focus particularly on resources that provide an image or representation of our number system which is intended to aid understanding of number concepts and provide insights into ways of calculating, either mentally or in written form. This is a focus that is widely viewed as important but it has a particularly high profile in the UK at the time of writing with the introduction of the National Numeracy Strategy (NNS). In the NNS, a strong emphasis is placed on understanding the number system in order to facilitate confidence and competence with mental and written calculations. The writers of the NNS Framework (DfEE 1999a) believe that

> better numeracy standards occur when teachers … use and give pupils access to number lines and other resources, including ICT to model mathematics ideas and methods.
>
> (DfEE 1999a: Introduction p. 5)

Despite the focus on number resources, all of the key questions below and many of the points I make in this chapter apply equally to resources used within other areas of mathematics.

Key questions

In focusing on this issue, my overarching key questions in this chapter are:

- Do resources inevitably help in the learning and teaching of mathematics and where they do help, what can be said about the ways that they do?
- Are there social and political factors that affect the choice and use of resources?
- Are some resources better than others and is this affected by the context, e.g. by the type of calculation or by the belief systems of pupils and teachers?
- How can teachers develop their use and understanding of resources, recognise the strengths and weaknesses of particular resources and adapt them to differing circumstances, e.g. for demonstration by the teacher or individual use by the pupil?

How would you respond to these questions in relation to your own practice and beliefs?

Do resources inevitably help understanding?

An inanimate resource cannot, in itself, have any miraculous power beyond the teachers and pupils who use it. Furthermore, there is no mathematics actually in a resource. The mathematics is brought to the resource by those who interact with it, or is developed by them as they use it to support or challenge their thinking. Counters can be used to help a child to count but it is the teacher, parent or peer who draws the child's attention to aspects of the mathematics of counting, e.g. that each counter should be touched only once and in unison with a correctly ordered sequence of counting numbers. In addition, it is the child who has to own this awareness – nobody else can do it on his or her behalf.

There have been many criticisms of the inappropriate use of instrumental methods of teaching, where pupils are trained in a series of steps that will lead to the correct answer for various standard written arithmetic methods (or 'algorithms'). Resources such as base-10 blocks were introduced in some schools to help pupils understand the place value aspects of these calculations, but it has often been observed that 'pushing wood' in this way can be equally instrumental if it is done in a manner that emphasises the procedure rather than the underlying structure of the calculation (see, for example, Askew and Wiliam 1995: 11). Clearly, the actions as well as the intentions of the teacher are important when using apparatus.

> *Reflecting on the issue . . .*
> Before you get too far into this chapter, think about the reasons you might use resources in the classroom; what do you hope the children will gain from the use of the resource? Are there any differences between the various resources you might use? What differences are there between when you use a resource to 'demonstrate' some mathematics to a group and when you give a resource to children to 'manipulate' some mathematics?

There is certainly a consensus (see Liebeck 1984; Hughes 1986; Skemp 1989; Pimm 1992; Askew 1998; Edwards 1998; Thompson 1997, 1999) that, in thoughtful and skilful hands, apparatus of different kinds can help; in fact it is hard to see how some mathematics could be taught at all without visual or manipulative aids of some kind. Over many years, thoughtful teachers have experimented with teaching aids, observed the results and developed a number of 'local theories' concerning the use and benefits of certain apparatus in mediating mathematical understanding.

Let me look at one example, that of Cuisenaire rods. My own observations of some of the major strengths of using Cuisenaire rods, as revealed by conversations with teachers and analysis of video material, could be summarised as follows (Delaney 1992a, b, c, d):

- They offer a very powerful image for representing and understanding number operations which children are able to internalise and subsequently use for mental calculations.
- They are a resource that both children and teachers can use to demonstrate concretely what they are trying to express about numbers.
- They enable teachers to follow and interact with children's thinking more directly.
- They make relationships between numbers more apparent.
- They emphasise and draw attention to the base-10 structure of our number system.
- They give powerful insights into the underlying algebra of calculations.
- They have a strong visual and tactile appeal that relates well to how children learn.
- They enable young children to gain quicker access to larger numbers.
- They enable children to explore the properties of numbers independently of the teacher.

There are of course other contexts in which Cuisenaire rods might be useful – such as pre-algebra, area, number sequences etc. However, I will restrict my attention in this chapter to their use in developing number concepts. At present, they receive limited attention in the UK but they remain a useful resource and one that is adaptable to a large range of contexts.

Reflecting on the issue . . .
Consider one of the resources that you use or have seen used most frequently and go through the list above. To what extent are these points true of the resource you have chosen? Consider whether the points apply equally well in situations where the resource is used to as a teaching aid and when it is used as a learning aid.

Broader theories concerning the nature of learning can also be invoked to explore and explain how learning is mediated by apparatus or structured visual images. Jerome Bruner (1964) drew attention to three different modes of representation, which are important in terms of learners gaining knowledge – the enactive, iconic and symbolic modes. The enactive mode involves representing mathematical ideas or structures by means of actions, such as manipulating physical apparatus for example. The iconic mode involves the representation of these ideas through pictures or images whereas the symbolic mode involves more abstract representation through words or language. Particular children may of course need a different balance of these experiences but Jerome Bruner suggests they are mutually supportive for achieving fuller understanding. In mathematics learning the enactive and iconic modes relate well to manipulative and image based resources. Lev Vygotsky (1978) is another theorist whose work throws light on the ways that adults can support pupils, at an appropriate level, to reach out and make new connections in their learning – David Wood (1988) has described this process as 'scaffolding'. More recently, the principles of 'constructivism' have caused much interest in the areas of science and mathematics education (see, for example, Ollerenshaw and Ritchie 1993). The underlying tenet of constructivism is that a learner must construct meaning for himself or herself rather than be a passive recipient. However, the teacher can act as a guide, suggesting paths that may be profitable. In the context of teaching aids, the constructivist teacher's role would be to scaffold or facilitate pupils' use of the aid through language and actions in order to help them make sense of some aspect of mathematics. Tony Harries and Mike Spooner (2000) provide a concise overview of the different branches of constructivism for those who would like to read further.

Theories of various kinds reflect the efforts of teachers and researchers to make sense of what is observable about the ways that we learn. In the area of mathematical learning, the interactions between manipulating objects, the language of teachers and pupils and the use of pictures and mathematical symbols are perhaps most clearly observed in situations involving young children and so it is not surprising to see that, amongst others, Pamela Liebeck (1984), Martin Hughes (1986) and Suzanne Edwards (1998) all draw attention to how the teaching and learning of mathematics can be mediated by images and physical apparatus. It is worth considering Suzanne Edwards' diagram of the interconnections between four modes of experience that she describes as symbols, pictures, language and handling objects as an example (see Figure 9.1).

She suggests that:

> the growth of mathematical understanding . . . is brought about by children making connections between the four types of experience, handling objects, language, pictures and symbols at every stage.
>
> (Edwards 1998: 18)

The Open University's *Do, talk, record* (Open University 1982a) and *Manipulating, getting a sense of, articulating* (Open University 1982b) frameworks have the same message of encouraging teachers to provide the four types of experiences in Figure 9.1. These frameworks are described as follows:

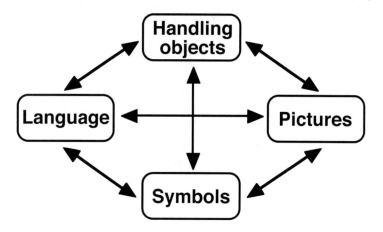

Figure 9.1   Four modes of experience.

Do, talk and record

Doing	Action and concrete experience, in multiple embodiments (i.e. offering the experience with different types of physical apparatus).
Talking	Language patterns injected, explored, listened to, developed.
Recording	Stories written in pictures and words, successive shorthanding (i.e. making the recording more concise and symbolic), ultimately leading to standard notations.

Manipulating, getting a sense of, articulating

Manipulating	Confidence-inspiring entities, which may be objects, numbers, letters, images.
Getting a sense of	what underlies the specific examples.
Articulating	the sense of an idea, crystallising it in succinct form.

(Open University 1982c)

Within the *Do, Talk, Record* approach the use of physical apparatus or useful images is crucial. It is the manipulation of objects or images which enables a pupil to 'get a sense of' mathematical ideas and provides a clear and appropriate focus for both the talk and the subsequent stages of recording. The teacher's language often determines the initial frames of reference for exploring apparatus or images, but in situations where children talk with other children and with teachers, shared meanings and language can be arrived at within the context of a particular classroom. The shared language may be non-standard (I have heard children working with Cuisenaire describe subtraction as 'chopping off' for example) but can always be related back to more widely accepted terms by the teacher once children have grasped underlying concepts. With repeated use it seems that the apparatus or image itself can become an 'anchor' for a whole network of interconnections between language, pictures, symbols and the resource itself. By thoughtful planning, intervention and evaluation accomplished teachers can make links and decide which aspects need to be visited and re-visited, using careful observation and reflection-in-action to nurture this process.

David Pimm (1992) offers the observation that touch is a key sense for us and that this is especially so for young children. He points out that many common phrases to do with understanding emphasise this connection and draw on our use of physical metaphors. It is recognised that the use of metaphors is more than a surface feature of linguistic style, but representative of deeper structures (Lakoff and Johnson 1980: 6). George Lakoff and Mark Johnson have argued that the metaphoric dimension of language plays a central role in the way we construct meaning.

> Metaphors are conceptual in nature. They are among our principle vehicles for understanding. And they play a central role in the construction of social and political reality.
>
> (Lakoff and Johnson 1980: 159)

For example, the use of spatial metaphors is more than a mere figure of speech, since 'most of our fundamental concepts are organised in terms of one or more spatialisation metaphors' (Lakoff and Johnson 1980: 17). George Lakoff and Mark Johnson describe how metaphors are used to '*allow us to understand one domain of experience in terms of another*' (1980: 117). The focus is upon 'basic levels of experience' which they suggest are:

- Our bodies
- Our interactions with the physical world
- Our interactions with other people within our culture.

(Lakoff and Johnson 1980: 117)

Hence, we grasp concepts and are able to handle new ideas and keep in touch with the latest developments. There is a sense in which resources are introduced as objects but may later develop an independent metaphorical existence. Actions taken with resources can be internalised and used to process mathematics when the resource is not physically present. The words that we use may well indicate the 'virtual resources' we are using to inform our communications, but hand and eye movements are also worth observing. Children may well point to an imagined number line or 100 square – indeed one can encourage them to! It is also worth observing children's eye movements – people often look up or de-focus their eyes when making internal images and it can be informative to ask them about what they see internally.

It is entirely possible that we will one day have a neurological appreciation, perhaps through brain scanning, of the ways that the integrated use of our kinesthetic, auditory, speech and language faculties increase our learning potential and enable us to understand, for example, the structure of our number system in ways which interlink with each other and with previously acquired knowledge. Win

Wenger (1992 and 1996) gives a hint of how we may eventually come to appreciate this. He draws attention to the work of psychologist Donald Hebb, who discovered in the 1940s that when two adjacent neurones become accustomed to firing signals to each other in the course of some activity, neurological changes take place in both cells, which makes interaction between them easier than between neurones not involved in that activity. Over a period of time, those neurones involved in particular activities form long-lasting connections. Win Wenger presents evidence that multi-sensory activities, such as those implied in Suzanne Edwards' diagram, enable 'pole-bridging' between significant areas of the brain such as Broca's Area (speech), Wernicke's Area (understanding of language) and the motor cortex (body movements), leading to powerful networks of Hebbian connections that criss-cross the brain. The implication is that a richer understanding develops as a result.

The bigger picture

It is worth considering the interactions that take place when mathematics is taught and learnt in terms of the following fairly well-known diagram (see Figure 9.2).

This simple but useful diagram serves to remind us that what some see as a non-problematic 'delivery' of a body of knowledge called mathematics is in reality much more complex.

If we consider the two-way interactions between mathematics and teacher, for example, there are any number of possibilities which will affect what happens in a particular classroom. Teachers will have different beliefs about mathematics depending on their experiences, particularly of being taught mathematics themselves. Some teachers believe that mathematics is a set of facts and techniques to be conveyed as efficiently as possible, while others have a constructivist view of learning mathematics, believing that the mathematics they offer has to be re-made (constructed) in the mind of the pupils they offer it to. Clearly, teachers at either end of this spectrum will have a very different view of the uses and purposes of resources and are likely to organise their classrooms and structure classroom activities rather differently.

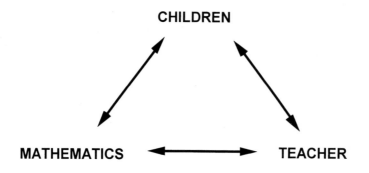

Figure 9.2   Triangle of interactions.

The interactions between pupils and teachers will also offer many possibilities, depending on the views of either party, about the nature of teaching and learning. Teachers who have beliefs that encompass the possibility of pupils helping each other, and even helping the teacher to learn or see things differently, will operate very differently from teachers who believe that they are solely responsible for the learning that happens in their classroom. Resources may offer possibilities for individual and shared use as well as for demonstrating; teachers at different places on this continuum will have different sensitivities to these possibilities.

I consider the interactions between pupils and mathematics last because it seems to be so vulnerable to the interactions considered above. How pupils interact with mathematics seems strongly influenced by their confidence and this in turn is affected by how their view of learning and the nature of mathematics develops through working with particular teachers. If pupils have been encouraged to believe that resources are open to them to make of what they will, they are in a very different position to those who feel, for example, that some resources are too 'babyish' and that to use them implies that they are rather stupid.

It is informative to view the triangle in Figure 9.2 in the context of the research of Mike Askew and colleagues (Askew *et al.* 1997; Askew 1999) since it throws light on effective primary teachers' beliefs and practices in terms of both mathematics and of pupils. Mike Askew and his colleagues investigated the practice of primary teachers of classes where the pupils made better than average gains when tested at the beginning and end of a two-term period, using a specially designed test of numeracy. They observed that effectiveness in this study was not a consequence of a particular style of organisation in maths teaching nor was it related to higher levels of qualifications. What seemed to distinguish many effective teachers of mathematics was 'a consistent and coherent set of beliefs about how best to teach mathematics whilst taking into account children's learning' (Askew 1999: 98). In particular, these teachers were likely to pay attention to

- connections between different aspects of mathematics;
- connections between different representation of mathematics, moving between symbols, words, diagrams and objects;
- connections with children's own methods – showing interest in them and sharing them with others.

These teachers were termed as having a 'connectionist orientation' within the project and were characterised in one way by their emphasis on children using an appropriate method for calculations (more on this can be found in Mike Askew's chapter in this book).

Clearly, the pairs of interactions considered in the triangle diagram in Figure 9.2 are not independent of each other. There is also a larger social context within which the interactions shown are set and this is likely to influence how individual teachers feel able to do choose resources and put them into operation.

The wider social context

Resources appear to go in and out of fashion, at least in the sense that some have been more often mentioned in print at particular times in history. Dienes base-10 blocks, Cuisenaire rods and calculators have all had their time in the spotlight internationally although I suspect that their sustained and informed widespread use has never reached significant levels despite the attention they have received in print. In the UK at the time of writing, however, the National Numeracy Strategy, although not technically mandatory (only the daily lesson of maths is laid down by law), will possibly herald the more widespread use of a set of recommended resources. For example, in the *National Numeracy Strategy Framework for Teaching Mathematics from Reception to Year 6*, we find the following:

10 What resources do we need?

Beside a board each classroom should have a large, long number line for teaching purposes, perhaps below the board . . . A 'washing line' of numbers strung across the room, number tracks with spaces numbered to 20 rather than number lines . . . Equip each child with a pack of digit cards 0 to 9 to hold up when answering questions in a whole-class setting . . . place value cards are equally useful . . .

(DfEE 1999a: 29–30)

The document goes on to include: addition and subtraction cards, symbol cards, 100–squares, counters, interlocking cubes, wooden pegs, wooden cubes, pegboards, straws, rulers, coins, dominoes, dice, calculators, squared paper, number games, measuring equipment, shapes, construction kits, base-10 apparatus, spike abacus – and interest books and dictionaries (DfEE 1999a: 30).

This unprecedented pressure to take on particular resources is created by a detailed numeracy framework document that makes multiple references to many of them and advocates a direct style of teaching. It is reinforced by the existence of many training videos in schools that demonstrate their use and by the OFSTED inspection system, which is likely to have the expectation that schools will follow the recommendations. Is this a desirable situation? Some would argue that a nationally imposed curriculum and teaching approach, based on resources that were carefully researched and piloted over a reasonable length of time, would help many pupils to avoid the effects of poor or uninspired teaching. Others would argue, however, that the National Numeracy Strategy (NNS) was introduced hurriedly for political motives and that its claims to be research-based are open to question (see, for example, Brown *et al.* 1998). Since the Framework makes strong recommendations for resources it is worth exploring how considered and research-based the Strategy was able to be in the circumstances that gave rise to it.

The NNS was developed from the National Numeracy Project (NNP), which took place in 750 schools in England during 1996–9 (Straker 1999). In structural and philosophical terms, the NNS and NNP are very similar, and differ markedly from approaches to mathematics teaching that were generally used in primary schools until that time. The NNP was intended to run for five years but the final two years were subsumed into the NNS, presumably before a full evaluation of the Project had been carried out. When it became an urgent political objective to put a National Numeracy Strategy in place it would seem that, within the time scale decided on, the only real choice available as a framework to build such a strategy around was the NNP, particularly since the Office for Standards in Education (OFSTED), the Qualifications and Curriculum Authority (QCA), the Teacher Training Agency (TTA) and the Basic Skills Agency (BSA) had been involved in its development. There has been a great deal of debate about whether the NNS is 'getting it right' (see, for example, Hughes 1999) and about whether it is sufficiently research-based. To explore this global issue is outside the scope of this present chapter but it is possible to look at how the question of teaching resources is dealt with in supporting materials for the strategy.

It is clear that in the NNS some pieces of apparatus are favoured and others are not. There is a strong bias towards more abstract representations such as number lines, place value cards and 100–squares with no substantial mention of Dienes base-10 blocks (at least in the example sections, although they are listed in the recommended section) and none at all of Cuisenaire rods. If this is the result of considered reflection rather than personal preference one would expect to see some rationale for the inclusion of certain pieces of apparatus and not others and some discussion of the advantages and disadvantages of those resources which are selected for inclusion in the strategy. Chapter 5 of Book 2 of the training pack for the NNS (DfEE 1999b) would be the place to develop such arguments, but this chapter is extremely general and offers no real insights into these important matters. There is also a need for written discussion of the potential for misusing the various resources. In the worst cases, resources can be misused in ways that result in confused pupils and highly instrumental approaches to learning.

By contrast, in Germany, for example, the Dortmund based 'Mathe 2000' project, which could perhaps be seen as similar in intention to the National Numeracy Project in this country, has adopted a much more sensible time scale with what appears to be much more coherent and grounded outcomes (Wittman 1995). It may be, of course, that this could have been true of the NNP if it had been allowed to run its natural life and had been evaluated in a more detailed way. In the event, however, a National Numeracy Strategy was required and in the absence of any serious rivals, the NNP was prematurely elevated to this status. The political will to have the NNS succeed is huge; it is a pity then that more time was not taken to develop a more focused approach, supported by a longer period of research and evaluation.

In our present context it is informative to learn from the German Mathe 2000 project's highly considered approach to teaching resources, as reported by one of its major developers, Erich Wittman (Wittman 1995). Working within the principle of what we might translate into English as 'Guided Active Discovery', Erich Wittman lays down a set of criteria for the selection of teaching aids as follows:

- The visual aids offered within a given school year should be compatible and small enough in number for pupils to deal with them thoroughly in the available time.
- Any specific aid should incorporate the basic ideas of the topic under consideration and should be exploited intensively over a long period of time so that the structure it offers can be assimilated.

- Teaching aids should be structured as clearly as possible and be easy to handle.
- As far as possible they should be available as a large model for class demonstration and as a small model for individual pupil use, with dialogue concerning different examples using these two versions encouraged.
- Every pupil should have their own personal set of resources (it is suggested that this is generally only possible where the resource is made of paper).

Reflecting on the issue . . .
At this point, you might want to think carefully about Erich Wittman's criteria in relation to some of the resources or teaching aids you use or have seen used in the classroom. Do they all fit with his five criteria? Which do and which do not? What advantages would it offer if all the aids that you had access to fitted all five criteria? (I am deliberately here not focusing on any negative aspects. My expectation is that you will do that instinctively anyway!)

Erich Wittman suggests that the most important criterion is the second. Most teaching aids they use in this project were well enough known about in Germany but have not necessarily been used extensively in the UK. However, when incorporated into the teaching approach of Guided Active Discovery, careful explanation was necessary to distinguish their new uses from those which had been traditional.

In Mathe 2000 various versions of what is often called the Slavonic Abacus are used. The version for 7-year-olds deals with numbers up to 20 and is intended, amongst other things, to draw attention to stressing grouping in fives. This piece of apparatus, referred to as the Twenty Frame, is an array of dots big enough to accommodate counters as shown in Figure 9.3.

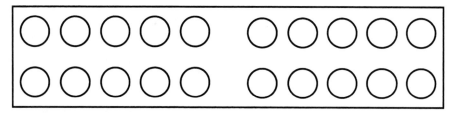

Figure 9.3   Twenty frame.

Erich Wittman (1995) considers the use of the Twenty Frame to represent different ways of calculating 7+5 such that different underlying strategies for addition are revealed. In Figure 9.4 the two sets of counters are laid in separate lines and the structure of the dots draws attention to the fives and enables a child to see the two fives as making ten.

In Figure 9.5, the counters are laid in one continuous line until 'bridging through ten' occurs.

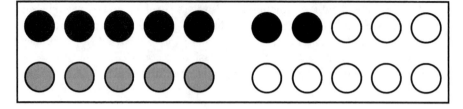

Figure 9.4　Representing 7 + 5 – identifying 'the hidden five'.

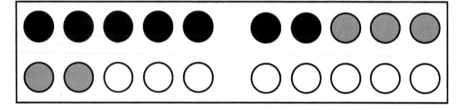

Figure 9.5　Transforming 7 + 5 to 10 + 2 – bridging through ten.

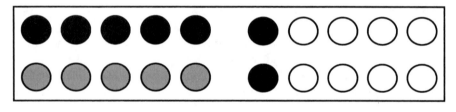

Figure 9.6　Showing 7 + 5 as 6 + 6 – drawing attention to doubling.

In Figure 9.6, counters are again in two lines, but are rearranged to draw attention to the doubling sum 6+6.

The intention in using this Twenty Frame is to allow children to explore different ways of formulating the sum 7+5 and

> in the course of practising and discussing with other children they will themselves establish which is the right way for them. This can vary from example to example.

(Wittman 1995: 38)

What is revealed by the Dortmund approach is that time has been available to think through important things regarding the fine detail of their approach to numeracy and in particular to the provision of teaching and learning aids. The Mathe 2000 project began in 1987 and, even at that stage, was based upon substantial prior research by key members of the assembled team. This is a luxury that the developers of our numeracy strategy have not had. There are certainly some thoughtful and talented mathematics educators working within the NNS organisation but it is clear that what they might achieve is compromised by the limited time scale for development. Enormous amounts of money have been put into setting up training materials for schools, but political objectives have compressed the development time. The overall effect of taking things more slowly could have netted results that would have been so much more cohesive and less stressful for teachers and children.

With such a monolithic structure in place, there is now the danger that, because so much money has been invested, the NNS will acquire an authority that encourages inertia and stifles future development. One hopes that teachers still have sufficient energy to re-examine decisions arrived at in this hasty way, that issues such as the choice of appropriate resources to support teaching will continue to be productively debated and that some enabling structures for this can be put in place.

Are some resources better than others?

Clearly, the answer to this question depends on who is using a resource, what they are using it for and with whom they are using it. Teachers naturally might feel less comfortable with some resources than with others but this may be because they have not fully considered the range of possibilities offered. There is certainly a need for informed sharing of ways to use resources and the NNS is potentially a wonderful catalyst in this regard, at least for the resources that it recommends.

Images or resources have advantages and disadvantages that derive from their inherent structure. A detailed analysis is inappropriate here but Ruth Trundley and Helen Edginton (1999) point to the fact that place value cards, for example, provide a good model for the way that the number names are written and allows the numbers to be split into tens and ones, but they are fairly abstract and offer no sense of the size of the number. Number lines provide a good image for estimating and rounding as well as for addition and subtraction but do not show number patterns easily and are not very powerful images for multiplication or division, where an array offers much more potential (see for example Pinel 1992a and b), or for doubling and halving. In addition to this, regardless of the apparatus, there are some children who respond better to a particular piece of apparatus rather than another in a specific context.

It is worth looking in detail at modelling a situation with one particular apparatus – in this case Cuisenaire rods – to derive some sense of when a specific apparatus can be more useful than another. Cuisenaire material comprises sets of ten rods of different colours and lengths from 1 cm to 10 cm that represent the numbers from 1 to 10. After an initial period learning the number values of the rods and their relationships to each other, children can explore a number of different number concepts and calculations.

A few years ago I worked with two pupils, Shelley and Georgie, both 6-year-old girls who had been using Cuisenaire rods for a year. I set them some problems, which were similar to those that I had seen their teacher set them. Although Georgie had no problem in solving open sentences like $4 \times \square = 8$, I needed to talk through what was required with Shelley. Once she had realised that she was being asked to find a rod that would fit into 8 four times, she used a trial and improvement process to quickly arrive at the correct answer (see Figure 9.7) and then tackled similar problems with growing confidence.

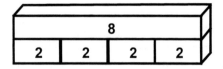

Figure 9.7   Modelling $4\times\square=8$.

With a child of this age I do not know of a more convenient a way to tackle such a problem. It does of course rely on familiarity with the rods but as I explore elsewhere (Delaney 1992a) this takes much less time than many teachers fear. It is true that one could arrive at a solution to the problem by using other forms of apparatus such as counters or Unifix but they would require more organising. In certain circumstances this might be beneficial but if your main focus is on finding a solution to $4\times\square=8$ then there is more work and more ways to get lost with counters or Unifix.

I tried different problems with the girls until I arrived at this one for Georgie: $3\times\square=+5=20$ She set out some rods as shown in Figure 9.8, indicating that she had understood the problem as being '*what rod will fit three times into 20+5?*' As I began to explain that '*three lots of something and another 5 make 20*' she was ahead of me and moved the rods as shown in Figure 9.9. She then went on to find a rod that fitted three times into the gap.

It seems to me that for a six-year-old there is some impressive algebraic understanding happening here. There is a sense in which Georgie cannot yet really solve problems like this, but with the scaffolding offered by the rods, she can worry about only those things needed to solve the problem and thus deal directly with the underlying algebra.

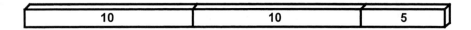

Figure 9.8   Representation of $10+10+5=25$

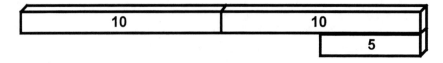

Figure 9.9   Modelling $3\times\square+5=20$.

When I showed the video of Georgie tackling this at an in-service event, one teacher said that she would have asked her children to solve the problem using interlocking cubes such as Unifix or Multilink. I asked if she would try it out and report back, but unfortunately, she never did. Reflecting afterwards, however, with a colleague, I considered the stages needed to solve $3\times\square+5=20$ using Multilink. First, you need to make a stick of 20 Multilink cubes (with possible counting errors). Next, it is necessary to make a stick of 5 possibly in a distinguishing colour. Following this there is the task of estimating what will fit into the gap 3 times, making up lengths of Multilink to fit your guess and adjusting these if unsuccessful. It is not impossible, of course, but it is not straightforward and there are several places where you might miss your step. Using a calculator provides an alternative way but only if the child has a clear image in their mind for $3\times\square+5=20$.

In tackling problems such as $3\times\square+5=85$ one also reveals the limits of Cuisenaire rods – it is possible to solve it but is somewhat unwieldy. However, I believe that the real purpose of structured apparatus is to provide a model, using straightforward calculations, which will offer insight into the algebraic structure of the situation. In this sense, it would become highly appropriate to use a calculator for the above calculations once an internalised image had been established using Cuisenaire rods.

In other situations, of course, Unifix or Multilink offers a versatile resource to explore the nature of arithmetic operations. Kathy Richardson (1971) offers many valuable activities to this end and makes it clear in the detailed nature of her commentary how much mathematical awareness one needs to bring to a lightly structured apparatus of this kind.

Reflecting on the issue . . .

You could try working with a small group of pupils for yourself on the sorts of problem I have outlined above. There is plenty to explore here, e.g.

- How the apparatus helps your demonstration and modelling (scaffolding).
- How the apparatus helps (or hinders or deflects) the child's engagement with the mathematics.

It is useful to make a distinction between the use of a resource to demonstrate to a class, and the use of a resource to engage children. The first of these seems to use resources as an aid or support for teaching, whereas the latter seems more akin to using a resource as a support for learning. Both of these are laudable and entirely justifiable – but they are different in the purpose they ascribe to the resource, and therefore the role ascribed to the teacher and to the learner.

Teachers demonstrating with resources

When teaching a group, resources can be used for (and this is enshrined in, and taken from, the training material for the National Numeracy Strategy).

Demonstrating or modelling a piece of mathematics – showing children how something works, how to do something or providing an image – static or dynamic – to help them 'see' something.

Directing or giving instructions – explaining what has to be done, running through a procedure or process to be followed.

Explaining and illustrating a piece of mathematics – giving examples, providing reasons.

Evaluating children's responses – giving them feedback and dealing with misconceptions.

(DfEE 1999b: Book 2, OHT 1.1 and 1.4)

These are 'traditional skills' which all teachers are likely to aspire to, although one could note that, in mathematics, they have not always had a high profile in the classrooms of teachers where children have worked individually through textbooks. There seems an underlying assumption in the list above that the teacher has appropriate insights into the nature of some mathematical idea or procedure which he or she will pass on to pupils. In this idealised picture, the pupil is initiated into these insights by demonstration of ideas or processes using appropriate resources. Explanations and illustrative examples are provided and the child's responses measured against a range of correct responses that the teacher has in mind. If this were the only diet offered it would be viewed as a purely transmissive mode of teaching mathematics with all the limitations that that implies.

In balance with other modes of teaching that involve pupils more actively, the categories listed seem entirely appropriate. It seems perfectly reasonable for a teacher who understands the mathematics being taught to offer their view of how things could be fitted together. For those children who are able to make sense of the connections that teachers draw to their attention, by their choice and use of resources and language, such demonstrations are worth having. Of course, despite the teacher's intention of 'pre-digesting' the mathematics presented, any child still has to re-construct the mathematics present in the demonstrations, explanation and illustrative examples in their own mind. There is a worry, however, about those children who are not able to make these connections so easily. For these children opportunities to engage with the resource individually will give space for making connections in a different way, but other children are likely to benefit from this opportunity as well.

Enabling children to engage with resources

There is nothing more frustrating than being forced to watch somebody else manipulate a resource when you want to explore it in your own way. And probably the least productive way of engaging in your own meaningful way with a resource is during a fast-paced, direct teaching session, where somebody else has the resource and your attention is constantly being called to their concerns. Even in the context of whole-class teaching, slowing the pace and *asking questions* that invite children to *notice* and *describe* are likely to engage children more in making meaning for themselves from the resource. However, for many contexts it is likely that the larger space provided by working individually, in pairs or in groups will be needed. Ultimately we all have to make individual sense of the mathematics we learn. Those teachers who have observed children at work in groups will have noticed how children often engage with the group for a while and then withdraw to consider the matters under discussion and make sense of them individually before re-engaging with the group.

Earlier there was a list considering the way that resources can be used with an emphasis on *demonstrating*. A complementary list focused on children *engaging* with resources would include:

- *Playing around with and getting a sense of* – how does this resource help me see this calculation, these patterns, this relationship . . .?
- *Noticing and describing* – structures, patterns, similarities, differences . . .
- *Discussing and showing* – this is how I do/see it, how do you do/see it? Is there some way that we could make sense of this?
- *Articulating* – putting relationships of different kinds into words.
- *Asking questions* – of yourself and others and trying to find answers. How does this work? Why does it work? Does it always work? Are there other ways to do this?
- *Testing out* – hypotheses, ideas and approaches, both your own and those of other people.
- *Convincing* – yourself, then others, about these hypotheses, ideas and approaches.
- *Practising and consolidating* – Can I do some more examples with increasing understanding, fluency and confidence? Can I carry out this procedure reliably time after time?
- *Developing new situations or contexts* – What would happen if . . .? Are there any other situations like this?

There is a different sense with this list. The demonstrating list involves somebody else presenting you with their view of the world but with the engaging list there is a feeling of personal involvement in making choices and decisions. Highly focused engaging with resources is probably best done individually and in a situation where time is available. However, part of the organising skill of a teacher is to set up situations so that when you go into that individual space ideas have been seeded and your reflections are as productive as possible. When you can make no sense of, for example, the fact that any two numbers added together give the same result independently of the order of adding, it may be no use to contemplate this on your own with no supporting structure. A useful structure for this might involve an initial demonstration of, for example, 3+5 and 5+3 having the same total, with an invitation to find out if this is true for any other pairs of small numbers. As part of this invitation, work with a partner to produce such pairs of numbers is likely to produce helpful discussion. Where there is a problem an intervention by the teacher may produce a different focus that helps; at this stage the intervention is likely to be more helpful if an appropriate question is asked rather than simply another demonstration using the resource. The question may lead to discussion that is more helpful with a partner. However, throughout all these events the final making sense belongs to the individual who must retreat for however short a time into some more private space to convince herself that the new awarenesses are true and fit with her previous knowledge in some way. The resource plays a crucial role in this process.

Looking at the overall picture, it seems that for some children demonstration is enough, although it seems likely that engaging with a resource may be enriching in many other ways. For many children, however, there needs to be a variety of experiences that support them in gradually making sense of a new situation. Work with a resource individually, in pairs or in groups allows more space for this. The teacher's role in these activities is also crucial; if intervention is limited to a further demonstration rather than fostering the possibilities in the second list an opportunity is lost. If, for example, Wayne in the video clip discussed earlier were able to facilitate the use of the available resources in a different way there would be more possibility for the children involved to make connections from the strength of their own insights rather than those of somebody else. Mary, however, by asking children to visualise, enables them to make connections in an individual way to the experiences they have had in a variety of contexts.

How resources might be constraining

(This section has been written with contributions from Peter Gates.)
The use of resources for teaching mathematics is not, however, restricted to primary schools. Mathematics teachers in secondary schools do use a variety of resources, although their use is much less common or frequent than in primary schools – and the way resources are used can be quite different as well. In many cases where resources are used they are often restricted to pupils who experience greater difficulty with learning mathematics. In other cases, resources seem to be used solely for demonstration purposes in the early stages of establishing some new mathematical idea or concept. This probably means the opportunities still exist for mathematics teachers in secondary schools to adapt and develop the way they use resources.

So why do teachers make use of teaching resources? It would seem that some of the main reasons are:

- Using some physical apparatus helps to make learning easier – and this possibly relates to Jerome Bruner's enactive mode of mental representation.
- Using something tangible and visible helps pupils draw connections more easily, and makes the learning experience more memorable by relating different sensory areas of experience.
- Encouraging the child to manipulate some physical resource can help to make otherwise more abstract ideas more concrete.

However, whilst each of these might be seen as an advantage, resources do have some potential drawbacks as well:

- The use of some physical resource might place the mathematics in an inappropriate and contrived concrete context. This can occur if the metaphor that the resource rests on stretches the association too far.
- The physical nature of the resource might divert the child's attention and disrupt the learning the teacher has in mind. In other words, what are pupils actually focusing on in using or watching the resource?
- The way the resource is presented can influence how the children are to engage with the resource. How are they to use it and interact with it? What do they need to be thinking about as they make use of the resource?

Hence, what we might usefully ask therefore is what the resource or apparatus is actually used *for*, and how it fits into the progressive development of mathematical concepts. This is quite a searching and challenging question, which all teachers both in primary and secondary classrooms need to ask of themselves. For example, are resources used to support or to challenge? A Piagetian approach – or a constructivist approach – would possibly want to encourage children to engage with resources in order to create dissonance or cognitive conflict, where children are confronted with the situation where their existing knowledge is shown to be insufficient, incorrect or conflicting with their experience.

One particular piece of research is illuminative in this respect – the 'Children's Mathematics Frameworks' (CMF) project, financed by the Economic and Science Research Council (ESRC) during the years 1983–5 and undertaken at Chelsea College (now King's College, London) by Kath Hart and her colleagues (Hart *et al.* 1989). The aim of the research was 'to monitor children's transition from concrete or practical work to the more formalized or symbolic mathematics commonly used in subsequent levels of the British schools system' (Hart *et al.* 1989: 2). This research was particularly important because of the widespread belief, at least in the UK, though undoubtedly much more widely held, that practical or concrete experiences are essential for children to learn mathematical concepts. Such a belief has permeated teacher education and teacher resources for decades and is possibly partly a result of Jean Piaget's influence and his identification of a 'concrete operations' stage in children's development.

One of the main findings of this research was to highlight 'the difficulties many children had in moving from the concrete or pictorial representations to the more formal (general) aspects of mathematics and the inability to link these stages of the teaching learning process' (Hart *et al.* 1989: 218). In particular, many children fail to see any connection between the concrete experiential stage and the development of a formal, symbolic relationship or formula. This was eloquently summed up by one pupil who told the research team 'sums is sums and bricks is bricks' (Hart *et al.* 1989: 1).

One example of this bricks versus sums dilemma that the research team explored, and which must be common in many classrooms across the country, is in the teaching of the formula for the volume of a cube or cuboid. The research team found many classrooms in which children were using bricks or blocks to build up cubes and cuboids, counting the bricks in each layer and the numbers of layers, and subsequently working out the total number of cubes. The teachers then showed how this (pre-formalisation) process was really just the same as the formalized $V=L\times B\times H$.

The difficulty, however, was that many children did not make this connection between the 'bricks' and the 'sums'. In one classroom, three months after the teaching took place, none of the children interviewed could link the formula to the practical work and when asked where $V=L\times B\times H$ came from, one pupil responded with 'I've no idea, somebody invented it for us' (Hart 1987: 18) – an indication that pupils often see the pre-formalisation work as not significant or not related to the formalisation. Hence, 'the fallacy of assuming that students will automatically draw the conclusions their teachers want simply by interacting with particular manipulatives' (Ball 1992: 17) has to be a serious consideration for all those engaged in teaching mathematics.

It is a fact of teachers' professional lives that pupils come to schools not only with a wealth of experience, but also with contrasting social and cultural background and competences and have different ways of responding to the school and classroom tasks (as is discussed in various chapters in this book, in particular the chapters by Barry Cooper, Carrie Paechter and Robyn Zevenbergen). This diversity has some implications for how they view the use of classroom resources. The example above illustrates that resources might be irrelevant or constraining to pupils' cognitive development.

I began this chapter by saying that there is no mathematics actually *in* a resource and that the mathematics is created by those who interact with it in order to make connections. The Children's Mathematical Framework research highlights the situation where children fail to make the connections that teachers assumed were inherent in the use of a particular resource to demonstrate some aspect of mathematics. Paul Cobb, Erna Yackel and Terry Wood suggest that:

> teachers might in practice challenge the assumptions that give rise to the learning paradox by attempting to see beyond their expert interpretations of instructional materials. They might then consider the various ways that students actively interpret the materials as they engage in genuine mathematical communication in the social context of the classroom. The materials would then no longer be used as a means of presenting readily apprehensible mathematical relationships but would instead be aspects of a setting in which the teachers and the students explicitly negotiate their differing interpretations as they engage in mathematical activity.
>
> (Cobb *et al.* 1992: 5–6)

As Kath Hart and her colleagues remind us, their research does not simplify the tasks of the teacher. On the other hand 'teaching mathematics effectively requires considerably more effort than is usually acknowledged by those both inside and outside the profession' (Hart *et al.* 1987: 224).

Reflecting on the issue . . .

It is highly possible that pupils you come across might similarly experience the problems illustrated above. Try to devise some small-scale research or information-gathering task (possibly involving some colleagues). Consider exploring the following questions, which are related to the points I raised earlier in this chapter.

- Are there actual examples of where a resource has helped a pupil develop some mathematics? Are there examples of where the resource 'gets in the way' or hinders development in some way? How might you overcome the limitations of the latter?
- What differences are there in how your pupils engage with resources? Consider age and capability differences that might be related to maturity or to social or cultural contexts.
- Do your pupils use the resource in the way that you (or the teacher) intend them to?

This will be further developed in the final Invitation to reflect.

Conclusion

Resources are an essential part of teaching and learning mathematics but their effective use is not always straightforward and they can be used in unhelpful as well as helpful ways. Resources can be used solely for demonstration purposes but when this approach is combined with individual use the potential for learning increases.

It would be easy, particularly for beginning teachers, to believe that the NNS in primary schools and its counterpart in secondary schools is able to provide a set of clear answers to the challenges of helping children advance in confidence and competence in their mathematics. However, even if this were true, as Mike Askew observes in his chapter, some teachers, despite the detailed nature of the Framework, have somehow overlooked a fundamental NNS message about choosing appropriate strategies for calculating. The reality is that the current Frameworks for mathematics in primary and secondary schools are frameworks in the very literal sense and that there is still much development work to be done.

The focus on a range of resources is to be welcomed. The high profile given to these resources provides an unprecedented chance for teachers to discuss wider issues concerning the nature and use of resources, rather than attempt to replicate a set of practices popularised by training video clips. Constructivists present the view that children have to make their own sense of the mathematics they are offered. Similarly, teachers need to make their own sense of what they are offered in terms of teaching approaches and the choice and use of resources. Continued reflection, analysis and an informed openness are needed to explore whether the recommended list of approaches and resources are necessarily the most appropriate for any given context. This chapter is intended to contribute to that exploration.

Invitation to reflect

Select a resource for number that you use regularly in your work with children. Consider the ways that you have used it in the past and reflect on these questions:

- When has it worked well? What is the evidence that it has worked well in terms of the children's understanding? Can you work out why it has been successful on these occasions? Many factors can have a bearing – for example, perhaps this resource is particularly well suited in some way to the topic dealt with.
- When has it not worked to your satisfaction? Can you pinpoint why? Is there something that you might have done differently? Might another resource have worked better?
- Do you use the resource for demonstration purposes only? If you do, is it possible to adapt it for individual use so that pupils can engage with it more effectively?
- How do you use language to bring out the mathematical ideas within the resource? How do you encourage children to interact with the resource and talk about mathematical ideas by using it?
- Is it better with some topics than with others?
- Is it sufficient on its own or might it benefit from the complementary use of other resources?

Having reflected on past use of resources, turn your attention to the future:

- Are there any other appropriate resources that you might consider for a topic you usually support with the resource you selected? Is it worth exploring the use of this?
- At what stage would you anticipate pupils moving away from the resource as a support and how might you facilitate such a move, if appropriate?

Further suggested reading

Pimm, D. (1992) *Mathematics: Symbols and Meanings*, Milton Keynes: Open University Press. There are relatively few books that consider the use of images and physical apparatus in depth but David Pimm's is a source of many useful reflections in this area. Several pieces of physical apparatus are considered along with diagrams and images. Computer programs that use images as learning devices are also included.

Hughes, M. (1986) *Children and Number*, Oxford: Basil Blackwell. This book also remains a readable and interesting account of the ways that the use of apparatus and images helps young children to get to grips with mathematics.

Thompson, I. (ed.) (1997) *Teaching and Learning Early Number*, Buckingham: Open University Press. This book contains many useful chapters on the issues I have discussed in this chapter. In 'Teaching for strategies', Chapter 13, Ian Sugarman looks at several resources that help children with a variety of topics and in 'Approaching number through language', Chapter 10, Alan Wigley takes a detailed look at the Gattegno Grid.

Thompson, I. (ed.) (1999) *Issues in Teaching Numeracy in Primary Schools*, Buckingham: Open University Press. In this second book edited by Ian Thompson, Meindert Beishuizen gives a detailed account of the development of the empty number line in 'The empty number line as a new model', Chapter 13.

More detail about the use of Cuisenaire rods can be found in a series of articles that I have written in the journal *Strategies* (see references for further details). In the same journal, Volume 3, Issues 2 and 3, are two interesting articles by Adrian Pinel that describe the development and use of arrays for teaching multiplication in practical and powerful ways. They also provide an excellent resource for supporting the development of the grid method of multiplication in the NNS examples.

References

Askew, M. (1998) *Teaching Primary Mathematics*, London: Hodder and Stoughton.

Askew, M. (1999) 'It ain't (just) what you do: Effective teachers of numeracy', in Thompson, I. (ed.), *Issues in Teaching Numeracy in Primary Schools*, Buckingham: Open University Press, pp. 91–102.

Askew, M. and Wiliam, D. (1995) *Recent Research in Mathematics Education 5–16*, London: HMSO.

Askew, M., Brown, M., Rhodes, V., Johnson, D. and Wiliam, D. (1997) *Effective Teachers of Numeracy: Final Report. Report of a Study Carried out for the Teacher Training Agency*, London: King's College.

Ball, D. (1992) 'Magical hopes: Manipulatives and the reform of math education', in *American Educator* 16(2), 14–18, 46–7.

Brown, M., Askew, M., Baker, D., Denvir, H. and Millett, A. (1998) 'Is the National Numeracy Strategy research-based?', in *British Journal of Educational Studies* 46(4), 362–85.

Bruner, J. (1964) *Towards a Theory of Instruction*, London: Belknap Press.

Cobb, P., Yackel, E. and Wood, T. (1992) 'A constructivist alternative to the representational view of mind in mathematics education', in *Journal for Research in Mathematics Education* 23(1), 2–33.

Delaney, K. (1992a) 'Number by colours', *Strategies* 2(2), 32–4.

Delaney, K. (1992b) 'Cuisenaire and infants', *Strategies* 2(3), 33–5.

Delaney, K. (1992c) 'Seeing is believing', *Strategies* 2(4), 27–9.

Delaney, K. (1992d) 'The missing piece', *Strategies* 3(1), 28–9.

DfEE (1999a) *The National Numeracy Strategy: Framework for Teaching Mathematics from Reception to Year 6*, London: Department for Education and Employment.

DfEE (1999b) *The National Numeracy Strategy: Professional Development Materials 1 and 2*, London: Department for Education and Employment.

Edwards, S. (1998) *Managing Effective Teaching of Mathematics 3–8*, London: Paul Chapman.

Harries, T. and Spooner, M. (2000) *Mental Mathematics for the Numeracy Hour*, London: David Fulton.

Hart, K. (1987) 'Children's mathematical frameworks. The volume of a cuboid is $V = L \times B \times H$', *Mathematics in School* 16(3–May 1987), 16–19.

Hart, K., Johnston, D., Brown, M., Dickson, L. and Clarkson, R. (1989) *Children's Mathematical Frameworks 8–13. A Study of Classroom Teaching*, Nottingham: Shell Centre for Mathematical Education.

Hughes, M. (1986) *Children and Number*, Basil Blackwell: Oxford.

Hughes, M. (1999) 'The National Numeracy Strategy. Are we getting it right?', *Psychology of Education Review* 23(2), pp. 3–7.

Lakoff, G. and Johnson, M. (1980) *Metaphors We Live By*, Chicago: University of Chicago Press.

Liebeck, P. (1984) *How Children Learn Mathematics*, Penguin: London.

Ollerenshaw, C. and Ritchie, R. (1993) *Primary Science: Making it Work*, David Fulton: London.

Open University (1982a) *Developing Mathematical Thinking (EM235) – Topic 1, Subtraction*, Milton Keynes: The Open University.

Open University (1982b) *Developing Mathematical Thinking (EM235) – Topic 2, Setting up and solving*, Milton Keynes: The Open University.

Open University (1982c) *Developing Mathematical Thinking (EM235) – EM235 Bookmark*, Milton Keynes: The Open University.

Pimm, D. (1992) *Mathematics: Symbols and Meanings*, Milton Keynes: Open University Press.

Pinel, A. (1992a) 'Go forth and multiply', *Strategies* 3(2), 31–3.

Pinel, A. (1992b) 'In the mind's eye', *Strategies* 3(3), 26–8.

Richardson, K. (1971) *Developing Number Concepts Using Unifix Cubes*, London: Addison-Wesley.

Skemp, R. (1989) *Mathematics in the Primary School*, London: Routledge.

Straker, A. (1999) 'The National Numeracy Project 1996–1999', in Thompson, I. (ed.), *Issues in Teaching Numeracy in Primary Schools*, Buckingham: Open University Press.

Thompson, I. (ed.) (1997) *Teaching and Learning Early Number*, Buckingham: Open University Press.

Thompson, I. (ed.) (1999) *Issues in Teaching Numeracy in Primary Schools*, Buckingham: Open University Press.

Thompson, P. (1994) 'Concrete materials and teaching for mathematical understanding', in *Arithmetic Teacher* **41**, 556–8.

Thompson, I. (ed.) (1997) *Teaching and Learning Early Number*, Buckingham: Open University Press.

Thompson, I. (ed.) (1999) *Issues in Teaching Numeracy in Primary Schools*, Buckingham: Open University Press.

Trundley, R. and Edginton, H. (1999), *Think Maths!*, Exeter: Devon County Council.

Vygotsky, L. (1978) *Mind in Society. The Development of Higher Psychological Processes*, Cambridge Ma., Harvard University Press.

Wenger, W. (1992) *Beyond Teaching and Learning*, Gaithersburg, MD: Project Renaissance.

Wenger, W. (1996) *The Einstein Factor*, Rocklin, CA: Prima.

Wittman, E. (ed.) (1995) *Mit Kindern Rechnen*, Frankfurt-am-Main: Der Grundschulverband e.V.

Wood (1988) *How Children Think and Learn*, Oxford: Blackwell.

10 Dealing with misconceptions in mathematics

Malcolm Swan

Introducing the issue

In this chapter, I focus on the development of conceptual understanding, and consider the design of lessons that enable pupils to reflect on the meaning of representations in mathematics. After looking briefly at some typical pupil mistakes and their possible causes, I consider the nature of understanding and the notion of misconceptions. This leads me on to consider the role of discussion in learning and a review of a number of research studies which have attempted to modify teaching methods to include specific types of pupil–pupil discussion into mathematics lessons. From this I draw a number of principles that suggest how one might design more engaging, effective mathematics lessons. The chapter concludes with some comments on the difficulties of implementing such principles on a wider scale.

Key questions

The chapter focuses on six key questions:

- Why do people make mistakes in mathematics?
- What does it mean to understand a concept in mathematics?
- What can we do about misconceptions? Can they be avoided?
- How do we help pupils to modify their understandings?
- How can we structure lessons to facilitate this modification?
- What obstacles are there to this form of teaching?

Mistakes in mathematics

People make mistakes for many different reasons. Some may be simply due to lapses in concentration, hasty reasoning, memory overload or a failure to notice salient features of a situation. Others, however, may be symptoms of deeper misunderstandings or may not be mistakes at all – they may be the result of alternative interpretations of a situation.

The following four examples illustrate errors made with fractions and percentages. I want to stress that each one is based on an actual occurrence.

Reflecting on the issue . . .
Read carefully through each of the four examples and consider what 'error' has been made. Consider what you might say to the person making the error.

Example 1

In a department store in Derby, you see a shirt that you like in a sale. It is marked '20% off'. You decide to buy two. The assistant does some mental calculations:

20 per cent off each shirt . . . that will be 40 per cent off the total price.

Example 2

In a newspaper article, a farmer claims that:

If I can produce 20% more milk per cow, I can decrease my herd by 20% to produce the same amount of milk.

Example 3

In a classroom, Leslie and Gil are given a square divided into nine pieces as shown in Figure 10.1 and are asked to represent each piece as a fraction of the whole

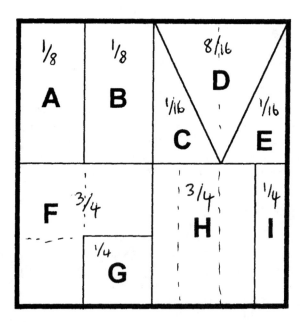

Figure 10.1   Fraction of a square.

square. They produce the solution shown and check their work by adding the fractions together to see if they make a whole. They add the tops and bottoms to obtain 20/80. Leslie justifies their answer:

Gil: Twenty-eightieths?
Leslie: Yes, but if you add eighty plus twenty, that will be one hundred. Eighty plus twenty would be one hundred.
Gil: Uh-huh.
Leslie: And a hundred equals a whole thing . . .

Example 4

In another classroom, several pupils are adding fractions and have responded to 3/20 + 9/20 with 12/40. When asked to justify this Sanjay answers:

Say you've got three out of twenty for one test and nine out of twenty for another test . . . that makes twelve right out of forty doesn't it?

In each of these examples, the person making the error has manipulated fractions or percentages without paying sufficient attention to the size of the unit that they refer to. Thus in Example 1 the shop assistant adds percentage reductions as if they are absolute quantities; in Example 2 the percentages refer first to an increase in the productivity of a smaller herd and then to a reduction in the size of a larger herd; in Example 3 the boys begin by interpreting A, B, C and E as fractions of the whole square, but then relate the remaining fractions to a quarter of the square; and in Example 4 the fractions refer to first one test then two tests (it *does* make sense to say that 3/20 of one test+9/20 of one test=12/40 of the two tests).

So how would *you* respond as a teacher in each case? In (1), assuming you are not dishonest, you might try to alert the shop assistant to the error and give a detailed explanation of how percentages work and the need to recognise the size of the unit. This would take a long time and the assistant would probably not have the time or inclination to listen. This is what I call 'the didactic approach'. Maybe it would more interesting to simply say 'I've changed my mind, I think I'll buy five shirts' and let the shop assistant explore the implications of his or her own beliefs. This may induce what is called 'cognitive conflict' as the assistant sees that the outcome conflicts with her intuitive solution. More of this later.

The teacher's position in the classroom is similar. It may be difficult to find the time to explain sources of error when they arise unexpectedly, especially when other pupils are demanding attention. One temptation is to stop a class and re-teach the concept again from the beginning. I recently observed one experienced teacher attempting to teach the addition of fractions to a class of 16–19 year old GCSE retake pupils. She patiently began reminding them *again* about the concept of equivalence and gave them an exercise to do. Many pupils, like Leslie and Gil, continued to add tops and bottoms. After 45 minutes, the teacher sighed and stopped the whole class:

Teacher: Let me take you back to where we don't care *why* we did it, I'll just tell you *how*. You can forget the *why* if you want and just remember the *how*. This is the way I was taught.

She wrote: $\dfrac{1}{3} + \dfrac{3}{4}$

Teacher: Now you just go $3\times3=9$ and $4\times1=4$.
Pupil: Why didn't you tell us that before?
Teacher: Because there is just a chance that you might understand why one day.

Throughout the lesson the pupils had appeared to listen well, but they remained unable to see what the teacher was getting at. The teacher, sensing defeat, resorted to teaching by rote – by telling. These pupils had probably been learning (and failing) to add fractions for the best part of ten years, so perhaps it is unlikely that this lesson made any permanent impact. Where does a teacher go from here?

One argument we often hear is that conceptual difficulties are a result of poor teaching. Maybe the pupil has not had enough concrete experience of manipulating fraction shapes or maybe the concept of a fraction has not been made sufficiently relevant to the real world. 'Good' teaching would perhaps avoid such difficulties – or so the argument goes. Yet the same mathematical mistakes occur all over the world, whatever curriculum is being followed and whatever pedagogical strategies seem to be adopted. Pupils seem to create their own alternative meanings for mathematics in spite of what they are taught. In the remaining sections of this chapter, I shall consider the nature and cause of mistakes and misconceptions and explain why I believe that far from being avoided or prevented, they must be welcomed, made explicit, discussed and modified for long-term learning to take place. This cannot happen, I believe, until teachers and pupils renegotiate the social nature of the classroom.

I recognise that this is far from easy and that there is a natural resistance from teachers and pupils to discursive approaches to learning. As John Mason and David Pimm (1986) point out, such methods can take more time, reduce apparent 'control', create insecurity and fundamentally challenge one's view of mathematics.

Reflecting on the issue . . .
How do you respond to each of the objections to classroom discussion given below?

'I haven't got time to lose whole lessons in chatter.'
'What about the noise? Frankly, I'm afraid of losing control.'
'Pupils won't want to be seen to be wrong.'
'They are likely to ask questions I can't answer.'
'If they understand it, there is nothing to discuss and if they don't, they're not in any position to discuss anything.'
'In maths, answers are right or wrong – its not a subject for discussion.'

The nature of 'misconceptions' and 'understanding'

The early 1980s witnessed a growing fascination with the nature of pupils' errors in mathematics and attempts were made to codify these and look for underlying 'misconceptions' which would explain their cause. Useful summaries of work at this time appeared in the reports of the Assessment of Performance Unit (APU 1980), the Concepts in Secondary Mathematics and Science Project (Hart 1980; 1981) and in research reviews (e.g. Dickson *et al.* 1984; Bell *et al.* 1983). This was rapidly followed by a number of research studies on how such errors might be remediated or avoided (e.g. the work of the Strategies and Errors in Secondary Mathematics (SESM) project, Booth 1984; Hart 1984; Kerslake 1986).

Terms like 'errors,' 'misconceptions,' 'remediation,' and even 'diagnosis and prescription' (Rees and Barr 1984) were commonplace at that time. Considerable efforts were made to pinpoint the exact sources of errors with surgical precision and to suggest suitable treatments that would eradicate them. I also remember the fears of teachers who were afraid that if they displayed mistakes on the board, then pupils might in some sense catch them, as if mistakes were somehow contagious. The medical metaphor suggests that we should try to find better ways to teach so that errors and misconceptions do not arise – 'prevention is better than cure'. The DfEE requirements for courses in initial teacher training seem to agree with this when they assert that

> trainees must be taught to recognise common pupil errors and misconceptions in mathematics, and to understand how these arise, *how they can be prevented*, and how to remedy them.
>
> (DfEE 1998: 57, emphasis mine)

The circular then goes on to list ten such 'errors and misconceptions', which presumably can be prevented by remedial work by the teacher. Amongst this list are several pupil 'errors' that are considerably widespread internationally; indeed many of these 'errors' are so common and so widespread that we see them reported from various countries across the world. For example:

iv. An expectation that the outcome of division always gives a smaller value *e.g.* $4 \div \frac{1}{2} = 2$;

v. Lining up columns of numbers for operations against a left hand margin, irrespective of the position of the decimal point;

vi. Thinking that numbers are larger if there are more decimal digits *e.g. 3.16 is larger than 3.2*;

> (DfEE 1998: 57)

The position taken by the DfEE here seems to assume that standard procedures are available which can be delivered to trainee teachers so that they can eradicate the problem. This is far too simplistic. Teaching is not like administering a medical 'treatment'. Take a few moments to reflect further on the nature of the problem yourself before reading on.

Reflecting on the issue . . .

Below are the ten examples of errors and misconceptions listed by the DfEE. (DfEE 1998: 57). Choose two or three. Design some classroom tasks that will enable you to see how prevalent these are amongst the pupils you teach. Suggest some alternative 'remedies'.

- counting on 3 from 7 to get 9 as result of starting with the 7;
- reading 206 as 26 as a result of misunderstanding about the number system and place value;
- misunderstanding the order of the subtraction operation *e.g.* $3-7=4$;
- an expectation that the outcome of division always gives a smaller value *e.g.* $4 \div 1/2 = 2$;
- lining up columns of numbers for operations against a left or right hand margin, irrespective of the position of the decimal point;
- thinking that numbers are larger if there are more decimal digits *e.g. 3.16 is larger than 3.2*;
- stating that two identical angles are unequal because the length of the arms are different in each, as a result of thinking that an angle is the distance between the ends of the lines;
- misreading the scale on a ruler, starting at 1, rather than 0, as a result of not understanding that the measure starts from 0;
- not using the scale when interpreting a graph, treating the graph as a picture rather than a scaled representation;
- thinking that, when throwing a dice, a 6 is harder to get than other numbers, through not understanding the nature of equally likely and independent events.

Before explaining why I believe the medical metaphor is misguided, I will first look briefly at what we mean by 'understanding a concept'.

One of the main tasks of a teacher is to help pupils interpret mathematical representations (including verbal and symbolic representations) and understand the meanings of the concepts and relationships that they are intended to designate. The teacher's task is not merely to explain a new word or symbol in familiar terms, but to help the pupil to create and shape a conceptual framework. This involves the creation and development of links and multiple perspectives. In this sense, a concept is not a single perception or even the notion of a particular mathematical object, but is rather

> a convenient capsule of thought that embraces thousands of distinct experiences and that is ready to take in thousands more.
>
> (Sapir 1970: 35)

Concepts are essentially organic; that is, they are an individual's attempt to make sense of the world and as such they constantly change and evolve. Think of multiplication, for example. A young child may build the concept of 3×4 by thinking of 'three groups of four objects' or 'four groups of three objects'. Multiplication takes on the sense of repeated addition. Naturally, the child quickly develops a sense that 'multiplication makes things bigger' and is the 'opposite to division'. The concept is initially built on discrete processes, but is then extended to continuous ones. We try to make sense of multiplying lengths to produce areas, then negative numbers (why *do* two negatives multiply to give a positive?) and rational numbers (why does multiplying sometimes make things smaller?). Irrational numbers present a particular practical problem. If it is impossible to write down numbers like π or e fully and completely, how can we go about multiplying them? Later, we extend the concept to multiplying vectors (why are there two forms of multiplication?), then matrices (why can't we multiply every pair of matrices?) and so on. The concept evolves and raises new questions as the concept of 'multiplication' is enlarged and reinterpreted with reference to new domains.

Reflecting on the issue . . .
Think of different mathematical words and concepts and describe how your own understanding of them has evolved. You might choose 'fraction', 'function', 'volume', 'probability' . . .

In this light, it becomes much less clear what is meant by 'understanding' a concept such as multiplication. Some educational theorists avoid using the term 'understanding' altogether because it tends to convey a static sense of closure and completeness and, as we have seen, one perhaps never really *fully* understands anything. Anna Sierpinska (1994: 32) suggests that people feel they have understood something when they achieve a sense of order and harmony, where there is a sense of a 'unifying thought', of simplification, of seeing some underlying structure and, in some sense, feeling that the 'essence' of an idea has been captured. Mathematicians, for example, feel that they have understood something when they have built a model of it. David Pimm (1995: 179) refers to the double meaning of the French word for understanding, *comprendre*, which also conveys a sense of 'inclusion' or 'incorporation'. Thus when we understand something, it becomes part of us, we own it. Similarly in Portuguese and Spanish (and it may be so for other languages too) the word for learn, *aprender*, is closely connected to *prender* – to grasp, unite, catch etc.

Anna Sierpinska (1994) lists the four mental operations involved in understanding as

- Identification: we can bring the concept to the foreground of attention; we can name and describe it;
- Discrimination: we can see similarities and differences between this concept and others;
- Generalisation: we can see general properties of the concept in particular cases of it;
- Synthesis: we can perceive a unifying principle.

This may also begin to clarify the nature of what are commonly called 'misconceptions'. Personally, I dislike the term, as it appears to delineate a fixed boundary between 'right' and 'wrong' ways of thinking. Some prefer the term 'alternative mathematical framework' to emphasise that the concept the pupil has is distinct from the culturally accepted one, yet is still reasoned and connected to other concepts. Frequently, a 'misconception' is not wrong thinking but is a concept in embryo or a local generalisation that the pupil has made. It may in fact be a natural stage of conceptual development. Thus 'multiplication makes bigger', for example, is a valid generalisation in one domain (that of natural numbers) that is often misapplied to a wider domain (that of rational numbers).

Although I do not believe it is possible to prevent misconceptions arising, a skilled classroom teacher will plan ahead when giving explanations so that he or she does not actively encourage pupils to believe that learning mathematics is about following an extensive set of unrelated, arbitrary rules. Indeed, it is worthwhile offering 'rules' to pupils and asking them to discuss their domain of validity.

Reflecting on the issue . . .
Write down a list of rules that teachers often use, either explicitly or implicitly. When are they valid and when are they invalid? Here are some to start you off:

'The bigger number is the one with the most digits';
'When you multiply by 10, you just add a nought';
'You always take the smaller number from the larger';
'You always divide the bigger number by the smaller number';

I vividly recall the 'multiplication makes bigger' misconception arising with Gareth, a year 9 pupil in the top set at his comprehensive school. I asked him to imagine that 1 kg of a product costs £1.50 and then invited him to calculate the cost of 2.2 kg and 0.7 kg respectively. Using a calculator, he confidently calculated $1.5 \times 2.2 = 3.3$ and answered '£3.30' for the first part. For the second part, he divided 1.5 by 0.7 and obtained 2.142857 . . . Clearly puzzled by this second answer, he stared silently at it for some time. I asked why he had multiplied for the first part and divided for the second and he told me that the second answer should be less than £3.30 and he thought division would make £1.50 smaller. He told me that the answer 'should be £1.05', but he couldn't see how to get this with his calculator. Seeing my surprise that he already knew the answer, he explained that he had worked the problem out mentally:

From the first question, 2 kilograms would be £3, so 0.2 kilograms must be 30p, so 0.1 would be 15p. Seven lots of 15p is £1.05.

He warned me that the batteries on his calculator might be wearing out and perhaps that was the cause of the error in the second answer. I congratulated him on his mental dexterity and asked him to try multiplying 1.5 by 0.7 using his calculator to see if he would get the same result. He immediate replied 'Why?', since he was convinced this would not work, but he tried it anyway to pacify me. When he saw the result, his jaw dropped: 'I never expected that!' This appeared to be a significant moment for Gareth, though he remained unable to explain what had happened. This example made me realise the power of presenting pupils with carefully engineered examples that provoke confrontation with conceptual obstacles. Here again cognitive conflict had been induced when the calculator display did not agree with an intuitive response. This was a dramatic event that captured his attention and created conditions in which he wanted to learn. I wondered if ways could be found of systematically engineering events like this into normal classroom practices.

Of course, not all common errors indicate misconceptions. David Wood, a psychologist who has worked extensively with young children's learning strategies, quotes the example where a pupil answered a question as if she believed that 'multiplication makes bigger', but when asked to reflect on her answer, she changed it and gave a correct, carefully argued response. He claims that her only 'error' was not to think carefully enough about the problem and this in turn is a symptom of a pupil's lack of self-regulation (Wood 1988: 196). Overcoming impulsive first thoughts and reviewing one's initial attempt at solution does not come easily or readily to pupils. Perhaps, as Lev Vygotsky would suggest, such self-monitoring activity only arises out of social interactions with others. When I was at school, my teacher continually prompted me to review and check my work, look for more elegant solutions and so on. I seem to have internalised his voice and now prompt myself with his words.

The role of discussion in learning

The only way to avoid the formation of entrenched misconceptions is through discussion and interaction. A trouble shared, in mathematical discourse, may become a problem solved.

(Wood 1988: 210)

Mathematics lessons have many different purposes. Lessons may be designed to develop fluency with skills, such as the ability to do arithmetic or solve an equation using a given algorithm, develop an understanding of concepts and their representations, develop strategies for problem-solving or investigation and/or develop an awareness and appreciation of the uses (and abuses) of mathematics in society.

It may seem equally evident that teachers need a broad repertoire of teaching strategies for achieving these purposes. If the purpose of a lesson is to develop fluency with a particular skill, there may be a place for practice exercises that allow the pupil to develop a fluent, confident, almost automatic pattern of activity that may be carried out with little mental effort. When the purpose is to develop understanding, strategies or awareness, then the classroom must become a place where meanings are created, problem-solving approaches are shared and values are debated. This necessitates a different kind of classroom environment, in which discussion and negotiation predominate.

This is not what we see when we visit most classrooms. In the everyday routine of the job, the purposes of particular lessons often remain tacit and a narrow range of teaching styles are deployed. Even when teachers try to broaden their repertoire, we frequently observe them using activities that are incompatible with their particular purpose, such as when pupils are given apparent freedom to 'investigate' a situation, while the teacher wants them to 'discover' a culturally valued result or learn a particular skill. In this case, pupils are asked to engage simultaneously in divergent and convergent activity that can eventually lead to pupils commenting: 'Tell us what you want us to discover.' It is clearly important, but not always straightforward, to choose a teaching strategy appropriate for the purpose of the lesson.

Developing pupils' understanding is a distinct activity from learning skills for fluency or from developing strategies for 'investigation' or 'problem-solving' and, as such, it requires a distinct classroom methodology. As you might expect, psychologists and educators have a variety of views on how this may best be achieved. While some view learning as coming about through cognitive conflict, others view learning as an apprenticeship.

In a reaction against traditional transmission approaches to teaching, involving 'explanation and imitation', Jean Piaget advocated a form of discovery learning in which

> . . . to understand is to discover, or to reconstruct by rediscovery, and such conditions must be complied with if in the future individuals are to be formed who are capable of production and creativity and not simply repetition.
>
> (Piaget 1975: 20)

Piaget held the view that individuals need time to interact with their environment (including the social environment) in order to construct concepts through assimilation and accommodation. Briefly speaking, 'assimilation' refers to the absorption of new ideas while 'accommodation' refers to the modifications that the child's cognitive structure makes as a result of 'fitting' new ideas into an existing framework.

His view is one where the child is an active constructor of his or her own understanding. For him, the most effective form of social interaction is co-operation between equals in which each tries to understand and modify the other's point of view. He felt that if pupils were unequal partners, then they might resign their position too readily and accept the opposing view without verification. Jean Piaget thus believed that learning through cognitive conflict comes about through the logical evaluation of differences of opinion. This may be interpersonal or intrapersonal, but, as Collette Laborde, a French Mathematics educator notes:

> The contradiction coming from two opposite points of view is more readily perceived and cannot be refuted so easily as the contradiction coming from facts for an individual. The latter may either not perceive the contradiction or not take it into account when wavering between two opposite points of view and finally choosing one of them. In order to master a task, pupils working jointly are committed to overcoming conflict. When attempting to solve the contradiction, they may manage to coordinate the two points of view into a third one overcoming both initial points of view and corresponding to a higher level of knowledge.
>
> (Laborde 1994: 149)

Jean Piaget acknowledged that it may be possible for a teacher to develop a relationship with pupils which allows for the free examination and discussion of ideas, but pointed out that this would involve the teacher in taking the role of an equal – unlikely in an authoritative, constraining classroom atmosphere (Piaget 1977). Some ways in which teachers might do this are suggested by David Wood (1988), who showed that pupils can become more active in verbal participation when teachers replace controlling commands and closed questions with open questions and when they allow increased time for responses. The gap in status is reduced as teachers reveal their uncertainties.

The Soviet psychologist Lev Vygotsky criticised Piaget's theory for reducing development to a continual conflict between antagonistic forms of thinking (Vygotsky 1987: 176). Lev Vygotsky saw learning as more akin to an apprenticeship. He emphasised the central role that language and symbols play in concept development. To him, the relationship between thought and words is a vital, living process:

> Thought is not merely expressed in words; it comes into existence through them.
>
> (Vygotsky 1996: 218)

To Lev Vygotsky then, thinking and language develop one another. People not only express what they think through language, they also use language to develop and refine their thinking. Words or symbols are used as a means of focusing attention on specific features of a concept and enable analysis and synthesis to take place.

In Vygotsky's theory, the novice works with an expert in the zone of proximal development (ZPD), which he saw as that zone of creative tension between what the learner can accomplish unaided and what he or she can achieve with support from the teacher. Thus Lev Vygotsky saw the most effective form of social organisation for learning as one between *unequals*; the experienced teacher and his or her apprentice.

One way of coming to terms with these apparently conflicting views is to consider the alternative domains of interest of Jean Piaget and Lev Vygotsky. As Barbara Rogoff points out, (Rogoff 1999: 73), Piaget was concerned with shifts in cognitive perspective while working on conceptual problems in science and mathematics. Lev Vygotsky was more concerned with the development of culturally valued tools for thinking. The nature of guided participation may differ according to whether a situation involves a pupil's shift in perspective or development of understanding or skill. In Barbara Rogoff's terms, learning a skill means the integration and organisation of component acts into plans for action under relevant circumstances (for example, learning to tie shoes, or learning to read). These are acts that require practice for fluency. Shifts in perspective mean giving up one understanding of a phenomenon to take up another contrasting one. Barbara Rogoff suggests that the development of skills may occur with the aid of 'simple explanation or demonstration' but changes in perspective require a deeper, shared communication. Whereas developing appreciation and skill may be attained through eavesdropping or observing actions and statements made by the more capable, changes in perspective may be best facilitated by the shared exploration of possibilities among peers.

In short, the implications are that apprenticeship models of learning might seem more appropriate for developing skills to fluency, but discussion among equals is more appropriate for facilitating the reformulation of concepts. In the next section I examine some examples of my own research into children's learning that attempted to modify existing classroom practices to encourage such shifts in perspective.

Shifting perspectives through 'cognitive conflict'

So how might we design teaching to encourage pupils to share, discuss and develop their own interpretations of mathematical concepts? Over the past 20 years, along with many colleagues, I have been working on developing a distinctive teaching methodology which we called 'diagnostic teaching'. This has evolved through many refinements and incarnations, but the essential distinctive feature is that pupils' own ideas and methods are acknowledged and discussed *before* any teaching input is given. The main design principles are listed below.

1   **Before teaching, assess pupils' existing conceptual frameworks**
    Usually teachers assess pupils with 'tests' at the end of a teaching sequence and do little in response to what they find. Here, we attempt to assess pupils' intuitive interpretations and methods before teaching. This can be quite short, involving just the posing of a few critical questions, or may take on the form of a more elaborate test. We also try to talk to the pupils about the thinking that went into their answers. This is done with pairs of pupils so that explanations are evoked in a natural context.

2   **Make existing concepts and methods explicit in the classroom**
    At the beginning of a lesson, offer pupils a task focused on some well-known conceptual obstacle. This is intended to make pupils more aware of their own intuitive interpretations and methods and expose common errors and misconceptions. Pupils are asked to attempt the task individually, with no help from the teacher. No attempt is made, at this stage, to teach anything new or even make pupils aware that errors have been made.

3   **Share methods and results and provoke conflict discussion**
    Feedback is provided to the pupils in at least one of three ways:

    - by asking pupils to compare their responses with those made by other pupils;
    - by asking pupils to repeat the task using one or more alternative methods;
    - by using tasks which contain some form of in-built check.

    If the task has been well designed, this feedback often produces cognitive conflict as pupils begin to realise and confront inconsistencies in their own and each other's interpretations and methods. Time is spent in groups and/or as a class reflecting on and discussing the nature of this conflict. Pupils are asked to describe inconsistencies and possible causes of errors and difficulties.

4   Resolve conflict through discussion and formulate new concepts and methods
A whole class discussion is held in order to resolve the conflict. Pupils are encouraged to articulate conflicting points of view in a non-judgemental atmosphere and reformulate their ideas. *After* this, the teacher may need to suggest, with reasons, a mathematician's viewpoint acknowledging cases where this is an arbitrary convention.

5   Consolidate learning by using the new concepts and methods through problem-solving
New learning is utilised and consolidated by:

- offering further problems to consider;
- inviting pupils to create and solve their own problems within given constraints;
- asking pupils to analyse completed work and diagnose causes of errors for themselves.

A number of classroom studies have been conducted in which features of this model were developed and tested and compared with more traditional teaching methods. The results from these studies were surprisingly consistent. The main finding was that, although both traditional and diagnostic teaching methods achieved short-term learning gains, only the diagnostic approach achieved significant longer-term learning. The greater effectiveness of the *discussion methods* was perhaps due to a number of factors:

- the identification of and focus on specific conceptual obstacles;
- the emphasis on oral rather than textual explanation;
- the increased level of challenge offered;
- the intensity of the discussion and involvement generated;
- the valuing of intuitive methods and explicit recognition of conceptual obstacles.

Although most of the traditional lessons progressed with few apparent difficulties, there was a remarkable change in the motivation and attitude of pupils from highly enthusiastic at the outset to bored and lethargic at the end. In one study (Bell 1994), where pupils were using gently graded, guided discovery materials (SMP 11–16), there was a considerable amount of teacher–pupil discussion, but very little pupil–pupil discussion, owing to the fact that they were working at different rates through the material. Completing booklets took precedence over comprehending ideas. There was a much greater sense of involvement in the diagnostic teaching lessons. The teacher's role was more prominent, requiring an expertise in managing discussion and in encouraging the reticent pupils to participate. There was a greater intensity of pupil–pupil discussion, resulting in a sometimes noisy atmosphere, which the teacher found quite stressful.

Other studies additionally showed that conflict discussion methods may be more effective than other methods of teaching which focus on conceptual obstacles, and which produce enthusiasm and involvement (for example, Onslow 1986).

I undertook a small-scale study with two year 8 classes in the curriculum area of decimal place value (Swan 1983), when I compared the diagnostic style of teaching with a more traditional approach, which focused entirely on teacher explanations followed by intensive practice. Although both teaching styles appeared effective in enabling children to answer questions about decimal place value immediately following the teaching programme, the diagnostic approach appeared significantly more effective at achieving longer-term learning, as shown by a delayed post-test given to the pupils three months later.

These research studies suggest that the value of what I call diagnostic teaching lies in the extent to which it values the intuitive methods and ideas that pupils bring to a lesson, offers experiences which create inter- and intra-personal conflict, and creates the opportunity for pupils to reflect on and examine inconsistencies in their own interpretations. This constitutes a first phase of 'preparing the ground' where existing conceptual structures are taken apart and examined for viability. The second phase, the resolution phase, involves pupils in reconstructing concepts through reflective discussion.

From these studies it seems reasonable to claim that the following principles emerge for the construction of effective classroom activities:

- Activities should be focused on known conceptual obstacles. This facilitates a convergent meaning-making discussion. One should not pose too many questions in one session but encourage a variety of interpretations to emerge, become explicit and thus be compared and evaluated.
- Activities should pose, or allow pupils to pose, questions that are challenging. Attempts to smooth the path by gradually ramping questions in difficulty (as we can see in many textbook schemes) fail to create conditions for conflict and learning.
- Questions or stimuli should be posed or juxtaposed in ways that create a tension that needs resolving. Contradictions arising from conflicting methods or opinions create an awareness that something needs to be learned. Pupils are thus sensitised to class discussions that follow.
- The activities should provide multiple opportunities for meaningful feedback to the pupil on his or her interpretations. This moves us beyond providing solutions or superficial information, such as the number of correct or incorrect answers. In the more successful diagnostic lessons, feedback was provided by the pupils themselves using and comparing results obtained from alternative methods, or through group discussion.

The invitation to reflect at the end of this chapter illustrates the diagnostic approach, and you might like to try it out and evaluate it in your own classroom.

Concluding remarks

The types of lesson I have described in this chapter are expected to provoke reflection on and the reformulation of mathematical concepts. As I have emphasised, this is only one of many purposes in teaching mathematics and they supplement, rather than stand opposed to, approaches that are designed to improve fluency in skills, develop strategies for investigation and problem-solving or aware-nesses of uses and abuses of mathematics in society. A discussion-based teaching approach will remain unpopular with many teachers because it is perceived as taking too much time and requiring a less authoritarian classroom. Explanation and practice approaches may seem to cover ground more quickly, but progress is often illusory (and hence long-term learning elusive) as imitative methods usually develop dependency and a fragile fluency that is lost when practice ceases. Methods which involve the sharing and renegotiation of ideas in an atmosphere of mutual trust may appear slow initially, but learning becomes meaningful, connected and stable over time. The atmosphere in these lessons has to involve respect and mutual trust if pupils are to feel able to share poorly articulated ideas without fear of ridicule. Discursive approaches, however, can sometimes conflict with pupils' expectations of what constitutes appropriate mathematics teaching and they may at times complain that they are not getting enough 'done'. As Desforges points out, many children see their task as 'producing work' rather than 'developing meaning' (Desforges *et al.* 1987). The way forward must therefore involve a renegotiation of what it means to learn mathematics in our classrooms.

Invitation to reflect

As an opportunity to reflect upon the issues in this chapter, I would like to invite you to try the following lesson concerning pupils' interpretation of decimals and fractions with a class of your own choosing, and then reflect on the questions which follow.

1 Making existing concepts explicit.

Ask pupils to do the following two questions on their own, without discussion:

1   Write down these decimals in order of size, from smallest to largest. Describe and explain your method for doing this.

    0.75   0.4   0.375   0.25   0.125   0.04   0.8

2   Write down these fractions in order of size from smallest to largest. Again, describe and explain your method.

$$\frac{3}{4} \qquad \frac{3}{8} \qquad \frac{2}{5} \qquad \frac{8}{10} \qquad \frac{1}{4} \qquad \frac{1}{25} \qquad \frac{1}{8}$$

My experience suggests that most pupils (from most classes) will do this incorrectly. The intention here is to make existing interpretations and misconceptions explicit – not to evoke correct answers. Allow pupils adequate time to compare and describe their methods without indicating correctness or judging responses.

2 *Sharing methods and producing 'conflict discussion'*

Next, sit pupils in pairs or threes (with pupils who obtained different answers to questions 1 and 2 sitting next to each other to encourage more discussion) and give each group the following set of cards to cut out and sort (see Figure 10.2). To begin with, just give out the sets labelled A to D. Pupils must first try to place the cards in groups, so that each group represents the same number. This involves

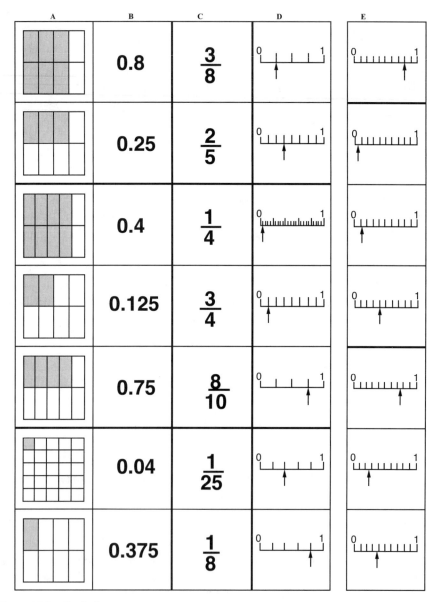

Figure 10.2   Cards for sorting.

moving between multiple representations and should encourage discussion of the meanings of each number. (Pupils may find it easy to match set A to B and C to D, but combining these may prove more difficult. If pupils are really stuck, then set E, where all the scales are marked in tenths, might help.) Now pupils should try to place each group in order of size.

For pupils to learn from this activity, emphasise that they should give an explanation every time they match a card. As they do this, listen to the discussions and arguments that ensue. See if conflicts are resolved. When groups finish, ask them to reflect again on their answers to the original questions and change them if necessary. They should also try to write down and explain any faults they had in their initial reasoning.

3 Resolving conflicts through discussion and formulating new concepts

Finally, hold a full class discussion on what has been learned, drawing out the common misconceptions and discussing them explicitly. Ask pupils to describe how disagreements were resolved and if there are any still outstanding that the whole class might discuss. Ask pupils to make notes for you on what they feel they learned and to comment on how they felt about learning in this way.

Reflection

Now consider the following issues:

- How far does this lesson expose conceptual obstacles in comparing decimals and fractions? What misconceptions become evident through the opening questions?
- Was cognitive conflict evident? How did it manifest itself?
- How did pupils' understandings develop during the lesson?
- How did pupils respond to the lesson emotionally?
- Now plan a second lesson that will involve pupils reflecting on the mistakes illustrated in the earlier parts of this chapter.

Further suggested readings

Although now a little dated, Dickson *et al.* (1984) and Hart (1980) offer many examples of errors and misconceptions that may form the basis for interesting discussions in mathematics lessons. You may find these in a library. A little more recently, the grey folders of In-service resources produced by the National Curriculum Council (1992) (now part of QCA) contains several lists of common misconceptions. You may still find this lurking on the shelf somewhere in a school mathematics department. There are also examples in Nickson (2000).

For discussions of diagnostic teaching applied to particular topics, the series of articles that appeared in *Mathematics Teaching*, the journal of the Association of Teachers of Mathematics, between June 1986 and September 1987 (numbers: 115, 116, 118, 119 and 120) will provide a useful start.

References

Assessment of Performance Unit (APU) (1980) *Mathematical Development, Primary Survey Report*, London: HMSO.

Bell, A. W. (1994) 'Teaching for the test', in Selinger, M. (ed.), *Teaching Mathematics*, London: Routledge, pp. 41–6.

Bell, A. W., Costello, J. and Küchemann, D. (1983) *Research on Learning and Teaching*, Windsor: NFER-Nelson.

Booth, L. (1984) *Algebra; Report of the Strategies and Errors in Secondary Mathematics Project*, Slough: NFER-Nelson.

Desforges, C. and Cockburn, A. (1987) *Understanding the Mathematics Teacher*, London: Falmer Press.

DfEE (1998) *Teaching: High Status, High Standards. Requirements for Courses of Initial Teacher Training. Circular 4/98*, London: Department for Education and Employment.

Dickson, L., Brown, M. and Gibson, O. (1984) *Children Learning Mathematics*, Eastbourne: Holt, Rinehart and Winston (Schools Council).

Hart, K. (1980) *Secondary School Children's Understanding of Mathematics (Research Monograph). A Report of the Mathematics Component of the CSMS Programme*, Chelsea College: University of London.

Hart. K. (1981) *Children's Understanding of Mathematics 11–16*, London: John Murray.

Hart, K. (1984) *Ratio: Report of the Strategies and Errors in Secondary Mathematics Project*, Slough: NFER-Nelson

Kerslake, D. (1986) *Fractions; Report of the Strategies and Errors in Secondary Mathematics Project*, Slough: NFER-Nelson.

Laborde, C. (1994) 'Working in small groups: A learning situation?' , in Beiler, R. *et al.* (eds), *Didactics of Mathematics as a Scientific Discipline*, Dordrecht: Kluwer, pp. 147–57

Mason, J. and Pimm, D. (1986) *Discussion in the Mathematics Classroom (PM644)*, Milton Keynes: Open University Centre for Maths Education.

National Curriculum Council (1992) *Mathematics Programmes of Study, INSET for Key Stages 1 and 2, 3 and 4*, York: National Curriculum Council.

Nickson, M. (2000) *Teaching and Learning Mathematics. A Teacher's Guide to Recent Research and its Applications*, London: Cassell.

Onslow, B. (1986) 'Overcoming conceptual obstacles concerning rates: Design and implementation of a diagnostic teaching unit', unpublished Ph.D. Thesis, University of Nottingham.

Piaget, J. (1975) *To Understand is to Invent. The Future of Education*, New York: Viking Press.

Piaget, J. (1977) 'Logique genetique et sociologie' in *Études sociologiques*, Geneva: Librairie Droz.

Pimm, D. (1995) *Symbols and Meanings in School Mathematics*, London: Routledge.

Rees, R. and Barr, G. (1984) *Diagnosis and Prescription: Some Common Maths Problems*, London: Harper and Row.

Rogoff, B. (1999) 'Cognitive development through social interaction: Vygotsky and Piaget', in Murphy, P. (ed.), *Learners, Learning and Assessment*, Buckingham: Open University Press, pp. 69–82

Sapir, E. (1970) 'Language and concepts', in Stones, E. (ed.), *Readings in Educational Psychology: Learning and Teaching*, London: Methuen, London, pp. 33–43.

Sierpinska A. (1994) *Understanding in Mathematics*, London: Falmer Press.

Swan, M. (1983) 'Teaching decimal place value – a comparative study of "conflict" and "positive only" approaches', in *Proceedings of the 7th Conference of International Group for the Psychology of Mathematics Education*, Jerusalem, Israel, pp. 211–16.

Vygotsky, L. S. (1996) *Thought and Language* (A. Kozulin, ed. and trans.). Cambridge, MA: MIT Press. (Original work published 1934.)

Vygotsky, L. S. (1987) 'Thinking and speech', in Rieber, R. W. and Carton, A. S. (eds), *The Collected Works of L. S. Vygotsky*, (N. Minick, trans.), New York: Plenum Press.

Wood, D. (1988) *How Children Think and Learn*, Blackwell: Oxford.

11 Adjusting to the newcomer

Roles for the computer in mathematics classrooms

Janet Ainley

Introducing the issue

> In many schools today, the phrase '*computer aided instruction*' means making the computer teach the child. One might say the *computer is being used to program* the child. In my vision, *the child programs the computer* and, in doing so, both acquire a sense of mastery over a piece of the most modern technology and establishes an intimate contact with some of the deepest ideas . . . from mathematics

If this quotation is not immediately familiar to you, you might like to try, before reading on, to make a guess at *when* it was written – and, of course, by whom. Take a moment also to think carefully about the images it offers for the role given to the computer, and the pupil's relationship with it. How do they match your own experiences and expectations as a teacher? How do they match your experiences as a computer user? In this chapter, I explore some of the ways in which the role of the computer (and other technological tools in mathematics) may be constructed by teachers, by pupils and by the wider community. I also discuss implications for the roles of teachers in the use of technology in the learning and teaching of mathematics, and for social interactions in the classroom.

Key questions

I have four key questions in my mind as I write this chapter:

- How might the role of the computer in mathematics classrooms be seen by teachers, and by pupils?
- How do perceptions of this role affect social interactions between teachers and pupils, and amongst pupils themselves?
- How might the teacher's role be altered by the presence of computers?
- How might differing constructions of these roles affect children's learning?

Potential roles for the computer

You may be surprised that the quotation in the introduction was written as long ago as 1980 (by Seymour Papert in the introduction to *Mindstorms*). The clues which perhaps give away its early date are the word 'instruction' and the reference to programming, both of which are somewhat out of fashion in educational discussion, at least in the UK. What does not feel at all out of date is the tension expressed between computers being seen primarily as rigid and mechanistic tools for teaching, and as tools for learning that are within the control of (even primary school) pupils. It is also interesting to note that the teacher is not mentioned, and yet it is the teacher who may be most closely affected by this tension.

The developments in technology since 1980 have been enormous. In education, these developments continue to put pressure on teachers to learn new skills. The most obvious, and the ones which generally attract public attention, are skills in operating the technology itself. Much less obvious are the requirements to address new areas of curriculum content, and new styles of teaching and interaction in the classroom. Ambiguity about the computer's role and the teacher's role in a computer-classroom continue to be causes of anxiety for many teachers.

Reflecting on the issue . . .
Before you read any further take some time to think about your own role in the classroom and how you use or might use computers in your teaching. How do you use the computer? What role does it play? Does the use of a computer change the nature of the mathematics you teach – or does it merely act as a substitute teacher?

In this chapter, I deliberately take a narrow focus, and consequently there is a danger of over-simplifying in at least two ways what is, in reality, a very complex situation. First, lack of clarity about relative roles of teacher and computer (and, of course, learner) is only one of a long list of factors that affect the extent and quality of the use of computers in mathematics classrooms. Issues to do with access to appropriate hardware and software, curriculum constraints and assessment requirements, attitudes to technology and management issues at both classroom and school level are all extremely significant. It is clear that even when high levels of access are available, and curriculum pressures relaxed, teachers' confidence in integrating technology within their existing classroom practice remains a key issue (Ainley and Pratt 1995).

A second over-simplification is that of treating 'technology' or 'the computer' as a single entity. Clearly, this is not the case. Particular pieces of hardware and software will make subtle and not-so-subtle changes to the role that the computer may be given in the classroom. Even the size and physical location of the computer may be significant: think about a desktop machine with a large, visible monitor which can only be plugged in at one corner of the room, in contrast to a small portable machine which fits comfortably on a table where the screen can be read by only two pupils. There is perhaps an even greater contrast between personally owned graphic calculators, with their very specific mathematical function, and the impersonality of a large computer room, used by the whole school for the whole curriculum.

In order to acknowledge this diversity, without getting distracted by discussion of particulars, the focus here will be on issues relating to the role of the computer which are common to many different technological settings, drawing on examples from across this range. Generally, the word 'computer' will be used as a placeholder, unless attention is being drawn to particular distinctions. I want now to discuss three main roles for the computer in the classroom: the computer-as-teaching-aid, the computer-as-tool and the computer-as-tutee.

Computer-as-teaching-aid

Perhaps the most obvious way in which to construct the role of the computer in a mathematics classroom is as a teaching aid. This refers not to particular kinds of software or hardware, but rather to the roles that the computer is seen to fulfil. This may parallel, and extend, those of existing teaching resources. The computer might be used as an 'electronic blackboard', for demonstration and as a stimulus for discussion: some software is designed specifically for this purpose, but in fact almost any software could be used in this way. Like an ordinary blackboard, the computer could be used in this way under the teacher's control, or used by pupils for sharing ideas.

The computer might also be used as a source of information, through access to CDs and to the Internet. Interactive software can also give pupils access to a range of (simulated) experiences, which might replace practical apparatus or pencil and paper in mathematical investigations, or might provide consolidation and practice of skills in the form of games and exercises.

At first glance, in this role the impact of the computer on pedagogic practice may seem relatively unproblematic, because it is performing functions that are already familiar to teachers and to learners. However, a more considered examination reveals some difficulties. Some characteristics of technological teaching aids lead to them being regarded differently from their more familiar counterparts. Their motivational power, and the fact that they are relatively scarce and expensive (except, of course, calculators), mean that issues of equality of access become critical for pupils, and perhaps even more so for parents who may be concerned that their children get a 'fair share' of computer time, particularly if they have been involved in the fund-raising necessary to buy the machines. The issue of 'fair' access within school becomes more problematic when unequal access to computers at home is taken into account (Robyn Zevenbergen discusses similar issues related to the acquisition of 'capital' in her chapter). Pupils with ready access to computers at home can more easily develop the know-how, the confidence, awareness and expertise required to use computers most effectively in school. Furthermore, there are likely to be issues related to gender which influence pupils' involvement with computers in the classroom and their familiarity with the equipment and procedures. In addition, most technological teaching aids (except, of course, calculators) are valued *per se* by our society, regardless of ways in which they are used. It is clear from the high profile given by governments in the UK and elsewhere to the provision of hardware that almost magical properties have been attributed to computers as teaching aids, as though mere access to them will ensure improvements in educational standards.

This puts enormous pressure on teachers to ensure that computers *are* used. In most classrooms, the level of resourcing means that it is only possible to give access to the computer for restricted periods of time. This may have the effect of isolating work done on the computer from the main work of the class. If only one group of pupils is able to work on the computer within the classroom, the teacher may be unable to give much attention to their work. For this reason, software that pupils can use independently is often popular with teachers and with pupils. Indeed one strand of development in educational software is towards packages that are designed to be largely teacher-independent. Integrated Learning Systems (ILS) are an extreme example of this trend. Such systems are not only capable of setting exercises, but also are capable of 'marking' them, evaluating and recording progress, and directing the pupil to the next appropriate level of work. (For an accessible description of an ILS approach, see Steen 1998.) The title Integrated Learning System seems disturbingly ambiguous: the system may indeed be integrated, but any learning that takes place may in fact be isolated and disjointed.

The use of such software can effectively put the teacher into the role of manager, and perhaps occasional troubleshooter, while the computer's role may be constructed (by pupils at least) as that of teacher. What is more, it is possible to put forward an argument for the advantages of the computer-as-teacher over a human teacher. The computer can be infinitely patient; it can simultaneously provide work at an appropriate level for every pupil, and keep a complete and detailed record of his or her work. (It is left as an exercise for the reader to find the bugs in this argument.)

Some teachers may appreciate what such technology can contribute to the motivation of pupils who thrive on the success they experience. Additionally, such a system can provide detailed information on pupils' progress. Yet, the computer may also feel like an intruder in the classroom. The software designer will have made decisions about both presentation and content that, however well intentioned, are beyond the teacher's control (see, for example, Goldstein 1998). Although the same is true of other resources, such as textbooks, there is something very powerful about the interactive nature of the computer, and its inflexibility about the answers it accepts, which leaves little scope for interpretation and professional judgment.

Computer-as-tool

In contrast to the previous section, other developments in mathematics education are pointing towards a contrasting role: the computer as a mathematical tool. The increasing use of generic software (such as word processors, spreadsheets and databases), often designed primarily for commercial rather than educational uses, offers a different image of the relationships between teacher, learner and computer. Here the teacher's traditional role is not obviously threatened by the technology, since the role of the computer remains passive and neutral.

For young pupils, the experience of using the computer in this way may initially be at odds with their expectations of technology as 'clever': thus there are opportunities not only to learn about mathematical ideas, but also to learn important lessons about control and responsibility in the use of technology. For example, in a fairly standard classroom activity, a group of year 2 pupils measured their heights, and recorded them on a spreadsheet. Their teacher used this activity to introduce them to the process of making graphs with the spreadsheet. When they looked at the graph (Figure 11.1), they noticed that it did not look as they had expected, since the pupils' heights were not shown 'correctly'.

In describing the graph, Kati said that the graph is not quite right, because Oliver ('oliva') is actually the tallest, and Kim and Tom are about the same size. She went on to say that this had gone a bit wrong because people had measured themselves wrongly. These comments are interesting on at least two levels. In terms of the mathematics curriculum, working with the computer was providing Kati with feedback about a measuring activity that might otherwise have gone unquestioned. If, as is often the case, the pupils' measurements had been recorded on paper and checked by the teacher, the relatively small inaccuracies in their results would probably have gone unnoticed. However, the immediacy of the graphical presentation prompted the pupils to compare the appearance of the columns of the graph with the physical evidence amongst themselves. This provided an opportunity for the teacher to talk in a meaningful way about accuracy and measuring techniques.

Kati's response is also interesting in what it reveals about her understanding of the limitations of the computer as a tool. Other pupils in the group felt that the computer had 'made a mistake'. Kati's teacher used this incident to reinforce an ongoing message about their relationship with the computer, and empowering pupils to decide when and how technological tools could be used most effectively.

There is a dialectical relationship between the tools available for learning and doing mathematics, and the curriculum within which these tools are used, which continues to be problematic. John Costello (1992), discussing the reasons for the failure of the use of calculators to have a significant impact on the mathematics curriculum in the UK, draws attention to the very different nature of change in terms of technology and of the curriculum.

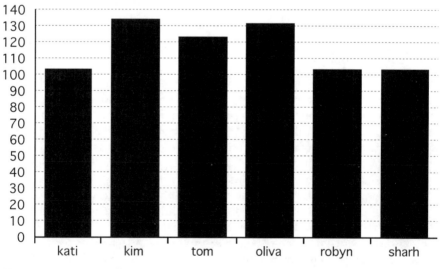

Figure 11.1   Kati's graph

Technological change and curriculum change are promoted in somewhat different ways. In technological terms, sudden, radical innovation can boost the pace of progress in a spectacular fashion. The school curriculum, however, is a conservative social institution. In this context, decisive change, . . . is likely to be resisted. Some aspects of school activity are treasured as fundamental; and proposals which appear to devalue these aspects encounter a backlash of personal and political prejudice.

(Costello 1992: 23)

In the UK at least, the political backlash since 1992 has been even more extreme than he may have envisaged. One reason for this seems to have been a failure, on the part of those outside the education community, to understand the relationship between the introduction of new tools and curriculum change. The following anecdotes may illustrate this point.

In discussion, one student in the early stages of a teacher education course accused his lecturer of being 'stupid' for suggesting that calculators should be available for pupils to use throughout the primary school, starting from their entry in the reception year. When the lecturer explored with the student how he thought calculators were used in schools, it emerged that his image was of a traditional 'pencil-and-paper' curriculum, in which pupils worked through pages of 'sums', and simply used a calculator to get the answers. In these circumstances, the use of calculators would indeed be stupid. It had never occurred to the student to think about how the curriculum, and the activities in the classroom might be changed because of the availability of the tool.

A second anecdote illustrates another difficulty in public perceptions of some technological tools. A year 11 pupil had her graphic calculator confiscated by a teacher who taught modern languages. When the pupil asked for it to be returned, she was told that it would 'do her good' to be without it for a few days. She naturally appealed to her mathematics teacher for help, and a heated staffroom discussion ensued. Eventually, the mathematics teacher convinced her colleague of the importance of the calculator by making a comparison with the use of a dictionary in language lessons.

It is interesting to consider why a dictionary was seen as an acceptable tool, and the calculator (initially) was not. One factor is certainly the familiarity of the tool: the function of a dictionary is well understood. In contrast, most adults will never have used a graphic calculator, and in fact only used a four-function calculator in fairly limited ways, so they have little idea of how the tool may be used.

A second, and perhaps more influential, factor is the perception of the difficulty of using the tool, and the prior knowledge required. It is 'obvious' that a dictionary is not simple to use: within the school curriculum pupils are explicitly taught the skills needed to use it efficiently, and teachers recognise that, far from becoming 'lazy' and 'dependent', pupils will learn further language skills through the use of a dictionary. The contact that most adults will have had with calculators may lead them to see a calculator as a very simple tool: you 'just press the buttons'. Since there is apparently nothing that needs to be taught about its use, it is not obvious that any further skills can be learnt through using it.

However, because computers are perceived as complex and difficult tools, their use in education is constructed quite differently. Attitudes to their use contrast sharply with the backlash against calculators, even though within mathematics there are other instances where the use of software may parallel the way in which the use of calculators may supersede traditional number skills, such as the use of symbol manipulators in algebra.

Despite this public perception, the complexity of computer tools is not unproblematic. Many teachers may feel anxious about the need to learn to control and use powerful and sophisticated pieces of software, and this, rather than pedagogic issues, may dominate their approach. The following comments from primary teachers involved in a spreadsheet project illustrate this anxiety:

Eve: I've always felt afraid of spreadsheets – they seemed so complicated. I never realised you could do things so simply.

Martha: I feel I need to learn to use the software properly before I use it with the children.

Both these comments were made at an early stage in the project, before the teachers had tried using spreadsheets in their classrooms. Both teachers were offered support by the project team, in terms of their own use of the software, and in terms of planning classroom activities. For both of them, time to explore the software on their own was very important in building their confidence. However, the key factor in turning them into enthusiastic spreadsheet users was the relative confidence with which pupils used and explored the software, and the quality of the mathematical work they were able to do. Martha soon decided that using the software 'properly' did not involve understanding every item on every menu, and concentrated much more on making changes to her teaching approach.

Computer-as-tutee

Seeing the computer as a potential tutee may initially seem a strange way in which to construct its role, although this view is implicit in the quotation used at the start of this chapter. In Seymour Papert's discussion of Logo, 'teaching the computer' becomes a natural metaphor for programming. Putting the learner in the role of teacher has been recognised in many areas, from studies of formal peer tutoring to less structured discussion, as a powerful way of supporting and reinforcing learning.

The computer differs from a human tutee in a number of ways that intensify the learning benefits for its teacher. It has no common sense: it obeys instructions without evaluating or elaborating them, or making assumptions. It forces the 'teacher' to be explicit and precise. Therefore, a pupil trying to teach the Logo turtle to draw a shape has to give numerical values to distances and angles. The computer is very patient: it will not criticise, and it will wait all day while many versions of a procedure are tried.

However, the computer is also pedantic: it disciplines the communication with its teacher by only accepting instructions that follow particular conventions. Turns must be given as numbers of degrees to left or right, values can be entered as decimals, but not as fractions. Finally, the computer provides immediate feedback about what it has been taught: the image produced on the screen can be used directly to see how successfully instructions have been given.

Exploring the metaphor of computer-as-tutee

One example of the application of this metaphor was integrated into the Primary Laptop Project, in which primary pupils, and their teachers, were given continuous access to portable computers over substantial periods of time, so that they became as natural a part of the classroom as pencil and paper. A significant feature of the project was the development of purposeful tasks that exploited the potential of the computer for learning mathematics. (For more detail of the Primary Laptop Project see Ainley *et al.* 1998; Pratt and Ainley 1997.) In the Primary Laptop Project, the pupils' personal relationships with portable technology are seen as a key element. The pupils' sense of 'ownership' of their computer (shared in a group of two or three) is encouraged by giving them responsibility for taking care of the machine, for taking it home regularly, and for making decisions about when and how it is used (Pratt and Ainley, 1997). The metaphor of teaching the computer has been used with pupils working in a number of different computer environments.

Reflecting on the issue . . .
It is likely that the practice adopted in the Primary Laptop Project of sending laptops home with pupils will be outside of the experience of many teachers. Perhaps this is understandable – it is often difficult enough getting all the pencils back in at the end of the day! However, just consider how it might potentially alter your practice as a teacher if some (or all!) your pupils were able to take a laptop home with them. What different sorts of tasks could you offer them? What different engagement might they have with mathematics?

Another issue of course is that of how many pupils have access to a PC at home. You might care to find out: Who has access and who does not? What pupils are 'PC confident'? Hence, is there an equity issue here? Could these be overcome? Have you tried setting a computer-based homework task? What about a graphic calculator task? (e.g. sending calculators home with data sets for pupils to explore at home with parents or carers or each other.)

The following extended examples from research within the Primary Laptop Project illustrate the powerful way in which the metaphor of 'teaching the computer' may support mathematical learning.

The sheep-pen problem

This activity involves pupils in manipulating a physical model of a sheep-pen made from flexible fencing to form three sides of a rectangle against a wall. They then take measurements, and enter these on a spreadsheet which they set up to calculate the area of the pen (see Figure 11.2). They can then graph this data to explore the maximum possible area. (For a detailed description of this activity, see Ainley 1996; Ainley *et al.* 1998.)

At some point during this process, most groups realised that they could manage without using the physical model: they could choose a width for the pen, and calculate the corresponding length. At this point, the teacher intervened to encourage the pupils to encapsulate their method of calculation in a spreadsheet formula, using the metaphor of teaching the computer. The following extract of a discussion between two pupils – Jordan and Stellios – is typical of these interactions.

Teacher: . . .What you are trying to do is to tell the computer how to work the length out, given some width. So if you knew what that width was, you're trying to work that length out (*pointing to the length column*).

Jordan: You have to add these together (*pointing vaguely at the length and width column*) . . . double it (*pointing to the width*) . . .

Stellios: How do you double it?

Jordan: . . . and then you work out the length.

Stellios: Zero point five add zero point five or something.

Jordan: Yeah but they don't know . . . (*pointing at width cell*).

Jordan: I know B eleven (*typing*) B 11, B11, . . . right B 11, add, . . . B11 add, oh no, B11 times 2 . . .

Stellios: Oh yeah times 2.

Jordan: . . . so then that doubles it , and . . .

Stellios: Add A 11 . . .

Jordan: B11 times 2 add . . .

Stellios: . . . add A11 equals C11.

Jordan: No we need to . . . if there's 30 in the ruler right, it's all doubled though, we need to tell it how to work out what's left.

	A Length	B Width	C Area
1	Length	Width	Area
2	20	5	100
3	10	10	100
4	24	3	72
5	26	2	52
6	14	8	112
7	12	9	108
8	16	7	112
9	13	8.5	110.5
10	29	0.5	14.5
11			0
12			0

Figure 11.2 The sheep pen spreadsheet.

The task of teaching the computer was familiar to the pupils, and they are able to engage with it immediately. They quickly realised that they needed to express their method in terms of the formal notation of the spreadsheet. Their mental method was to choose a width for the pen (S starts trying to use zero point five as the width), double this, and take that length away from 30, (the total length of the fence). After struggling for some time to express this method clearly, and trying several slightly different verbal formulations, they typed:

$$=30 \quad B11 * 2$$

Their problem being they couldn't work out how to express 'take it away from 30'. The computer gave them a message 'Bad formula', and they quickly deleted this formula and typed:

$$=B11 * 2 - 30.$$

Stellios:	. . . You can't take 30 from . . . um . . .
Jordan:	Times it by 2 take it from 30.
Stellios:	Times it by 2 and take it from 30.

They try putting in 13 for the width and get length -4 and area -52.

Jordan:	It's probably 52.
Stellios:	The minus, shouldn't have put the minus in.
Jordan:	I don't know. B11 times it by 2 take it from 30 . . . but this looks like take away 30, and we don't . . . It should have been 4, so it's nearly right.

At this point, the pupils had an efficient method for performing the necessary calculation themselves, but it was not in a form that the spreadsheet would accept. Imagine a different scenario, in which they had reached this point in an activity and the *teacher* required them to express their method in formal mathematical notation. In this case, there seems little purpose for the formal notation, and the teacher's judgements about what is acceptable may seem arbitrary: after all, the teacher *can* make sense of the instruction 'take it away from 30', and the pupils know that this method works perfectly well.

With their attention on teaching the computer, the pupils were apparently quite happy to accept that the spreadsheet needed information in an unambiguous, standardised form, and were eventually able to make the link between this notation and their more idiosyncratic method.

The drawing-kit

The second example involves the use of dynamic geometry software, which combines basic drawing elements such as lines, points and circles with the possibility of constructing geometric relationships (such as the perpendicular bisector of a line segment), which remain constant when points of the figure are dragged around the screen. When some groups first explored dynamic geometry software they used it spontaneously to make pictures, but as these were essentially static, the pupils saw no purpose in construction rather than placing points and lines by eye. (For a fuller discussion of this, see Pratt and Ainley 1997.) In response to this, an activity was designed to help pupils to see some purpose in using geometric construction. A group of 11-year-olds was given the task of making a drawing kit that younger pupils could use to make their own pictures. (The pupils were using an early version of *Cabri Geometry* that offered a more limited set of primitives than more recent versions, in which the drawing-kit activity may actually make little sense.)

After discussing what shapes such a kit might contain, they considered how these shapes had to behave. It was important that each shape could be moved around on the screen, that its size could be altered, and that it could be produced many times. Their aim was not just to draw a single square or wheel, but to teach the computer methods to produce these shapes. In an introductory demonstration of how to construct an equilateral triangle, the teacher also introduced the possibility of making macros to record their constructions.

Understanding the difference between drawing and construction proved to be difficult for most of the pupils, because initially the visual impression on the screen was much stronger than other considerations. The idea of teaching the computer was helpful for distinguishing between the two modes of working. One group had constructed a circle, placed points by eye onto the circle and joined them to the centre to produce a wheel with four spokes. However, when they tried to drag a point on the wheel to change its size, the image came apart (Figure 11.3).

In trying to explain what he saw, Marco commented '. . . those points aren't stamped on . . . the computer doesn't know about them'. This was an important moment in his transition from drawing to construction, as he saw that the computer had not 'learnt' about these points. Marco's understanding of his relationship with the computer supported his understanding of a potentially difficult mathematical idea.

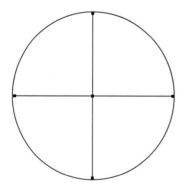
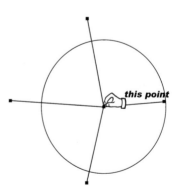

Figure 3   The wheel before and after dragging.

Extending the metaphor of computer-as-tutee

These examples indicate ways in which the idea of the computer-as-tutee may be helpful in supporting pupils' learning of mathematical ideas, and also in helping them to understand something of the nature of those ideas. In particular, the distinction between mathematical conventions and logical necessity may begin to emerge.

This metaphor might substantially alter perceptions of a range of uses of technological tools. For example, imagine pupils solving a problem involving calculating value added tax, using a calculator. One perception of this activity is that the calculator actually does all the 'work': all pupils have to do is to press buttons. In fact, this does not accurately convey what happens. It is the pupil who has to decide which operations to use to model the problem correctly, and in which sequence the instructions must be given to the calculator. An alternative description of the pupil teaching the calculator how to solve the problem offers a strikingly different perception of the balance of intellectual control.

However, in considering the complexity of the interactions with the computer, the metaphor of computer-as-tutee may be too simplistic. The computer is being 'taught' by accepting instructions, but it is doing much more. It is providing feedback in response to those instructions, in ways that may offer both validation for correctness, and support for reformulation. In both the examples in the previous section, feedback from the computer was crucial in supporting mathematical thinking. The computer is also offering a different, but equally important, form of validation through its insistence on the use of notation that follows mathematical conventions. The computer might be seen as offering a purposeful context for practising the use of such notation (Ainley 1996).

Conclusion

In this chapter, I have examined three different models for thinking about the role of the computer in mathematics classrooms. 'Computer-as-teaching-aid' reflects many of the strengths of the computer, and appears non-threatening to the traditional role of the teacher. However, the pragmatic requirement for software that is teacher-independent opens the way for a slide in perception from 'teaching-aid' to 'teacher', potentially resulting in alienation for the teacher, and isolation for the learner.

'Computer-as-tool' offers a more neutral role for the computer, and more autonomy for the learner. However, too much attention on mastery of the tool may prove intimidating for many teachers, and focus concern away from mathematics.

'Computer-as-tutee' offers a very different perspective, which may be powerful for learners, but challenging for teachers. It is only a partially successful metaphor. The difficulty of finding a better one is perhaps an indication that its role does not have obvious human parallels: the closest might be critical-listener, or perhaps critical-friend. The presence of such a critical friend may have enormous benefits in terms of pupils' autonomy, but may also make considerable demands on teachers to review their role in the classroom. The shift in control towards pupils' independence may seem intimidating, but can also be empowering, opening up possibilities for genuine discussion and insights into pupils' thinking. The critical friend for the pupil can also become an ally for the teacher.

Invitation to reflect

- Think about one piece of software (or a specific piece of technology, such as a graphic calculator) that you use in your teaching. Which of the three categories suggested here, 'teaching aid', 'tool', 'tutee', best fits the way in which you have used it in the past? Could you plan different ways in which you might use it, fitting the other two models? What might the effects on pupils' experiences be?
- List the different physical settings in which you have used, or observed the use of, technology in mathematics lessons (e.g. a computer lab, one calculator per child, laptops in the classroom). How much does the physical environment influence the ways in which the role of the technology is seen? How does it affect your role as teacher? How does it affect the social interactions in the lesson? Think about what you would like to change: could altering the environment enable you to do this?
- Think about an occasion on which you have used a computer or other technology when you were working on a piece of mathematics. Try to recall as vividly as you can how and when you used the technology, and when you moved away from it. How did you feel about your interactions with the computer? How did it support, or hinder, your access to the mathematical ideas? Use this experience to think about the kinds of experiences your pupils do, or might, have of using technology for doing mathematics.

Further suggested reading

Papert, S. (1980) *Mindstorms: Children, Computers and Powerful Ideas*, Brighton: Harvester Press. If you haven't read this book before, you really should do. Despite its age, it still offers a refreshingly innovative view of technology and learning. And if you have read it before, it is probably time you reminded yourself about what it actually says.

Ainley, J. (1996) *Enriching Primary Mathematics with IT*, London: Hodder and Stoughton. This book illustrates a range of uses of technology to support and extend the mathematics curriculum some of which, despite the title, would be applicable to Key Stage 3.

References

Ainley, J. (1996) 'Purposeful contexts for formal notation in a spreadsheet environment', in *Journal of Mathematical Behavior* 15(4), 405–22.

Ainley, J. and Pratt, D. (1995) 'Supporting Teachers' and Children's Mathematical Thinking', in *Journal of Information Technology in Teacher Education* 4(1), 81–92.

Ainley, J., Nardi, E. and Pratt, D. (1998) 'Graphing as a computer mediated tool', in Olivier, A. and Newstead, K. (eds), *Proceedings of the Twenty-Second Annual Conference of the International Group for the Psychology of Mathematics Vol. 1*, Stellenbosch: University of Stellenbosch, pp. 243–58

Costello, J. (1992) 'The failed revolution', in *Micromath* 8(1), 21–3.

Goldstein, R. (1998) 'ILS – an anecdote', in *Micromath* 14(3), 21.

Papert, S. (1980) *Mindstorms: Children, Computers and Powerful Ideas*, Brighton: Harvester Press.

Pratt, D. and Ainley, J. (1997) 'The construction of meanings for geometric construction: Two contrasting cases', in *International Journal of Computers for Mathematical Learning* 1(3), 293–322.

Steen, T. (1998) 'Getting under the skin of an ILS', in *Micromath* 14(3), 15–20.

12 Reading mathematics texts

Paul Dowling

Introducing the issue

At the beginning of their book *Children Reading Mathematics*, Hilary Shuard and Andrew Rothery described reading as 'getting the meaning from the page' (Shuard and Rothery 1984: 1). Yet of course we are all aware that even apparently very straightforward texts can generate innumerable and often very different readings depending upon who is doing the reading, for what purpose and so forth. So, an important issue in using school mathematics textbooks has to be, whose 'meaning' are pupils intended to get?

In this chapter, I look at the reading of school mathematics texts from a sociological perspective. That is to say, I am concerned with relations of authority between categories such as the author and the reader. I am also concerned with the distinctive forms that mathematical and non-mathematical practices can take and with the manner in which mathematical texts can be understood to 'mythologise' non-mathematical practices. I am, finally, concerned with the tendency of at least some school mathematical texts to reflect patterns of social class in their differentiation between 'high ability' and 'low ability' readers.

In this chapter I use illustrations and examples that are mainly (but not exclusively) taken from secondary school mathematics texts. However, I claim that the issues are of direct relevance to mathematics teaching at all levels.

Key questions

In this chapter I address four main key questions.

- How can we conceptualise different forms of mathematics that appear in mathematics texts and classrooms?
- What are the relationships between mathematics and non-mathematical practices such as shopping?
- How do school texts enable and deny access to mathematical principles?
- On what basis are students differentiated by school mathematics texts?

Before you begin to read the chapter, you might usefully consider how you view the relationships between some non-mathematics practices (such as shopping for example) and the mathematics that is undertaken in classrooms under the guise of this practice.

Two forms of mathematical activity

In this first section, I will make some suggestions for how we might view the types of mathematics that might appear in school classrooms. Some time ago a beginning teacher described to me an incident in a mathematics lesson that she had been teaching. The year 7 students had been constructing triangles to measurements that had been put on the board: 8 cm, 7 cm, 6 cm and so forth. As a final example, the teacher had included 6 cm, 3 cm, 3 cm. Having arrived at this example, one of the students announced that this was not a triangle. Another student – a girl – responded: 'Oh yes it is, and what's more I've drawn it.'

The teacher invited her to draw the triangle on the board using a board ruler. The girl first constructed a line of length 6 units horizontally. She then tilted the ruler very slightly and drew a 3 unit line from one end of the first line and finally joined this to the other end of the first line by constructing another line of similar length.

'But those lines are more than 3 cm', observed one of the boys in the class. A number of the others agreed with him. 'OK, I'll make them smaller', the girl said and duly constructed a somewhat flatter triangle.

But the other students remained unconvinced. One of them tried a different argument:

> You can't draw that triangle, because 3 cm and 3 cm make 6 cm so the two short sides have to be on the same line as the long side or they won't join up.

A debate ensued with most of the class joining in. Eventually, everyone had sided with the sceptics. Everyone, that is, except the girl who had drawn the 'impossible' object on the board. She remained, throughout, stubbornly attached to her claim that she had in fact achieved the impossible and that her triangle was to be allowed.

Reflecting on the issue . . .
How would you respond in this situation? What might you say to the girl? What might you say to the rest of the class? What might you do next?

She was, of course, entirely correct. The task that the teacher had set was a practical one. In assessing the students' work, she would have had to measure the lengths of the sides of the triangles that they would have drawn. In doing this, she would have had to allow – explicitly or tacitly – a margin of error, a millimetre either way, perhaps. This would have been quite enough to enable the girl to produce an acceptable 6, 3, 3 triangle. The boy who had declared the task to be impossible had, in fact, changed the rules of the game. Unfortunately, under the new rules, none of the triangles could be drawn; they were all impossible. In this game, triangles are idealised objects and not physical objects. A drawing of a triangle is really a representation of a formal object. We might say that it is a metaphor for a triangle.

This incident raises a number of issues that are crucial to the reading of mathematics texts. The first issue concerns the nature of 'reading'. As I suggested earlier the interpretation of reading as simply accessing the meaning that is given on the page is naïve. It separates the 'meaning' of a text from the 'form' in which it is expressed. Furthermore, it is an interpretation of reading that considers the link between what a writer writes and what a reader reads as simple and straight-forward. In my interpretation of 'reading' things are somewhat more complex. Reading involves the reader in actively – though not always consciously – impos-ing contextual boundaries to what is being read. In this way, the text is always referred to something else outside of itself – let's call this the reader's interpretive framework. In the triangles classroom the girl, the rest of the class, and the teacher had their own, different interpretive frameworks.

The girl was referring to the text on the board – the list of measurements – to a practical activity that involved the manipulation of a ruler, pencil and paper or their analogues on the board. In a sense she was working on pictures, images or physical representations of triangles. The rest of the class were referring to an activity that concerns making statements and drawing conclusions about formally defined objects – in this case abstractly defined formal triangles. The girl was correct in the sense that only in her interpretation was the task actually physically doable. The rest of the class were correct in the sense that their interpretation more closely coincided with the rules of the mathematics classroom. She was working on physical objects realised in practical activity; they were working on mathematical principles expressed through language. Now these two approaches actually represent two different ways of viewing or interpreting mathematics – that is, two different interpretive frameworks or domains of mathematical activity – a *practical domain* and what I refer to as the *esoteric domain*.

However, the 'rules' that pupils need to follow in order to be successful at school mathematics require them to learn to recognise the need to work at the level of formal principles that define and relate mathematical objects – that is, working at the level of language, rules, principles – in other words at the level of what we call discourse – that is in the esoteric domain of mathematical activity. (Robyn Zevenbergen addresses a related point in her chapter when she discusses the different linguistic expectations on pupils from different social class back-grounds.)

These two interpretive frameworks illustrate two other features. First, in its construction of formally defined objects and principles, mathematical practice makes its principles available within language; that is to say discursively. These formally defined objects and principles are, therefore, generalisable to a range of situations and contexts. On the other hand, the manipulation of drawing instruments involves manual skills that are not available within or acquired through language. The objects of manual practices such as this are not generalised, but are localised instances. Crudely, the teacher cannot mark the students' work by calling out the answers; she has to engage physically with each one separately. School mathematics generates both kinds of practice, the generation of discursive, generalised principles and objects, and the production of non-discursive, localised skills and objects. However, the esoteric domain of mathematics is heavily dominated by such discursive practices and pupils need to recognise that they have to work at this level, and they must demonstrate their capacity to do so.

Let us look again at the triangles activity. Even though it is supposedly about drawing triangles, this is not necessarily the intended or real activity behind the task the teacher has set the pupils. The real task is about working on the possibility of drawing triangles using rules and general principles. This real task is, to all intents and purposes, fully realisable within discourse and does not depend at all on the physical act of drawing. In other words, the activity is charged to the fullest possible extent – it is saturated – by discursive principles. This is what I call *discursive saturation*. Where the discursive practices have priority over, or are minimally dependent on the non-discursive practices, we have an example of high discursive saturation. Where the non-discursive, localised skills and objects have priority or where the task is heavily dependent on material practices, is an example of low discursive saturation. (You can find more about this in my book *The Sociology of Mathematics Education. Mathematical Myths/Pedagogic Texts*, especially Chapters 5 and 6.)

School mathematics generates tasks and draws on practices that can have high discursive saturation and others that can have low discursive saturation – but they are not necessarily equally privileged or valued.

Reflecting on the issue . . .
Take another *practical* task (from a textbook for example) and identify the rules or principles that it is intended to convey. How might over-concentration on the practical elements inhibit the move to the formal or abstract mathematical principles? You might try out the task with a group of students and see how they respond.

Public and esoteric mathematics

In this second section I will discuss the different purposes to which mathematics can be put. In school mathematics, the objects and principles of the esoteric domain are routinely projected onto non-mathematical practices. The projection of number and algebraic relations onto supermarket shopping is quite common, for example, to produce what we might refer to as a 'mathematised world'. I refer to this 'mythical' world as the *public domain* of school mathematics. In what I call the public domain, there is an appearance of a real world application of mathematics. Yet the principles that control and regulate the acceptability of the mathematics are still subject to the esoteric domain. (In Barry Cooper's chapter, the test question about the lift is another example of this public domain.) This creates a very false world in which pupils have to assume that mathematics is all around us and that it is actually useful for routine activities in our everyday life. Of course teachers may actually know differently.

Reflecting on the issue . . .
One inroad into the public domain for pupils is often the practice of decorating a room. In the public domain, pupils are encouraged to use a range of mathematical practices in order to calculate the amount of paint, paper and carpet required, and even to plan furniture moving and arrangements.

Identify the public domain of mathematics in a decorating context. Then identify the actual practice in the domestic setting. What do pupils gain from the public domain? What do pupils lose by the transformation of the domestic setting into a mythologised world?

Such a transformation of the real world also happens in geometry. So, formal, discursive objects such as triangles are projected onto the world to interpret and describe drawings, parts of buildings and other structures, even the positions of footballers in a game, as if these interpretations were actually the formal objects. The physical practice of drawing triangles is also part of the public domain of mathematics, so a world of physical shapes and manual activity is constructed as the public domain of school geometry.

Now the crucial thing about the public domain of mathematics is that it is always a transformed version of the non-mathematical world. The nature and behaviour of drawings, buildings and footballers are not fully or even accurately captured by their description as being positioned in triangles. In constructing the public domain, mathematics always transforms, simplifies and recontextualises the world.

In the rest of this chapter, I shall illustrate my arguments by referring, mainly, to a popular series of mathematics textbooks, *The School Mathematics Project (SMP) 11–16*. The textbooks that I specifically refer to are: *SMP Book Y1* (1985); *SMP Book Y4* (1987); *SMP Book Y5* (1987); *SMP Book G6* (1987); *SMP Book G7* (1987); *SMP 11–16 Teacher's Guide to Book G* (1985). All are authored by the School Mathematics Project and published by Cambridge University Press, Cambridge. Figure 12.1 is an example from one of the textbooks.

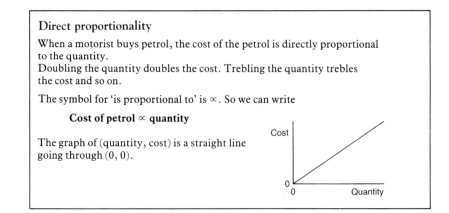

Direct proportionality
When a motorist buys petrol, the cost of the petrol is directly proportional to the quantity.
Doubling the quantity doubles the cost. Trebling the quantity trebles the cost and so on.

The symbol for 'is proportional to' is $\propto$. So we can write

Cost of petrol $\propto$ quantity

The graph of (quantity, cost) is a straight line going through (0, 0).

Figure 12.1   Page 62 from textbook SMP 11–16 Book Y4.

Now the activity that involves motorists in buying petrol is an example of an everyday domestic activity. I make a distinction between this kind of activity and pedagogic activity that takes place in schools as institutions for the purpose of teaching and learning. Now in the petrol example, the author of the textbook has acted transformatively on the practices of what is clearly a domestic activity. These practices have been dislocated from any local context (a particular filling station at a particular time and a particular motorist in particular circumstances and so forth). The result is a rather specialised form of commentary upon the practice of buying petrol. This commentary in the book involves proportionality and graphs and is of a generalised nature that is quite different from the actual practices of buying petrol. The commentary has been achieved by the privileging of a particular form of mathematical discourse – the esoteric domain. The commentary that results is part of the public domain of school mathematics. In this example, the public domain is presented as a way of entering mathematical discourse rather than as a way of conducting the purchase of petrol. The direction of the text is from domestic activity (purchasing and paying for petrol), to the public domain (imposing some mathematical principles onto the activity) and onto the esoteric domain (applying the principles of proportionality). Furthermore, in working through this book, the pupil has a career within the esoteric domain; it is the esoteric domain that is developed systematically in the chapter and similarly in other chapters of the book and in the Y series of books as a whole.

The precise nature of the setting in the public domain of mathematics is actually irrelevant to the completion of the mathematical task. In the above case, all that is necessary in order to complete the task is constructing the graph and answering the questions that follow. It does not follow of course that all pupils will necessarily recognise the significance of the transformation from domestic setting to esoteric domain. A very long tradition of research suggests that setting-independent and setting-dependent contexts for mathematical tasks are likely to be distributed on a sociocultural basis (for example Barry Cooper's and Robyn Zevenbergen's chapters; also see Luria 1976; Bernstein 1977; Cooper and Dunne, 2000). Consequently there are pupils who may not fully recognise that a game is being played here, let alone recognise the rules by which they have to play. It is perhaps not surprising that many such pupils become alienated from school mathematics.

Reflecting on the issue . . .
Review some of the domestic setting of tasks in a textbook that you are using or have available. Does the text place greater emphasis on the setting itself or on the esoteric domain of mathematics? How?

In the case of the motorist example we have a particularly radical transformation of the world. That is the recontextualising of a domestic exchange activity (the purpose of which is economic) into a pedagogic activity (the purpose of which is educational). This entails a reorganising of the social relations that give the activity its meaning, because moving from the domestic exchange activity to the mathematical esoteric domain shifts authority from the 'consumer' to the 'vendor' – in other words from the pupil to the teacher. The two forms of activity are structurally different. The petrol consumer decides whether, how much, and from whom to buy (which is also the basis for limited consumer authority with respect to price via competition between vendors). Should the pupil manage successfully to claim an equivalent form of authority then their mathematical failure is likely to be assured.

There is a further effect of the recontextualising of petrol buying. As I have pointed out, mathematics is dominated by strategies that prioritise practices with high discursive saturation. Consumer practices, such as shopping and buying petrol, are more appropriately described as deploying low discursive saturation strategies. This is because the principles that are deployed by the customer are generally localised in terms of the specific context in time and place, the particular purpose and resources of the customer and so forth. As well as the structural difference between the pedagogic activity – school mathematics – and the domestic exchange activity – buying petrol, then there is a strategic difference in that they privilege discursive and non-discursive practices respectively.

What sort of mathematics is valued in schools?

In this third section, I want to look at how mathematics texts can value some forms of mathematical activity in preference to others. The extract in Figure 12.2 is from the same school mathematics scheme as the example above, but is taken from a book that targets 'lower ability' students.

This task is accompanied by a photograph showing a large and a small box of Persil Automatic Washing Powder.

The first point to be made here is that the approach to 'best buy' decisions implied in this text is not one that is usually applied in the world outside the classroom. A more general approach, I suspect, is illustrated in the following extract by the response of an actual shopper doing actual shopping.

A3 Here are two packets of washing powder. The small size contains 930 g of powder. It costs 84p. The large size contains 3·1 kg of powder. It costs £2·56.

(a) How many grams do you get for 1p in the small size?

(b) How many grams do you get for 1p in the large size? (Remember you must work in **grams** and **pence**.)

(c) Which size gives more for your money?

Figure 12.2   Page 2 from textbook SMP 11–16 Book G7.

A shopper considered two rolls of paper towels, one costing 82 cents, the other 79 cents. The shopper noted the number of sheets in each roll, 119 versus 104, and proceeded to reformulate the problem, saying, 'That would be three cents more and you get 11 more, 15 more sheets.' She concluded that the larger roll was 'probably a better . . . buy.' The shopper's decision is, precisely, whether to spend an additional three cents for 15 sheets. That is, she must judge whether the marginal value of the additional quantity is worth the marginal cost, a different and more relevant question than whether the larger or smaller size has the lower unit price.

(Murtaugh, quoted in Lave 1988)

The strategies deployed by the shopper are quite different from those that are introduced in the Persil question. Indeed it is not possible to address the shopper's question – is it worth spending 3 cents for 15 extra sheets – in mathematical terms. The criterion that determines the answer is the shopper's own perception of the relative worth of 3 cents and 15 paper towels. Quite clearly, this cannot be interpreted mathematically.

As a pedagogic institution, the school privileges a specific body of knowledge that constitutes the principles against which pupils' performances are to be assessed. Now this is a very different situation from the supermarket, which certainly presents the shopper with a selected array of goods and services, but does not evaluate the performances of its clients against these goods and services. We could, of course, reformulate the Persil question as 'which would you buy?' However, whereas the supermarket leaves this as an open question, the school must foreclose on a privileged set of answers that maps onto its curriculum. In general, a mathematics curriculum must entail the privileging of mathematical principles. This relates to the structural difference between pedagogic and exchange activities.

In fact, the textbook that contains the Persil question also includes tasks that do not have fixed solutions. Generally, these tasks are bounded from the main text by a border and the title 'Discussion point'. Here in Figure 12.3 is an example.

The 'Teacher's Guide' to the first textbook book in this series includes a general introduction to the materials. In this introduction, 'discussion' is marked out as being particularly important.

Discussion between pupils, and between pupil and teacher, is perhaps the most useful mathematical activity possible; 'talking through' with the teacher may

—discussion point —

Look at each of the tins and packets in question A5.
Look at the packets that give you **less** for your money.
Some people might prefer a packet that gives you **less** for your money.
Who might prefer a packet like this?

3

Figure 12.3   Page 3 from textbook SMP 11–16 Book G7.

be the only way to make the work relevant. Discussion should always precede a teacher-led lesson, and discussion can often follow a class game or investigation. Pupils may be asked to explain how they solved a particular problem, and the different methods used by pupils can then be compared. Often for these pupils, there is no single 'correct way' of doing things. Rather there is one method which suits a particular pupil best for a particular problem.

...

Discussion of how to solve problems will be almost as valuable as actually solving them. A discussion of how to avoid congestion in the school corridors, which would be the best local school to amalgamate with, where to go to buy a bike cheaply – all these represent the sort of problem whose solution is mathematically valuable. They are, of course, absolutely specific to the pupils' own environs and interests. 'Problems' may arise topically from a newspaper or TV of a local incident. Valuable discussion can come out of unpromising territory.

(SMP 11–16, Teacher's guide to Book G1: 8–9)

Now one point to note here concerns a statement in the second paragraph, '. . . all these represent the sort of problem whose solution is mathematically valuable'. On the face of it, this seems to propose the same kind of trajectory that characterised the petrol example, that is, from public to esoteric domains. However, this interpretation is questionable once we look in more detail at the SMP 'Green' series as a whole. Less than 10 per cent of the page space of the series is occupied by esoteric domain text (Dowling 1998). Nevertheless, there is a clear privileging of mathematical principles, here – 'Valuable discussion can come out of unpromising territory' – and there is again evidence of retention of the principles of evaluation of performances – that is, retention of authority – by the teacher who is to supervise the comparison of student methods.

In the 'discussion point' example quoted above, there is no obvious privileging of mathematical principles. It seems to refer more closely to the generation of relevance and to the principle that the method should suit the situation. Superficially, this might be interpreted as an attempt to get at precisely the kind of context-dependency that characterises non-discursive activities such as shopping. However, such an interpretation misses two points. Firstly, the discussion by necessity dislocates decision making from its immediate context. It represents a move from what is called practical logic to theoretical logic (Bourdieu 1990). Thus, introduction of discussion in this way is a strategy that shifts the practice away from non-discursive practices and towards discursive practices. The school is a form of institution that, in the main, is characterised by its strategic privileging of practices characterised by high discursive saturation. It generates generalised forms of communication even where it appears to be engaging in highly localised practices. It is important to emphasise that I am referring to that which is formally privileged in and by the school. Clearly, in the day-to-day practices of the school there will be many instances of context-dependent decision making.

Different kinds of practice for different students

To summarise the main claim that I am making here, the school and the super-market are institutions that can be understood as being dominated by logically opposite modes of social activity and that deploy strategies that privilege opposite modes of practice. The supermarket is a domestic exchange activity that, in the main, locates the principles of evaluation of practice with the customer. In general, the supermarket privileges localised and context-dependent practices. The school, by contrast, is dominated by the pedagogic mode that locates the principles of evaluation of practices with the teacher/textbook. Official school discourse deploys strategies that privilege context-independent practices. These structural and strategic disparities between school and supermarket pose a challenge to the contention that the school is or can be a site for the transmission of skills that are generalisable in any simplistic way to sites such as the supermarket.

Reflecting on the issue . . .

From a mathematics textbook, select a public domain task that involves a non-mathematical setting other than shopping.

1   What are the structural characteristics of the real setting (is it more like shopping or more like mathematics in terms of where the authority lies)?
2   What are the strategic characteristics of the real setting (does it privilege high or low discursive saturation)?
3   Reformulate the task to: (a) make it more realistic; (b) allow movement into relevant esoteric domain mathematics.
4   Are 3(a) and 3(b) mutually exclusive?

I do not want to go so far as to claim that school mathematics can be of no use to shoppers. The evidence of Jean Lave and her colleagues (Lave *et al.* 1984) is that shoppers make use of the resources that are available to them in the context of the supermarket. This may generalise to discursive resources and these may include school mathematics. This is, of course, an empirical question: I have often thought it would be interesting to investigate whether mathematics teachers shop differently from the rest of the population. My argument, however, does challenge the claim that mathematics occupies a privileged position in respect of the optimising of everyday domestic activities. Furthermore, to the extent that mathematics is to become available as a generalisable resource, it would seem to be incumbent upon teachers and the authors of textbooks to concentrate upon providing a more even distribution of access to the esoteric domain of mathematics rather than on the public domain as mythologised shopping. This is because only in the esoteric domain are mathematical principles fully discursively available for generalisation to other mathematical and non-mathematical contexts. The context-dependency of the public domain more or less severely delimits its range of application.

In practice, being able to interpret and work in the esoteric domain of mathematics is a function of 'ability'. The petrol example is taken from a textbook targeted at 'high ability' students, so that the shift from the public domain to the esoteric domain is consistent with this targeting. The shopping examples are taken from a textbook directed at 'low ability' students. Here, the partial substitution of mathematical discourse by general discussion on shopping is again consistent with this targeting. Essentially, 'high ability' students get mathematics whilst 'low ability' students get *ad hoc* principles that lay claim to, but which clearly do not constitute, official school knowledge. This effect reproduces the strategic disparity between school mathematics and the supermarket, between high discursive saturation and low discursive saturation.

Insofar as the *SMP 11–16* books are representative of school mathematics more generally, it would seem that mathematics for 'higher ability' students privileges highly discursive over non-discursive practices and the esoteric domain over the public domain. In the case of the classroom debate that I introduced at the beginning of this chapter, this would privilege the formal interpretive framework that was applied by the majority of the members of the class as 'correct'. From this perspective, mathematics is knowledge and must be acquired explicitly via language that may or may not be accompanied by practical work. The interpretive framework that was applied by the girl who had drawn the 'impossible' triangle would be regarded as 'incorrect'. From this perspective, mathematics is skill and can be acquired only through practical engagement with relevant apparatus and contexts. To take another example, you can't learn to ride a bicycle by reading a book; you have to get on the thing and try it out.

Discovery and discourse in primary mathematics

With the distinction between these interpretive frameworks in mind, I would like to consider the following explicit 'assumptions' about the teaching and learning of mathematics that are made in another school mathematics scheme – a primary level text this time – *Nelson Mathematics*, published by Thomas Nelson and Sons, and dated 1992.

> Children need concrete experiences if they are to acquire sound mathematical concepts.
>
> Like adults, children learn best when they investigate and make discoveries for themselves.
>
> Children refine their understanding and develop conceptual structures by talking about their own thinking and what they have done.
>
> Children will become more mathematically able if allowed to develop reliable personal methods of working; the formal recording used by mathematicians is very difficult for most children to understand.
>
> The conventions of mathematics should be taught only when children are confident in their own knowledge, concepts and skills.
>
> (Nelson Mathematics 1992: 5)

Now the first of these 'assumptions' grounds mathematical knowledge in concrete experience. However, as I have already discussed, concrete experiences are open to the application of multiple interpretive frameworks, not all of which are likely to approximate to the kind of knowledge that is privileged by school mathematics. The second and third 'assumptions' do not necessarily refer to non-discursive practices and the third quite explicitly involves language. Nevertheless, mathematical knowledge is characterised by the explicit nature of its principles – we can define mathematical objects and relations in words. This being the case, just what is it that might lead us to suppose that investigation and discussion will lead children to similarly defined objects and relations?

The fourth and fifth 'assumptions' entail the exclusion of esoteric domain discourse until children will have developed fluency within another domain. Now is this other domain the public domain of school mathematics? As I have described it, the public domain is the product of the projection of esoteric domain principles onto the non-mathematical world. That is to say, it is the reading of the world in terms of a highly discursive mathematical interpretive framework. It is unclear how children might be expected to arrive at such readings unless and until they are already in possession of such an interpretive framework. The public domain, then, is the product of the textbook author's or teacher's knowledge, not that of the children. This 'other domain', then, is the result of the children's reading of the world according to their own individual interpretive frameworks. Having formulated such readings, children will not necessarily be any closer to mathematical knowledge than they were before they started investigating and discovering.

There is no doubt that children are learning something in their mathematics lessons, no matter what kinds of tasks and texts they are given. The school, however, is a pedagogic institution rather than an institution set up to engage pupils in domestic activities and thereby to learn more about such realistic social practices. This is because the school privileges certain kinds of practices and reserves the authority to evaluate performances in these practices. The particular kind of practice that is privileged by school mathematics is highly discursive esoteric domain knowledge that is explicitly principled and specialised. Students will not gain access to this privileged practice unless teaching, teachers and their texts provide this access.

Access and social class

There are two further and related points that I need to make. Firstly, my analysis of the *SMP 11–16* texts revealed that the distribution of esoteric/public domain practice follows not only an 'ability' hierarchy, but also one that can be associated with images of social class. For example, the public domain settings contained in the Y ('high ability') and G ('low ability') books have a tendency to emphasise intellectual and manual activities, respectively. However, this tendency, whereby 'high ability' and 'low ability' are associated with intellectual and manual labour is often quite subtle and I shall describe one example, briefly.

Books G6 (the sixth book of a series of eight) and Y5 (the final book in the Y series) both include whole page tasks that relate to the police practice of measuring skid marks on the road in order to estimate the speed of a vehicle immediately prior to an accident (see Figures 12.4 and 12.5). As is the case throughout these books, they differ in the extent to which they involve generalisation and specialisation.

F   Skids

When a car is in an accident,
there are often skid marks on the road.
The police measure the length
of the skid marks.
Then they can work out how fast
the car was going when it started to skid.

This formula tells you roughly how long a skid will be.

$$\text{length of skid} = \frac{\text{speed} \times \text{speed}}{75}$$

The car's speed must be in **miles per hour** (m.p.h.).
The skid length will be in **metres**.

F1   A car is moving at 30 m.p.h. and then skids to a stop.
Roughly how long will the skid marks be?

F2   (a) Work out how long a skid
will be from 20 m.p.h.
Check you get this display
on your calculator.

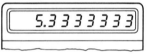

   (b) **Roughly** how many metres long will a 20 m.p.h. skid be?

F3   (a) Copy and complete this table.
It shows the length of skid
from different speeds.

   (b) The police measure
some skid marks.
They are 27 m long.
About how fast do you
think the car was going?

Speed (m.p.h.)	Skid (metres)
20	
30	
40	
50	
60	
70	
80	

F4   Here is a picture of some skid marks.
1 cm on the picture is 1 m on the real road.

About how fast do you think the car was going?

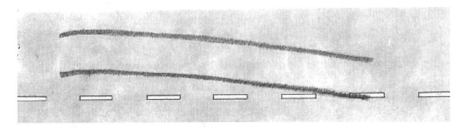

Figure 12.4   Illustration from textbook SMP 11–16 Book G6.

M13

When measuring skid marks, the police can use this formula
to estimate the speed of the vehicle.

$s = \sqrt{(30fd)}$

s is the speed in miles per hour (m.p.h.).
d is the length of the skid, in feet.
f is a number which depends on the weather and the type of road.

This table shows some values of f.

		Road surface	
		Concrete	Tar
Weather	Wet	0·4	0·5
	Dry	0·8	1·0

(a) A car travelling on a wet concrete road makes a skid mark
of length 80 feet. How fast was it travelling?

(b) (i) When the road surface is tar and the weather is dry, the
formula may be written

$s = \sqrt{(30d)}$

Complete this table to show the values of s for the given
values of d, to 1 decimal place.

d	50	100	150	200	250
$30d$	1500				
$s = \sqrt{(30d)}$	38·7				

(ii) Draw axes, with d from 0 to 250 (use 2 cm for 50) and
s from 0 to 100 (use 1 cm for 10).
Draw the graph of (d, s).

(iii) Use your graph to find how many feet a car would skid on
a dry tar road at 75 m.p.h.

Figure 12.5   Illustration from textbook SMP 11–16 Book Y5.

The G text refers only to 'cars', the Y text generalises to 'vehicles'; the G6 police use a formula that 'tells you roughly how long a skid will be'; the Y5 police 'estimate the speed of the vehicle'. Now this might be a trivial difference in a single instance. However, the impact of these localising/generalising strategies is cumulative in each series taken as a whole. The G text expresses the formula in words; the Y text employs conventional mathematical symbols.

$$\text{length of skid} = \frac{\text{speed} \times \text{speed}}{75}$$

(SMP 11–16 Book G6: 6)

$$s = \sqrt{(30\ fd)}$$

(SMP 11–16 Book Y5: 181)

Furthermore, the orientation of each text in terms of the domains of mathematical practice is very different. The Y5 text begins with a very mathematical form of expression that makes the recontextualisation of the police activity very visible. The central task in the Y5 text moves on the construction of and estimation from a parabolic graph. This foregrounding of esoteric domain practice privileges the esoteric domain over the public domain setting that thereby acquires a degree of arbitrariness.

The G6 text, by contrast, does not foreground the esoteric domain at any point. Indeed, the final task is about as close as one might get to the real police activity whilst remaining between the covers of a school textbook. There is a sense, then, in which the G6 text presents the task as *for* the police activity: its purpose is to enable the student to be a potential practitioner in the public domain setting. The Y5 task is clearly *for* mathematics operating in the esoteric domain.

This opposition of orientations is emphasised by the illustration that heads each page. The G6 text shows a photograph of a real policeman using a tape measure on the road. The camera angle positions the viewer – the student – at the shoulder of the policeman, squatting down beside him, learning the trade.

The Y5 text is a line drawing of two faceless police officers (one of each gender). We suspect that the artist, unlike the photographer, did not produce their image from life but from an imagined representation of life. Furthermore, the angle of vision in the Y5 text places the reader above and looking down on the scene. The student is not being apprenticed to a police officer. Rather the student is, metaphorically, standing alongside the textbook author, casting a mathematical gaze on the non-mathematical activity. This student is apprenticed to the mathematician.

The point that I am making is that here and in general in these books, the orientations of the textbooks tend to identify the G series readers with future manual work and the Y series readers as future mathematicians. Where there is an apprenticing to a non-mathematical activity in the Y Books, it tends still to be to an intellectual activity – a geologist in Book Y1, for example.

The second point that I need to make is associated with this and derives from my earlier discussion. As I have suggested, the G Book reader is, in general, textually apprenticed into public domain settings – shopping and other domestic practices, police work and so forth – rather than into mathematics. But, as I have shown, these public domain settings are recontextualisations of the practices to which they refer. The effect of these recontextualisations is to radically transform them, often in terms of the structural relations between participants – that is to say, recontextualising an exchange activity by importing it into a pedagogic one. The apprenticeship of the G Book readers is, in other words, to 'mythical practices'.

Conclusion

I have made a number of claims in this text. I have made claims about the way in which school mathematics privileges the esoteric domain and its highly discursive practices over public domain practices and distributes these to target groups of students on an 'ability' basis that has some grounding in images of social class. I have claimed that public domain practices are always recontextualised from non-mathematical activities and that the effect of recontextualisation is to transform them, to construct mythical practices. I have claimed that the greatest impact of recontextualisation occurs where a non-discursive domestic practice, such as shopping, is recontextualised by a discursive, abstract activity, such as mathematics, or where the practices of an exchange activity – again, such as shopping – are recontextualised by a pedagogic activity – again, such as school mathematics.

The most fundamental claim, I believe, is that which asserts that the meaning of a text is given in and by its referral to an interpretive framework. Here, I have been deploying my own interpretive framework in the analysis of school mathematical texts. We might say that I have recontextualised them as the public domain of my own theory.

Invitation to reflect

In terms of mediating this theory via this chapter, I am hampered in at least two respects. That is, in terms of space and in terms of the very diverse audience that I am attempting to address. To an extent, then, this chapter is itself a recontextualising of my own interpretive framework. Specifically, I have been able to provide only limited access to its esoteric domain; most of the chapter is clearly located in the public domain. In reading it, you will be referring it to your own interpretive framework. To the extent that your interpretive framework and mine differ, then our readings of this chapter will differ. This matters to you only to the extent that you are interpreting the relationship between author (me) and reader (you) as pedagogic. In this case, the reader is constructed as, in a sense, 'apprenticed' to the author's principles of interpretation. If the relationship is to be constructed as one of exchange, then you will appropriately privilege your own principles.

I will, therefore, ask you to reflect on this analogy between your reading of this text and your students' readings of your mathematical texts (in textbooks and in other forms in which you deliver mathematical knowledge). In reading the text, were you attempting to access the principles that I have used in constructing my readings of school mathematics texts? If so, to what extent and in what ways have

I assisted or hindered you? On the other hand, were you reading the text as an evaluator in terms of your own principles? If so, how is it possible for this text – any text read in this way – to tell you anything, at least anything fundamental, that you did not already know?

Further suggested readings

Dowling, P. (1998) *The Sociology Of Mathematics Education: Mathematical Myths/Pedagogic Texts*, London: Falmer Press. In his preface, Paul Ernest, the editor of the series of which this book is a part describes it in the following way

> This book develops and exemplifies a systematic approach to the analysis of texts which is extendable to a wide range of empirical settings within mathematical education, to education more generally, and to wider social settings ... [Its] primary focus is the semiotic analysis of mathematics texts. This is an important innovation which links the sociology of interpersonal and class relations with a central tool in social reproduction through education: the school mathematics text.

It has been put to me that this book presents quite a challenging read, especially for those who may be unfamiliar with the sociological and semiotic principles that it employs. I have not deliberately set out to obscure – we all would like to be read as widely as possible – but the complexity of the practices that I examine in the book has, I feel, demanded a level of complexity in the analysis.

References

Bernstein, B. (1977) *Class, Codes And Control: Towards a Theory Of Educational Transmissions. (Vol. 3), (Second Edition)*, London: Routledge and Kegan Paul.

Bourdieu, P. (1990) *The Logic Of Practice*, Cambridge: Polity Press.

Cooper, B. and Dunne, M. (2000) *Assessing Children's Mathematical Knowledge. Social Class, Sex and Problem-solving*, Buckingham: Open University Press.

Dowling, P. (1998) *The Sociology Of Mathematics Education: Mathematical Myths/Pedagogic Texts*, London: Falmer Press.

Hodge, R. and Kress, G. (1988) *Social Semiotics*, Cambridge: Polity Press.

Lave, J. (1988) *Cognition In Practice: Mind, Mathematics and Culture in Everyday Life*, Cambridge: Cambridge University Press.

Lave, J., Murtaugh, M. and de la Rocha, O. (1984) 'The dialectic of arithmetic in grocery shopping', in Rogoff, B. and Lave, J. (eds), *Everyday Cognition: Its Development in Social Context*, Cambridge, Mass.: Harvard University Press.

Luria, A. (1976) *Cognitive Development: Its Cultural and Social Foundations*, Cambridge, Mass.: Harvard University Press.

Nelson Mathematics (1992) *Toward Level 2*. Teachers' Resource File, Walton-on-Thames: Thomas Nelson and Sons.

Shuard, H. and Rothery, A. (1984) *Children Reading Mathematics*, London: John Murray.

13 Personal, spiritual, moral, social and cultural issues in teaching mathematics*

Jan Winter

Introducing the issue

Mathematics is sometimes thought of as a neutral, objective, pure subject in which the messiness and imperfections of society and humanity do not feature. In this chapter, I reject that view and look at the learning of mathematics in the context of the societies which created it and which use it. I consider ways in which pupils can be encouraged to use mathematics in contexts that help them to develop more than just decontextualised skills. I argue that as a teacher one has a wider duty to children's development and that mathematics can be a rich and real subject, which can help children to understand and to enjoy their world more fully.

Key questions

This chapter is based upon the following key questions:

- Why do we learn mathematics? What are the contexts in which we use it in our lives?
- How can mathematics help us to become fuller members of society?
- How can we develop spiritually through working on mathematics?
- Can mathematics reach parts of the pupil that other subjects do not reach?
- What can teachers do in classrooms to address these key questions?

Setting the scene

I feel that in mathematics education we are being pulled in two directions at the moment. On the one hand, we are being pulled in the direction of skills and knowledge, often in a very mechanistic way, and on the other hand we are being pulled in the direction of personal development, responsibility within society and fostering citizenship. I'll begin setting the scene by illustrating the first pull, with a quote from the National Numeracy Strategy.

---

* This chapter has been adapted – and considerably enlarged – from the opening address I gave to the Annual Conference of the Association of Teachers of Mathematics in April 2000. The transcript of that address can be found in *Mathematics Teaching* 172: 21–27.

Numeracy is a proficiency which involves confidence and competence with numbers and measures. It requires an understanding of the number system, a repertoire of computational skills and an inclination and ability to solve number problems in a variety of contexts. Numeracy also demands practical understanding of the ways in which information is gathered by counting and measuring, and is presented in graphs, diagrams, charts and tables.

(DfEE 1999b: 4)

It seems to me that within this framework we could interpret the demands of mathematics as being quite mechanistic. This is one side of the story. The other side is that of personal and moral issues, and those of citizenship in particular, and I will illustrate this with a quote from the DfEE Standards for the Award of Qualified Teacher Status that presents 'Standard B4k(xii)':

Those to be awarded Qualified Teacher Status must, when assessed, demon-strate that they use teaching methods which sustain the momentum of pupils' work and keep all pupils engaged through . . . exploiting opportunities to contribute to the quality of pupils' wider educational development, including their personal, spiritual, moral, social and cultural development.

(DfEE 1998: 13)

In this chapter, I explore how we can make these two potentially conflicting imperatives compatible and mutually supportive. What can we do in classrooms so that both can be achieved? What is important is how we do this within the framework for developing pupils' skills. Perhaps the best place to begin is to look at what the National Curriculum requires of us as teachers:

The examples below indicate specific ways in which the teaching of mathe-matics can contribute to learning across the curriculum.

Promoting pupils' spiritual, moral, social and cultural development through mathematics

For example mathematics provides opportunities to promote:

- *spiritual development*, through helping pupils obtain an insight into the infinite and through explaining the underlying mathematical principles behind some of the beautiful natural forms and patterns in the world around us
- *moral development*, helping pupils recognise how logical reasoning can be used to consider the consequences of particular decisions and choices and helping them learn the values of mathematical truth
- *social development*, through helping pupils work together productively on complex mathematical tasks and helping them to see that the result is often better than any of them could achieve separately
- *cultural development*, through helping pupils appreciate that mathe-matical thought contributes to the development of our culture and is becoming increasingly central to our highly technological future, and

through recognising that mathematicians from many cultures have contributed to the development of modern day mathematics.

(DfEE 1999a: 8)

I was pleased to see this in the new National Curriculum; we are encouraged to promote students' spiritual, social, moral and cultural development through mathematics – personal development seems to have got lost here though! I find it interesting, when working with student teachers over the years, that when we get to this issue the response is often, 'Oh that one can't be meant for us – that must be for R.E. teachers'. So perhaps it is important to look again at the requirements laid down in the government circular 4/98, for all (primary and secondary) courses of initial teacher education for those studying to be teachers of mathematics:

All courses must ensure that that pupils' progression in mathematics depends upon teaching which emphasises that mathematics

ii.   is intriguing and intellectually exciting and can be appreciated by pupils of a wide range of ability as an activity in itself.

(DfEE 1998:. 105)

Later on in the same government circular we find more specific detail, though it is only in secondary schools that b and c are deemed to be important.

[T]rainees must be taught the importance of engaging all pupils' interest in mathematics including:

a.   developing pupils' enthusiasm for mathematics;
b.   being aware of gender differences in attitude, performance and take-up of mathematics subjects post 16 and looking for effective ways of motivating all pupils so that they make satisfactory progress in mathematics;
c.   helping pupils to recognise the contributions of different civilizations to our knowledge and to value the work of mathematicians from different cultures.

(DfEE 1998: 108)

Although Circular 4/98 will not remain indefinitely as the often used assessment criteria for qualified teacher status, the spirit of this quote will remain enshrined in what many of us believe about teacher education.

So it is important for me in my role as a teacher educator to encourage new mathematics teachers to see the development of pupils' personal, spiritual, moral, social and cultural development through mathematics as part of the teacher's duty – and the inclusion of this chapter in this book has to be seen as part of that duty.

Defining the area

First I want to explore what is meant by personal, social, moral, cultural and spiritual development. I think this will vary between us since we will all have our own ideas of what we mean. John Costello, in his book *Teaching and Learning*

Mathematics 11–16 (Costello 1991), identified the following five issues related to culture and the teaching of mathematics – and these seem to address very much the same issues as I want to address here:

- Mathematics is generally taught in a narrow context, with little concern for its historical and cultural setting. Would the subject be enriched by such concern?
- Is the mathematics curriculum in Britain racist, in the sense of discriminating against the needs, values and best interests of certain ethnic groups?
- To what extent can and should school mathematics be used politically, to promote certain values or social developments; and is it being used in this way?
- It is a common complaint that school mathematics is remote from the familiar experiences of many pupils. Could it usefully be more closely based on the pupils' culture, however that might be identified?
- Is studying the mathematics of a particular culture or society a reasonable and productive way of understanding that society?

(Costello 1991: 158)

Reflecting on the issue . . .
Before going much further, try to set out your own responses to those five questions. Then on your own, before reading my interpretations of the five terms, decide what role you feel you have as a teacher of mathematics in pupils' *personal, social, moral, cultural* and *spiritual* development. Discuss your ideas with others and try to identify the differences in our views.

I will begin by outlining my own perspective on each of these aspects of a pupil's development.

Personal development

I take this to mean our development as independent, autonomous, powerful individuals with control over our own lives. Mathematics has an enormous part to play in this as adults who do not understand and feel confident in dealing with mathematics, both numerical and spatial ideas, are open to being controlled by those who do. So a key question for us is, how can we teach mathematics in such a way that learners have personal control over it and so that they can independently value their achievements?

Social development

By 'social development' I mean our pupils' development as members of society and I think there are two main aspects to consider. First there are the 'local' aspects of their development as social beings within the context of groups and their local environment. Second there are the 'global' aspects – developing pupils' understanding of their place in a global community and the complex network of issues and responsibilities this brings with it.

So, looking first at the local aspect, it is incumbent on teachers to consider how mathematics teaching can develop pupils' abilities to work in social settings, to learn with and from others, to give and take, to value and respect other. You may think of this as linked to personal development – of course it is – I'm distinguishing them for my purposes by considering social development as those aspects of a person's development which look outward from themselves and consider the needs of others and the interactions with others around them, rather than the personal aspects which consider looking inwards into a person's development.

Taking the second aspect, we also want to develop pupils' understanding of the social context they live in and to see how mathematics contributes to this. The teacher's task here is to show pupils how their use of mathematics helps them to understand and take part in society. We can be guilty of offering simplistic contexts that do not encourage questioning or analysis – so to avoid this we need to be clear how we can balance the need for straightforward starting points with the need to understand the complexity of society. I don't think I am just talking about the needs of older pupils here – I think this kind of orientation to the world around us begins very young. And I am also talking, vitally, about society on a global scale as well as closer to home.

Moral development

Here is an area where mathematics teachers have often feared to tread. We are not always very good at being political (with a small p) – it is the job of the geography teacher to talk about inequality in the world; the job of the English teacher to work with the gritty reality of drug abuse through literature; it is the job of the PSE teacher to deal with sexually transmitted diseases, smoking, teenage pregnancy . . . and so on. 'It's not me guv! I just teach Maths'. Yet all of these issues have both moral and mathematical components – why is the world like it is? At least by engaging with and understanding some of the statistics we could help pupils think through their own moral positions on some of these issues.

Cultural development

Perhaps this is the one on the list that mathematics teachers feel most comfortable with. It is reasonably easily to find a range of cultural contexts through which to teach mathematics. Islamic art, Rangoli patterns, mathematics in nature, all those old Greeks – they all provide ways of brightening up our teaching and producing some wall displays when OFSTED are coming. I am not criticising this – it is part of what makes mathematics accessible to all. But perhaps we can broaden our horizons to think about culture more widely so that we are more effectively inclusive for all our pupils.

Spiritual development

Well, here is the really knotty one! One's spirituality is very personal and, perhaps, inaccessible to anyone else. I would find it very difficult to articulate what I mean by my own spirituality and I certainly find many other people's interpretations quite incomprehensible. For me, spirituality is about making contact with the outer reaches of my understanding. It is about beauty, peace and wholeness – and I can find all of these in mathematics on a good day. I know for other people this might sound like post-hippy claptrap and I would possibly feel the same about their descriptions. So, in the mathematics classroom, perhaps all we can do is offer some experiences that are important to us and, even more crucially, help pupils engage in their own activities that inspire and excite them and perhaps give them some access to their own spirituality. Greg Morris, whom I once worked with as an Advisory Teacher, and who is now an LEA inspector in Milton Keynes, put it nicely for me:

> In mathematics lessons, students have the chance to meet something so large they cannot easily comprehend it, to be struck by something of such beauty and elegance they cannot fail to appreciate it, to appreciate something of such power that they are humbled by it.
>
> (Morris 1995: 36)

That is the spiritual in mathematics!

Reflecting on the issue . . .
What are the implications of taking this view of mathematics and the teacher's responsibilities? Consider discussing with a group of colleagues what difficulties these implications might present to teachers. Where might conflicts arise? How can the range of views that you identified previously be reconciled with pupils' entitlements as described in the DfEE documents quoted above?

Putting it into our teaching

Now I want to go on to offer some examples from my own work in each of these five areas. I've learned a lot from my involvement in the Association of Teachers of Mathematics (ATM) over the years, so many of the things I will offer will have come from ATM sources and materials. So, I'm not claiming originality – this is just a collection of ways of working and of ideas that have been of interest and importance to me over the years. As I have already suggested above, there is a lot of overlap between the five aspects, so my examples can perhaps be thought of as being in five overlapping sets – you can decide if they fit better into other sets than the ones I am going to put them in. The National Curriculum offers some advice on how teachers can promote pupils' spiritual, moral, social and cultural development through mathematics in the quote I used earlier (DfEE 1999a: 8). Unfortunately, the NC does not go further by giving detailed statements in the programmes of study. Hence mathematics teachers have to interpret for themselves how this can be achieved.

The cultural dimension in mathematics

First, a simple association of ideas that delighted me when I discovered it: Gelosia multiplication – my favourite method of multiple digit multiplication. Here's an example of the Gelosia method of multiplication; see how long it takes you to work out how to do it, and why it works.

I include the Gelosia method here as a cultural example of a method developed by Arab mathematicians around the thirteenth century and later introduced into Europe where it became known as multiplication '*per gelosia*' or 'by jealousy' – the name coming from the grid on which it is carried out. The grid resembles the wooden or metal lattices through which jealous husbands or wives could watch their spouses. The word '*jalousie*' for shutters is the French equivalent. The connection between the method and its Italian name enriched the idea for me. This is what seems important to me about teaching mathematics effectively – that connections, context, and background can give meaning to useful mathematical ideas. Whatever makes an idea memorable is useful in helping people learn.

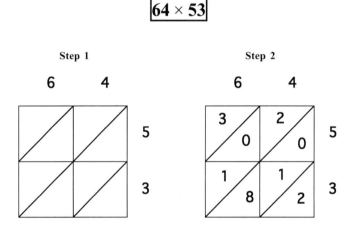

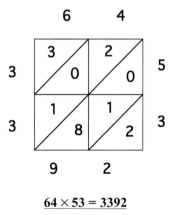

Figure 13.1   Example of Gelosia method of multiplication.

A fuller description and discussion of the 'jealousy' method of multiplication can be found in Georges Ifrah's book, *The Universal History of Numbers* (Ifrah 1998: 567–70) where he gives an extract from an Italian text from 1468. One cultural aspect that we can easily exploit is that of the global nature of mathematics itself and of its unifying properties – we all use numbers in much the same way. Here is a comment from Georges Ifrah's vast and fascinating book.

> I hope that the reader will recognise in this History that numbers, far from being tedious and dry, are charged with poetry, are the very vehicle for traditional myths and legends – and the finest witness to the cultural unity of the human race.
>
> (Ifrah 1998: xxiv)

The idea of mathematics as representing the unity of the human race is a very powerful one. We can find lots to divide us but we can see mathematics as something that unifies us. The history of mathematics, as well as just of number, is a rich source of stimuli through which ideas can be linked to the diversity of their sources. The white southern-English male did not, for the most part, discover or invent much mathematics!

I should also mention the issue of the recognition of pupils' own cultures, which is not a simple issue as, in many cases, most of the children we teach may have a substantially different culture from our own. I don't just mean in terms of their families' origins, but also simply the wide variety of cultures that exist even among people who may 'look the same'. This is a factor in many schools where older children particularly can resent the more materially privileged teachers who, they feel, come into communities and lecture children on conforming to irrelevant ideals. This is a tricky issue for all teachers, not just those of mathematics, and one that in my own teaching I have always felt to be a very difficult one. I will leave cultural ideas there for now because of all the five ideas, it is the one with most overlap with the others, so I will be revisiting it many times.

The moral dimension in mathematics

Given the power of mathematics as a controlling influence in all our lives, it seems to me really important that we do not teach it in a moral vacuum. My first example of this involves some research I have carried out with Rosamund Sutherland and others at Bristol, looking at case studies of teaching in the new post-16 Free Standing Mathematics Units. These are units were piloted for two years and were implemented fully in September 1999. They are intended to provide some mathematics learning in addition to and alongside students' other studies. For students who have been unsuccessful in mathematics when younger, the lower-level units can provide a fresh start while the higher-level units can provide students who are perhaps already taking A levels in other subjects with some mathematics to support these studies. They are wide ranging in their application and use. Students learn mathematics closely allied to contexts that are real and meaningful for them and use the mathematics to understand these contexts better.

The contexts may come from students' other studies – in GNVQs or A levels perhaps – or from the students' own experiences. For one group I met, being taught a Unit on 'Managing money', this meant a discussion of interest rates on loans. The issues that came out of this discussion were illuminating – some, as young adults who would soon be encountering student loans and the need to manage their own financial affairs, had very little idea of what borrowing money involved. Their experience was of their parents, in some cases, borrowing money from 'loan sharks'. They had no idea what different kinds of interest rates they might pay by borrowing money in different ways – a credit card, a shop finance deal, a mortgage or a bank loan for example. The Muslim students in the group were able to add their cultural perspective – that the reality of modern life means that Islamic restrictions on borrowing money and paying interest cannot be strictly adhered to and that often loans are made within the family or close community. These ideas are therefore not just about learning formulas to calculate interest and repayments, they are about considering the moral contexts of access to money in our society.

Another powerful example, also linked to money, comes in an idea from UNICEF called '*The Trading Game*' published in an NCC document on *Mathematics and Economic and Industrial Understanding at Key Stages 3 and 4* (NCC 1992: 22). It is a simulation game intended to help students understand economic relationships between richer and poorer countries. (The game is now published by Christian Aid.) There are other resources offering similar opportunities to help teachers situate pupils' mathematics learning into a moral dimension. Christian Aid, for example, produces 'The Debt Game' which aims:

- to help players understand how countries become trapped in debt
- to explore some outcomes of the operations of major economic powers and financial institutions
- to enable players to understand that economic structures are not inflexible and can be changed to become more just

(Christian Aid 1999: 2)

Such resources are more than just 'add-on' luxuries to an already overcrowded curriculum; issues such as these can be found in 'official' curriculum guidance documents. Take for example the DfEE document on *Developing a global dimension in the school curriculum* (DfEE 2000), which describes its purpose as:

. . . to show how a global dimension can be incorporated into both the curriculum and the wider life of the school. This means that the content of what is taught is informed by international and global matters, so preparing pupils to live their lives in a global society. It means addressing such issues as sustainable development, interdependence and social justice at both the local and global level.

(DfEE 2000: 1)

More specifically, it offers guidance on how this might be interpreted within the mathematics curriculum at each key stage.

Key Stage 1:   pupils 'can learn to appreciate the mathematical ingenuity of other cultures' (p. 4).

Key Stage 2:   pupils 'can learn what different cultures have contributed to the development and application of mathematics' (p. 6).

Key Stages 3–4: pupils can 'apply their mathematical skills to interpreting statistics relevant to international current affairs such as international debt and fair trade' (p. 10).

While we might want to criticise the limitations of the suggestions made here – I believe we can be considerably more imaginative in applying mathematics to such local and global contexts – we cannot overlook the significance of the issue. Of course, there are many other contexts in mathematics through which we can, and I believe, should, challenge pupils to understand inequality and injustice. Teachers of other subjects do this: so why do we often retreat into drawing scatter graphs of height against shoe size when we could use GDP against the number of doctors per thousand of the population? I would argue that we should be looking for wider, richer and more significant data sets to use with pupils so that we enrich their moral and cultural development as well as teaching them those statistical skills. Of course, relevance to pupils is still important so maybe we could make more use of the masses of local data now available on the Internet to understand more about our own society too. (I could of course mention the National Lottery at this point – a very complex and subtle example that I know is used in many classrooms.)

On the international level there are many sources of ideas and activities – Sharanjeet Shan and Peter Bailey's book, *Multiple Factors. Classroom Mathematics for Equality and Justice* (1991) and the multiple-authored *Multicultural Mathematics* (Nelson *et al.* 1993) being two very rich sources.

Another example related to shape and space that incorporates wider moral issues is a map from the Open University Press called *The Third World Atlas* (Thomas 1994). This shows, amongst a host of alternative representations and projections other than Mercator's and Peter's Projections, in the colouring and shading of a country, per capita income and, in the area occupied, its population. Looking at the sheer size of the low-income economies we can see in this map a graphic illustration of the number of people in the world living in poverty. (Low income on this map is defined as below $545 per capita per annum.) Such a resource can be a valuable tool in the mathematics classroom for raising issues of data representation.

The spiritual dimension in mathematics

One important aspect of the development of one's spirituality is the way it helps one locate one's place in the world. Hence this section will be a little more personal than others, since I am responding in a personal way. One aspect of mathematics that has always been really important to me personally is that of its beauty, both visually and structurally. Many mathematicians have written about this over the years. Here is a quote from a novel you may have come across when it was published in 2000. The publisher's hype on its launch included the offer of a million dollars to anyone who could solve Goldbach's conjecture – it's worth reading the book before settling down to try to do this one weekend! While I don't exactly share this view of mathematics I think it illustrates what many mathematicians feel about something inside mathematics which is inherently beautiful and which is a real driving force for some mathematicians.

> 'Mathematicians find the same enjoyment in their studies that chess players find in chess. In fact, the psychological make-up of the true mathematician is closer to that of the poet or the musical composer, in other words of someone concerned with the creation of Beauty and the search for Harmony and Perfection. He is the polar opposite of the practical man, the engineer, the politician or the . . .' – he paused for a moment seeking something even more abhorred in his scale of values – '. . . indeed, the businessman.'
>
> (Doxiadis 2000: 29)

Given the massive expansion of mathematics in the last century I think the following quote from the mathematician Arthur Cayley is also interesting, and is a nice way of thinking about the landscape of mathematics.

> It is difficult to give an idea of the vast extent of modern mathematics. The word 'extent' is not the right one: I mean extent crowded with beautiful detail – not an extent of mere uniformity such as an objectless plain, but a tract of beautiful country to be rambled through and studied in every detail of hillside and valley, stream, rock, wood and flower. But, as for everything else, so for mathematical beauty – beauty can be perceived but not explained.
>
> (Cayley 1883, quoted in Ifrah 1998: 598)

If there was a 'vast extent' in 1883 it is interesting to think how he would see mathematics now. So if, as I said earlier, spirituality is to do with beauty, what can some of the mathematical images we see offer to us as teachers? There are very many that I could have chosen to show you at this point and I want to show a few which make the link for me between mathematics and aesthetics or beauty.

The artist Maurits Cornelis Escher can also provide us with a rich source of mathematics, beauty and wonder. Perhaps what we can do with Escher is to use the images to help pupils who may think of themselves as artists also to recognise that they can also think of themselves as mathematicians (and not just vice versa). Escher's 'Metamorphosis' (see Escher 1990; Hofstadter 1979: 14) is intriguing as he moves from tessellating hexagons to tessellating squares. How does he make that transition?

> Infinity plays a large role in many of Escher's drawings. Copies of one single theme often fit into each other, forming visual analogues to the canons of Bach. Several such patterns can be seen in Escher's famous print *Metamorphosis*.
>
> (Hofstadter 1979: 15)

So there is a whole range of 'pretty things' to use to demonstrate the beauty – and the spirit – of mathematics. How might we use them in our teaching? Here we might have to think quite carefully about what we might be teaching pupils if we use such images in our teaching – aesthetic appreciation? Colouring in? I believe that both of these have a place in learning in their own right – and that a teacher can develop activities which go way beyond these starting points. I wonder if the constant emphasis on pace, important as this is, can cut out thinking time which a little bit of 'colouring in' might make time for again. Mathematics is creative and artistic for me – and gives spiritual meaning to my life.

Which leaves me with personal and social development so far largely untouched although there are aspects of social development at the macro scale present in activities such as the trading game – a reminder of the overlap in these areas?

Working on wonder and wondering

This section is adapted from Watson (1999)
It is quite likely that a sense of adolescence as a particular phase of development, with its own concerns and preoccupations, will be quite strong amongst many new teachers, and passages from *Mathematics Curriculum 5 to 16* (HMSO 1985) give some shape and language to this sense, in relation to mathematics teaching. This also serves to show (a) that this sensitivity is worthy and important and (b) that those in 'authority' in education need not always speak with the current predominant discourse of targets, levels and standardisation. The following two paragraphs give a flavour of this:

> There is a fascination about mathematics itself . . . which it is possible to develop to some degree in most if not all pupils. This fascination will not, of course, be the same for all pupils but most aspects, if considered within a suitable context and at an appropriate level, can have such appeal.
>
> (HMSO 1985: 3)

> The aim should be to show mathematics as a process, as a creative activity in which pupils become fully involved, and not as an imposed body of knowledge immune to any change or development.
>
> (HMSO 1985: 4)

It is important to think seriously about such high-status, authoritative support for valuing students' sensitivities, because when learners find themselves voicing opinions which contradict current orthodoxy, they may need more than the reassurance of a teacher or tutor to believe their views are worthwhile – yet such cases can leave teachers in conflict between the way they want to teach and the pressures of covering syllabi.

Steven Downes has written an interesting article on 'Mathematics and collective worship' (Downes 1997), which can help teachers see that people approach the spiritual from different positions and different prior knowledge. The article was about a 'maths week' in a school that used the requirement for collective worship as a framework within which pupils considered mathematical questions arising from contexts such as rainforest destruction, malnutrition, trading inequities and clean water. A question arises in such cases of exactly what vision of mathematics is being explored. It can too often be limited to calculations of varying complexity and data-handling, and such activities based upon a specially structured piece of work might not be seen as part of the usual curriculum.

One does not have to leave a consideration of the spiritual in mathematics teaching at the level of one-off activities, or to using collective worship as a framework for dealing with socially responsible mathematics, nor to leave it to those who have randomly dipped into the Charis materials written by members of the Association of Christian Teachers (Shortt *et al.* 1996). The idea that spirituality could link mathematics with a liberal Christian concern with charity and social justice does not appear to do justice to the human sensitivities that might drive us fundamentally to seek for explanations of the world in terms of religion, philosophy, science and mathematics. I want to link spirituality with our propensity to regard the world with wonder, and to follow this with wondering.

In order to address the spiritual dimension you might care to consider what aspects of mathematics filled you with awe and wonder. Might it be 'infinity' or some other wide-ranging aspect of the subject? There is an article by Nitsa Movshovits-Hadar in which she writes about using surprise in her teaching by, for example, introducing Pythagoras' theorem as a surprising special case of adding the squares on the sides of general triangles (1988). Consider what this might mean for the teaching of mathematics and whether ordinary, unsurprising, lessons and unsurprising work would encourage learning.

> The tie between wonder and learning is clear in the moment when after long confusion and study you suddenly say, 'Now I get it!' Plato ... uses mathematics because the moment of 'getting it' is extremely clear in mathematics.
>
> (Fisher 1998: 21)

Again, think about what that might mean for mathematics lessons, and of the meaning and purpose of the somewhat traditionally fragmented 'step-by-step' approach to mathematics teaching. Steps need not be devised which smooth the path to a solution (Wigley 1992). Indeed, such small steps may not result in learning at all. Instead, steps could be devised which offered opportunities for wonder and wondering.

Try the following activity for yourself, with some colleagues and with some of your pupils.

Reflecting on the issue . . .
Mark a point P inside a circle of radius 8 cm. fairly close to the edge. Fold and crease the circle so that the circumference just touches the point, draw the crease in pencil. Fold at different places and repeat the creasing and drawing procedure several times. What happens?

This activity can often cause such surprise that one is confronted with cries of delight that can potentially attract others in a teaching group to the activity.

Before long, others might be tempted to begin to explore it for themselves; working on paper, using dynamic geometry software; there are often several conjectures around about the position of the foci and directrices of the resulting figure. The result might be described as 'wonderful', and in this case, I suggest, wonder can obviously be an effective motivator for some people to work in a sustained way on the situation, raise new questions, look for ways to explain their insights to others, and even attempt to communicate their enthusiasm to others.

After working with that activity, one might actually reconsider what aspects of the mathematics curriculum one *now* felt could be taught through generating a sense of wonder among pupils. Of course, not every pupil will respond similarly, nevertheless it is appropriate to construct situations that *might* engender wonder. Support from authority, which is important, comes again from HMSO:

> The spark may come from a feeling for order, the appreciation of pattern, an interesting relationship, the power of a formula, the simplicity of a generalisation, a curious or unexpected result, the conciseness of an abstraction, the aesthetic appeal of mathematical designs or models in two or three dimensions, or the elegance of a proof.

> (HMSO 1985: 4)

Reading this extract, one gets a heightened sense of the beauty and wonder that lies possibly dormant in much of our 'bread-and-butter' mathematics. The extract both legitimates and encourages the recognition of personal 'sparks' which are often more wide-ranging and exciting; far more emerges than the obvious choice of 'infinity'. Consider for example the following as examples of possible 'sparks' of wonder:

- π
- $\sin^2 + \cos^2 = 1$
- circle theorems
- internal and external angles of polygons
- properties of graphs
- trigonometry
- sum of arithmetic series
- iterative solutions
- sequences
- probability theorems
- the uncertainty of probability
- difference between two squares
- tessellations
- binomial expansion
- symmetry
- Pythagoras' theorem
- The formula: $e^{i\pi} + 1 = 0$ that links arguably the five most basic constants in mathematics

... and so on. In fact pretty soon it becomes a problem knowing when to stop. The real tasks for mathematics teachers here is to turn these sparks of wonder into the flames of learning.

Personal and social development

What I want to address here are issues of social development at the personal level – learning to co-operate and work with others, learn from others and share ideas. Pupils' personal development is something that we have to be aware of in our classrooms all the time. Are we supporting them in growing into happy, motivated and successful people? I do think we have a duty to do this and it does not just come from featuring in the school league tables as one of the percentage who gained level 4 at age 11 or 5 or more A* to C grades at age 16. Some things, such as a good education for life, are considerably more important than that.

Personal development also comes from feeling valued; feeling as though you have something worth saying and that others will listen. I've already referred to assessment in this context and increasingly believe that self-assessment is the only real answer to the teacher dependency I mentioned earlier on. By this I don't mean marking your own book! I mean pupils having a real understanding of what the objectives are for a piece of work and, through open dialogue between teacher and class, being enabled to understand the extent to which those objectives have been met and how to get closer to achieving them.

So, to conclude – are these ways of thinking about mathematics teaching just as an optional extra; as little more than something for the end of term? (I do not know whether to be depressed or annoyed when I hear people talking about doing things that are fun at the end of term!) On the contrary, I believe that we cannot teach children to be numerate if we do not pay attention to the broader experience of their learning. The mathematical skills that are so highly prized are meaningless if a pupil does not have the personal, social and moral education to make sense of the world and thus know when to use them. So, at all levels, mathematics and real life are all part of the whole experience of children and it is up to us to find ways of making our teaching of mathematics reflect that.

Invitation to reflect

Finally I'm going to ask you to think about this in terms of your own practice. Consider your own experiences so far. What have you been doing that has contributed to the personal, social, spiritual, moral and cultural aspects of your pupils' development? What activities and ways of working have you used? How might you develop the features you identify so they can contribute more directly to broadening pupils' experiences? Consider making notes of your ideas both to keep as reference and to share with others.

Further suggested reading

Collins, J. (1992) *Maths and the Tropical Rainforests, Set 1* and *Set 2*, London: Pearson Publishing. This consists of two sets of classroom resources, this time focused on the environment and sustainability.

Westwell, J. (1999) 'Getting the whole picture', in Johnston-Wilder, S., Johnston-Wilder, P., Pimm, D. and Westwell, J. (eds), *Learning to Teach Mathematics in the Secondary School. A Companion to School Experience*, London: Routledge, pp. 187–200. This chapter is from the companion series to this book, and it discusses the contribution teachers of mathematics can make to the development of the whole child through the role of mathematics in the whole curriculum.

Wright, P. (ed.) (1999) *The Maths and Human Rights Resource Book*, London: Amnesty International. It is often difficult finding sources of ideas, and more specifically actual photocopiable classroom resources and activities. This book consists of thirty ready-to-use activities at key stages 3 and 4. Not only does it consist of classroom activities, but it also has Teachers' Notes, lists of other resources and a simplified text of the 320 Articles of the United Nations Declaration of Human Rights. (www.amnesty.org.uk)

Some resources

The following resources all offer potentially useful ideas and suggestions for teachers wishing to enhance the areas of pupils' development discussed in this chapter.

Bell, R. and Cornelius, M. (1988) *Board Games from Around the World*, Cambridge: Cambridge University Press.

Howse, J. (1976) *Maths or Magic: Simple Vedic Arithmetic Methods*, London: Watkins.

Nelson, D., Joseph, G. G. and Williams, J. (1993) *Multicultural Mathematics*, Oxford: Oxford University Press.

Nock, D., Riding, M. and White, N. (1988) *Mathematics for All*, Trowbridge: Wiltshire Education Authority.

Shan, S. and Bailey, P. (1991) *Multiple Factors*, Stoke-on-Trent: Trentham Books.

Shortt, J. (ed.) (1996) *Charis Mathematics, Units 1 to 19, Age Range 11–16+*, St Albans: Association of Christian Teachers.

V and A Education (1996) *Teaching Maths through Islamic Art*, London: Victoria and Albert Museum.

Zaslavsky, C. (1973) *Africa Counts*, New York: Lawrence Hill Books.

References

Christian Aid (1999) *The Debt Game*, London: Christian Aid (www.christian-aid.org.uk).

Costello, J. (1991) *Teaching and Learning Mathematics 11–16*, London: Routledge.

DfEE (1998) *Teaching: High Status, High Standards. Requirements for Courses of Initial Teacher Training. Circular 4/98*, London: Department for Education and Employment.

DfEE (1999a) *Mathematics. The National Curriculum for England. Key Stages 1–4*, London: Department for Education and Employment/Qualifications and Curriculums Authority.

DfEE (1999b) *The National Numeracy Strategy. Framework for Teaching Mathematics from Reception to Year 6*, London: Department for Education and Employment.

DfEE (2000) *Developing a Global Dimension in the School Curriculum*, London: Department for Education and Employment.

Downes, S. (1997) 'Mathematics and collective worship', *Mathematics Teaching* 159, centre insert.

Doxiadis, A. (2000) *Uncle Petros and Goldbach's Conjecture*, London: Faber and Faber.

Escher, M. C. (1990) *The Graphic Work*, Berlin: Benedict Taschen.

Fisher, P. (1998) *Wonder, the Rainbow and the Aesthetics of Rare Experiences*, Cambridge, Mass.: Harvard University Press.

Hofstadter, D. (1979) *Gödel, Escher and Bach: An Eternal Golden Braid. A Metaphorical Fugue on Minds and Machines in the Spirit of Lewis Carroll*, London: Penguin Books.

HMSO (1985) *Mathematics from 5–16*, London: Her Majesty's Stationery Office.

Ifrah, G. (1998) *The Universal History of Numbers*, London: Harvill.

Morris, G. (1995) 'Developing the spiritual in mathematics', *Mathematics Teaching* 153, 36–7.

Movshovitz-Hadar, N. (1988) 'School mathematics theorems – an endless source of surprise', *For the Learning of Mathematics* (8)3, 34–40.

National Curriculum Council (1992) *Mathematics and Economic and Industrial Understanding at Key Stages 3 and 4*, London: NCC.

Nelson, D., Joseph, G. and Williams, J. (1993) *Multicultural Mathematics*, Oxford: Oxford University Press.

Shan, S. and Bailey, P. (1991) *Multiple Factors: Classroom Mathematics for Equality and Justice*, Stoke-on-Trent: Trentham Books.

Thomas, A. (1994) *Third World Atlas*, Milton Keynes: Open University Press.

Watson, A. (1999) 'Working on wonder and wondering: making sense of the spiritual in mathematics teaching', *Mathematics Education Review* 11 (November 1999), 25–34.

Wigley, A. (1992) 'Models for teaching mathematics', *Mathematics Teaching* 141, 4–7.

Part IV

Issues in the assessment of mathematics

14 Making judgements about pupils' mathematics

Anne Watson

Introducing the issue

As a teacher one frequently makes judgements about pupils for all kinds of reasons during mathematics teaching. For example, you have to decide whether pupils are responding appropriately to your teaching; who needs more support; who would benefit from some more challenging work; how you could respond to similar questions from different pupils. You are also expected to keep some kind of record of individual pupils' achievements arising from normal classroom work, as well as from tests and other formal assessment activities.

This chapter is not about practical ways in which this might be done, but questions whether teachers, or anyone else, can make fair judgements about pupils' learning. In looking at how some experienced teachers in primary and secondary schools make judgements, I shall identify how interpretation, and therefore possible bias, are inevitable aspects of the processes. My view is that if teachers are not aware of the possible flaws in their judgements, some pupils may be disadvantaged by being inappropriately taught within the classroom. Unfortunately, because teachers' informal judgements can be incorporated into formal and summative assessments, unfairness, which arises quite naturally in the classroom, can contribute to major decisions such as setting, examination entry and future educational opportunities, and therefore should be professionally scrutinised. I have found that these potential sources of social injustice are not usually discussed systematically in the context of teacher assessment. Nevertheless, in a situation in which teacher assessment is, for very good reasons, an integral part of the education system, it is possible to suggest ways in which teachers, co-ordinators and subject departments might ensure that they are as fair as possible in their judgements.

Key Questions

I have several questions in mind for this chapter:

- What are the purposes of teacher assessments?
- How do teachers make judgements about their pupils' mathematics?
- What possible issues about fairness arise in practice?

- What is the potential for bias in teachers' judgements?
- How is unfairness avoided in existing practices?
- What further professional practices might help teachers ensure they make just decisions?

In order to more fully engage with the ideas I discuss in this chapter, you might care to consider some of the judgements you make about pupils – how you come to these judgements and what influences your judgements.

The purposes of teachers' assessments of pupils' mathematics

In order to teach anyone anything, it is necessary to have some idea of the pupils you are going to teach. You may wish to know the number of pupils of the class, their ages, their behaviour and motivation, what the aim of your teaching ought to be, their past experience of teachers and teaching styles and so on. This information will help you build a picture of possible social and curricular aspects of the lessons you will teach. You plan lessons accordingly, but it is likely that your main aim in the early lessons is to 'get to know' the pupils. What is it you need to know, and how are you going to find it out?

Many teachers start teaching a new group with activities specifically designed to 'get to know' something about the learners' mathematics. These can vary from written tests of various kinds to open-ended explorations of mathematical or everyday situations. The justification for using written tests is generally expressed in terms of finding out what pupils already know; the justification for asking learners to explore situations is generally to find out something about their mathematical thinking.

The belief that it is possible and desirable to find out what pupils already know is found throughout educational literature. David Ausubel, for example, says 'The most important single factor influencing learning is what the learner already knows. Ascertain this and teach him accordingly' (Ausubel 1968: 36).

This same belief is enshrined in the assessment and testing regime relating to the UK National Curriculum; that it is possible to find out what someone knows, design teaching to build on that, and make definitive statements about states of knowledge. Learning, after all, usually involves adjustments and additions to what has been experienced previously.

However, the assumption that it is possible to find out what a learner knows is one I would question. The teacher can never see with certainty what goes on in the pupils' minds. Nevertheless Derek Blease, a teacher-educator, pointed out in 1983:

> Teachers are led to believe, through their professional training, that they are able to make accurate judgements about children. They occupy a status in society whereby it is thought legitimate for them to make such judgements.
>
> (Blease 1983: 124)

Since he wrote this, teachers' judgements have been further legitimised by being included in the statutory assessment procedures which mark a pupils' progress through school at ages 7, 11, 14 and 16. There may be some distance between finding out about the pupils in your classes in order to teach them effectively, and making summative statements about their mathematical achievements.

The Standards for Qualified Teacher Status (DfEE 1998) reflect the prevailing view of assessment at the time of writing. They describe the setting of targets for pupils' learning within the aims of the National Curriculum, assessing whether those targets are met, monitoring difficulties, strengths and weaknesses and using this information in planning for future teaching. In addition, the teacher keeps records of achievements, records pupils' progress, reports to parents and eventually ascribes levels of attainment to each pupil. This technical view of teaching as a set of procedures to make observable outcomes match curriculum aims, omits many aspects of teaching and learning. It leaves out the individuality of pupils, the lack of predictability about the outcomes of any teaching situation, and the social and emotional issues surrounding children, learning and schooling. These aspects are hard to predict and measure, and even harder to incorporate into statements about pupils' understanding of mathematics.

The temptation is to reject this technical view and say that teaching and learning are human activities, and human beings, on the whole, do not fit neatly into such procedures. The technical view does, however, fit the market-place philosophy of public life introduced formally into the UK during the 1980s and 1990s. This philosophy substituted categorising, labelling, scrutinising, shaming and rewarding for more interpretative, holistic, flexible and social approaches to human endeavour (Ball 1997; Brown 1993). In education, raw measures of national test scores and examination passes were introduced to compare schools to schools, teachers to teachers, and could also be used to compare pupil to pupil. The imposition of targets that do not take starting conditions into account causes resentment in the teaching profession. The crudity of test score comparisons masks real differences between resourcing, class and other issues which affect teachers' work and makes those who work in socially fractured areas feel blamed for matters over which they have no control. Adherents to the market-place view may see few problems in a technical approach to teaching. It may seem obvious to outsiders that all the teacher has to do is teach a certain way, and pupils will learn. To experienced educators this is a naïve approach that could lead to the alienation of many pupils. These factors, and others, can lead to a wholesale rejection of the technical view of teaching and learning among educators.

However, I am going to argue that a technical approach to assessment can make some sense viewed from a perspective of social justice. In order to assess pupils' mathematics fairly all we can use as evidence is what we can see, hear and read; we cannot and should not imagine we can have access to others' minds except by inference. The temptation to substitute what a teacher thinks about a pupil for what can be seen in written and oral evidence should, perhaps, be resisted. Instead, the best we can do is to interpret the evidence carefully and professionally and use it to inform teaching and grade-giving. In this sense, the technical business of assessing formal learning outcomes becomes a useful and honest part of a more holistic approach to developing teaching and trying to be fair about the demands of grade-giving.

A technical approach also provides the shared, common framework for teaching within which learning, as making sense of experiences, will take place. This framework also enables teachers to generate specific, if incomplete, information about progress towards external, socially empowering, standards that can be fed back to the learner. Such frameworks go some way towards providing educational entitlement.

A further point to consider is that teachers see themselves as having certain expectations of pupils. They make inferences about learning from their observations of pupils' behaviour and the mathematics they can see, hear and read. They report being surprised or not by pupils' achievements. The language of 'expectation' and 'observation', used in a humanistic view of education, is not so very different from the language of 'targets' and 'assessment outcomes' used in a technical view.

For these reasons, I argue, it is unrealistic to reject totally a technical view of education. Rather, it could be recognised as extant in many teaching and assessment practices and adapted critically for more humanistic use.

Reflecting on the issue . . .
It may be useful for you to consider here how far you regard teaching, learning and assessment as technical matters and how much personal interpretation, by you, is involved in the way you teach.

In many countries as well as the UK it is now the case that assessment of pupils' mathematics is a combination of teachers' assessments and externally produced written tests of various kinds. I am not going to discuss testing here, except to point out that the disadvantaging of some pupils by being assessed solely on written timed tests has been well known for some time. Caroline Gipps and Patricia Murphy (1994) summarise the main sources of unfairness as being the artificiality and stress of the testing context; language difficulties in test questions; some questions appealing more to one gender than another, or excluding people from certain social backgrounds, and so on. The incorporation of teachers' judgements in statutory assessment has been seen as a way to redress imbalances introduced in written timed tests. Some of the reasons given are that teachers' own judgements can:

- assess application of knowledge, as this is more relevant to life and work than reproducing it in an examination;
- assess pupils' performance in longer, more complex tasks than can be assessed in traditional tests;
- value communication of mathematics in a variety of forms, rather than limiting it to written answers;
- alleviate the effects of bias in written tests by providing other assessment environments;
- value the processes and the dynamics of doing mathematics explicitly, perhaps in contexts;
- assess pupils' learning over time, not just a pressured performance of specially prepared skills.

Since teachers will generally teach in ways that enable pupils to do well in assessments, the form of the assessment will affect the way pupils are taught. Hence, one way to ensure pupils are taught to adapt and apply mathematics is to include assessment of those abilities in the assessment system. Another reason for requiring different forms of assessment is to enable more pupils to enjoy and feel confident in mathematics and thus continue to study it with some interest and effort, acquiring more skills than if they had been bored and uninterested. All of these are arguments used by those who believe education to be about providing a suitably qualified, flexible, future workforce.

An argument which might be put forward by mathematicians is that the kind of mathematics which can be shown in timed written tests is a subset of the wider meaning of mathematics, and a travesty of how mathematics is really 'done' by mathematicians and by others who use mathematics in their adulthood. Assessment formats that encourage attention to doing and exploring mathematics are therefore valued alongside traditional methods.

The practices of teacher assessment and teacher judgement

So how do teachers do the job of assessing? I will look at this question on two levels: first, how they assess and monitor their pupils' learning and, second, how they contribute to the statutory assessment requirements.

The first level arises from the kind of assessment reflective teachers have always done within their classrooms to help them make decisions about what and how to teach: ongoing, day-to-day judgements about pupils, either as a group or individually, which inform their planning. I call these 'teacher judgements' in order to differentiate them from the word 'assessment' which has more formal connotations.

It is important to start by looking at teacher judgements because they determine how individual pupils are taught, what is expected of them, how their work is interpreted and even what they are taught. Judgements, therefore, contribute to assessments by being used to decide what targets the pupil should aim to reach and to develop the expectations the teacher has of that pupil. By using these judgements to contribute to decisions about which set pupils should be in for mathematics, they are also used to control access to the curriculum, differentiated access being given to different pupils. Further, judgements contribute to assessments by providing a picture for the teacher of the pupil as a mathematician in general terms. Research in social psychology, in education, and in mathematics education has shown that teachers tend to retain early impressions they have of pupils, even in the light of later contradictory evidence (McIntyre *et al.* 1966; Watson 1998). I shall return to this point later, but it shows how important informal judgements are in possibly skewing the way the teacher sees the pupils' subsequent work.

In my own research I found that teachers make their judgements by combining their observations of pupils with their views of mathematics and their existing knowledge of the child (Watson 1998). Hence the judgement is cumulative, previous judgements contributing to how the teacher currently sees the pupil. Observations include oral interactions, written work, actions which relate to mathematics, and unprompted, unexpected use of a concept in another context.

These are interpreted by the teacher to indicate mathematical knowledge of some kind. At first this may seem self-evident, but each of these components of judgement is problematic in some way.

Interpretation and oral interactions

Evidence from oral interactions, though highly valued by all the teachers, is time-consuming to organise. Language difficulties, diffidence or fear might prevent some pupils from showing the best they can do orally, also it is rare to overhear useful remarks in a busy classroom, although such remarks often give insight into a pupil's thinking before they are able to record what they think on paper. Over-reliance on oral interaction for judgements may leave the teacher vulnerable to criticism, since there is no hard evidence to support the teacher's claims.

However, many teachers use oral interactions to make sure a child understands or to find out what led to errors in written work; some are unwilling to believe pupils understand unless they explain 'in their own words'. But teachers' reported reliance on oral work can be seen critically in the light of Basil Bernstein's work (for example, Bernstein 1971). He describes how middle-class pupils are at an advantage in school because the kind of elaborated codes of language on which school depends may be what they are used to at home. Working-class pupils, however, are expected to communicate at school in a way very unlike the restricted codes of language used at home. (Robyn Zevenbergen discusses this issue in more detail in her chapter.) This theory relies on a very stereotyped view of language use outside school, yet it does prompt a closer look at language forms in mathematics classrooms. For example, 'explain how you did something', a common requirement in teacher–pupil discourse, is a rare form of speech outside school in any social grouping. Hence reliance on pupils' ability to use acceptable forms of language, in terms of the teachers' mathematical understanding, expects a keen awareness of different ways to talk as well as mathematical ability. (Candia Morgan discusses a similar phenomenon in her chapter.)

Reflecting on the issue . . .
It might be useful to review the kinds of questions you ask pupils, and how you expect them to answer, and to examine how language use in your classroom might make participation easier for some and harder for others.

Interpretation and written work

Written work is regarded as a reliable form of evidence which can be held up to scrutiny. Many teachers want more than 'right answers' in order to be convinced that pupils understand a topic. Ideally, written work would be supplemented with oral explanations as well. However, it is also recognised that many pupils have considerable difficulty in recording in writing what they could do mentally or practically. Sometimes they just omit anything they do not consider of value, although it may reveal much about thinking processes to an alert teacher

(MacNamara and Roper 1992). Any assessment based on written work has to be seen in the light of Candia Morgan's research (Morgan 1998 and her chapter in this volume). She shows that well-meaning, experienced teachers in a collegial discussion can reach widely differing interpretations of the mathematics represented by written work.

Interpretation of actions

Observed actions provide no permanent record of achievement. Organising observation in a busy classroom is difficult but such observations can reveal that the pupil is using particular methods, such as counting instead of using number bonds. Observation of actions depends in part on the teachers' notions of how mathematical activity *might* be observable. Sometimes this is clear, such as when one sees a pupil use a ruler correctly and read a measurement. At other times it has to be interpreted, such as when a pupil is trying to make a cube from six squares and may appear to be doing it in an obscure way, but nevertheless succeeds. At other times, there is little to interpret; the pupil who is gazing motionless at a problem may or may not be thinking about it, and the thought may or may not be productive. On the other hand, avid writing may not indicate that anything useful is being done.

How the teacher interprets the actions can be influenced by many factors. In the examples just given interpretation depends on what the teacher expects to see, and on what the teacher expects from the particular pupil and from pupils in general. Interpretation also depends on what is noted by the teacher and this, in turn, depends on the teacher's existing impressions of pupils' 'ability'. Teachers are assailed by information in the classroom from all sides and rarely have the time to make considered decisions in the moment. Derek Blease warned about this twenty years ago: 'In the heat of the moment they may more readily accept their own first impressions or the judgements of others without question – myth becomes reality' (Blease 1983: 124).

Unprompted use

Unprompted and unexpected use of mathematics is seen as a very strong form of evidence of knowledge, but is difficult for teachers to plan; teachers like some sort of time gap between teaching a topic and seeing unprompted use, the theory being that the use will spring from an internalised understanding of a concept rather than short-term memory alone. In order to encourage unexpected use, teachers need to be providing open, exploratory situations and to be open-minded about the approaches pupils take. Unfortunately this contradicts the current target/ outcome view of teaching, and the philosophy of aims and assessment under which teachers are inspected, and the hierarchical progress implied in the National Curriculum. Nevertheless teachers may find ways to notice, recognise and record when unexpected things happen in their classrooms.

Issues arising from practice

The evidence which teachers use to reach their judgements, described above, is haphazard. In addition, the process of forming a judgement from it involves much interpretation. I shall now describe some features of one pupil's work and show that the teacher, and I as researcher, both acting in good faith, interpreted her behaviour to give rather different views of her mathematics.

Sandra: a case study

I sat in on one lesson a week for the first term during which the teacher, Andy, taught Sandra. In those lessons I watched Sandra in much more detail than the teacher could possibly have done, so had more information about behaviour and actions than the teacher did. For oral evidence, Andy's and my experiences overlapped, but not completely, as we both heard her contributions to whole class discussions, but there were some other remarks I could not hear, such as those to Andy, and some he could not hear, such as those to her neighbour. For written work we both had access to the same evidence although sometimes I knew more about what had been achieved but not written down, or what had led to the written work. We discussed the pictures we were forming of Sandra's work throughout the term.

Andy, while being vaguely aware that Sandra sometimes altered the written answers of the mental arithmetic tests he gave in class, was not aware of the extent of the alterations and had a view that she was mainly good at mental arithmetic. This view came from her enthusiasm about giving some answers, she would call out and wave her hand energetically in the air, and from the fact that they were largely correct. My view was that Sandra wanted to appear to be good but was making and hiding errors regularly. Nearly all of her enthusiastic contributions to class arose from work done at home or, very occasionally, from discussions that Andy had already had with her. It was as if she knew that to get approval from the teacher she had to show right answers publicly, but that she was skilled in getting those right answers not from her own head but from her father or the teacher. In one session she gave the answer '225' for 'the product of 100 and 125'. When shown it was not she muttered 'but my dad says . . .'. In another homework feedback session she correctly said that a sequence goes 5/8, 5/16, 5/32 and that it was a 'denominator thing'. In the same lesson she described a sequence as generated by 'multiplying by point 9'. Later, when asked to continue the work on sequences by explaining her methods she did nothing for a long time and then reported that she did it with her dad and 'can't remember how we did them'.

I had further evidence to support my impression of weakness in number work in her use of fingers, particularly for subtraction, in situations where a competent arithmetician may have known number bonds or have developed some patterning strategies. Andy's estimation of her arithmetic, initially low as a result of an initial test, had risen to a relatively high level as a result of her oral contributions to class. My estimation was that she lacked skills, lacked useful internalisation of arithmetical facts, and had relied on performance of algorithms that she failed to remember. She was interested in arithmetic enough to want to look good at it but had to depend on help, asking and 'cheating' to do it, but did have some sense of underlying links and connections within mathematics. Andy was also unaware of how much time Sandra spent carrying out mundane parts of the activities, or simply not working. She had successfully created the impression that she was a keen worker, if frustrated and in need of support. Andy agreed that he had a neutral view of her until something outstanding happened, namely her enthusiastic contribution to homework feedback sessions. Once there had been an event that allowed him to differentiate her mathematics from that of other pupils, the view he formed remained strongly with him so that subsequent events were interpreted in that light. Her alteration of answers became under-represented in his picture of her and the pattern of her responses was not as obvious to him as it was in my more systematic methods.

In contrast, Andy believed that she was weak in the skills of exploring and reasoning with mathematics, and did not 'look for new ways' to do things, needing direction and reassurance. However, I saw at least four incidents where she was able to devise strategies, reuse strategies that had been effective in the past, describe patterns and make conjectures about mathematics. For example, when she was trying to fit pentominoes together to make a rectangle she calculated an appropriate width and length and then used those as constraints within which to work.

To me, Andy appeared to overestimate skills in the area of mathematics in which Sandra wanted him to be interested; he appeared to underestimate her skills of reasoning, perhaps because she was less confident about them or had less opportunity to articulate them, or perhaps because she asked for help so often, hence creating a negative impression in that respect. Seeing her work always in the context of what the rest of the class did and what his own expectations were, Andy made a judgement that was compared to what she had done before and to the rest of the class. But 'what she had done before' included creating an impression in his mind; therefore his judgements are relative to the picture already formed.

However, Sandra had also succeeded in helping me to create a different picture of her. Neither picture need be 'correct'; both are interpretations of available evidence. Andy and I discussed these differences often. Andy was constrained, as all teachers are, by the realities of classroom situations. No teacher can see everything all the time. I was constrained by not knowing anything about what the rest of the class were making of the tasks he set. I could not achieve the overview a teacher has, so had no real understanding of the context within which Sandra was working.

For each of us, seeing the other's point of view required a huge effort of the imagination. On the whole, my views were based on more detailed information and Andy's on more contextual information. For most teachers, the detailed information is not available in any systematic form.

Reflecting on the issue . . .
It can be an interesting exercise to try to keep detailed notes about one student, as I suggest at the end of this chapter. You might find it useful to do the sort of research activity I described above with a colleague. Naturally this is time-consuming, but may illuminate potentially crucial issues in the different judgements teachers make when faced with different points of view and when the observers have different personal knowledge on which to base their interpretations.

Potential for bias in teachers' informal judgements

None of the points made above are intended to be criticisms of the teacher; rather they are criticisms of the practices of the profession and the magnified effect of these practices when they are incorporated into assessment that contributes to decisions about pupils' futures. For example, decisions about which school to go to, which set to be in for mathematics, which future educational opportunities are on offer, what jobs might be available, and so on, depend on a mathematics grade. The grade itself depends on flawed testing procedures and also on teachers' judgements and assessments. Therefore it is important for teachers to understand the limitations of the grounds on which they make judgements.

All the teacher has knowledge of is what can be seen, heard and read; everything else is inferred. There is nothing wrong with inference; it is essential to inter-human communication. Also there is nothing wrong with forming impressions, *per se*, since they are essential to all our decisions about interacting with others. But how are inferences made? On what basis? A teacher who has a view of mathematics as a technical subject requiring correctly written algorithms, neatly laid out, might draw different inferences about a pupils' mathematics to one who sees mathematics as a subject requiring oral argument or physical representations. All teachers really know is the effect that a pupil's work and interactions has on them, the teachers: how they react to this pupil, to this way of doing and representing mathematics, to this particular way of tackling a mathematical problem. It becomes important, therefore, for teachers to identify their own beliefs and attitudes about mathematics and learning as much as it is to identify pupils' characteristics as a mathematics learner. Your reaction to reading about Sandra, for instance, would be influenced in part by your beliefs.

Further problems, as shown in the example of Sandra above, arise because what a teacher sees and hears is dependent on what else is going on in the classroom, and what the teacher expects to see and hear from that pupil. It is important, therefore, for teachers to imagine that the information they have is only partial, and a different picture of the pupil might be constructed if different ways to observe her were possible.

Reflecting on the issue . . .

Try focusing on one or more pupils you know. Having read my discussion about Sandra, what other information might be useful (crucial?) if you are to be able to make more robust and reliable judgements? How might you realistically adapt your practice – possibly along with colleagues – to have more access to that information?

Making sure judgements are fair

I want to discuss here several approaches to helping teachers to ensure judgements are fair through some form of moderation procedure. How can busy teachers ensure their judgements are fair without being frozen into indecision by self-doubt in the classroom? An obvious way to do this would be to have professional discussion with colleagues about their judgements. All UK schools have some kind of mechanism for moderating teachers' assessments of pupils, so it would be during these meetings and procedures that teachers' judgements might also be subjected to scrutiny. Such meetings have several purposes, the following of which could contribute to the fairness of the final decisions made about grading pupils:

- interpretation of externally imposed criteria;
- interpretation of the mathematics in a range of pupils' work;
- scrutiny of individual teachers' assessments against the criteria;
- scrutiny of teacher judgements (Gipps 1994; Clarke 1996; Watson 1998, 1999).

I will now look at each of these in more detail.

Interpretation of externally-imposed criteria

In order for a judgement to be fair it ought to correspond to some agreed set of standards, but standards need consistent interpretation in practice, in actual examples of pupils' work, and in the expectations generated by teachers in their classrooms. It may be impossible to expect every school in the country to interpret, for instance, the level descriptors of the National Curriculum in the same way, but it might be possible for teachers within a school to get close to agreement. Agreement on interpretation goes some way towards ensuring fairness when giving a grade or level to a pupil, and may influence how teachers see individual pupils by giving them a different vocabulary with which to describe mathematical achievement.

Interpretation of the mathematics in a range of pupils' work

In general, moderation meetings are attempts to validate interpretations of work, but most are limited to written work produced in particular circumstances, namely special assessment tasks. Some kinds of evidence which teachers use for informal judgements, such as oral and action evidence, could be included at this stage for moderation and scrutiny by colleagues, but in a study of moderation at seven schools I observed no instances of such scrutiny (Watson 1998). However, if observational evidence were included as a component of a range of pupils' work, as is done in primary schools, it would go some way towards ensuring scrutiny of this aspect of teachers' judgements as well as providing another source of information about achievement.

Scrutiny of individual teachers' assessments against the criteria

The focus of the meeting is to come to agreements about the kinds of standards individual teachers might apply when assessing pupils' work. Usually the meetings are not used for detailed problem solving, but there is an expectation that teachers will scrutinise their own assessments in the light of the discussions at the meeting. I saw no scrutiny of individual assessments at the meetings I attended, but at all of them there was discussion about 'going away and looking at levels again', and remarks about other informal discussions which may have taken place about assessment.

Scrutiny of teacher judgements

It would be unusual for a teacher's informal, classroom-based judgements to be discussed at moderation meetings. In fact, the opposite seems to be the case, teachers' informal judgements being used to justify other decisions made about more formal assessments. Rather than being moderated, challenged or justified at these meetings, teachers' judgements are often used as validation or explanation for results. For instance, in one school teachers agreed that no pupils in a particular class could be expected to achieve anything on level 3 or above at Key Stage 3 because they were a lower set. The fact that the teachers had themselves assigned these pupils to the lower set was not discussed. These two occasions of exercising their judgement, setting and grading written work, were used to confirm each other. Explanations of individual's grades given at moderation meetings included 'he works slowly' and 'she doesn't do well in tests' and 'he's one of my brighter ones'. Again, these remarks were not elaborated, the teachers' professional wisdom and judgement being taken as a yardstick for other results.

The second level, the contribution teachers make to formal grades, is therefore worth critical consideration. The relationship between the judgements teachers make, based on normal classroom evidence, and teacher assessments is a complex one. Pupils' achievements in special assessment tasks can add to, or alter, the view a teacher already has. However, existing judgements can influence assessment directly through interpretation of criteria for assessment and indirectly by applying non-criterion-related judgements to areas of doubt.

Reflecting on the issue . . .
Given that the practices described above are common, and taking into account the real work pressures of teachers, how might you develop ways to examine critically your own judgements of pupils?

Professional practice

If existing moderation systems do not provide mechanisms for examining teachers' informal judgements, how can the profession avoid unfairness? I offer the following suggestions:

1   Teachers can incorporate systematic self-criticism into their casual judgements, informed by awareness of how they form such judgements; this could go some way to preventing hasty decision making, or decisions based on a selection of evidence influenced by an initial impression.

2   Schools can incorporate systematic examination of teachers' judgements, including exploration of other possibilities, into their moderation procedures; this could enhance the professionalism of decision making to include criticism as well as experience, and ensure that judgements are made by more than one person.

3   Irrevocable decisions and actions based on teachers' judgements (such as setting or curriculum discrimination) can be avoided; this would reduce the long-term effects of flawed decisions and might also generate flexible expectations.

4   Hierarchies of mathematics teaching and learning promulgated in the National Curriculum and associated testing can be questioned as a normal part of professional practice; this could help teachers develop a more flexible view of mathematical progress so that expectations of pupils are not based on the limitations of one curricular model.

5   Cultures of individualism, judgement, selection and elitism in school mathematics can be replaced with cultures of professional self-doubt and an open-minded approach to the potential achievement of all.

Conclusion

In this chapter I have outlined the function and purposes of teachers' judgements about their pupils' mathematics. Teachers need to make judgements in order to make many day-to-day classroom decisions. However, their judgements are unavoidably based on a selection of what the pupil does, partly because the classroom is so busy that the teacher cannot see and hear everything, and partly because teachers subconsciously select and interpret what they hear, see and read in their pupils' work. Different interpretations arise because teachers have different viewpoints about pupils, mathematics, what it means to learn mathematics and so on.

Teachers' assessments of pupils' achievements are incorporated into formal assessment at every level throughout school. It is therefore possible that some pupils' mathematical strengths, weaknesses and potential achievement are systematically under- or overestimated. This can lead, through setting, differentiated curricula and tiered examination entry, to social inequity by influencing access to further educational opportunity or employment.

In this chapter I have not suggested that teacher assessment should be excluded from assessment systems, nor that teachers are culpable as assessors; rather, I have pointed out that such inevitable features of the system should be alleviated as much as possible by building discussion and critique into informal aspects of practice, as a norm. This can start by individual teachers questioning their own assumptions about pupils, and their own views about how mathematical learning is manifested in various aspects of pupils' work.

Such developments would enhance the professional life of mathematics teachers, and improve mathematics teaching and learning.

Invitation to reflect

My purpose in offering this activity is to invite you to engage in a more sustained and systematic way in some of the reflections I have so far offered in this chapter.

Keep as detailed a diary as you can of the actions, interactions and other observed behaviour of a pupil you might regard as average in one of your classes. Do not attempt to interpret the actions, try to keep your notes neutral. For example, 'Kate wrote four lines about her method of counting squares' is more neutral than 'Kate *only* wrote four lines . . .'.

If you can get someone to help you, try to find out what sorts of things you are missing in your observations of the pupil.

Create a discussion between you and the other observer about the pupil's mathematics; one of you to take a positive view, using the evidence; the other to take a negative view, also using the evidence. What is revealed about different kinds of evidence and different views of what is of value in mathematics learning?

Having learnt more about an 'average' pupil, you could now select someone whom you believe to be a 'good' mathematics pupil. Describe, in terms of mathematics rather than behaviour, what contributes to this view. Look at the features you have chosen and decide if they really do indicate strong mathematics, rather than good social skills, neatness, or some other less relevant characteristics.

Select an 'average' pupil in a group you teach frequently. Identify a positive attribute about this pupil, plan to focus on this attribute in a future lesson, e.g. if the pupil likes spatial work, plan to introduce percentages using a spatial representation. Does this affect the lesson, the learning, the success of this pupil and others? Do you still feel the pupil is 'average'? Why? Or why not? The idea behind this activity is to see if you can challenge your own preconceptions about pupils.

Further suggested readings

Gipps, C. (1994) *Beyond Testing: Towards a theory of educational assessment*, London: Falmer Press. This book summarises research on bias in testing and goes on to examine critically the whole field of educational assessment.

Morgan, C. (1998) *Writing Mathematically: The Discourse of Investigation*, London: Falmer Press. This book offers a detailed discussion about pupils' extended writing of mathematics, and how teachers might differ in their reactions to it.

Watson, Anne (1999) 'Paradigmatic conflicts in informal mathematics assessment as sources of social inequity', *Educational Review* 51(2), 105–15. This paper elaborates on some of the issues in this chapter, and says much more about how different viewpoints about mathematics, teaching and learning influences teachers' judgements.

References

Ausubel, D. (1968) *Educational Psychology: A Cognitive View*, New York: Holt, Rinehart and Winston.

Ball, S. (1997) 'Markets, equity and values in education', in Pring, R. and Walford, G. (eds), *Affirming the Comprehensive Ideal*, London: Falmer Press.

Bernstein, B. (1971) *Class, Codes and Control. Vol 1*, London: Routledge and Kegan Paul.

Blease, D. (1983) 'Teacher expectations and the self-fulfilling prophecy', *Educational Studies* 9(1), 123–35.

Brown, M. (1993) 'Assessment philosophy and practice in the UK', in Niss, M. (ed.), *Cases of Assessment in Mathematics Education*, Dordrecht: Kluwer.

Clarke, D. (1996) 'Assessment', in Bishop, A. (ed.), *International Handbook of Mathematics Education*, Dordrecht: Kluwer.

DfEE (1998) *Teaching: High Status, High Standards. Requirements for Courses of Initial Teacher Training. Circular 4/98*, London: Department for Education and Employment.

Gipps, C. (1994) *Beyond Testing: Towards a Theory of Educational Assessment*, London: Falmer Press.

Gipps, C. and Murphy, P. (1994) *A Fair Test*, Buckingham: Open University Press.

McIntyre, D., Morrison, A. and Sutherland, J. (1966) 'Social and educational variables relating to teachers' assessments of primary pupils', *British Journal of Educational Psychology* 36(3), 272–9.

MacNamara, A. and Roper, T. (1992) 'Attainment Target 1 – is all the evidence there?', *Mathematics Teaching* 140, 26–7.

Morgan, C. (1998) *Writing Mathematically: The Discourse of Investigation*, London: Falmer Press.

Watson, A. (1998) 'An investigation into how teachers make judgements about what pupils know and can do in mathematics', unpublished D.Phil. thesis, University of Oxford.

Watson, A. (1999) 'Paradigmatic conflicts in informal mathematics assessment as sources of social inequity', *Educational Review* 15(2), 105–15.

15 The place of pupil writing in learning, teaching and assessing mathematics

Candia Morgan

Introducing the issue

Traditionally, school mathematics has been a subject in which pupils have done relatively little writing. Although they may have covered pages of their exercise books with calculations and manipulation of algebraic symbols, writing in 'natural language' has generally been very brief, often restricted to copying definitions or rules from a textbook or blackboard (Britton *et al.* 1975; Spencer *et al.* 1983). Indeed, this lack of writing is a reason some give for preferring mathematics to other subjects. However, recent reform movements in mathematics education, both in the United Kingdom and elsewhere, have begun to change the overwhelmingly symbolic nature of school mathematics, encouraging greater use of both oral and written language. These changes have been prompted by the belief that learning can benefit from talking and writing about mathematics. The introduction of more varied and 'authentic' mathematical activities into the classroom has also brought with it increased demand for writing, for example, reporting the results of problem-solving and investigative work.

Assessment in mathematics has always relied heavily on pupils' written work. At a time when the consequences of assessment are ever greater for pupils and teachers, the complexity and difficulty of the writing demanded by new forms of assessment are also increasing. There are two major concerns about this development that I shall discuss in this chapter. First, there are questions that must be raised about the way pupils' writing is interpreted by teachers and other assessors – can it be a transparent, valid representation of understanding? Second, it is widely acknowledged that many pupils find it difficult to write effectively – how can they learn to write in ways that will lead to them being assessed as highly as possible? I shall suggest that these concerns with increased use of pupil writing in assessment practices may particularly affect the chances of pupils from disadvantaged groups in society.

Key questions

This chapter is based on the following three key questions:

- Why should teachers of mathematics bother about writing? In other words, what are the benefits (and problems) that writing may bring to learning and teaching mathematics?
- How may pupils' writing skills affect the ways teachers assess their mathematical attainment?
- How can pupils learn to write mathematics effectively and what can teachers do to help?

Benefits of writing for mathematics learning

Why should mathematics teachers concern themselves with writing? Surely this is the domain of English and humanities teachers? Indeed, many of those who choose to study mathematics at advanced levels have heaved a sigh of relief as they think they have put writing behind them and can concentrate on using the simple means of pure symbolism to express their mathematical meanings. In contrast, the importance of oral communication for mathematical learning is widely agreed among teachers and curriculum developers. Speaking and listening are the primary means by which pupils learn to participate in mathematical communities, explaining, questioning, justifying, clarifying their ideas, listening to the ideas of others, and working with others to construct mathematical arguments. So what does writing have to offer pupils and teachers of mathematics?

Of course, writing shares with speaking the important quality of externalising the pupil's thinking. This not only puts the thinking into the public domain to be shared with other pupils and the teacher but it also helps pupils to clarify their own ideas through struggling to find the words to communicate them to others. However, writing has some useful characteristics that it does not share with most spoken language; it does not take place face-to-face in interaction, it produces a lasting record, it bears some similarities with doing mathematics. I will look at these in turn.

Writing does not take place face-to-face with its audience

While this has some disadvantages (for example, the writer does not get immediate feedback about whether what they are writing makes sense), it does mean that the writer generally has more time to think about what they are writing and hence to clarify and refine their thinking. It also means that what is written has to be more complete and precise than spoken communications because the reader cannot ask for clarification or more information. Completeness and precision are particularly important to mathematical communication and to the development of mathematical thinking. Mathematical definitions, explanations and justifications that are constructed and communicated in face-to-face situations are often informal and incomplete because the participants become aware that they share underlying understandings and assumptions that do not need to be spoken. Similarly, oral arguments may not be presented in the most logical order because the process of constructing the argument is recursive, filling in gaps that are identified during the conversation. A definition or argument that is to be communicated in written form cannot rely on such implicit joint construction of meaning but must be complete and logical in itself (although writers have to make some assumptions about the amount of information required by their expected audience).

Writing produces a lasting record

This record can be useful both for pupil-writers and for their teachers. During the writing process, writers can look back at what they have already written, reflect on whether it really communicates their intentions, revise and redraft it. This process can help develop the ideas that are being communicated. As Frank Smith says, in discussing the roles that writing plays in thinking and learning:

> Things happen when we write. Ideas can be generated and developed in the interaction between writer and what is being written that would not be possible if the ideas were left to flower and perhaps fade in the transience of the mind.
>
> (Smith 1982: 16)

Because pieces of writing have a physical existence, they can be read at different times and in different places. Texts produced at different times or by different pupils can be brought together and compared and discussed or combined. For example, a group of pupils might compose their individual definitions of a mathematical concept they are studying, read each other's definitions, discuss what is necessary and sufficient, and construct an agreed, better definition (see, for example, the work on definitions described by Raffaella Borasi 1992). The permanent record also provides pupils with a source for revising the subject matter at a later date. Teachers, of course, use pupils' written records of their work for assessment purposes. Assessment issues will be discussed later in this chapter.

Writing and mathematics are similar activities

Parallels between writing and mathematics have been noted by a number of authors over the years. Jerome Bruner, for example, suggests that both are used for 'ordering thoughts about things and thoughts about thoughts' (Bruner 1968: 112). Others have claimed that the processes of writing and mathematical problem-solving are similar, involving recursive development of clarity about the nature of the problem and its solution (Elsholz and Elsholz 1989; Kenyon 1989). These parallels do not necessarily imply that writing is a useful activity for learning mathematics: they do, however, suggest that mathematics teachers should not dismiss writing as irrelevant and alien to their subject.

Benefits to developing mathematical understanding

Those teachers who have used writing activities in their classrooms are often enthusiastic about the improvements they have seen in their pupils' mathematical understanding and achievement. The nature of these improvements depends, of course, on the type of writing activity. For example, primary pupils who engage collaboratively in writing, revising and publishing their own 'word problems' develop familiarity with the structure of such problems, know how to look for the essential information, and can solve harder problems than before (Ford 1990). Getting pupils to explain in writing what they find easy and what they find difficult about solving mathematical problems seems to help pupils to develop their problem-solving skills (Bell and Bell 1985). More general claims have been made about the depth of understanding that can be achieved when pupils write about the mathematics they are studying. These claims are hard to substantiate because of difficulties in assessing understanding. One interesting attempt to investigate this is reported by David Clark and his colleagues. They analysed mathematical journals that pupils in an Australian secondary school wrote over an extended period of time, concluding that the pupils' writing demonstrated movement towards greater reflection on their personal understandings and mathematical activity (Clarke *et al.* 1993).

Benefits to attitudes towards mathematics

Another benefit claimed for some kinds of mathematical writing activities is improved attitudes towards mathematics. We are all familiar with the negative feelings that some people have about their mathematical experiences. At least some of these feelings seem to arise from the impression that mathematics is abstract and cold – separated from other, more human aspects of experience. Many of those who have used expressive forms of writing in their classrooms (such as journals, stories or 'free writing', where pupils are encouraged to be creative and questioning without being subjected to assessment) are enthusiastic about the changed attitudes of their pupils (Borasi and Rose 1989; Powell and López 1989; Stempien and Borasi 1985; Tobias 1989).

Most of the published accounts of writing in mathematics classrooms have been written by innovative teachers about activities they have introduced into their own classrooms. Their successes are likely to be due at least in part to their own enthusiasm and talents, though many of their suggested writing activities seem worth trying. We need to be aware, however, that there are many variables likely to affect the types of effects that using writing in mathematics classrooms may have. Obviously the purpose and nature of the task and the genre of writing expected will be a major variable, but teachers also need to consider their pupils' writing skills and attitudes to writing and the ways in which writing activities are to be integrated into the curriculum. The issue of pupils' writing skills will be returned to later in this chapter. In the next section, I turn to the question of how teachers make use of their pupils' written work as evidence of their mathematical achievement.

Assessing mathematics through written work

The public and lasting nature of pupils' written work means that it is conveniently available for teachers to use for assessing their pupils' mathematical knowledge and understanding. Traditional forms of assessment, such as marking work done in class, homework exercises, tests and examinations, have usually been in a written format. The types of response expected from pupils have generally, however, been limited to sequences of steps of symbol manipulation, leading to numeric or other symbolic answers. It is now widely recognised that such short responses to closed questions can provide only a very partial picture of pupils' achievement and there has been international interest in developing a wider range of methods to produce fuller and more valid assessments (see, for example, Leder 1992; Lesh and Lamon 1992; Niss 1993).

Many teachers who have introduced less traditional forms of mathematical writing into their classrooms have found that it helped them to gain different insights into their pupils' mathematical understanding and achievement (Borasi and Rose 1989; McIntosh 1991; Meyer 1991; Richards 1990; Wilde 1991). Diane Miller worked with high school teachers who used five minutes of writing at the beginning of every lesson in response to a prompt, for example, 'Why is $\frac{0}{5}=0$? Why is $\frac{5}{0}$ undefined?' or 'How can the property of zero help you to compute mentally $[(5+7\times13-6)-15]\times(36-12\times3)$?' She found that the teachers were often surprised by the pupils' responses and felt that they had learnt more about the pupils' understanding of the topics studied than they would have done by using only traditional methods (Miller 1992). This allowed the teachers to modify their teaching to address misunderstandings.

Reflecting on the issue . . .

To appreciate how much you can learn about pupils' understanding, it is worth trying writing prompts with one of your classes. The prompts you use should be related to the topics the pupils are studying and should demand understanding of the under-lying concepts. Here are some more examples:

(a) Why does the pair of simultaneous equations $2x+3y=5$ and $3y=6-2x$ not have a solution?

(b) Can a triangle have both a right angle and an obtuse angle? Explain.

(c) How does knowing that $17^2=289$ help you calculate 16×18 quickly?

When using such prompts, it is important to do so on a regular basis so that pupils get used to writing in mathematics and develop the skills to communicate their understanding. Remember that a poor response to a prompt does not necessarily indicate a lack of understanding. This issue of pupils' writing skills is discussed further below.

A rather different way of using writing activity as a source for assessment is described by Andrew Waywood. Pupils in his school made regular entries in journals, summarising and discussing work done in lessons, asking questions and collecting examples. The quality of the mathematical reflection and analysis in the journals contributed to pupils' profiles and constituted a substantial proportion to their summative assessments (Waywood 1994).

Since the introduction of the General Certificate of Secondary Education (GCSE) in 1988, pupils in England and Wales have been expected to be assessed on their ability to 'carry out practical and investigational work, and undertake extended pieces of work' (DES 1985: 2) as part of the examination process at age 16+. The main means of assessing this aspect of pupils' mathematical activity has been through written reports, providing evidence of processes as well as of the results of the investigational work. Some have expressed concern about pupils' ability to write well enough to provide evidence of the full quality of their mathematical thinking (Ball and Ball 1990; Bloomfield 1987; MacNamara and Roper 1992). Nevertheless, concerns about the reliability of other forms of evidence, such as oral discussion or teacher observation, and the difficulties these pose for moderation have meant that extended pieces of writing form an important part of this 'high-stakes' assessment for most pupils.

More varied forms of assessment clearly provide teachers with more opportunities to gain insight into pupils' understandings and achievements. Written reports of problem solving and investigation have the potential to allow pupils to display the mathematical processes they have gone through and their reasoning skills. Unfortunately, however, communication is not a simple matter of transmission from writer to reader, preserving the writer's meanings and intentions. Teachers and examiners who read pupils' work have to make sense of it by drawing on their personal experiences, expectations and values. This process of making sense is dependent on the form in which the work is presented as much as on the content. If there is a mismatch between the type of writing a pupil produces and the expectations of the teacher who reads and assesses that writing, it is possible that the pupil's understandings and achievements will be undervalued.

I will illustrate some of the problems arising from such mismatches with examples taken from a study I undertook of teachers assessing GCSE coursework (for more details of this study see Morgan 1998). All those involved were experienced and committed teachers, trying hard to make sense of the pupils' writing and to give full credit for their achievement. Each of the following examples relates to a piece of advice often given by mathematics teachers to their pupils to help them to produce acceptable reports of problem-solving or investigative work. As you read each section, you might like to think about times you feel compelled to offer such guidance, why you do it, and what you expect as a result.

'Write down everything you have done'

The purpose of this advice is to provide evidence of the mathematical processes the pupil has gone through in order to achieve their results. Many pupils, however, find it difficult to judge what 'everything' includes. The pupil whose work is shown in the example below failed to match teachers' expectations in two ways. First, she included too much detail of things she and her partner did that were judged to be non-mathematical and irrelevant. One teacher responded to this extract: 'That's one of my pet hates. It's the sort of, you know, "Miss put this task on the board and we copied it down" but not quite that bad.' At the same time, there is too little detail of the mathematical processes gone through to 'discover' the relationship between the variables. This pupil's attempt to follow her teacher's advice has resulted in a readable and lively narrative of her experience of working on this problem, but has failed to bring her credit for her mathematical thinking. It has also opened up the possibility that she will be condemned for lack of mathematical judgement because she has followed her teacher's advice too literally.

Example
Once Suzanne and I had completed tasks 1 and 2, we set out to discover if there was any connection between the triangular area and the lengths of the sides. First we lettered the sides:

a = slant line
b = base line
c = top line
d = area

In a very short time we had discovered a relationship between the lengths of the sides and the area (triangular). We were able to put this into a formula:

$$ab + ac = d$$

'Explain why it works'

Being able to explain, justify and prove mathematical results is generally considered a sign of high achievement. It also seems to be one of the aspects of mathematical writing that pupils find most difficult. While there may be problems in the reasoning itself, particular difficulties may arise from pupils' lack of control of the language needed to construct written arguments. When arguments are presented informally and orally, the reasoning is often left implicit – the premises and the conclusions are simply listed and logical relationships between them may not be explicitly stated. Formal written genres, however, signal the logical structure of arguments by using linking words such as 'because,' 'but,' and 'so,' or phrases such as 'the reason is . . .' (Martin 1989). Academic writing by mature mathematicians tends to highlight reasoning strongly, starting many sentences with 'thus' or 'hence' (Morgan 1998). Pupils whose writing skills are still immature are likely to produce arguments that, like the spoken forms with which they are more familiar, fail to make the reasoning explicit. I found that teachers responded positively to one pupil who used 'the reason is . . .' and 'because . . .' – even though the explanation itself was inadequate – but did not even recognise other pupils' attempts, which did not make use of such explicit language, as being explanations. Without awareness of the different requirements of spoken and written expression of reasoning, pupils run the risk of failing to communicate their understanding of the logical basis of their conclusions.

'Use diagrams'

Diagrams are an important medium of mathematical communication but they can serve a wide variety of purposes for those producing them and for their readers

(Morgan 1994). They may be used, for example, as a source of data (to be measured or counted), to demonstrate a method used, to illustrate a definition, or to aid the explanation of a solution. The status of diagrams serving different functions varies: a diagram as a source of data may be seen as evidence that a pupil has engaged in relatively low-level mathematical activity, while a diagram that demonstrates the structure of the situation being investigated and helps to communicate a proof of a generalisation may be valued highly by teachers. Among the coursework texts that I have asked teachers to assess was one that contained a large number of very carefully drawn and coloured diagrams of the arrangements of Cuisenaire rods that the pupil had used to gather data for a practical investigation. Teachers reading this work generally saw these as evidence of hard work but as irrelevant to the solution of the mathematical problem. One responded that it was typical of a girl, commenting 'they waste their time doing things that are absolutely nothing to do with the task'. The pupil herself was probably not aware of the negative response her writing would elicit from teachers. She may well have felt that following the advice to use diagrams, presenting her work attractively and recording her many examples accurately would be valued. Indeed, these features often are valued in other areas of the work of the mathematics classroom.

These three examples raise some issues about the validity of using pupils' written work as a primary source of evidence for assessing their achievement in mathematical problem solving and, by extension, in other aspects of mathematics. The expectations of mathematical writing are different from those in other genres with which pupils may be more familiar, so their attempts to follow the advice they are offered may not result in effective writing. The examples also highlight the influence that students' lack of relevant linguistic knowledge and skills can have on the ways teachers evaluate their mathematical achievement. This raises important questions about the fairness of assessment systems that make use of pupils' written work as an important source of evidence of achievement. The introduction of coursework at GCSE in England and Wales (demanding extended writing from all pupils) may have benefited those groups of pupils who were already more successful within the education system as a whole (Abrams 1991). Assessing mathematical understanding by depending on written work is likely to benefit those children who come to school with a rich variety of language experiences. Such children are more likely to be aware of the different ways in which language may be used and to have the skills needed to adapt their own language use to the demands of the new genres they meet in school, including those of mathematical writing. They can thus communicate their achievement in ways that will be recognised by their teachers and evaluated positively. Other children, lacking such linguistic awareness and skills, are likely to be disadvantaged when assessed through writing because they are unable to communicate their mathematical achievement effectively. The questions we must ask are: Which groups are advantaged or disadvantaged by written forms of assessment? And what can mathematics teachers do to help all their pupils write mathematics effectively?

Learning to write

How can pupils learn to write mathematics effectively? Of course, many of the skills involved in writing are generic and will be taught by those who have expertise in language development. However, teachers of English have neither the time nor the expert knowledge needed to help pupils acquire the specialist language and genres needed for writing in mathematics (and science, geography, history, etc.). Producing a definition that is both necessary and sufficient, a complete, logical proof, or an explanation of mathematical ways of working demands specialist knowledge of mathematical language as well as general linguistic skill. The pupil whose work was discussed in the example above was clearly competent at writing in a general narrative genre but appears to have been unable to adapt her skills to the demands of mathematical writing. Skills that are highly valued in creative writing in the context of English lessons may even be completely inappropriate in mathematics. For example, the use of rich, varied vocabulary to avoid repetitiveness and elicit imagery is at odds with the need in mathematics for consistent use of clearly defined terminology. Judging whether mathematical writing is effective – and communicating the criteria for effective mathematical writing to pupils – has to be done by teachers of mathematics.

It is sometimes argued that, just as all children learn to speak without explicit instruction, pupils will 'pick up' the knowledge and skills they need to write effectively. Unfortunately, this does not seem to happen. Unlike spoken language, writing does not saturate the everyday environment and, for many pupils, writing is a distinctly 'unnatural' activity (Marks and Mousley 1990). Some pupils, of course, do pick up the linguistic skills necessary for writing mathematics well, just as they do in other subject domains. These pupils, however, are most likely to be those who come to school with the advantage of a home background of experience in a range of ways of using language, including the abstract and formal kinds of language that are valued in school. (This is also discussed in Robyn Zevenbergen's chapter.) Basil Bernstein argued that children from working-class families and from other non-dominant groups in society are less likely to be able to distinguish the various kinds of language that are highly valued in school contexts (lacking access to the criteria or 'recognition rules') and are less likely to produce texts of their own in forms that will be evaluated positively (lacking the 'realisation rules' that would enable them to do so) (Bernstein 1996). In mathematics education, Barry Cooper and Máiréad Dunne have shown that working-class children may fail to demonstrate their mathematical capabilities when assessed through 'realistic' questions because they do not make appropriate decisions about which aspects of their 'everyday' knowledge should be used (Cooper and Dunne 2000; see also Barry Cooper's chapter in this volume). The examples in the previous section showed that the rules pupils are given for writing coursework are not sufficiently explicit to enable them to produce acceptable writing. If the implicit rules of mathematical discourse are not made explicit in the classroom, these disadvantaged groups of pupils are most likely to be even further disadvantaged.

One of the reasons that many mathematics teachers find it difficult to help their pupils is that the teachers themselves have never been taught explicitly how to write mathematically and therefore lack ways of analysing and communicating about the various mathematical genres. While all teachers can identify mathematical vocabulary, notation, graphs, charts and diagrams and can advise their pupils how to use these accurately, they do not, on the whole, find it so easy to describe the ways in which these various components need to be combined to construct a convincing, rigorous proof, a concise definition, or an account of the problem solving processes leading to the discovery of a general result. Further work is needed to produce useful analyses of effective mathematical writing in the genres used in schools and to find ways of helping pupils to acquire knowledge and skills in writing mathematically.

Conclusion

In this chapter, I have raised questions about writing in mathematics classrooms that make it clear it is not a simple matter. Nevertheless, recent changes in the mathematics curriculum have encouraged a wider range of classroom activities involving both oral and written language. This has broadened the kinds of learning experiences that pupils encounter and may open up mathematics to some who previously felt excluded by the emphasis on abstract symbolism. It seems likely that the opportunities that writing provides for reflection and expression of personal understandings can have benefits both for pupils' learning and for their attitudes towards mathematics. At the same time it is important to recognise that, just as with any other style of working in the classroom, some pupils will respond less positively.

Tasks that result in pupils writing about their understanding of mathematical ideas or about their problem-solving processes can provide teachers with much richer evidence of a range of pupil achievement than traditional exercises or tests. However, we must be very careful of making unfounded assumptions about the correspondence between what pupils write and what they know and understand. Any mode of communication involves interpretation and mismatches between writers' and readers' meanings, and expectations are less easily resolved than those that arise in face-to-face situations. The examples of teachers' responses to pupils' written reports of investigative work suggest some areas where pupils' writing skills are likely to be inadequate to meet the expectations of mathematics teachers – and areas where the advice that mathematics teachers give is likely not to be specific enough to help pupils to communicate their mathematical thinking effectively. There may well be other areas of difficulty and mismatch when pupils are asked to write in other mathematical genres.

As the range of kinds of writing used in mathematics classrooms becomes wider, pupils need to master the linguistic knowledge and skills required by different mathematical genres. I have argued that we cannot expect these to be simply 'picked up' as if by osmosis by most pupils, nor can we expect the particular requirements of mathematical writing to be addressed by general language teaching. Moreover, we need to be aware that pupils from disadvantaged groups within society may be further disadvantaged by the mismatch between the types of language with which they are familiar and the types of language valued by their teachers. Mathematics teachers are responsible for teaching their pupils to write in the mathematical genres they use in their classrooms. This means that teachers need to be aware of the characteristics of various kinds of mathematical texts and need to develop classroom activities that will help their pupils to develop similar awareness of mathematical language.

Invitation to reflect

Revising writing can help develop deeper understanding of the subject matter and greater awareness of the ways in which the choices writers make affect meanings. Try getting pupils to write a definition or an explanation of something they have been working on in class. They can then work in pairs or small groups to rework what they have each written and agree on one revised text. Compare the originals with the final version. What has changed? Repeat the activity after studying another topic. What do the pupils seem to be learning – about the topic and about mathematical writing?

The paragraph below is an example of a report produced by a pupil who had been investigating area and perimeter of rectangles:

> The observation I've learned is that the area can change while the perimeter stays the same. Also, the perimeter is the amount around the shape. While the area is the inside of the shape. The area would usually be square units. The maximum perimeter of a shape would usually be a square. To get the area you can multiply the length and width of a shape. You can make a chart to find the length, width and area of a shape.

Before reading further, evaluate this report and consider what feedback you might give the pupil concerned. Now read and evaluate the paragraph below:

> Area is the inside of a shape. It is measured in square units. To get the area of a rectangle you multiply the length by the width. Perimeter is the distance around a shape. I made a chart to record the length, width, area and perimeter of rectangles. I've learned that the area can change while the perimeter stays the same. The maximum area for a given perimeter is a square.

Most mathematics teachers would agree that the second paragraph is 'better' (and more mathematical), yet it was constructed simply by reordering the sentences in the first paragraph and rewording them slightly. (Reordering and rewording can also be a useful exercise for pupils.) Identify the changes that have been made and explain how they affect the mathematical nature of the paragraph. You should consider the roles of particular words or phrases that have been changed as well as the structure of the whole report and the function that each sentence serves within it. (You may also want to suggest some further or alternative revisions.) If the two paragraphs had been written by two different pupils, what judgements could you have made about their mathematical understanding and reasoning?

Further suggested readings

Connolly, P. and Vilardi, T. (eds) (1989) *Writing to Learn Mathematics and Science*, New York: Teachers College Press. This collection includes theoretical discussion of the benefits that writing activities may have for learning mathematics and practical suggestions of varied writing activities, mostly from secondary or tertiary education but many could be adapted for use in primary contexts.

Morgan, C. (1998) *Writing Mathematically: The Discourse of Investigation*, London: Falmer Press. This book analyses some of the characteristics of mathematical writing and applies this analysis to the writing of reports of investigations in the secondary school. Teacher assessment of pupils' writing is investigated critically.

Mousley, J. and Marks, G. (1991) *Discourses in Mathematics*, Geelong: Deakin University. A wide range of uses of both oral and written language in primary and secondary mathematics classrooms is discussed. This should help teachers reflect on their language practices.

References

Abrams, F. (1991) 'GCSE fails to eliminate inequality', *Times Educational Supplement*. 15/2/91.

Ball, B. and Ball, D. (1990) 'How do you cheat at coursework?', *Mathematics Teaching* 133, 9–12.

Bell, E. S. and Bell, R. N. (1985) 'Writing and mathematical problem solving: arguments in favour of a synthesis', *School Science and Mathematics* 85(3), 210–21.

Bernstein, B. (1996) *Pedagogy, Symbolic Control and Identity: Theory, Research, Critique*, London: Taylor and Francis.

Bloomfield, A. (1987) 'Assessing investigations', *Mathematics Teaching* 118, 48–9.

Borasi, R. (1992) *Learning Mathematics Through Inquiry*, Portsmouth, NH: Heinemann.

Borasi, R. and Rose, B. J. (1989) 'Journal writing and mathematics instruction', *Educational Studies in Mathematics* 20(4), 347–65.

Britton, J., Burgess, T., Martin, N., McLeod, A. and Rosen, H. (1975) *The Development of Writing Abilities (11–18)*, London: Macmillan Educational.

Bruner, J. (1968) *Towards a Theory of Instruction*, New York: W. W. Norton.

Clarke, D. J., Waywood, A. and Stephens, M. (1993) 'Probing the structure of mathematical writing', *Educational Studies in Mathematics* 25(3), 235–50.

Cooper, B. and Dunne, M. (2000) *Assessing Children's Mathematical Knowledge: Social Class, Sex and Problem-Solving*, Buckingham: Open University Press.

DES (Department of Education and Science) (1985) *GCSE: The National Criteria – Mathematics*, London: HMSO.

Elsholz, R. and Elsholz, E. (1989) 'The writing process: A model for problem solving', *Journal of Mathematical Behaviour* 8, 161–6.

Ford, M. (1990) 'The writing process: A strategy for problem solvers', *Arithmetic Teacher* 38(3), 35–8.

Kenyon, R. (1989) 'Writing is problem solving', in Connolly, Paul and Vilardi, Teresa (eds), *Writing to Learn Mathematics and Science*, New York: Teachers College Press, pp. 73–87.

Leder, G. (ed.) (1992) *Assessment and Learning of Mathematics*, Victoria: Australian Council for Educational Research.

Lesh, R. and Lamon, S. (eds) (1992) *Assessment of Authentic Performance in School Mathematics*, Washington DC: American Association for the Advancement of Science.

McIntosh, M. (1991) 'No time for writing in your class?', *Mathematics Teacher* 84(6), 423–33.

MacNamara, A. and Roper, T. (1992) 'Unrecorded, unobserved and suppressed attainment: Can our pupils do more than we know?', *Mathematics in School* 21(5), 12–13.

Marks, G. and Mousley, J. (1990) 'Mathematics, education and genre: Dare we make the process writing mistake again?', *Language and Education* 4(2), 117–35.

Martin, J. (1989) *Factual Writing: Exploring and Challenging Social Reality*, (2nd edn), Oxford: Oxford University Press.

Meyer, R. (1991) 'A classroom note on integrating literacy activities into the mathematics classroom', *Mathematics and Computer Education* 25(1), 38–41.

Miller, L. D. (1992) 'Teacher benefits from using impromptu writing prompts in algebra classes', *Journal for Research in Mathematics Education*, 23(4), 329–40.

Morgan, C. (1994) 'What is the role of diagrams in communication of mathematical activity?', in *Proceedings of the British Society for Research in Mathematics Learning*, London: Institute of Education, pp. 80–92.

Morgan, C. (1998) *Writing Mathematically: The Discourse of Investigation*, London: Falmer Press.

Niss, M. (ed.) (1993) *Cases of Assessment in Mathematics Education: An ICMI Study*, Dordrecht: Kluwer Academic Publishers.

Powell, A. and López, J. (1989) 'Writing as a vehicle to learn mathematics: A case study', in Connolly, P. and Vilardi, T. (eds), *Writing to Learn Mathematics and Science*, New York: Teachers College Press, pp. 157–77.

Richards, L. (1990) 'Measuring things with words: Language for learning mathematics', *Language Arts* 67(1), 14–25.

Smith, F. (1982) *Writing and the Writer*, London: Heinemann.

Spencer, E., Lancaster, J., Roy, J., Benvie, J. and McFadyen, I. (1983) *Written Work in Scottish Secondary Schools: A Descriptive Study*, Edinburgh: The Scottish Council for Research in Education.

Stempien, M. and Borasi, R. (1985) 'Students' writing in mathematics: Some ideas and experiences', *For the Learning of Mathematics* 5(3), 14–16.

Tobias, S. (1989) 'Writing to learn science and mathematics', in Connolly, P. and Vilardi, T. (eds), *Writing to Learn Mathematics and Science*, New York, NY: Teachers College Press, pp. 48–55.

Waywood, A. (1994) 'Informal writing-to-learn as a dimension of a student profile', *Educational Studies in Mathematics* 27(4), 321–40.

Wilde, S. (1991) 'Learning to write about mathematics', *Arithmetic Teacher* 38(6), 38–43.

16 Social class and 'real-life' mathematics assessments

Barry Cooper

Introducing the issue

In recent years, it has become taken for granted in official reports and in much academic writing on 'good practice' that the teaching and learning of mathematics should be related to its uses in everyday life and work settings (Cockcroft 1982; HMI 1985). This position often assumes that the majority of children will find mathematics more interesting if it is related to supposedly realistic contexts, but also that one purpose of schooling is to prepare children for their future lives (Hayman 1975). There is not space in this chapter to consider in full the overall case for and against a realistic approach. However, in England, the degree to which mathematics has been related to everyday tasks and anticipated working lives has been related to the social class of pupils, with working class pupils typically being seen as those who would benefit most from this approach (Cooper, 1985; Dowling, 1998).

Assessment items, and National Curriculum (NC) tests in particular, demonstrate this preference for supposedly realistic settings. Test items typically set mathematics in such contexts as shopping, sport and work. As a result children have to make choices – though some may not be at the conscious level – about how realistically to respond to such items. One study suggests how social class might affect children's responses to such supposedly realistic tests. Janet Holland (1981), working with the sociologist Basil Bernstein, asked primary age children to sort twenty-four pictures of food items into groups and to give reasons for their decisions. She found that middle-class children were more likely to use general principles of classification, e.g. 'the same kind of thing, both made from milk'. Working-class children were more likely to refer to their everyday life, e.g. 'that's what we have for Sunday dinner'. Given a second chance to classify the pictures, the middle-class children often switched to an everyday classification, while the working-class children stayed with this form of classification.

Key questions

I will concentrate on four key questions in this chapter.

1 How clear are the messages carried to teachers and pupils by supposedly realistic test items and their marking schemes concerning what counts as correct answers?

2   Are the messages, in so far as they are clear, ones of which we should necessarily approve?
3   Are tests employing supposedly realistic items likely to be valid measures of
what children understand and can do in mathematics?
4   Are tests employing supposedly realistic items likely to favour some social
groups over others?

Since these questions are related closely to one another, I will address them
together through the discussion of three test items and their marking schemes. I
will point to some contradictory aspects of the messages they carry, and will also
present some data on children's responses. You will be asked to stop at several
points in your reading in order to undertake a NC test item. Please do not skip
these three tasks. You will gain more from this chapter if you reflect on your own
responses.

Children, class and test items

Example 1: the lift question

I begin with the Key Stage 3 item shown in Figure 16.1

Reflecting on the issue . . .
Before reading further, you should attempt to solve the test question in Figure 16.1,
reflecting carefully on your answer (you are allowed to use a calculator). Please do
this now, and only then read on.

This is the sign in a lift at an office block:

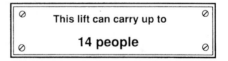

In the morning rush, 269 people want to go up in this lift.

How many times must it go up?

Figure 16.1   The lift question.
Source: SEAC 1992.

The official answer scheme gives as 'appropriate evidence' of achievement the following:

> Gives the answer to the division of 269 by 14 as 20, indicating that they have interpreted the calculator display to select the most appropriate whole number in this context. Do not accept 19 or 19.2.
>
> (SEAC 1992: Band 1–4, Paper 1)

You may or may not have thought there was a single number that could reasonably be taken as the correct answer here. While the answer scheme is based on this assumption, there is an alternative perspective that might be considered. This alternative is based on an understanding of the principles for the mathematical modelling of real problems. According to one approach, when faced with the task of mathematically modelling a real problem, one should begin by 'generating variables or features', 'selecting variables or pruning features', 'formulating questions', 'generating relations between variables', and/or 'selecting relations' (Mason 1988). In the case of the lift, we can consider the question of possibly relevant variables. These might include whether the lift was always full, whether there were stairs as an alternative, whether being full always means fourteen people can be carried (consider a wheelchair or child's buggy). It is not difficult to see how, were the problem to be taken as involving a serious reference to a real context, we might want to answer in terms of a range of possibilities, noting that the actual outcome would depend on the specific details of the 'morning rush' in this particular 'office block'.

We therefore have two possible modes of response to consider. One of these – that approved by the answer scheme – assumes that it is a good thing for the child to understand a set of peculiar 'rules of the game' for testing 'realistic' understanding in school mathematics. These rules involve bracketing out considerations that would be relevant in the case of a real 'realistic' problem. The second mode of response involves reference to recommended principles of mathematical modelling but, were it to be followed, would result in a non-unique answer which would be marked as 'incorrect'.

Looked at more generally, the choice between these two modes of response seems to involve two different interpretations of what might count as 'intelligent behaviour'. Alice Heim (1970) has argued that intelligent activity consists in grasping the essentials in a situation and responding appropriately to them. Here the answer scheme, and by implication the subject experts who have designed the item, seems to have opted for a conception of intelligent activity which comprises decoding the peculiar rules of such test items rather than one that involves bringing together arithmetical understanding with knowledge of the world outside of school to generate a reasoned response to a problem that is potentially open-ended. It is particularly ironic in this case that, though the child would be penalised for bringing in the sorts of realistic considerations outlined above, they are expected to bring in the particular realistic consideration that fractional lifts do not make much sense. (I have written about this elsewhere, in Cooper 1992.) A homeopathic dose of realism is required, but no more. We are left to wonder why ruling out fractional lifts does matter to the item designers while the possibility of bored people in a queue turning to the stairs does not. More generally we are left to wonder about the ways in which school mathematics sometimes does and sometimes does not accommodate realistic considerations.

An account of what is going on in the case of the lift item can be developed in terms of the idea of 'obviousness'. Before reading further, assuming you gained the 'approved' answer of 20 for this item, you might ask yourself whether you achieved this via a process of careful reflection about the item or in a more habitual manner. An habitual approach typically would involve dividing 269 by 14, generating 19.2142 . . ., and then rounding this up to 20 to accommodate one realistic consideration implicit in the context of a lift. Thoughts concerning other variables would not have arisen. The former, more reflective, approach might have involved some awareness of other variables. However, you will have decided, after some deliberation, that you were not expected take these into account. For me, and probably for most mathematics teachers, it may have been 'pretty obvious' what was required. This sense of what is 'obvious' will have been developed over the long years of a relatively successful educational career. The ground rules for understanding the context and its demands will be understood (Bernstein 1973). Furthermore, some readers may be predisposed to stand back and consider explicitly, or metacognitively, the possible different readings of the demands of the item, as I did earlier. S/he may wonder whether we want the assessment of mathematics to be transformed partly into the assessment of the 'feel for the game' involved in decoding the peculiar demands of such items. Whatever one's views on this question – which concerns the goals of schooling – it is important to hold in mind that this sense of the 'obvious' or the 'appropriate' has to be learned, either in the home or the school. Basil Bernstein's work (see Bernstein 1996, and the earlier example from Janet Holland) suggests that opportunities for learning what is appropriate in school mathematics may not be equally distributed across social class cultures, with the result that children and adults are differentially prepared, and therefore differentially predisposed, to read such questions in the required way. (Robyn Zevenbergen discusses related issues in her chapter.)

I suggest you end this section by returning to my key questions 1 and 2. It seems that the message carried by items like that in Figure 16.1 is ambiguous. On the one hand realistic considerations matter. On the other they do not, since an extended realistic analysis here would produce zero marks. Whether we should approve of the implicit message – realism, but in homeopathic doses – is something for you to consider against the background of your own values and educational aims.

Reflecting on the issue . . .

Look through a textbook you might use with some of your classes. Find a task that refers to an everyday context such as sport or shopping. Can you reword it

    (a) so that it becomes a modelling question and
    (b) so that the intention of the question becomes clear to all?

Try your reworded task out with some pupils.

Example 2: the traffic question

We have seen that, in the case of the lift question, taken from tests for 13–14-year-olds, a child who introduces a little realism will achieve a better mark than the child who, writing 19.21, does not. I now consider another test item. In Figure 16.2 we have an item intended for 10–11-year-olds concerning chance in the context of a traffic survey. This was intended to test the objective 'Use appropriate language to justify decisions when placing events in order of "likelihood"'. The item refers to a common topic in school mathematics – the traffic survey – and therefore refers to an area in which children are likely to have some previous school experience alongside their experience of traffic in everyday life.

Reflecting on the issue . . .
Before reading on, please solve the problem, including the additional task of writing down your reasons for each choice.

The children in Year 6 conduct a traffic survey outside the school for 1 hour.

Type	Number that passed in one hour
Car	75
Bus	8
Lorry	13
Van	26

When waiting outside the school they try to decide on the likelihood that a **lorry** will go by in the next minute

Put a ring round how likely it is that a **lorry** will go by in the next minute.

| certain | very likely | likely | unlikely | impossible |

They also try to decide on the likelihood that a **car** will go by in the next minute.

Put a ring round how likely it is that a **car** will go by in the next minute.

| certain | very likely | likely | unlikely | impossible |

Figure 16.2 The traffic question.
Source: SEAC 1993.

The marking scheme gives the answers 'likely or very likely' for the car, and 'unlikely' for the lorry, with one mark for each. This marking scheme, notwithstanding the appearance of the word 'order' in the objective, pays no attention to the ordering of the two likelihoods by the child. Neither does it, or the question, seem to address the justification of decisions, though I asked you to do so. It is also unclear that there is any good mathematical basis for the linking of the given data with these answers. It is unclear why two responses are allowed for the car, but only one for the lorry (see Cooper 1998a for a fuller discussion of this question). Here, however, I want to refer to one aspect of children's response to this item when they are asked, in an interview, to give reasons for their choices. You will see how, unlike the responses demanded by the test question, the interview allows some investigation of children's reasoning.

Here is how one year 6 child, Diane, from a professional middle-class background, explains her reasoning to me. She has circled lorry and car, gaining two marks.

BC: Right, why have you chosen those two?
Diane: Well, because in an hour, if there were, if there were 60 minutes in an hour, then if there were only 13 lorries in one hour, it's not very likely that, um, you're going to get a lorry just in one minute. And the cars – cos there were 75 cars, more than one a minute, so it's more likely that you'd [pauses, stops].
BC: It's not certain though?
Diane: It's not certain but there's, I mean, – I don't know, there could be a traffic jam [laughing].

Diane refers to the given table of data, reasoning from the figures in a way that shows she believes that the car is *more* likely than the lorry to appear in the next minute. However, when I probe her understanding of 'certain' she does introduce a consideration not given in the table of data. She does what any rational individual would do when considering such a problem in everyday life. She asks whether we can assume that the conditions under which the survey was taken can be assumed to be those holding 'in the next minute'. Often, of course, in the absence of additional knowledge, it is best to assume that the conditions will continue to hold. Nevertheless, such questions are rational ones to ask, especially given the way in which traffic accumulates around schools at particular times of the day! But the key point about Diane's overall response – and it applied to those she made to other items – is that, although she raises a realistic consideration, she seems to understand that it is not what typically is required in answering 'realistic' NC test items. In fact, Diane shows repeatedly in the interview that she knows explicitly that she should not import everyday considerations such as the possibility of a traffic jam into her solutions (see Cooper 1998b).

Diane's response can be contrasted with that of Mike, a working-class boy. He has circled 'impossible' for lorry and 'certain' for car, common errors in responding to this item. He gains no marks.

Mike: A traffic survey outside the school. One hour. . . . Impossible. Cos it would
        probably take him a minute just to get past.
BC: Right, why have you put those two then?
Mike: Cos, lorries, you don't come across lorries very often, only if they've been
        delivered somewhere, or something like that. But cars, people use them all
        the time and things.

What differentiates this justification from Diane's is the use of his everyday knowledge to generate his answers. As in the case of the lift item we can consider which
is the more intelligent response – to use just the given data or to draw also, or
instead, on one's everyday experience. As I have noted, in the world outside of
school we might draw on a range of considerations as well as the given data. Some
year 6 children use just the given data, some just their everyday knowledge and
experience, while some employ both. Diane and Mike were taking part in pilot
work for a large research project that explored the relation between children's
mode of response and their social class backgrounds. Table 16.1 shows the relation
between social class and mode of response of 10–11-year-olds in the context of an
individual interview (see Cooper and Dunne, 2000a for full details of this
research). The service class broadly comprises professional and managerial parents.
Working-class children are much more likely than others in this sample to employ
their everyday knowledge alone in explaining and, we must assume, generating
their answers.

   As it happens, for this particular item, children who completely ignore the
given data, and employ instead their everyday knowledge, can gain full marks.
Rick, for example, a working-class boy, circles 'unlikely' for lorry and 'very likely'
for car, gaining two marks.

BC: Now how did you decide on those two?
Rick: Cos, because the lorry, there's not as many lorries around as there is cars.
BB: What were you thinking of, whereabouts?
Rick: Outside of school, more parents would come to like collect a child in a car
        than they would in a lorry.

Tabl 16.1   Distribution of response strategies of year 6 children by social class (traffic item)

	Uses given data alone	Uses everyday knowledge and given data	Uses everyday knowledge alone	Numbers of children
Service-class	38	10	11	59
Percentage	*64.4*	*16.9*	*18.6*	
Intermediate-class	16	10	4	30
Percentage	*53.3*	*33.3*	*13.3*	
Working-class	16	6	10	32
Percentage	*50.0*	*18.8*	*31.3*	
Totals	70	26	25	121
Percentage	*57.9*	*21.5*	*20.7*	

BC: That's true, right, OK, did you look at these numbers at all here? Did you read that part?

Rick: No.

BC: OK so you did the question without looking at that part?

Rick: Yep.

Rick draws on his everyday experience, seems to pay no attention to the given data, and yet gains two marks. Perhaps he should be seen as lucky, since this question, if written slightly differently, might have differentiated by social class not because of children's different competence in respect of reasoning from the data, but rather – or at least partly – as a result of differences in their choice of response mode. To see this, just assume that the given data were to be made less like that which would have been produced around a typical school. Assume that the number of lorries and cars were swapped. Then, typically, children drawing on their everyday knowledge might no longer produce the 'right' answers, which would now be, on the model provided, 'very likely' or 'likely' for lorries and 'unlikely' for cars. With the item revised in this way it would tend to produce greater social class differences in performance than the original. This thought experiment illustrates a general point. The results of measurement depend on the measuring instrument, and some instruments may produce systematic errors. In the context of assessment some items may be differentially valid, more validly measuring mathematical knowledge from some social groups than others. My key question 3 asked about threats to the validity of assessment that might arise from supposedly realistic contexts. The discussion of the traffic item has suggested that children's failure to respond 'appropriately' to an item – in choosing to bring in their everyday experience – might generate one threat. The relation of this response mode to social class suggests that key question 4 might deserve further examination, though of course evidence from one item hardly provides a final answer! In the next section I consider another case.

Reflecting on the issue . . .

Using either the lift item or a similar one chosen from a textbook you use, choose some higher- and lower-attaining pupils, and interview them while they attempt the task. Probe for their reasons for answers. You might then challenge them to approach the task in other ways and note their responses.

Example 3: the tennis question

The discussion of the traffic item included some speculation about how slightly rewriting a test question might have significant effects. We can now consider an item where differential validity seems to have actually arisen, with the result that the item tended to underestimate children's actual understanding, and particularly so for working- and intermediate-class children rather than those from professional and managerial backgrounds. The NC level 6 item concerns an imagined tennis competition (Figure 16.3).

Reflecting on the issue . . .
Please solve the tennis question, and write down the reasons for your answer. Only then, read on.

Organising a competition

David and Gitas's group organise a mixed doubles tennis competition. They need to pair a boy with a girl.

They put the three boys' names into one bag and all the three girls' names into another bag.

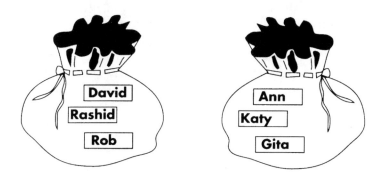

Find all the possible ways that boys and girls can be paired.
Write the pairs below. One pair is already shown.

Rob and Katy

Figure 16.3   The tennis question.

Source: SEAC 1993.

The marking scheme states that 'there should be exactly nine pairings, all different'. They are set out in the answer scheme thus:

Rob & Katy
Rob & Ann
Rob & Gita
Rashid & Katy
Rashid & Ann
Rashid & Gita
David & Katy
David & Ann
David & Gita

Clearly, none of these discrete sets of three pairs could engage in tennis as usually practised! The item seems to be based on the assumption that the children will not be misled by acting in a common-sense way – by imagining, for example, that they might be acting physically on the 'names' on the cards in the context of an imagined real competition. On the contrary, in order to be successful, they are expected, having abstracted the mathematical problem from its pictorial setting, to approach this in a Piagetian 'formal operational' mode. The problem is that, even where children are capable of undertaking the abstracted combinatorial act, they might not demonstrate it in this case. After all, objects put in such bags are normally there to be taken out (as, for example, in televised draws for the FA Cup). If children were to operate on this assumption they would have, in their imagination, to put the 'names' back in order to generate all the possibilities. It seems clear, therefore, that to succeed here, the child must treat this as a mental exercise in combining names and must avoid being side-tracked by imagining features of real sports draws. The bags must not be taken to signify the request for the 'empirical' three pairs that might seem implicit in the physical act of removing names *without* *replacement* (as in the case of real draws for knock-out competitions), when a step into mathematical discourse *with* *replacement* can allow the production of nine.

In the pilot work with fifteen children, a further problem of interpretation appeared alongside that of whether a realistic three pairs might be the required answer. Some children read the sentence 'Find all the possible ways that boys and girls can be paired' as an instruction to focus on methods of pairing the children as a process. One suggested shaking the bag. Another suggested blindfolding the children. In most cases these children nevertheless went on to write down some pairs as a product, sometimes after I had pointed out the next sentence (Cooper 1998a). These children, and others, together totalling seven of the fifteen, wrote just three pairs. However, several of the seven possessed the competence to produce nine. Rebecca, for example, initially wrote three pairs but on being asked whether she had found 'all the possible ways that boys and girls can be paired?' wrote six more. She appeared to have no idea why she had stopped at three.

Mike, having stopped after writing three pairs, was asked whether there were any more to be found:

BC: . . . if I said, here, write down all the pairs you think you could get, of boys and girls – all the possible ones – do you think there are more than three? Or just three?

Mike: There'd be nine.

He proceeded to write them down. Mike seemed able to carry out the operation required by the Statement of Attainment given for the item, i.e. 'identify all the outcomes of combining two independent events', once he had understood it was required. However, his initial performance did not reflect his underlying competence. He suggested a realistic three pairs, after first considering methods of generating the pairs. An invitation to reflect further led to the production of nine, along with an account of why nine boy-girl pairs exist (Cooper 1998a).

How common is Mike's mode of response, i.e. moving from three pairs initially to nine after a cue to reflect further? In the pilot work, four out of fifteen children did this (Cooper 1998a). In the subsequent larger-scale project some ten per cent of the sample of 10–11-year-olds did so, and they tended to be intermediate- and working-class rather than service class children, as is shown in Table 16.2 (Cooper and Dunne 2000a: 114). These twelve children, producing initially three but subsequently nine pairs, behaved in a way compatible with an everyday or realistic response to this item. This mode of response would lead to zero marks in a test context where no further reflection is encouraged. In fact, if we use the initial response in the interview as the basis for awarding a mark to each child, then the mean marks for service-, intermediate- and working-class children are, respectively, 0.83, 0.80 and 0.64 (one mark being available for nine pairs, none for any other response). The gap between the classes narrows if we award marks for the better of either the first or second cued response. The final marks become 0.88, 0.97, 0.76 respectively. As in the case of the traffic item, working-class children are much more likely to respond realistically to this item than service-class children

Table 16.2   Social class distribution of first and second responses on the tennis item in the interview

Response pattern		Service class	Intermediate class	Working class	Total
Other	count	6	1	5	12
	column %	10.0	3.3	15.2	9.8
3 then 3	count	1	0	1	2
	column %	1.7	0	3	1.6
3 then 4 to 8	count	0	0	2	2
	column %	0	0	6.1	1.6
3 then 9	count	3	5	4	12
	column %	5.0	16.7	12.1	9.8
9 pairs first time	count	50	24	21	95
	column %	83.3	80.0	63.6	77.2
	Total count	60	30	33	123

(Cooper and Dunne 2000a). These realistic responses largely comprise the production of just three pairs, producing marks of zero, though we have seen that a considerable number of these children can demonstrate the required mathematical competence once they have understood the intended goal of the item. We have here evidence that this particular type of 'realistic' item may well tend to favour some social class groups over others, as a consequence of children's habitual ways of responding to the clues provided by its supposedly realistic content. Importantly, children who draw on everyday knowledge for the traffic item are more likely to respond realistically to the tennis item, suggesting a predisposition to behave in this way across items (Cooper and Dunne 2000a). If you wish to see how Key Stage 3 children cope with this item, see Cooper and Dunne 2000b.

This discussion of the tennis item provides some grounds for an affirmative answer to my key question 4, 'Are tests employing supposedly realistic items likely to favour some social groups over others?' At this point you might like to consider the pros and cons of an alternative way of asking children to undertake the combinatorial task embedded in the tennis item. Here it is: 'Find the Cartesian product of the sets {a, b, c} and {d, e, f}'.

This clearly provides a quite different image for children of the nature of mathematics. Which image we prefer is partly a matter of our personal values and beliefs concerning what mathematics is. However, I hope I have demonstrated that, in so far as you share the values associated with equal opportunities in education, the decision might also need to be informed by research into the social implications of some assessment practices that, at first glance, might seem neutral.

Reflecting on the issue . . .
Designing tasks is not easy. Taking the context of sport as an example, and combination and/or permutations as the mathematical operation, design two tasks, one of which seems likely to cause similar problems for some children as the tennis item did, and one that seems likely not to do so. Try these with a range of children, and reflect carefully on the lessons learned.

Conclusions

I have shown statistically elsewhere that, for a sample of 125 year 6 children, a sample of NC 'realistic' test items produced larger differences in measured achievement between the social classes (and sexes, to a lesser extent) than NC non-'realistic' items (Cooper and Dunne 2000a). Controlling for the measured ability of children, the word count of items and the difficulty level of items did not lead to the disappearance of this effect. Here I have shown that part of this finding might be explained by children misreading the cues provided by supposedly realistic items. Contrary to appearances, often children are not expected to treat these problems as real problems. Instead they either have to ignore real world considerations, or introduce just a very well-judged small dose. There are also social class differences in another area. Working-class children, at both Key Stage 2 and Key Stage 3, faced with several items demanding an explicit explanation of their answer, were more likely than other children to give a truncated response that gained no marks. They were often able, however, to expand this truncated answer when cued to do so in an interview, demonstrating that they did understand the mathematics involved (Cooper and Dunne 2000a).

I began with four key questions. We have seen, in respect of these, that the message carried by some NC 'realistic' items, in conjunction with their marking schemes, may be far from clear; that the message might be seen as running against advice to teach mathematics realistically; that these items might cause us to underestimate children's mathematical capacities; and that this might be a particular problem for working- and intermediate-class children. These surely must be critically important issues for mathematics teachers to address.

Invitation to reflect

The material in this chapter is relevant to a number of important educational and often political issues.

- Choose some schools you know which have different proportions of the various social classes in their intakes. Consider whether it is fair to compare these schools with one another, using league tables derived from tests comprising mainly supposedly realistic test items. Is this merely a technical issue to be left to test designers?
- At KS3, in the 1996 tests, the proportion of items referring to people and/or everyday contexts decreased as one moved from Tiers 3–5 through to Tiers 6–8 of the tests (Cooper and Dunne 2000a). Working-class children are more likely to take the lower tiers of tests. In the light of the KS2 findings referred to earlier, does this matter? Why?
- Look through the textbook exercises and assessment items you use in the classroom. Identify key differences in the nature of these for different groups of your pupils. Consider whether such differences as you find can be justified, and on what grounds, or whether they are merely the result of traditional practice.
- Encourage your pupils to think about the sorts of issues raised in this chapter. What might they learn in class from considering the lift item as I have done here? About mathematics? About questioning authorities and experts? About 'intelligent activity'?
- I have shown that, from an equity viewpoint, there may be problems in assessing children using supposedly realistic items. However, as noted in the introduction, there may be other good reasons for using them both in teaching and assessing children. As is often the case, we have competing values here. Where do you stand? Is the relating of mathematics to realistic contexts a valuable enough pedagogic goal to override the equity concerns raised here?

Further suggested readings

Cooper, B. and Dunne, M. (2000a) *Assessing Children's Mathematical Knowledge: Social Class, Sex and Problem-Solving*, Buckingham: Open University Press. This book provides a detailed account of the research referred to in this chapter, both at Key Stage 2 and at Key Stage 3, funded by the Economic and Social Research Council. It also includes a critical account of research by others that has described the ways in which children frequently fail to bring realistic considerations to bear when items *do* require this. It also addresses sex differences alongside social class differences.

References

Bernstein, B. (1973) *Class, Codes and Control*, St Albans: Paladin.

Bernstein, B. (1996) *Pedagogy, Symbolic Control and Identity: Theory, Research, Critique*, London: Taylor and Francis.

Cockcroft, W. (1982) *Mathematics Counts. Report of the Committee of Inquiry into the Teaching of Mathematics*, London: HMSO.

Cooper, B. (1985) *Renegotiating Secondary School Mathematics: A Study of Curriculum Change and Stability*, Basingstoke: Falmer Press.

Cooper, B. (1992) 'Testing National Curriculum Mathematics: Some critical comments on the treatment of 'real' contexts for mathematics', *The Curriculum Journal* 3(3), 231–43.

Cooper, B. (1998a) 'Assessing National Curriculum Mathematics in England: Exploring children's interpretation of Key Stage 2 tests in clinical interviews', *Educational Studies in Mathematics* 35(1), 19–49.

Cooper, B. (1998b) 'Using Bernstein and Bourdieu to understand children's difficulties with 'realistic' mathematics testing: An exploratory study', *International Journal of Qualitative Studies in Education* 11(4), 511–32.

Cooper, B. and Dunne, M. (2000a) *Assessing Children's Mathematical Knowledge: Social Class, Sex and Problem-solving*, Buckingham: Open University Press.

Cooper, B. and Dunne, M. (2000b) 'Constructing the 'legitimate' goal of a 'realistic' mathematics item. A comparison of 10–11 and 13–14 year-olds', in Filer, A. (ed.), *Assessment – Social Practice and Social Product*, London: Routledge/Falmer, pp. 87–109.

Dowling, P. (1998) *The Sociology of Mathematics Education: Mathematical Myths/Pedagogic Texts*, London: Falmer Press.

Hayman, M. (1975) 'To each according to his needs', *Mathematical Gazette* 59, 137–53.

Heim, A. (1970) *Intelligence and Personality*, Harmondsworth: Penguin.

HMI (1985) *Mathematics From 5 to 16*, London: HMSO.

Holland, J. (1981) 'Social class and changes in orientation to meaning', *Sociology* 15(1), 1–18.

Mason, J. (1988) 'Modelling: what do we really want pupils to learn?', in Pimm, D. (ed.), *Mathematics, Teachers and Children*, London: Hodder and Stoughton.

Schools Examinations and Assessment Council (1992) *Mathematics Tests 1992, Key Stage 3*, London: SEAC/University of London.

Schools Examinations and Assessment Council (1993) *Pilot Standard Tests: Key Stage 2: Mathematics*, London: SEAC/University of Leeds.

Part V

Issues in the culture of mathematics teaching

17 Inclusion, learning and teaching mathematics

Beliefs and values

Mike Ollerton

Introducing the issue

There are three main premises upon which this chapter is based. The first is that equality of educational opportunity is embodied by inclusion. Second, that learning and teaching mathematics are exceptionally complex. Third, that teaching mathematics is a socially and politically charged business.

In this chapter, you are invited to consider ways you wish to teach mathematics, by comparison to how, at times, you feel you ought to, or are expected to teach mathematics. You are also asked to consider the issue of teaching in inclusive, all-ability groups, as a way of raising standards of learning mathematics for all pupils, and from a social justice perspective. I offer some experiences when, as a head of a mathematics department (1986–95), I chose to teach across the 11–16 age range in all-ability groups without textbooks, using, wherever appropriate, problem-solving, equipment-based approaches. I shall develop some of the teaching ideas that reflect my pedagogy.

Key questions

In this chapter I set out to answer three fundamental key questions that relate to the premises on which the chapter is based.

- If you believe in the importance of equality of opportunity, how does this determine the way you teach?
- How do issues relating to inclusivity impact on why and how you teach mathematics?
- If you are committed, both in principle and in practice, to inclusivity, how does this affect the way you operate in the classroom?

The importance of values

I have written some of my beliefs and values for learning and teaching mathematics below. You might care to consider where you and I converge or diverge in our beliefs and how this might indicate any divergence in underlying values we hold.

Reflecting on the issue . . .

First, before you begin to read the chapter, I have two questions to ask, about your teaching of mathematics.

   1   What are your beliefs?

   2   What are your values?

These are sizeable questions and you may wish to close the book to think about your answers. You could of course answer these questions on a relatively superficial level, but in reading this chapter, I hope that you will be challenged to consider just how your teaching of mathematics reflect your values.

My beliefs stem from events in my childhood and as a teacher. They are formed through experience and discussion with pupils and colleagues in schools, colleges and at conferences, and over the years, they have changed, been moulded, challenged and strengthened. However, there is always a tension between what I believe I am teaching and what different pupils learn in my lessons. What pupils learn will not only be affected by what *I* do. What they learn will be influenced by an array of other factors – and there are many of these (magazines, videos, radio stations etc.) over which I, and more generally the school itself, have no control.

To make matters worse, teachers, and in particular mathematics teachers, are faced with an incredible number of pressures from a variety of sources, about how mathematics should be taught. Sometimes it seems everybody knows better than the mathematics teacher himself or herself. These pressures come from the government, parents, the media, key stage test writers, OFSTED inspectors, TV personalities, locals in the pub and the next-door neighbour. Because all these

Table 17.1   Beliefs and values for learning and teaching mathematics

Beliefs	Values
I believe that learning should promote interest.	I value those teachers who made learning interesting for me.
I believe that active, practical involvement supports learning.	I value opportunities to have practical, hands-on experiences that enable me to access and understand mathematics.
I believe that throughout compulsory schooling, all pupils should be provided with equal opportunities to learn the same core body of mathematics, defined by NC.	I value teachers who treat me as an equal and find ways of enabling me to study mathematics at higher, more complex levels than those I currently operate.
I believe everybody can understand mathematics if they are given opportunities to start from simple beginnings and develop their thinking towards more complex ideas.	I value those teachers who provide me with ways of improving my understanding of mathematics.

people have at some time in their lives experienced school mathematics, some may consider themselves to be 'experts'. This pressure is further underpinned by a belief that mathematics is a logical, step-by-step, straightforward subject, where you are either right or wrong. So why can't we teachers teach mathematics in ways it can be easily learnt? That question itself flags up recognition of a real difference between teaching and learning. Often the focus of discussion and debate about mathematics in schools is on how and what the teacher *teaches*. What is overlooked is how (and what!) pupils *learn*. This is not an easy or simple step to make, but it does involve us in subordinating our thinking about teaching to thinking about learning.

To distinguish between teaching and learning, I offer a light-hearted story:

'I taught my five year old some prime numbers yesterday.'
'Oh really! How many does she know?'
'She doesn't know any yet.'
'But I thought you said you taught her.'
'I did – she just hasn't learnt yet.'

Of course some of these 'experts' described above do not understand the pressures involved and the enormous skills required, to teach the intrigues of Pythagoras' theorem to a class of adolescents some of whom will be more interested in magazines, mobiles, TV and radio, and 'sex, drugs and rock 'n' roll'. In addition teachers are expected to get pupils to achieve as high results as possible on tests at every stage of their development; the outcomes of these are distilled and published in national and local newspapers. Schools which do not come up to 'standard' are named and shamed. There are no hiding places. Life as a mathematics teacher isn't easy; we live in challenging times.

Reflecting on the issue . . .
Suppose, however, just for the moment, none of the pressures of tests, targets, national curriculum and league tables existed. Of course this is entering the realms of fantasy, but just suppose you had absolute responsibility for teaching mathematics in ways that matched your values, in the ways you chose to teach it. How would you teach? What changes might you make to existing structures in your department? What different strategies and resources might you use? What kinds of lessons would you plan? Would you choose to teach in inclusive groups or in setted groups? Why? With regard to the last question you are invited to consider whether, as a parent, you would support setting as a form of organisation in your child's school, particularly if you knew in advance your child would be placed in the 'bottom' set, say set 7 out of 7.

Earlier I described my decision as a head of department to teach mathematics to all pupils in inclusive groups. The two main reasons for this were first to develop the quality of pupils' learning, and second to foster equality in learning and teaching. I deal with the latter first.

Fostering equality in learning and teaching

One of the most divisive and iniquitous systems in operation in schools in the UK is that of setting pupils according to some notion of their measured 'ability'. The propensity to classify pupils and place them in 'sets' creates the conditions for under-achievement. (You might like to have a look at how Jo Boaler and Dylan Wiliam finish off their chapter in this book, by arguing that setting by ability could be the single most important cause of low levels of attainment in mathematics in Great Britain.)

However, keeping an open mind about each child's potential is consistent with a belief that everyone can achieve; my responsibility is to provide supportive conditions to make this possible. Children's attainment, interests, work-rates and achievements change and develop at different speeds. As such it is impossible to objectify, construct and apply fixed criteria that, under scrutiny, maintain integrity and equity, and subsequently use such criteria to place pupils in setted groups. The problem for many children is that once they are placed in a particular set, then this is most likely where they will stay and future potential is largely predetermined. The solution to this problem, offered by proponents of setting, is that movement between sets is part of the design; part of the flexibility of ability grouping. There is a clear anomaly here that is revealed in research findings: '. . . a child's chance of remaining in its initial grouping for the rest of its school career are 88–89%' (Dixon 1999: 1).

Were children to be separated out into learning groups by some other criteria, such as ethnic background, social class, parents' income or gender, this would rightly be described as some form of apartheid. However, not only is setting by 'ability' a form of educational apartheid, it also *does* serve the purpose of separating children by ethnic background, social class and gender, but it does this surreptitiously.

> Homogeneous forms of grouping reinforce the segregation of pupils in terms of social class, gender, race and age (season of birth). Consequently, low ability classes often contain a disproportionately large number of pupils from working-class backgrounds, boys, ethnic minorities and summer-born children.
>
> (Sukhnandan and Lee 1998: 43)

My values, with regard to equality of educational opportunity, are based upon the importance of working for social inclusion. I expect *all* pupils in a class to be capable of making contributions irrespective of notions I may have about their different abilities. I do not believe I have a right, simply because I have decided to work as a teacher, of restricting and limiting some pupils' opportunities for learning and for enjoying mathematics. In every group there will exist a range of perceptions, understandings and learning outcomes. However, no matter what any pupil has achieved in the past, I must be circumspect about assumptions I make about what anybody might achieve in the future. I cannot predict eventualities. For me this embodies equal opportunities, based on a belief that everyone has the potential to make progress in the present and the future. I believe all pupils can advance and all can gain from the same classroom environment.

A significant characteristic of teaching to inclusive groups, therefore, is the value given to the inevitable wide range of pupil contributions and how we respond to pupils' perceived needs. Making decisions, as a consequence of moment-by-moment classroom interactions, about whom to offer consolidation or extension tasks to, lies at the heart of effective teaching. Acting upon what pupils have recently done or are currently doing is significantly different to making decisions, effectively years in advance, about the level of curriculum input different children will or will not be able to cope with. Building pupils' confidence, to believe they can all achieve and make progress in mathematics, is central to differentiated learning. This important principle has been described by HMI as follows:

> Mathematical content needs to be differentiated to match the abilities of the pupils, but according to the principle quoted from the Cockcroft Report, this is achieved at each stage by extensions rather than deletions.
>
> (DES 1985: 26)

This is a critically important quote for understanding how we might organise mathematics teaching in inclusive classrooms. I develop the implications of this quote in the next section.

Planning for quality in learning and teaching

How do *you* go about planning lessons? Of course many of us have planned a lesson whilst walking down the corridor on the way to the lesson! However, how would you go about planning a lesson where you have the luxury of time to plan? What do you take into account when planning a single lesson or a sequence of lessons? It is at this stage that one's fundamental beliefs and values come into play – possibly covertly – to organise and structure how we conceive of the lesson.

Apart from the ever-present challenge involved in seeking to maintain positive classroom interactions with pupils, I find lesson planning one of the more interesting aspects of teaching. As a new head of mathematics, in 1986, I sought to apply to my teaching the aim from the Cockcroft Report *Mathematics Count* (DES 1982) of responding to pupil diversity through curriculum extension rather than curriculum deletion. I also set out to support colleagues who wished to translate this aim into their teaching. To achieve this it was necessary to analyse any constraints that existed in the department and to consider how to overcome them, I identified several constraining factors and these were:

- the limited nature of the scheme of work;
- an over-dependence upon textbooks and, in particular, the (then) relatively new SMP 11–16 booklets;
- a severe shortage of practical equipment and inadequate storage facilities for any equipment that did exist;
- few opportunities for department staff to share ideas and discuss best practice.

I believed a key feature in ensuring the success of this venture was to co-operatively develop a scheme of work that was based upon the following structures and ways of working:

- to construct a modularised framework of interconnected skills and concepts;
- to analyse each module in terms of skills involved;
- to develop 'story lines' (starter and extension tasks);
- to use a range of teaching strategies;
- to utilise a range of resource material;
- to use problem-solving approaches;
- to take risks in order to open up new possibilities.

I will now look at each of these in turn. At the beginning of each section I describe how the related aspect of the structure is supportive of pupils learning mathematics in inclusive classrooms. Of course, all the descriptions relating to structure are not exclusive to working with all-ability groups and can, obviously, be used in setted teaching groups, certainly the phrase 'all groups have a mix of abilities' is frequently heard when a debate ensues about whether or not to set. Setting by ability does not resolve the two usual concerns of the wide spread in the pace at which pupils work and the depths of understanding they subsequently gain (Ollerton 1995: 35). I seek, therefore, to demonstrate that it is perfectly feasible to teach in all-ability groups, as well as arguing for the desirability of working in this way.

Constructing a modular framework of concepts and interconnecting skills

A modular curriculum framework is supportive of inclusive learning because at the beginning of each module every pupil has a new opportunity to make a 'fresh start' and develop an understanding of the central concept within each module. The implication of this is that everybody can embark upon a journey to learn, for example, trigonometry. This challenges a hierarchical view of mathematics, and a belief that it is not feasible to understand trigonometry unless other concepts are in place. However, if the starting point to a module is accessible then the hierarchical issue becomes less crucial. I develop this issue of starting points below.

One way to construct a modularised framework is to begin with large sheets of blank paper and a number of coloured marker pens and decide which modules, or central concepts, ought to appear on a specific year group plan. For example, for year 10, typical module titles might be: Pythagoras, Circles and π, Graphs and Functions, and Statistics; in all there could be a dozen or so such titles. In a school year this translates into three to four weeks of curriculum time to devote to each module. Because different modules, describing central concepts, embody common, specific skills (e.g. measuring, estimating, rounding a result off to a number of decimal places, multiplying, etc.) an interconnected and holistic view of mathematics can be constructed.

However, because specific skills frequently appear within separate chapters of textbooks there exists a danger that such skills are taught in isolation. One outcome of this is that pupils may conceive of mathematics as a set of separate experiences and disconnected procedures. It is, therefore, important to teach mathematics in ways that underlying structures are revealed so pupils can see links between concepts. For example, any result gained by performing a division calculation (e.g. calculating a mean average, carrying out a trigonometric calculation) or by finding a square root (e.g. calculating the radius of a circle given its area, carrying out a calculation involving Pythagoras) offers opportunities for pupils to round off. Within such contexts, the purpose of rounding is much clearer than it is when pupils are presented with an exercise to practise, requiring them to round off ten or twenty values devoid of any context, real purpose or motivation.

In an inclusive classroom the teacher is encouraged to deploy a range of strategies to help pupils understand specific skills, such as rounding off to two decimal places. Some strategies are: to offer a brief reminder to some pupils, ask one pupil to explain this skill to another, spend an intensive two or three minutes working with a small group, ask pupils to make a poster (say for homework) which describes the process of rounding. This last strategy, of creating posters that explain specific skills, can be a powerful way of using display work towards which the teacher can subsequently direct pupils who need extra help.

Analysing modules and interconnected skills and concepts

It is useful to show how modules fit together into an overall curriculum framework. In an inclusive classroom it is important to consider those basic skills in which pupils will need to have some confidence at the outset of a module, and skills which they will engage with in different modules. As different modules are completed, pupils can be encouraged to consider the skills they have worked on, and, over time, to draw out a concept map of the curriculum, showing connections they make between different modules.

Drawing concept maps is an important part of the planning process. To illustrate this I offer a concept map for mensuration in 3-D. One well-known starting point is the 'Maximum Box' problem. This idea is referenced in many sources, e.g. *Points of Departure 1* (ATM 1980: problem 50), *Mathematics from 5 to 16* (DES 1985: 27, 62–4). It involves cutting equal-sized corners from a square (or rectangular) piece of paper then folding up the resulting net and calculating the volume of the open box thus created. As different-sized corners are cut off, so the volume of the resulting (open) box varies. The worth of this problem is that it can be used in Key Stage 2, as a context for counting and multiplying, and at A level as a context for calculus. This richness provides a wide range of possibilities.

Below is a diagram (Figure 17.1) showing one deconstruction of 'Max Box' into skills that can emerge as pupils set about solving the problem. However, before looking at this diagram you may wish to construct your list of the skills that can arise from 'Max Box'.

Each of these skills also appears in other contexts, for example 'Calculating with decimals', 'Constructing procedures', 'Writing formulae' and 'Approximating' will all be part of learning Pythagoras' theorem. Consequently, these skills can be practised in various contexts and become the links connecting different modules.

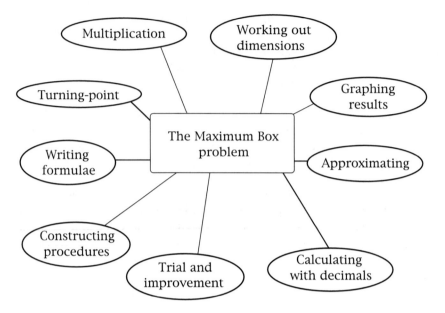

Figure 17.1   Mensuration in 3-D. The Maximum Box problem.

Deconstructing one's knowledge to decide where to begin to provide pupils with access to concepts is a process that can be applied to the entire curriculum. In the detailed planning, a shift from a broad overview of a concept, to a specific starting point needs to be considered. Subsequently, layers of knowledge about a concept are deconstructed and reconstructed in terms of the basic skills that must be in place for pupils to proceed from a chosen starting point.

This planning process is underpinned by the following principles that adhere to inclusion:

- Pupils can access concepts by building upon small amounts of previous knowledge.
- Opportunities exist for pupils to move speedily from a starting point.
- Pupils can work on a concept over several lessons, enabling them to achieve in-depth understanding.
- Interconnected skills, subordinate to the main concept, are met, practised and consolidated within different modules.
- Opportunities exist for pupils to use and apply process skills such as organising, specialising, generalising and proving.

The first of these principles leads to the question I raised at the beginning of this section, i.e. what basic skills do pupils need in order to have access to a higher-order concept? Deciding on what these basic skills are will guide decisions about the nature of the planned starting task; this is developed in the following section where pupils need to have the motor skills of cutting, sellotaping, and measuring with a ruler.

Developing 'story lines': starter and extension tasks

In an inclusive classroom, I have a key responsibility to construct starting point tasks to enable all pupils to access the main concepts I am planning for them to learn. In addition, and recognising that over the duration of each module different pupils will achieve different levels of cognition, I have a responsibility to plan a range of extension tasks, and questions and prompts (Watson and Mason 1998) that will support differentiated learning outcomes. Finding places for each module from whence all pupils can begin to construct knowledge to different depths is fundamental to planning in an inclusive classroom. Providing all pupils with opportunities to develop concepts to varying depths, according to their interest and potential I have described as a process of 'seeding' (Ollerton 1990: 32).

The example below describes a module based upon π, a concept taught in every mathematics classroom at some point in Key Stage 3. The initial task involves pupils doing the following:

- cutting out several thin strips of paper of different lengths, and measuring the length of each strip;
- forming a circle from each strip by carefully joining the two ends together with sellotape, so the length becomes the circumference of a circle (C);
- measuring the approximate diameter (d) of each circle;
- collecting information for each strip about its length and the diameter of the circle so formed;
- observing the data to perceive an approximate ratio of 'threeness' of C:d

The above plan forms the major whole-class teaching input. From this point onwards I plan a range of extension tasks to offer to individuals or small groups of pupils, as I perceive they are ready to develop the work further; this is the basis of planning for differentiation and progression.

Reflecting on the issue . . .
Having considered the circumference 'seed', consider, possibly with a group of colleagues, how you might organise and plan the first lesson. Try to do this before you read further.

How would you develop the seed in subsequent lessons? What possible avenues might be available for different pupils in subsequent lessons?

For me, typical developments from this seed would be:

- using a calculator to divide the measured length of the strip of paper by the length of diameter of the circle it forms, and repeating this for each strip;
- rounding off each calculation to two decimal places;
- finding the mean average of these results;
- graphing d against C, d against r and r against d;
- constructing formulæ to connect C with d, d with r, and C with r;

- asking pupils to construct their own and solve each other's problems, based upon knowing one variable (C, *d* or *r*) and calculating the other two;
- drawing circles on 1 cm squared paper, of different radii, and counting the area of each one;
- seeing how close these calculations are when the (given) formula for the area of a circle, $A = \pi r^2$, is applied;
- constructing more complex formulæ connecting the variables A, C, *r*, and *d*;
- pupils constructing and solving each other's problems based upon knowing one of the variables (A, C, *r* and *d*) and calculating the other three;
- considering how to calculate the volume of a cylinder.
- This list of extension tasks could be developed into 3-D mensuration.

At some point it is valuable for pupils to be explicit about what they have learnt, to write about and illustrate their work with diagrams, formulæ and graphs, to explain what they have understood. In this way opportunities are created for pupils to develop literacy skills and simultaneously consolidate their understanding of key concepts and subordinate skills. Alternatively groups of pupils could be asked to present their work to others in the class in a plenary lesson, possibly making posters or writing on overhead transparencies to aid dissemination. (You might care to consider how this approach fits in with suggestions made by Candia Morgan in her chapter on writing.)

The diagram below (Figure 17.2) is a further illustration of how this Circles and π module can be used as a context for pupils to use and develop a range of interconnected and subordinate skills.

Using a range of teaching strategies

In an inclusive classroom there exist valuable opportunities for using a range of teaching strategies. For example, asking one pupil to explain something to another automatically creates a situation where there is, temporarily at least, more than one teacher in the classroom. This is not only useful to the class teacher and of course the pupil receiving help, it is also advantageous to the pupil who offers the help. We will, no doubt, be able to recall an 'Aha!' teaching moment when something we have explained to a class has suddenly made much more sense to ourselves.

> *Reflecting on the issue . . .*
> What different strategies do you employ in your classroom? Perhaps before reading on you might list those you used in your last two weeks of teaching, or those you might consider using.
>
> Once you have done that, look over the list I offer below to see what strategies you seem not to have included. Why might you not have included them? (Remember my original question about your beliefs and values.)

The richness of my pupils' learning experiences depends upon the range of teaching strategies I use. Demonstrating something is one strategy, others include:

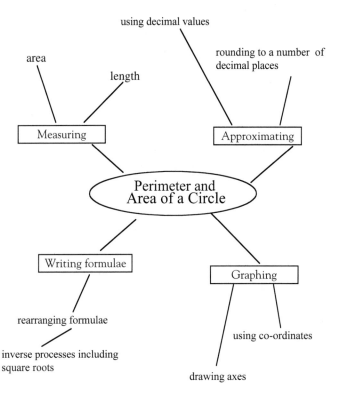

Figure 17.2 Using a 'Circles and π' module.

- small group discussion;
- pupils writing on the board;
- using a mind-imagery approach;
- rote learning;
- pupils planning presentations;
- pupils setting and solving each other's problems;
- pupils sitting in a ring to discuss a problem;
- in pairs sitting back to back and trying to describe a shape or a construction;
- pupils carrying out an experiment and sharing results;
- one pupil teaching another.

Only the class teacher can decide which strategies will best serve the intended purpose of the lesson. When planning a lesson, therefore, the teacher needs to consider how strategies and resources fit together into the overall lesson structure.

Using a range of resource materials

As with using a range of strategies, in an inclusive classroom there are good reasons for deploying a wide range of resources. This is because different, heterogeneous, groups of pupils require the support offered by opportunities to use different types of resources. Having a wide range of resources in the classroom helps create a vibrant and lively classroom atmosphere. Furthermore, when pupils know they are expected to use a range of types of equipment then they are able to exercise some independence with regard to making choices about the kind of resource they need to solve a problem.

What kinds of resources do you use to teach mathematics? In particular, what kinds of equipment, as well as calculators, rulers, protractors and compasses have you used in your teaching in the past few weeks? Equipment-based learning supports an active, practical, hands-on approach to knowledge. It provides all learners with opportunities to work towards abstract mathematical ideas from concrete experiences. It allows pupils to feel and touch mathematics as well as see and hear about mathematics.

The most widely used resource in mathematics classrooms is the textbook. However, the over-use of a textbook or a published scheme can monopolise learning and teaching and create a dependency culture which can steadily erode a teachers' responsibilities for lesson planning and likewise prevent pupils from being active, responsible learners. Of course routines need to be practised and knowledge consolidated, yet it is quite feasible to achieve such end-points without using a textbook. Learners need to know how to carry out a calculation, and when to use a specific skill if they are to achieve fluency and confidence in mathematics. The key issue is finding ways of enabling pupils to practise and consolidate knowledge whilst simultaneously maintaining their interest in mathematics.

The use of practical equipment, its value in different contexts, and the range of materials that can be used to support learning raise issues for debate. One perception is that equipment is more suited to the primary classroom than to the secondary phase. Another argument is that there is insufficient 'time' in lessons to 'get pupils through' the amount of content required to pass tests (sadly gradually becoming a feature at the primary phase). Consequently practical equipment is often viewed as a luxury that cannot be afforded. There is also the challenge of managing the behaviour of some pupils, who may choose to use equipment for more disruptive purposes.

Each of these is a valid concern and from my classroom experience I recognise similar tensions. Some pupils do see equipment as 'toys' from their childhood, others do dwell too long on using equipment, and delay getting around to the mathematics; in lessons involving paper folding, the occasional aeroplane has sailed through the air! Of course how I deal with such occurrences is all part of my style and my classroom culture. Not to provide pupils with opportunities to fold paper, to enhance their understanding of shape and space, because of the 'threat' of a paper aeroplane, would be to restrict their mathematical experience. There is a further issue in the use of practical equipment to foster inclusivity – that is to provide an environment in which pupils with different learning styles and preferences can benefit.

Some reasons in support of using different types of practical equipment such as coloured paper, pegs and pegboards, cardboard and scissors, Cuisenaire rods and Multi-link cubes are:

- to provide pupils with concrete experiences, something to physically manipulate, to construct understanding of abstract concepts;
- to offer pupils a focus of interest and provide a richness beyond verbal and written communication;
- to create an image which learners can at a later time revisit in order to reconstruct knowledge;
- to demonstrate that mathematics is a creative subject which exists beyond the pages of a textbook;
- to provide imaginative approaches to learning mathematics and create, for pupils, an investment in mathematics.

Practical equipment is a means to an end. Multi-link cubes, Geoboards and Cuisenaire rods are not imbued with power whereby the user automatically understands more about mathematics. How equipment is used and the way it forms part of the classroom culture are important considerations. Indeed, to grasp the intended concepts learners must at some point detach themselves from the equipment; they must know what it is they have learnt, and be explicit about this. (Kevin Delaney writes more about practical equipment in his chapter.)

Using problem-solving approaches

Because problem-solving, as a way of learning mathematics, is an excellent vehicle to enable learners to develop an idea to a level commensurate with their cognitive ability, the use of problem-solving in an inclusive classroom is particularly relevant and valuable.

Debate over the value of using problem-solving approaches, or discovery methods, has existed for decades. Unfortunately such methods are frequently polarised, in immature ways, by the media and Chris Woodhead a previous Chief Inspector of Schools (HMCI) alike, as progressive and, therefore, anti-educational. To polarise debate, however, is unhelpful. Finding ways of using progressive approaches to teach traditional concepts is necessary if we are to find ways of improving children's opportunities to learn mathematics.

Problem-solving methods, therefore, need to be merged with didactic approaches to support effective learning. Seeking potentially interesting problems with built-in opportunities for differentiated outcomes is important. A seemingly 'rich' starting point may not in itself be sufficient to support effective learning; this must be assisted by teacher interventions that, in turn, depend upon pupils' responses to the initial stimulus.

Too often open-ended work is misconstrued as a separate, bolt-on part of the curriculum where pupils are expected to discover ideas for themselves, with hints from the teacher; this is due, in part, to the way such tasks are used for assessment purposes at GCSE. Using problem-solving as a 'normal' way of teaching mathematics to aid pupils' understanding of the content is different to 'doing' an investigation as an end in itself.

Returning to the Circles and π module described earlier, a mixture of the problem-solving and didactic methods is exemplified. On one hand pupils are encouraged to 'discover' 'threeness' connecting the circumference with the diameter of a circle. Later in work on Area I will 'give' the formula: $A=\pi r^2$ then ask pupils to collect information to demonstrate this fact.

Whatever the teacher decides about balancing teaching styles between the investigative and the didactic, decisions about whether certain individuals might benefit more from exploring something, or from being given specific information are central to teachers' professionalism. The most important consideration is how learners come to know what they have learnt, and where this knowledge might lead.

Taking risks to open up new possibilities

If I only stick to 'tried and trusted' teaching methods I automatically limit my horizons and the possibility of something different happening; this, in turn, limits my pupils' horizons. Yet, whenever I try out something new I inevitably take some measure of risk.

One aspect of risk-taking is when the teacher does not know all the answers or is not able to predict all the mathematics that learners may elicit from a new (to them) idea. In terms of professional development it is important for teachers to try new ideas and new ways of working. For example, the first time I set up the Circles and π work, I realised that to maintain a desirable pace to the lesson I had to move quickly around the classroom and dispense several short strips of sellotape to pairs of pupils. However, this flurry of activity did not act as a signal for some pupils to misbehave, just the opposite. Indeed the air of amazement, at the speed at which I managed to cut off the first hundred or so pieces of tape, helped create a purposeful and relatively humorous atmosphere.

Risk-taking is supported by the strength of relationship the teacher has with a class; the more confident the teacher feels, the more risks can be taken and the more pupils can be relied upon to take initiatives and determine the shape of a lesson. As such, risk-taking is a process of renewal, of teaching concepts in different, more interesting ways compared to approaches used in the past. Experienced teachers learn how to weigh up situations and decide when conditions are favourable for taking a risk and departing from the *status quo*. However, newly qualified or trainee teachers do not, by definition, have the same depth of experience, and risk-taking for them can be a hazardous business. Usually the safe option is to give pupils work from a textbook, particularly if this is the common methodology used by the department. However, rigorous adherence to a published scheme or text can prevent new teachers from considering alternative approaches and from designing interesting lessons – which consequently inhibits the potentiality for professional development. Yet to take risks by departing too radically from the textbook and changing too many of the usual ways of working can lead to difficulties, often because some pupils themselves do not like change. The types of conditions that might be considered a change to 'normal' way of working are:

- a different seating arrangement;
- using practical equipment;
- adopting an investigative approach;

- group work and discussion;
- a shift from practising and consolidation of specific skills;
- pupils writing on something other than their exercise book;
- pupils writing about mathematics *per se*;
- using a resource other than a text book or a worksheet.

As always there is a balance to be found here. If a new teacher or student teacher is to broaden their horizons and experience alternative approaches, then risks need to be taken. If a 'risk' lesson is successful, the teacher can build on this. If the teacher has a difficult lesson, the tendency may be to teach 'safer' lessons in future; for this reason it is important for the teacher to recognise they are indeed taking a risk and, where possible, to try to maximise conditions for success.

Conclusion

In this chapter I have discussed beliefs and values about learning and teaching mathematics in inclusive, all-ability classrooms for pupils in compulsory education. I have connected inclusion to quality and equality of learning, through constructing schemes of work and relating this to writing 'story lines' to describe approaches to lesson planning. I have also developed the issue of planning concept modules using interconnected skills as an important part of the structure. I have illustrated this process with two specific curriculum concepts: Mensuration in 3-D and Circles and π. I have considered the major factors involved in planning including teaching strategies, resources, using problem-solving approaches and the importance of risk-taking with regard to professional development. Now the rest is up to you!

Invitation to reflect

You have been invited to examine your beliefs and values about they ways you want your pupils to learn mathematics and, therefore, how you teach mathematics. The main issues to reflect upon have been:

- setting as an equitable way of organising teaching groups;
- how you plan your teaching;
- the range of strategies and resources you use.

I recognise that setting is the most widely used organisational method for teaching mathematics. OFSTED and the government are strongly in favour of setting and it is now being operated in Key Stage 2 and even some Key Stage 1 classrooms. I find myself, therefore, in a marginal minority! However, not to be daunted, I challenge readers to consider the following scenario.

Imagine you are to walk into a new Y10 class tomorrow; you know nothing about the so-called abilities of individuals in the group, although you do know the pupils have not been placed into sets. You have been asked to teach them trigo-nometry. What would you do? What advance plans would you draw up? How would you set out to include everybody so that the issue of differentiation, with regard to pupils' cognitive differences, which is bound to exist, can be catered for? How will you start the lesson?

Further suggested reading

Because the essential issues about teaching in an inclusive classroom focus on planning for teaching mathematics, the following six ATM publications are likely to be of benefit to anyone looking for ideas. *Points of Departure 1, 2, 3* and *4*, *Questions and Prompts for Mathematical Thinking*, and *In Our Classrooms*.

Association of Teachers of Mathematics (ATM) (1980) *Points of Departure 1,2,3* and *4*, Derby: ATM. Collectively these four booklets contain 282 ideas, many of which can be used as starting points for lessons, or as extension tasks during lessons for mathematics classrooms. The value of them is that it is up to the teacher to decide how best to incorporate them into classroom practice and into departmental schemes of work. Although there are some ideas I personally have steered clear of, there are many more which provide a richness and a wide variety of possibilities for classroom practice.

Watson, A. and Mason, J. (1998) *Questions and prompts for mathematical thinking*, Derby: ATM. This is the perfect book to accompany the four *Points of Departure* booklets because it offers teachers a plethora of types of questions and prompts for developing pupils' understanding of mathematics. It would, however, be harsh to align this book too closely to *Points of Departure*: it is an excellent publication for use in any mathematics classroom where the teacher wishes to help pupils develop and deepen their mathematical thinking.

Association of Teachers of Mathematics (ATM) (1993) *In Our Classrooms*, Derby: ATM. This publication draws upon a range of approaches that different teachers have used. It is set out in common themes and contributors describe the ways they use ideas, strategies and resources in their classrooms.

There is one further seminal text for inclusive mathematics teaching, last published by Tarquin, but which is sadly out of print. However if you should find a copy of *Starting Points*, by Banwell, Saunders and Tahta, perhaps in a second-hand bookshop or collecting dust somewhere on a shelf, then grab it quickly. This is the most marvellous resource book, full of ideas, strategies, resources and stories that will provide any teacher of mathematics with much to consider and plenty to reinforce one's teaching.

References

Association of Teachers of Mathematics (ATM) (1980) *Points of Departure 1*, Derby: ATM.

DES (Department for Education and Science) (1982) *Mathematics Counts. Report of the Committee of Inquiry into the Teaching of Mathematics in Schools*, chaired by W. H. Cockcroft (the Cockcroft Report), London: HMSO.

DES (Department for Education and Science) (1985) *Mathematics from 5 to 16. HMI Series Curriculum Matters 3*, London: HMSO.

Dixon, A. (1999) 'A canker by any other name', FORUM 41(1), 1.

Ollerton, M. (1990) 'Seeding', *Mathematics Teaching* 132, Derby: ATM.

Ollerton, M. (1995) 'Mind the gap', *Mathematics Teaching* 152, 35–6.

Sukhnandan, L. with Lee, B. (1998) *NFER Review of Literature into Streaming, Setting and Grouping by Ability*, Slough: NFER.

Watson, A. and Mason, J. (1998) *Questions and prompts for mathematical thinking*, Derby: ATM.

18 Critical mathematics education

Paul Ernest

Introduction

The idea of a critical mathematics education is both an unusual and a controversial one. I explore here what a critical approach to mathematics and mathematics education is and what it might mean in the classroom. Looking critically at mathematics is important, not only philosophically, but because it impacts on the mathematics classroom. However, individuals do not just adopt philosophical positions on mathematics and associated classroom practices, for these positions are related to deep underlying ideas and ideological positions. I examine what these positions might be and how they are in conflict, both philosophically as well as in practice, over, for example, the introduction of the National Curriculum.

Of course ideologically diverse stances on mathematics and education see mathematical activity in quite different ways, and I conclude this chapter by offering practical activities suggesting how to make mathematics education more critical.

Key questions

Four sets of interrelated questions give an overview of what the chapter is about.

- What does 'critical mathematics education' mean? What is a critical attitude of mind?
- What different sorts of mathematics are there? What is mathematics? Can mathematics be conceptualised in more human and historical ways than it traditionally is? How should informal mathematics, street mathematics, and ethnomathematics be viewed? Do these alternative ways of conceptualising mathematics have different classroom implications?
- What are the aims of teaching and learning mathematics? What should they be? Whose aims dominate? For whom are they intended? Based on whose values? Who gains and who loses?
- How should learning mathematics empower learners? Can learning mathematics help people take more control of their lives? Could it aid democracy and help tackle injustice? What would having a critical mathematics classroom mean in practice? What different activities and resources could be used?

These four areas reflect the structure of the chapter, and you might find it useful to consider my questions and your own answers to them before moving on.

What is a critical perspective?

Modern times have seen not only an amazing growth in knowledge and information, but also the development of a critical attitude that questions some of it. This may be a result of some of the pronouncements of the old authorities such as the church being challenged in the first place by the findings of science. Indeed the questioning mind, which is supposed to underlie science, is the source of such a critical attitude. Of course criticism also lies at the heart of politics, in which contesting sides offer alternative political manifestos and critiques of each other's platforms. What has this to do with mathematics? Interestingly, Ancient Greek political argument is regarded by many as the source of proof in Euclid's Geometry. Although proofs appear to be the perfect polished results of reason, they emerge through the process of proposal and criticism through which they are improved enough to withstand the critical attitude of mind (Lakatos 1976). (Carrie Paechter discusses some of the implications of this historical perspective in her chapter.)

So what is this critical attitude of mind? This idea of 'being critical' is not the same as the popular meaning of being inclined to judge severely and find fault, calling attention to petty errors and flaws. Instead, 'being critical' is about engaging in a critique, making careful judgements, using all available evidence, reasoning and balanced arguments to evaluate claims and to reach conclusions. It also means not taking traditional explanations and views for granted but questioning them to see if they stand up. Above all it means independent thinking, drawing upon the larger contexts and implications of the issue under consideration, to make balanced judgements.

One implication of this critical approach is that we need to be prepared to have our preconceptions and our existing knowledge challenged, open to reappraisal and potential change. Such an attitude of mind may not sit too easily with a view of mathematics as a fixed body of eternal truths. Hence many scholars apply the philosophical tradition of critique to the traditional view of mathematics, and also think that there are important implications for the way we teach mathematics.

'Critical mathematics education' is about this critical attitude of mind applied to mathematics and its teaching.

Critical questions about the nature of mathematics

For some time one conception of mathematics has dominated both academic and popular thought – an 'absolutist' conception. Absolutist perspectives describe mathematical knowledge as an objective, absolute, certain and incorrigible body of knowledge. According to the absolutist conception, mathematical knowledge is:

- timeless, although we may discover new theories and truths to add;
- superhuman and untouched by social and historical developments, for, so it is claimed, the history of mathematics is irrelevant to the nature and justification of mathematical knowledge;

- pure, abstract, isolated and wholly logical knowledge, which it is claimed, happens to be useful because of its universal validity;
- value-free and culture-free, for the same reason.

Since this is the way that many teachers, philosophers and mathematicians describe their subject, it lends support to a public, and often negative, image of mathematics as cold, hard and inhuman. It is also seen as unfeeling and primarily masculine. Many researchers have pointed out the important part such views play in maintaining mathematics as a male domain, and in reducing women's participation in it (Burton 1986; Walkerdine 1997; Carrie Paechter in this book). However, although such a view may have negative consequences for many, it also needs to be recognised that the absolutist image attracts a minority of students to study mathematics; it views the subject as having reassuringly fixed rules and answers, providing a zone of safety from the uncertainties of life. For the pure mathematician, the absolutist image of mathematics often goes hand in hand with an appreciation of its austere beauty and elegance. Unfortunately, for many others, such a view denies the openness and creative processes that would make mathematics attractive to them.

In contrast, an alternative tradition in the philosophy of mathematics emph-asises the practice of mathematics and its human side. Because it rejects absolutist views of truth, this position is termed 'fallibilist'. A growing number of philo-sophers and mathematicians promote fallibilist views of mathematics (for example Davis and Hersh 1980; Ernest 1998). The argument is not that some or all of mathematical knowledge may be wrong, but that mathematics is a historically developing area in which ideas of truth and proof as well as mathematical theories, rules and results themselves are modified, changed and redefined over time. So mathematics is no more an area of timeless truth than philosophy, science or even history. In these areas of study we often have to re-evaluate the past in the light of our knowledge of the present. $1+1=2$ is true, but only for as long as we keep our definitions and rules fixed, and only so long as we only deal with the natural or real number system and their associated operations. If we subsequently define addition as in Boolean Algebra, or in base 2 modular arithmetic, then $1+1=1$ or $1+1=0$, respectively.

A more complex example is given by the equation $xy = yx$. Until the mid nineteenth century this was understood to represent an unquestionable truth, the Law of Commutativity, which had to hold for all numbers and other algebraic values. But after twenty years of struggle to extend imaginary numbers, William Hamilton made the decisive breakthrough by rejecting this law, which led to the important Theory of Quaternions, in which this previously 'unchangeable truth' is false.

In these two cases, fallibilism does not assert that the old mathematics is false; it is just that in the new system the old truth is no longer true. So these truths cannot be called absolute, eternal and beyond question!

Most versions of fallibilism view mathematics as the outcome of social processes. Mathematical knowledge is understood to be fallible and eternally open to revision, both in terms of its proofs and its concepts. Despite the rigour and precision of mathematical concepts and proofs, which humans have developed to extraordinary, austere and beautiful lengths, mathematical knowledge never attains a final, ultimate form. Fallibilist views reject the notion that there is a unique, fixed and permanent hierarchical structure comprising mathematical knowledge. Instead fallibilist views see mathematics as made up of many over-lapping structures. These, over the course of history, grow, collapse, and then grow anew like icebergs in the Arctic seas or like trees in a forest (Steen 1988). Fallibilism embraces as legitimate philosophical concerns the practices of mathe-maticians, its history and applications, the place of mathematics in human culture, including issues of values and education – in short – it fully admits the human face and basis of mathematics.

A feature of the fallibilist view is that mathematics is seen to be made up of (and in) different social practices, each with its history, persons, institutions, symbolic forms, purposes and power relations. Academic research mathematics is just one such practice (rather, it is a complex of shifting, interconnected practices). Likewise each of ethnomathematics (culturally embedded informal mathematics) and school mathematics is a distinct set of such practices. They are intimately bound up together, because the symbols and knowledge of one practice are taken into and used in another (Dowling 1988). This traffic is not all one way, from academic mathematics into other practices. For example, overweight and under-weight bales of goods are understood to have given rise to the plus and minus signs in medieval Italy. However, it was the acceptance of negative roots to equations in pure research mathematics in Renaissance Italy that finally forced the recognition of the negative integers as numbers.

Two important issues here are that first mathematics itself is controversial. Mathematics can no longer be taken to be above dispute. This in itself is sur-prising, in the light of the traditional view of mathematics as objective, superhuman and eternal. Second, mathematics is created by humans in their various cultures, and important contributions have been made in most parts of the globe, from China, India, Persia, Arabia and Africa, to the Americas and Europe. Mathematics is not a white European product but is genuinely a product of all of humanity.

Looking critically at the history and nature of mathematics leads to challenges both to philosophical and racial myths about the nature and origins of mathe-matics. This also begins to answer the critical questions asked above about the role of mathematics in society. (See Ifrah 1998 and Joseph 1992 for more on this.)

A current issue of interest is that of ethnomathematics – the culturally embedded mathematics outside the bounds of academia, from marble exchange values in British school playgrounds, symmetrical sand drawings in Moçambique, Islamic tiling patterns, Kabbalistic numerology in medieval Europe, to knotted Quipu strings in Central and South America. What is the relationship between ethnomathematics and modern academic mathematics? The traditional view of mathematicians is that it is their specialist knowledge that is applied to real world and other problems, and in watered-down form used in informal cultural contexts (i.e. ethnomathematics). The mathematicians, according to their view, own the pure 'essence' of mathematical knowledge, and 'dilute' versions are used by others.

In contrast, an ethnomathematical or cultural view of mathematics argues that mathematics is an intrinsic part of most people's cultural activities, and that academic mathematicians have appropriated, decontextualised, elaborated and concentrated that mathematics, until it seems to have a life of its own, thus denying its ethnomathematical origins. From the ethnomathematical perspective, this is a historical and philosophical falsification.

The importance of this controversy is that it concerns the ownership and origins of mathematics, and the legitimacy of cultural practices outside of the academic European tradition. Is it the case that ethnomathematics is irrelevant to 'real' academic mathematics, which was born with the Greek miracle, passed on by the Arabs, and developed to its present glory by modern Europeans? Are the ancient mathematical developments of China, India, the Middle East, Africa and Central/South America merely a backdrop for the *real* developments in mathematics? Or has a Eurocentric myth been foisted on the history of mathematics, and through it, on our school children? Many of us would agree with this latter viewpoint, and such an interpretation of history has more than a historical relevance. (As Derek Kassem points out in his chapter, it has implications for the value we place on the diverse cultures of pupils in our classrooms.)

Including a historical dimension in the teaching of mathematics can serve to counter the received Eurocentric view, and promote elements of a multicultural and anti-racist mathematics. Likewise, attending to ethnomathematics can also promote these perspectives and indicate the broad and living informal cultural presence of mathematics. The unique and universal characteristic of human beings is that we all have and make cultures, and every culture includes elements we can label as mathematical. Scholars in the history and culture of mathematics are quite clear about its nature. Mathematics is cultural knowledge that derives from humans engaging in the six universal activities of counting, locating, measuring, designing, playing and explaining in a sustained and conscious manner (Bishop 1988). There is no space to do justice to these questions here but a good place to begin to look for answers is in Skovsmose (1994) and in Powell and Frankenstein (1997).

A corollary is that if mathematics is a shifting complex of different practices, then school mathematics should not be seen as a fixed and unified subject that comes only in one form. It is a matter of decision which mathematical experiences, concepts, processes and applications are included in the mathematics curriculum for schools. Such decisions should perhaps be related to student age, aptitudes, interests, intended future study or work, cultural contexts and needs. What is needed is a varied mathematics curriculum responsive to the different wants and needs of students. This raises the problem of who is to decide what those needs are, but a flexible and responsive approach can be adopted. Of course a central shared set of knowledge and skills is needed by all, but in the eleven years of schooling from ages 5 to 16 years there is room for much more than this in the mathematics we teach.

These considerations provide the basis for a critique of the British National Curriculum in mathematics. Its structure is that of a single fixed hierarchy or 'ladder' of knowledge and skills. Mathematics is made up of a few topic strands (Attainment Targets) with eight or nine levels. All students in state schools from 5 to 16 years of age are expected to work their way up this same ladder. A single mathematics curriculum specification serves for all, irrespective of age, aptitude, interest and need. Elsewhere I have analysed and critiqued the National Curriculum in mathematics because of its ideological assumptions about the hierarchical structure of school mathematics, of learning and also of the way mathematical ability is distributed (Ernest 1991). There I argued that these views of mathematics, schooling and society lead to social reproduction. The analogy is with a fractional distillation tower as used in the petro-chemical industry, where different types of products (oil, petrol, etc.) are produced and tapped off at different heights in the tower. Likewise, pupils at age 5 are fed into the National Curriculum structure and emerge at different heights from the framework at age 16. 'Low-grade' products come out at levels 1–4 and these often are the future semi-skilled, unskilled and unemployed in society. 'Medium grade' products come out at levels 5–6 and these correspond to skilled blue- and white-collar workers. 'High-grade' products come out at levels 7 or above and these correspond to managerial and professional occupations. My claim is that both social class and future career prospects of students correlate with these levels, so the National Curriculum in mathematics serves to reproduce class, wealth and hence social opportunities.

It is of course false to claim that these correspondences always occur in a simple and deterministic way. But my claim is that there is a statistical correlation between mathematical achievement and future occupation. Indeed, the use of mathematical qualifications as a 'critical filter' controlling entry into higher education and higher paid occupations has long been noted, especially by researchers in the area of gender and mathematics (Sells 1976; Walkerdine 1997). It is in this way that a single fixed mathematics curriculum for all serves social reproduction purposes rather than defensible educational purposes.

Critical questions about the aims of teaching mathematics

In the previous section I began to raise issues about the aims and outcomes of teaching mathematics. In this section I want to consider more critical questions about the aims of teaching mathematics. Why do we or should we teach mathematics? What are the purposes, goals, justifications and reasons for teaching it? How can current mathematical teaching plans and practices be justified? What might be the rationale for reformed, future or possible approaches for mathematics teaching? What would be the aims of a critical approach to mathematical teaching? How could critical mathematical literacy or critical citizenship be fostered through mathematics teaching? Even though it is traditional to give mathematics a central place in the curriculum, surely we should have good reasons and justifications for doing so? A recent edited book on the subject called *Why learn maths?* (Bramall and White 2000) stirred up controversy when some of the authors argued that mathematics is overvalued and perhaps should be optional in later secondary school. Clearly mathematics is important, but exactly why do we teach it?

Of course the question 'why do we teach mathematics?' is not a million miles from the question 'why do we teach mathematics in the way that we do?'. Furthermore, this question leads almost naturally to 'why do we teach mathematics in the way that we do to whom we do?'. In arriving at such a question, we can begin to see that the teaching of mathematics has significant social implications.

Reflecting on the issue . . .

Consider the three questions in that last paragraph. What would your responses be?

   Now consider someone that you feel you have most disagreement with. This might be someone else in your school, someone else on a course, a relative, colleague, etc. What would their responses to these questions be and how would they differ from yours?

The aims of mathematics need therefore to be considered in relation to society, because aims reflect the intentions of individuals or groups. Different individuals would respond differently to those previous three questions, and these individuals might form different interest groups with diverse positions on the mathematics curriculum and its associated pedagogy. Aims embody their values, interests and ideologies, and not surprisingly, these views are often in conflict. In my book *The Philosophy of Mathematics Education* (Ernest 1991), I analysed the aims of what I saw as five different interest groups in modern Britain and related these to their views of mathematics. These groups and their aims and views are summarised in Table 18.1.

Reflecting on the issue . . .

You might want to consider where you would place yourself here given your responses to the 'Reflecting on the issue . . .' questions above. Do you fit neatly into one group or another or do you seem to span group boundaries? How do you think this influences your teaching? Do you know others who fit these profiles differently to you? How do you know? How does it seem to influence their teaching?

   You might also try to copy the table, cut it up and ask your colleagues to select descriptions they feel best fit themselves and use this as a focus for discussing the diversity of views amongst you.

The last group shown here (called the Public Educators) have the aim of developing critical mathematics education in schools. This group is also the only one with a fallibilist view of mathematics. Why, then, do we not see this view in schools today? Historically there was conflict between these five social groups who were engaged in a struggle over the nature of the National Curriculum in mathematics in the 1980s and 1990s (Brown 1996). The first three (whom we might call the 'more reactionary') groups managed to win a place for their aims in the curriculum. The fourth group (the progressive educators) wanted creativity and self-expression to be central in school mathematics, through problem solving, investigational work, and generally open-ended mathematical activity (at least

Table 18.1   Five aims for mathematics teaching and their interest groups

Mathematical aims	View of mathematics	Typical group members	Name for the Group
Acquiring basic mathematical skills and numeracy and social training in obedience (authoritarian, basic skills centred)	Absolutist set of decontextualised but utilitarian truths and rules	Radical 'New Right' conservative politicians and petty bourgeois	Industrial Trainers
Learning basic skills and learning to solve practical problems with mathematics and information technology (industry and work centred)	Unquestioned absolutist body of of applicable knowledge	Meritocratic industry-centred industrialists, managers, etc., New Labour	Technological Pragmatists
Understanding and capability in advanced mathematics, with some appreciation of mathematics (pure mathematics centred)	Absolutist body of structured pure knowledge	Conservative mathematicians preserving rigour of proof and purity of mathematics	Old Humanist Mathematicians
Gaining confidence, creativity and self expression through maths (child-centred progressivist)	Absolutist body of pure knowledge to be engaged with personally	Professionals, liberal educators, welfare state supporters	Progressive Educators
Empowerment of learners as critical and mathematically literate citizens in society (empowerment and social justice concerns)	Fallible knowledge socially constructed in diverse practices	Democratic socialists and radical reformers concerned with social justice and inequality	Public Educators

some of the time). However, they were forced to accept a compromise in the shape of an Attainment Target called 'Using and applying mathematics'. This focused on utilitarian aims: the practical skills of being able to use and apply mathematics to solve work-related problems, not the creative activities that they aspired to. In the revised National Curriculum of the year 2000 even this compromise component was eliminated. So this fourth group's main aim had little lasting impact on the school mathematics curriculum.

The fifth aim, the development of a critical mathematics education, however, has played no part whatsoever in the National Curriculum, and is absent from virtually all other curriculum developments too. It was rejected by the dominant interest groups. Thus the aim of developing critical citizenship and empowerment through mathematics is lacking from the National Curriculum, as is any awareness that pupils live in a society and in an unjust world in which citizens must use the mathematical knowledge and skills to critique misrepresentations and abuses of power.

The outcome of the historical contest between the five interest groups is that the National Curriculum is now based on an absolutist view of mathematics and can be said to be serve three main purposes:

1   communicating numeracy and basic mathematical skills and knowledge across the range of mathematical topics;
2   for advanced or high attaining students the understanding and use of these areas of mathematics at higher levels – an initiation into the abstract symbolic practices of mathematics;
3   development of the utilitarian skills of using and applying mathematics to 'real world' problems.

Each of these three outcomes is to a greater or lesser extent utilitarian, which should come as a surprise to no-one, because the whole thrust of the National Curriculum is towards scientific and technological competence. New Labour education policy has maintained this direction; the recent National Numeracy Strategy, which includes some useful ideas about developing children's mental strategies in mathematics, is also based on these utilitarian aims too.

Table 18.1 shows that underpinning the aims of the victorious groups in this contest are absolutist views of mathematics. It is therefore not surprising that the aims lack any elements of the appreciation of mathematics as a living strand in history and culture. Also lacking is any sense of the critical aspect of mathematics education. Such limited notions of mathematics are very widespread. Even in schools, it is seen as a study apart from others. For example, in a large-scale inspection of schools, the most widely made recommendation to mathematics departments (to 66 per cent) was that greater co-operation with other subject departments was needed (HMI 1979), thus illustrating the common perceptions and practice of isolation and 'apartness' of school mathematics.

Critical mathematics education questions these views of mathematics and the aims and nature of school mathematics. It questions the assumption that mathematics is nothing but developing skills and is all about 'doing' maths, consisting of working through the exercises in school maths books to solve book problems, perform algorithms and procedures, and to compute solutions. Given the major role that mathematics plays in the curriculum, a large capability element of this sort is necessary, for it serves a number of useful functions. But is there nothing more? From a critical mathematics education perspective there should be more. Students should be able to think mathematically, use it in their lives to empower themselves both personally and as citizens, and appreciate its role in history, culture, and the contemporary world. A critical mathematics education should encourage:

•   critically understanding the uses of mathematics in society: to identify, interpret, evaluate and critique the mathematics embedded in social, commercial and political systems and claims, from advertisements to government and interest-group pronouncements.

- being aware of how mathematical thinking permeates everyday and shopfloor life and current affairs;
- having a sense of mathematics as a central element of science, technology and all aspects of human culture, art and life, present and past;
- being aware of the historical development of mathematics, the social contexts of the origins of mathematical concepts, symbolism, theories and problems;
- understanding that there are multiple views of the nature of mathematics and controversy over the philosophical foundations of its knowledge.

However, this is not supposed to be a list of yet more content that is to be added to what is already there in the National Curriculum. The key issue is that these need to be *living* aspects of awareness. They need to link to the real interests, enthusiasms and experiences of students. All students bring an extensive range of knowledge and experience from everyday life, work and the social and cultural milieu in which they live. They are involved in and knowledgeable about local affairs, leisure activities, pastimes, hobbies, clubs, pop music, video games, television, films, magazines and newspapers. A wide range of issues is involved, including local, national and global politics, environmental issues, health, fitness, sport, nutrition, drugs, education, policing, law and order, finance, housing, transport, accidents, etc. These factors provide rich shared issues threading through students' lives, which can be drawn upon as meaningful resources for contextualising the teaching and learning of mathematics.

Authentic materials, social statistics and other resources also provide a basis for understanding how mathematics is used and applied outside school. They can be used to teach students to identify, interpret, evaluate and critique the mathematics embedded in social and commercial applications in advertisements and the mass media, and in political claims made by political parties and the government. This is not a partisan political aim, but merely the desire to equip all future citizens in society with the confidence, knowledge and skills to make informed and reasoned judgements. Citizens should not to accept the pronouncements of any authorities or interest groups on faith without applying their own critical judgement.

Teachers are often provided with resources to offer pupils that are far from authentic, but which are simplified, sanitised and trivialised (see many current mathematics textbooks). It is claimed that real materials introduce more complex and complicated mathematics than pupils are capable of, so the 'real world' has to be simplified. But this simplification is based on a presumed view of the learner, and what she or he is capable of, which subsequently creates the limitations of the learner. Children, usually those termed 'less able' but often those from more disadvantaged backgrounds, are not given real materials and so become un-accustomed to dealing with the real world in which they live. Mathematics thus becomes divorced from its purpose of enabling the critique and understanding of the world. As Paul Dowling argues in his chapter, the simplification of applied mathematics materials is not merely for simplification, but functions as a social positioning device. One advantage of authentic material is the very complexity they introduce into mathematics – and the way they foster a connectionist view of mathematics – which, as Mike Askew's chapter argues, is important and beneficial.

Developing critical mathematical literacy and citizenship through using authentic materials (and a critical pedagogy), independent critical judgement is fostered in students in ways that should be individually empowering. Empowered learners can not only pose and solve mathematical questions, but can also begin to answer important questions relating to a broad range of social uses (and abuses) of mathematics. Many of the issues involved will not seem primarily to be about mathematics, just as keeping up to date about current affairs from reading broadsheet newspapers is not primarily about literacy. Once mathematics becomes a 'thinking tool' for viewing the world critically, it contributes to the political and social empowerment of the learner, and ultimately to the promotion of social justice and a better life for all.

Recent National Curriculum developments in citizenship in the (DfEE and QCA 1999) provide opportunities for such approaches in secondary schools. For 14–16-year-olds the following two (reformulated) objectives are legal requirements.

1   Pupils should gain knowledge and understanding about becoming informed citizens, including human rights, the diverse national, regional, religious and ethnic identities in the United Kingdom, the media's role in society, including the internet, wider issues and challenges of global interdependence and responsibility, including sustainable development and Local Agenda 21.
2   Pupils should develop the skills of enquiry and communication including researching political, moral, social issues, problems or events by analysing information from different sources, showing an awareness of the use and abuse of statistics; expressing, justifying and defending orally and in writing personal opinions about them, and contributing to group and exploratory class discussions and debates.

Do pupils really need to see the world through mathematical eyes to be citizens in modern society, when most of these concerns are general? From a critical mathematics perspective they do, because the mathematisation of modern society and modern life has been growing exponentially. Virtually all human activities and institutions are conceptualised and regulated numerically, including sport, popular media, health, education, government, politics, business, commercial production and science. Sports records are numerical, as are music charts and those for best-selling books. Many aspects of modern society are controlled by complex hidden mathematical systems: supermarket checkout tills with automated bill production and stock control; tax and welfare benefits; industrial, agricultural and educational subsidies; voting; stock markets. These automated systems carry out complex tasks of information capture, policy implementation and resource allocation. Complex mathematics is used to regulate many aspects of our lives – our finances, banking and bank accounts, with very little human scrutiny and intervention, once the systems are in place. Only through a critical mathematics education can future citizens learn to analyse, question and challenge these systems that can distort life chances and reduce freedoms.

We already view our lives and the world through a quantified framework, framed by the clock, calendar, work timetables, travel planning and timetables, finances and currencies, insurance, pensions, tax, measurements of weight, length, area and volume, graphical and geometric representations, etc. Much of our experience of life is already mathematised. Unless schooling helps learners to develop the knowledge and understanding to identify these mathematisations of our world, and the confidence to question and critique them, they cannot be in full control of their own lives, nor can they become properly informed and participating citizens. Instead they may be manipulated by commercial, political or religious interest groups, or become cynical and irrational in their attitudes to social, political, medical and scientific issues.

Critical mathematical education aims to empower learners as individuals and citizens in society, by developing mathematical power both to overcome barriers to higher education and employment and thus increasing economic self-determination, and by fostering critical awareness and democratic citizenship via mathematics. The ultimate aim is social change towards a more just and egalitarian society via the empowerment of the citizenry.

What does this mean in practice? These aims of critical mathematics, require the use of a questioning and decision-making learning style in the classroom. Teaching approaches should include discussions, permitted conflict of opinions and views but with justifications offered, the challenging of the teacher as an ultimate source of knowledge (not in their role as classroom authority), the questioning of content and the negotiation of shared goals. Some of this is included in the new Citizenship curriculum. Learners should also be given the chance to pose their own problems and to initiate their own projects and investigations at least some of the time, as did the children of the School of Barbiana (1970). Learning materials should include socially relevant projects, authentic social statistics, accommodating social and cultural diversity and using local cultural resources. However, this approach must also honestly and openly address the instrumental life goals of the learners themselves, both in terms of needed skills and passing exams.

The counter-argument against such an approach is that it can become propaganda and a political misdirection of the young. But, as anyone who has taught contentious issues in the mathematics classroom or lecture hall knows, such an approach invariably results in dispute and heated argument rather than in passive acceptance. The pupils of today will not accept teacher propaganda without question.

Examples of critical mathematics education approaches are embodied in Marilyn Frankenstein's numeracy course for adults (Frankenstein 1989), and the Radical Statistics Group's publications (for example, Irvine *et al.* 1979). In schools, developments in anti-racist and anti-sexist mathematics perhaps have gone the furthest in this direction. A discussion of the underlying philosophy of critical mathematics education as well as accounts of project work with secondary school children in Scandinavia can be found in the work of Steig Mellin-Olsen (1987) and Ole Skovsmose (1994).

A successful critical mathematics education must empower learners, first to overcome internal inhibitions and perceptions of inadequacy, second to question the teacher, the subject and the constraints of school, and third to question the 'facts' and edicts of authority at large in society. Learners have an unquestioning acceptance of authority in school, society and mathematics which may be manifested in lack of confidence, passivity or even aggression. Students and even adult returners to education cannot become autonomous learners and confident critical citizens immediately.

Mary Belenky, Blyth Clinchy, Nancy Goldberger and Jill Tarule (Belenky *et al.* 1986) provide a useful model of the stages of empowerment of the knower. This model is relevant here because it charts the development of the knower/learner from the silenced subject completely dominated by authority, to the constructing knower, an autonomous, confident and empowered knower. Intermediate stages in this journey include (a) accepting the voice of others, (b) responding for oneself and then (c) beginning to connect different areas of one's knowledge. If we apply this to schoolchildren, most of them will best be described as being in the early stages. They may have acquired some of the knowledge and means of doing mathematics at school, but because of the separated way in which mathematics is usually taught it will probably just be a small compartment in their lives and a way of thinking that they bring out in the mathematics classroom. If they succeed in mathematics hopefully they develop the ability to apply some of the features of the intermediate stages, but this still leaves mathematics as something technical and little to do with their lives and experiences. Very few will be able to relate to mathematics through connecting different areas of their own knowledge. This is primarily about intuition and an 'inside knowledge' of mathematical concepts: getting inside mathematical ideas, and feeling that they have some life inside your imagination too. The ultimate goal, according to this model, is to become a 'constructing knower', where you can combine intuition and the procedures and skills of mathematics to make sense of the world and confidently apply mathematical thinking too.

Practical approaches to critical mathematics education

So how can these ideas be applied in the classroom? I think the key issue is to use examples, discussion points and projects within the standard mathematical curriculum with relevance for pupils: immediate personal relevance by getting learners engaged in activity; evident utilitarian and examination relevance; links with their out-of-school interests; connections with local, regional, national and global issues that affect learners or humanity more widely. Obviously teachers must decide what activities and projects would be best suited to their pupils, how often these kind of things can be done, and what is too risky in view of likely reactions from pupils, teachers and parents.

Aspects of such mathematical tasks would include activities which require co-operation, discussion, creativity, judgement, and for which there is no 'right' answer; pursuing cross-curricular links and avoiding demarcating subjects strictly; discussing the history and the cultural origins of mathematics.

Critical citizenship through mathematics

Resources that present activities from a critical perspective are available, but they are not widespread. This is possibly due to publishers not wishing to invest in potentially non-profit-making areas. One does not need, however, to totally depend on external resources, but instead to develop a critical frame of mind. Here are some ideas (some more can be found in Gates 2000).

Local Environment

- Local survey of shops: types including charity shops and closed shops; changes over the years.
- Parks and playgrounds: types, size, safety.
- Survey of homeless: local and national statistics.
- Analysis of accident black spot data.
- Should there be more children's parks, schools and shops on new housing estates? Are shops, post offices and postboxes placed in the best positions? What happens to local roads when a new housing development is built?
- Just how much does it cost to build a house in the area? How much is it sold for?
- Develop projects of local interest – publish the results in the local press to show that school projects are valued by the community.

Environment

Children are acutely interested in the local and global environment – it is their future after all. Particular topics could include:

- Pollution, destruction of the rainforest, comparative surface areas; local and national figures for recycling – is it actually worth driving to the recycling centre?
- Paper use in the school, county, country.
- Petrol usage – how much pollution is caused by different cars? Who causes most pollution? Who drives the most polluting cars? Which country pollutes more? Which countries suffer most?
- Discuss and challenge controversial statistics about the environment, etc. Is the world getting hotter?

Betting

The lottery is an obvious example of where mathematics might be used, but non-critical activities can easily dominate. For example 'Is the lottery fair' often relates to the frequency of numbers coming out. However, one might alternatively ask whether spending on the lottery is 'value for money'. Whether spending is equally distributed across social classes? Where does lottery funding go to?

Local 'folk' mathematics

What mathematics does the school caretaker use? What about a carpenter? Bricklayer? Nurse? Doctor? Find out where mathematics is used in different jobs by inviting people in and taking pupils on trips.

Health education

- Surveys of (i) smoking, (ii) drinking, (iii) drugs – class, school, street.
- Analysis of mortality, life expectancy by class, region in UK, in world.
- Estimate costs to the National Health Service each year of treating patients suffering from smoking-related illness.
- Find out the profits of the three main tobacco companies in the world.
- Given that it kills you, why do people smoke?
- How much does the tobacco industry get in profits for each person who dies from smoking-induced lung cancer?

Political data

- Discuss the British voting system. Is it fair? Is there a better way? Is it possible to develop a fair voting system? Test out different ways of voting (information from Electoral Reform Society).
- Racial statistics on employment, education, mental health.
- Gender and exam success: using DfEE data, local and national league tables – are they fair?
- Gender stereotypes in adverts and newspapers.
- Comparative spending in UK and abroad on education, health, defence, aid etc.
- Critical analysis of RPI index.
- Analysis of unemployment figures by region, qualification, social class, gender.
- Analysis of house prices, relationship to school league tables.
- Repossessions, bankruptcies by regions.

In conclusion

In this chapter I have introduced some of the key issues and questions concerning a critical approach to mathematics. This involves questioning mathematics and its uses and applications to see what assumptions lie underneath. The questions make a traditionally uncontroversial subject more controversial, and you will have to decide how much of this is right for the children you teach. What these questions show is that mathematics need not be the boring subject that many take it to be. From the critical perspective, mathematics must not be seen as separate from children's interests and social activities, and reconnecting it with their lives gives it a greater relevance and gives them more interest and confidence in using and applying it.

Invitation to reflect

Reflecting with and on your colleagues

You can expect to find a range of differing philosophical standpoints about mathematics and its role in society among your colleagues. I have already suggested that you explore these in this chapter. In order to bring the elements of this chapter together what you might usefully do now is arrange for some of your colleagues to discuss their responses to a variety of mathematical activities, including some of the ideas I have offered in this chapter, and in particular consider the following.

- What are your/their views on the appropriateness of the tasks?
- What are your/their views on the suitability of the tasks for their pupils?
- How would you/they implement the tasks or activities in the classroom? How would you/they structure the tasks? How would you/they develop, extend or restrict the tasks in different ways?

You could try taking this a step further and agree to work on an activity task or project and see how it gets interpreted differently by different teachers.

Reflecting with and on your pupils

You could explore the different stances taken by a range of your pupils. Different contributors to this book have suggested that pupils with different cultural and social backgrounds might see the world of mathematics education quite differently. You might find it illuminating to explore some of the issues I examine in this chapter with your pupils. Focus on gender, ethnicity and social class differences and on pupils positioned as having different abilities in mathematics.

- What views do they have of mathematics?
- How do these fit with the stances I outlined in Table 18.1?
- How do they respond to different mathematical tasks?

Recommended further reading and resources

Shan S. and Bailey, P. (1991) *Multiple Factors: Classroom Mathematics for Equality and Justice*, Stoke-on-Trent: Trentham Books. A valuable discussion of critical mathematics education emphasising anti-racist education. It includes useful classroom examples of data that can be discussed.

Wright, P. (1999) *The Mathematics and Human Rights Book*, London: Amnesty International. Contains practical activities that fit with the suggestions made here.

Ernest, P. (1991) *The Philosophy of Mathematics Education*, London: Falmer Press. This analyses views about the nature of mathematics, discusses the aims for mathematics teaching of different groups, and discusses critical mathematics education under the title of the Public Educators.

Joseph, G. G. (1991) *The Crest of the Peacock: Non-European Roots of Mathematics*, London: Penguin Books. Shows the important and neglected non-European roots of mathematics in history.

Powell, A. and Frankenstein, M. (eds) (1997) *Ethnomathematics: Challenging Eurocentrism in Mathematics Education*, Albany, New York: SUNY Press. Valuable collection on ethno-mathematics and critical mathematics.

References

Belenky, M. F., Clinchy, B. M., Goldberger, N. R. and Tarule, J. M. (1986) *Women's Ways of Knowing*, New York: Basic Books.

Bishop, A. (1988) *Mathematical Enculturation*, Dordrecht: Kluwer Academic Publishers.

Bramall, S. and White, J. (eds) (2000) *Why Learn Maths?*, London University Bedford Way Papers, London: Institute of Education.

Brown, M. (1996) 'The context of the research – the evolution of the National Curriculum for mathematics', in Johnson, D. C. and Millett, A. (eds), *Implementing the Mathematics National Curriculum: Policy, Politics and Practice*. London: Paul Chapman Publishing, pp. 1–28.

Burton, L. (1986) *Girls into Maths Can Go*, London: Holt, Rinehart and Winston.

Davis, P. J. and Hersh, R. (1980) *The Mathematical Experience*, London: Penguin Books.

DfEE and QCA (1999) *The National Curriculum for England: Citizenship*, London: HMSO.

Dowling, P. (1988) 'The contextualising of mathematics: towards a theoretical map', in Harris, M. (ed.), *Schools, Mathematics and Work*, London: Falmer Press, pp. 93–120.

Ernest, P. (1991) *The Philosophy of Mathematics Education*, London: Falmer Press.

Ernest, P. (1998) *Social Constructivism as a Philosophy of Mathematics*, Albany, New York: State University of New York Press.

Frankenstein, M. (1989) *Relearning Mathematics: A Different Third R – Radical Maths*, London: Free Association Books.

Gates, P. (2000) 'The social and political responsibilities of the mathematics teacher', paper presented to *Profmat2000 – Conferência da Associação de Professores da Matemática de Portugal*, 8th–11th November, Funchal: Universidade da Madeira.

Her Majesty's Inspectorate (1979) *Aspects of Secondary Education, Supplementary Information on Mathematics*, London: Her Majesty's Stationery Office.

Ifrah, G. (1998) *The Universal History of Numbers. From Prehistory to the Invention of the Computer*, London: Harvill Press.

Irvine, J., Miles, I. and Evans, J. (eds) (1979) *Demystifying Social Statistics*, London: Pluto Press.

Joseph, G. G. (1992) *The Crest Of The Peacock, Non-European Roots Of Mathematics*, London: Penguin Books.

Lakatos, I. (1976) *Proofs and Refutations: The Logic of Mathematical Discovery*, Cambridge: Cambridge University Press.

Mellin-Olsen, S. (1987) *The Politics of Mathematics Education*, Dordrecht: Reidel.

Powell, A. B. and Frankenstein, M. (eds) (1997) *Ethnomathematics: Challenging Eurocentrism in Mathematics Education*, Albany, New York: SUNY Press.

School of Barbiana (1970) *Letter to a Teacher*, Harmondsworth: Penguin Books.

Sells, L. (1976) 'The mathematics filter and the education of women and minorities', paper presented at the Annual Meeting of the American Association for the Advancement of Science, Boston, February 1976.

Shan, S. and Bailey, P. (1991) *Multiple Factors: Classroom Mathematics for Equality and Justice*, Stoke-on-Trent: Trentham Books.

Skovsmose, O. (1994) *Towards a Philosophy of Critical Mathematics Education*, Dordrecht: Kluwer.

Steen, L. A. (1988) 'The science of patterns', *Science* 240(4852), 611–16.

Walkerdine, V. (1997) *Counting Girls Out*, London: Falmer Press.

19 Comparing international practice in the teaching of mathematics

Paul Andrews

Introducing the issue

The Third International Mathematics and Science Study (TIMSS) indicated that the average mathematical attainment of 13-year-old children in Britain is poorer than the attainment of those from many economically and culturally comparable countries. Comparative research suggests that the styles of mathematics teaching found in many British classrooms bear little resemblance to those in other countries where pupils score more highly. Also, the curriculum and the manner in which it is presented in Britain is prone to a political influence unknown elsewhere, with the consequence that entitlement and curricular access have been compromised on the back of practices of dubious educational but highly politically rhetorical provenance.

In this chapter, I focus particularly on how mathematics is presented in those countries where, according to research like TIMSS, it is taught 'successfully'. My emphasis, because that is where much of the available research is focused, is on the teaching of mathematics to pupils at age 13. This also fits with the TIMSS data and therefore helps in the making of comparative statements. As I show, many of these successful practices contradict long-held tenets of British education and, in particular, the assertion by ex-Chief Inspector of Schools, Chris Woodhead, that setting, irrespective of age, is the appropriate means of grouping pupils for successful mathematics teaching. (Jo Boaler and Dylan Wiliam also demonstrate the drawbacks in ability grouping in their chapter.) Importantly, I hope to show also that there are ways forward that are premised on rationality rather than rhetoric (Ruthven 1999).

Key questions

This chapter addresses the three areas described above by focusing on the following three questions.

1 What was TIMSS, what did it find out and what importance can we place on the results?
2 How is mathematics taught overseas and are there general models of successful mathematics teaching?

3   How is British educational policy framed and is it likely to facilitate the learning of mathematics for all pupils?

What was TIMSS, what did it find out and what importance can we place on the results?

The Third International Mathematics and Science Study (TIMSS), undertaken during the mid 1990s, surveyed the attainment of 'more than half a million students at five grade levels in 15,000 schools and more than 40 countries around the world' (Beaton *et al.* 1996: 7). A detailed description of the study can be found at the TIMSS web site (http://timss.bc.edu/TIMSS1/AboutTIMSS.html). Conducted under the auspices of the International Association for the Evaluation of Educational Achievement (IEA), TIMSS was a multinational study in which substantial administrative, developmental and analytical parts were played by teams of researchers in the United States, Germany, Canada, the Netherlands and Australia plus, of course, many national organising bodies.

The main study was concerned with the educational attainment of pupils from around the world and it is on this that I focus initially. Also, the TIMSS video study and the survey of mathematics and science opportunities (SMSO) project yielded valuable insights into national pedagogic traditions that have informed greatly the latter part of this chapter. (Summaries of both can be found in Kawanaka *et al.* 1999 and Cogan and Schmidt 1999.)

Six topic areas of mathematics were tested and the results are of significant interest to teachers in Britain. You can see from the figures of Table 19.1 that the mean scores for both England and Scotland were below the international mean on five of the six topic areas. Indeed, the evidence indicates that the mathematical attainment of British pupils at age thirteen was substantially poorer than that of those from many other countries which could be regarded as economically and culturally similar to Britain. Sig Prais, in his interesting analysis of the TIMSS findings, argues that at age thirteen English pupils lag behind their more successful European counterparts by around one year and behind their contemporaries in the Pacific Rim by more than three years (Prais 1999).

Inevitably such studies court criticism although frequently they can be defended. Dylan Wiliam (1998) argues that the TIMSS sampling procedures militated against English participants mainly because of the practice in many countries of repeat years and the lower levels of pupil absenteeism reported by English teachers. Sig Prais (1999) argues that even when such things were taken into account, English pupils fared little better. Alternatively, overseas researchers could argue that the TIMSS sampling procedures favour the British by virtue of their having received an extra year of schooling – the British start formal schooling at least a year earlier than almost all other countries. (There are some people in the field of early years education, however, who might argue that starting formal education a year 'early' was a positive *disadvantage* to such young children.)

Dylan Wiliam (1998) and Christine Keitel and Jeremy Kilpatrick (1999) suggest that the United States' dominance of the study's processes militated against the interests of other participating countries. Dylan Wiliam writes of a process of '"horse-trading" whereby representatives of each country try to get items that reflect their own distinctive approaches to topics included in the tests' (Wiliam 1998: 34) and argues that such a process inevitably favours the strong. Christine Keitel and Jeremy Kilpatrick believe, despite claims to the contrary, that the use of English as the official language of the project may have militated against equity. An alternative perspective might be that the relatively poor performance of both England and the United States was indicative of little such bias.

Below, Table 19.1 is an adaptation of the table found on page 41 of Beaton *et al.* (1996) showing the overall and topic area mean scores for some of the participating TIMSS nations. A gap between rows indicates that some countries have been omitted from the original list. Also, those marked with an asterisk failed to satisfy the criteria for sampling as determined by the TIMSS researchers but have been inserted into the table to facilitate comparisons.

Christine Keitel and Jeremy Kilpatrick (1999) argue that the interest shown by many politicians and educators in studies such as TIMSS is selfish rather than altruistic – that it is little more than politicians trying to show that their educational system compares favourably with the best, and educators framing national findings in ways which persuade governments to fund their own particular research interests. Whether this is a realistic appraisal of the situation or a cynical

Table 19.1   TIMSS topic area mean scores

	Overall	Number	Geometry	Algebra	Data handling	Measure	Proportion
Items	151	51	23	27	21	18	11
Singapore	79	84	76	76	79	77	75
Japan	73	75	80	72	78	67	61
Korea	72	74	75	69	78	66	62
Belgium (Fl.)	66	71	64	63	73	60	53
Czech Rep.	66	69	66	65	68	62	52
Slovak Rep.	62	66	63	62	62	60	49
Switzerland	62	67	60	53	72	61	52
Hungary	62	65	60	63	66	56	47
Austria*	62	66	57	59	68	62	49
France	61	64	66	54	71	57	49
Bulgaria*	60	60	65	62	62	54	47
Netherlands*	60	62	59	53	72	57	51
Belgium (Fr.)*	59	62	58	53	68	56	48
Australia*	58	61	57	55	67	54	47
England	53	54	54	49	66	50	41
Scotland*	52	53	52	46	65	48	40
United States	53	59	48	51	65	40	42
Latvia (LSS)	51	53	57	51	56	47	39
Spain	51	52	49	54	60	44	40
International Average	55	58	56	52	62	51	45

response by two academics is, of course, an important issue on which you will no doubt have your own opinions.

Whatever the validity of the criticisms, my own conjecture is that few teachers would recognise the TIMSS questions below as being fully representative of the range of topics they teach. The issue then is whether the TIMSS study actually does represent 'mathematical attainment' or rather merely the attainment over a limited range of mathematical areas. The average (international) percentage success on each question is shown in brackets.

- The numbers in the sequence 2, 7, 12, 17, 22, . . . increase by fives. The numbers in the sequence 3, 10, 17, 24, 31, . . . increase by sevens. The number 17 occurs in both sequences. If the two sequences are continued, what is the next number that will be seen in both sequences? (45%)

- In a discus-throwing competition, the winning throw was 61.60 m. The second-place throw was 59.72 m. How much longer was the winning throw than the second-place throw?
   A. 1.18 m   B. 1.88 m   C. 1.98 m   D. 2.18 m (72%)

- The length of a rectangle is 6 cm, and its perimeter is 16 cm. What is the area of the rectangle in square centimetres? (40%)

- Last year there were 1,172 students at Beaton High School. This year there are 15 per cent more students than last year. Approximately how many students are at Beaton High School this year?
   A. 1800   B. 1600   C. 1500   D. 1400   E. 1200 (44%)

- A drawer contains 28 pens; some white, some blue, some red, and some grey. If the probability of selecting a blue pen is 2/7, how many blue pens are in the drawer?
   A. 4   B. 6   C. 8   D. 10   E. 20 (53%)

Reflecting on the issue . . .

Have a go at answering each of the questions above (I will not provide the answers – you should discuss and compare with your colleagues).

- What range of mathematical skills is being tested here? What do you consider to be important omissions in this list of questions?
- What issues might there be in designing test items for your list of omissions that could be used in a multi-national study such as TIMSS?

A detailed review of the TIMSS study is not the intention of this chapter. This can be found in, for example, Sig Prais' analysis (Prais 1999). Suffice it to say that the TIMSS study has identified some significant problems in respect of British educational attainment and my intention is to explore what we might do in our classrooms to improve the situation.

How is mathematics taught overseas and are there general models of successful mathematics teaching?

Recent research has hinted at the existence of distinctive national mathematics teaching traditions (Schmidt *et al.* 1996). Despite this there is also considerable evidence of generalities and commonalities in classroom practice in respect of effective teaching that I will present here in two parts. The first looks at how teachers manage their classrooms and structure their lessons. The second considers the ways in which mathematics itself is (re)conceptualised for teaching and learning. The evidence is drawn from observations undertaken in Japan, Hungary and France – all successful TIMSS countries. Other starting points could have been used; Frederick Leung's accounts of mathematics teaching in China (Leung 1995, 1999) or Fou-Lai Lin's descriptions of Taiwan (Lin 1988; Lin and Tsao 1999), for example. However, I made a decision to focus on just a few successful systems in order to offer detail and evidence of transferability.

Class management and lesson structures

The evidence, of research undertaken in Japan, France, Hungary and elsewhere would seem to suggest that where mathematics is taught successfully, the following effective practices can be found:

- Learners are generally taught in mixed-ability classes.
- Teachers expect to teach each class as a unit.
- Teachers dominate the lesson with their own talk, or by managing the talk of others, for the majority of the lesson.
- Learners are expected to operate in a public domain.
- Teachers constantly review what is being done, and what has been done during a lesson.
- Learners spend little time working alone from textbooks.
- Homework is a device to provide a coherent link between lessons.

Several of the ideas expressed here conflict with those propounded by the British government and OFSTED through the public statements of the then Her Majesty's Chief Inspector of Schools, Chris Woodhead. Two particular areas of conflict are the association of high mathematical attainment with the teaching of mixed-ability classes and the practice of teaching a class as a unit. In most countries education is underpinned by the principle that all children have equal rights to the curriculum. Indeed, equality of provision has constitutional authority for the French (Monchablon 1995) – a principle that is readily accepted by teachers on the basis 'that it is not essential for a child to demonstrate a well-defined knowledge and understanding of a topic before moving to the next' (Jennings and Dunne 1996: 50). This resonates with my own experiences of Hungary where there is a clear sense that all pupils will understand eventually – if not today then tomorrow. In Japan a similar philosophy exists supported by a belief that 'grouping by ability within classrooms is discriminatory' (Stevenson 1999: 117). However, the fulfilment of such principles demands ways of working different from those conventionally seen in Britain and it is on these that I focus next.

A typical Japanese mathematics lesson is based around a mathematical problem that is attempted either individually or in small groups before a public discussion in which pupils' ideas are presented on the board. The teacher summarises the discussion, the pupils work on several similar problems and homework is set (Cogan and Schmidt 1999; Jacobs *et al.* 1997; Kawanaka *et al.* 1999; Stigler *et al.* 1996; Whitman and Lai 1990). In general the format of the lesson is such that teachers conduct a discussion around the previous lesson's problem before posing the new one. The majority of the lesson is spent with pupils either attending to their teacher – in all its manifestations – or working collaboratively on the problems offered (Schmidt *et al.* 1996; Stigler *et al.* 1987). Little time is spent on textbook exercises. A Japanese lesson moves slowly because, for Japanese teachers, thinking about a problem, focusing on and sharing processes are more important than the final product (Stigler and Perry 1990).

French mathematics lessons typically comprise several phases. They generally start with the previous lesson's homework being publicly discussed and corrected. This is followed by the presentation of the new topic content before pupils begin a short period of individual working on problems set from a text. Lastly, the next homework is set (Schmidt *et al.* 1996). Sue Jennings and Richard Dunne (1996) write that the presentation element of the lesson frequently involves problems on which pupils are invited to work before the public sharing of ideas from which the general principles being introduced might emerge. At any time pupils may be called to the board to share solutions or to offer ideas because public sharing is seen as an integral part of the process (Pepin 1996; Schmidt *et al.* 1996). During the middle, or teaching, phase of the lesson pupils are frequently invited to work on tasks that verify that which has been introduced – proofs and confirmatory examples are discussed simultaneously (Jennings and Dunne 1996; Schmidt *et al.* 1996).

In Hungary, lessons begin with a review of the homework set the previous lesson. Solutions are shared with children being invited to the board (Andrews 1995, 1999; Hatch 1999). This may be followed by a brief period of revision or mental work with the teacher offering questions orally for immediate response before the day's work is introduced. The teaching phase of the lesson consists of several episodes in which a question or problem is posed, then children work individually for a few minutes before solutions are publicly shared and outcomes reviewed by the teacher. Occasionally, prior to pupils being invited to work on their problems, there will be a discussion, but this is rare. At the end of the lesson, homework is set in preparation for the next lesson. Pupils spend little time working through routine exercises or discussing their work in small groups (Hatch 1999) – teachers tend to view the whole class, rather than the individual, as the learner (Andrews 1999; Hatch 1999).

However, to focus solely on teachers' actions would be to deny other important elements of the story. The TIMSS video study identified similar teacher behaviours in both Germany and Japan but significant differences in mathematical attainment (Kawanaka *et al.* 1999). The differences appeared to lie in the nature of the tasks teachers set their pupils – Japanese teachers placing a greater emphasis on the encouragement of thinking. Also, and this is interesting from the British perspective, not only do the proportions of seatwork differ across educational systems but also the quality of the tasks that teachers offered their pupils diminished with increasing amounts of seatwork (Kawanaka *et al.* 1999). Further, where pupils share publicly their ideas teachers expect to spend little time on routine and repetitive exercises – in Japan far fewer problems are covered during the course of one lesson than in the United States where the number of problems covered is seen as a gauge of teacher success – the more the better (Stigler and Perry 1990).

Reflecting on the issue . . .
Having read those three scenarios from Japan, France and Hungary, try to construct a paragraph that could describe a 'typical' mathematics lesson in the UK as it might be written by someone unfamiliar with our system (for example a Japanese, French or Hungarian mathematics teacher).

Then consider what effect such diversity might have upon pupils' learning.

You might usefully experiment and plan a lesson based upon the alternative models in Japan, France or Hungary in your school. Plan a lesson collaboratively with your mentor or another teacher, and make a note of pupils' reactions.

Mathematics as conceptualised or structured for teaching and learning

As with teacher behaviours there are several generalities to be inferred from research concerning the manner in which mathematics is conceptualised for teaching in Japan, Hungary and France. I alluded to some of these above but the major issues seem to be among the following:

- Mathematics is acknowledged as difficult.
- Mathematics is viewed as a problem-solving activity.
- Problems are chosen to exemplify mathematical generality.
- Teachers expect to develop rather than state mathematical ideas.
- Teachers do not shy away from the vocabulary of mathematics.
- Pupils are expected to engage with proof and justification.
- The applications of mathematics are subordinated to the subject itself.
- Mathematical ideas are revisited constantly within the problems offered.
- Relatively little time is given to the practice of routine procedures.

The problems presented to Japanese pupils are mathematically challenging and unfamiliar but they will have learned any necessary concepts or procedures for dealing with them (Jacobs *et al.* 1997; Kawanaka *et al.* 1999). Teachers offer few explicit instructions, as the problems are intended to lead all pupils towards an understanding of the topic being studied (Jacobs *et al.* 1997; Schmidt *et al.* 1996). The problems, chosen to uncover generalities and emphasise process over product, are posed at the start of the lesson to allow time for solutions to be found before public sharing (Stigler and Perry 1990; Stigler *et al.* 1996). More than half of all lessons involve some elements of proof (Kawanaka *et al.* 1999; Stigler and Hiebert, 1997). Lessons are kept slow in order to encourage thinking and even during seatwork more time is spent on thinking creatively or applying concepts than on the practice of procedures (Kawanaka *et al.* 1999; Stigler and Perry 1990). A coherent lesson within a coherent sequence of lessons is the objective of all teachers (Jacobs *et al.* 1997; Stigler and Perry 1990; Whitman and Lai 1990) in order to give learners 'opportunities to infer connections between different topics in the mathematics curriculum' (Stigler *et al.* 1996: 155–6). Lesson plans are highly detailed and attempt both to anticipate and to provoke pupils' thinking (Stigler *et al.* 1996).

French children are 'offered formal and complex subject matter' (Schmidt *et al.* 1996: 130) which teachers organise in a variety of ways in order to scaffold learning (Pepin 1999) and which is premised on a belief in the power of discovery (Pepin 1996). All pupils are expected to engage with formal definitions, laws and principles; logical reasoning and proof; and problem-solving (Jennings and Dunne 1996; Pepin 1996, 1999; Schmidt *et al.* 1996) and to engage with the formal language of mathematics. Teaching is based on generalities rather than particularities (Jennings and Dunne 1996). Children frequently engage in investigational or experimental tasks where much emphasis is placed on process (Pepin 1998; Schmidt *et al.* 1996). Such tasks frequently serve either to establish a relationship that is then subjected to a formal treatment or to demonstrate in a concrete manner something already formally established. Overall the main objective for French teachers is to focus on the development of mathematical thinking through the exploration, development and understanding of mathematical concepts; an emphasis on mathematical reasoning and little time spent on routine procedures (Pepin 1998). French teachers acknowledge that mathematics is a difficult subject but, unlike their English counterparts, who offer their pupils a *reduction from* that complexity, offer an *induction into* that complexity (Jennings and Dunne 1996).

Hungarian lessons are purposeful with clear mathematical objectives (Harries 1997) towards which pupils are directed (Hatch 1999) by means of extensive use of open and closed questions (Andrews 1997). Teachers emphasise generality and highlight particular cases as problematic (Andrews 1999; Hatch 1999). They stress abstract ideas although real situations are used to validate the processes being taught with algebra being presented as the language by which mathematics is communicated so 'that for most Hungarian pupils algebra appears to be a natural form in which to express ideas' (Hatch 1999: 28). Lessons are structured around problems that facilitate proof strategies (Andrews 1997, 1999; Harries 1997; Hatch 1994) and the creation of 'links within the pupil's conceptual networks' (Hatch 1994: 30). Teachers do not see their task as passers-on of knowledge; pupils are expected to engage with problems, debate ideas publicly, agree a resolution and, ultimately, reach an understanding of the issue under consideration (Andrews 1999; Hatch 1994). The emphasis lies not in routine practice or applications but in the understanding of mathematical ideas coupled with reasoning and proof (Andrews 1997; 1999; Hatch 1994; 1999). Hungarian teachers offer a mathematically continuous experience incorporating constant revision of ideas covered previously (Andrews 1999; Harries 1997; Hatch 1999) – homework is used both to consolidate ideas and facilitate the transition from one lesson to the next (Andrews 1999).

In summary it would seem that there are several generalisable conditions which underpin the successful teaching and learning of mathematics. However, '. . .

systems of teaching are not easily transported from one culture into another'
(Stigler and Hiebert 1997: 19) because teaching is

> a system composed of tightly connected elements. And the system is rooted in
> deeply held beliefs about the nature of the subject, the way students learn, and
> the role of the teacher. Attempts to change individual features are likely to
> have little effect on the overall system. The changes often get swallowed up or
> reshaped.
>
> (Stigler and Hiebert 1997: 19)

Reflecting on the issue . . .
You might want to undertake this task with a group of colleagues. Collect together a
set of around three mathematical activities or tasks. Try to get some diversity in
format, style and the nature of the problem. Now adapt each of them so they could fit
into a Japanese, French or Hungarian classroom. This might in some cases require
considerable adaptation. Consider, for example, using a standard set of routine
exercises that one usually finds in UK mathematics textbooks. This will require some
imagination and creativity!

There are other issues that are discussed below which impact directly on pupils'
access to the curriculum and the rhetorical justification that successive British
governments offer for their decisions.

How is British educational policy framed and is it likely to facilitate the learning of mathematics of all pupils?

In the previous section, I illustrated how successful mathematics teaching is
undertaken in other parts of the world and how this conflicts with the traditional
British view of education in particular, the manner in which the curriculum is
presented to pupils. In this section I consider how recent UK policy decisions have
emerged and I argue that the UK government, its agents and those who support its
view, have little real interest in genuine, and rational, change. I will look at just
two issues – the organisation of pupils into ability groups and the marking of
pupils' work.

Ability grouping

A previous (1997) UK government White Paper, *Excellence in Schools*, outlined
the British government's intention to

> modernise comprehensive education to create inclusive schooling which pro-
> vides a broad, flexible and motivating education that recognises the different
> talents of all children and delivers excellence for everyone.
>
> (DfEE 1997: 38)

These are laudable aims – indeed, notions of inclusivity parallel the constitutionally demanded equality of opportunity of France. However, there seems to be a contradiction between the aims of the White Paper – in particular to deliver excellence for all – and the suggestions it puts forward for how schools ought to go about achieving those aims.

The White Paper asserts that mixed-ability teaching has been proved ineffective and suggests that 'unless a school can demonstrate that it is getting better than expected results through a different approach, we do make the presumption that setting should be the norm in secondary schools' (DfEE 1997: 38). No evidence is offered either for the rejection of mixed ability or the advocacy of setting – these are presented as appeals to an obvious common sense. A similar position is adopted by the UK Office for Standards in Education (OFSTED), whose head, Her Majesty's Chief Inspector of Schools (HMCI), is obliged to produce an annual summary of school inspections. In his summary in 1995 he wrote, as if it is uncontentious, that effective teaching involves pupils being 'taught as a whole class, in groups and individually' with 'selective and effective use made of ability grouping' (OFSTED 1995: 27). Three years later HMCI asserts, unequivocally, that even at primary level, 'a very large proportion of the schools inspected demonstrated a clear trend of rising standards for pupils of all abilities, once the use of setting had become established' (OFSTED 1998c: 5). (Details of the reports can be found in OFSTED 1995, 1996, 1997, 1998a, 1998b and 1999a.)

Yet research from around the world – and evidence from the TIMSS studies – offers, overwhelmingly, the opposite perspective. When we look at the evidence we are clearly drawn to different conclusions from that of the White Paper Chief Inspector. Indeed, as Jo Boaler comments, 'there is little, if any, research anywhere in the world, that supports this notion' (Boaler 1997: 576; see also Jo Boaler and Dylan Wiliam's chapter in this volume). At best, according to Susan Hallam and Inji Toutounji, in a review of the relevant research, the evidence from international studies indicates that pupil grouping is not 'a key characteristic of effective schools' (Hallam and Toutounji 1996: 63). This review indicated that more important features of successful teaching are related, for example, to the learning environment itself, purposeful teaching, high expectations and positive reinforcement. More recently Judith Ireson and Susan Hallam (1999) indicated that attainment appears to be related to pupils' access to the curriculum. Interestingly, all these aspects were highlighted above in respect of effective mathematics teaching in other countries.

Indeed, several substantial reviews of the international literature pertaining to ability grouping have been undertaken over the last few years (see Cahan and Linchevski 1996; Linchevski and Kutschev 1998). One of the better known was performed by Robert Slavin (1990). His detailed review concluded that grouping by ability led to no effective difference in children's achievement and that this was consistent across different forms of grouping. In the few studies that showed some minor, but not statistically significant, differences the tendency was for able children in ability groups to attain higher than comparable children in heterogeneous groups, but that this tended to be at the expense of poorer performance of average and lower-ability children.

Other reviews, Laura Sukhnandan (1998) and Susan Hallam and Inji Toutounji (1996), for example, came to similar conclusions. The latter conclude that the 'research suggests that turning the clock back and reintroducing selective education or highly structured systems of streaming will not provide a solution to the problem of underachievement and may lead to increased alienation' (Hallam and Toutounji 1996: 68). Also, as Robert Slavin notes:

> if the effects of ability grouping on student achievement are zero, then there is little reason to maintain the practice . . . arguments in favor of ability grouping depend on assumptions about the effectiveness of grouping, at least for high achievers. In the absence of any evidence of effectiveness, these arguments cannot be sustained.
>
> (Slavin 1990: 492)

Teachers of mathematics in the UK have traditionally viewed 'ability' as the main determinant of pupil achievement. This, along with a perception of mathematics as a hierarchical, serial or cumulative subject, has led to the teaching of homogeneous ability groups (Ruthven 1987). So strong is this belief that, following the White Paper's exhortation to schools to group by ability, it was noted that

> in mathematics, however, relatively few subject departments have needed to change back to ability grouping as the majority have remained faithful to practices of selection, even when they have been the only subject department in their particular school to do so.
>
> (Boaler *et al.* 1998: 2)

Such practices conflict with the evidence above that mathematics is best taught to mixed-ability groups.

Marking pupils' work

A further area of contrasting international practice is in the different emphases placed on teachers' marking of pupils' books. It is only the English who take piles of books home for marking (Pepin 1996). In many countries, as is indicated above, children's work is marked in class when individuals share their solutions on the board; children take a significant responsibility for marking their work in class. This contrasts with advice given by schools' inspectors in England and is indicative of a British perspective on marking – as something that should be done independently of, rather than contemporaneously with, teaching. So firmly held is this belief that schools' inspectors are cautioned against being influenced by 'superficially positive features' such as the frequent marking of books by children themselves (OFSTED 1999b: 6). In respect of homework this advice is unfortunate because the evidence above suggests that where mathematics is taught effectively, homework, as a transitional device between lessons and focus for the public sharing of ideas, is an integral element of teaching. Used in this fashion homework demands a particular form of response if pupils' ideas are to be properly exploited. Collecting in books for marking not only undermines the structural significance of homework within a teaching programme, but also reinforces the pernicious belief that grades, not ideas, are what matters.

Conclusion

Changes in British educational practices are unlikely to happen overnight. Like all systems it is bound by traditions, beliefs and perspectives that will require substantial effort and persuasion if change is to be effected. So, what are those traditions and perspectives and what are their influences? At the risk of being accused of recycling old arguments I offer three. Inevitably there are others but I focus on these three in particular because, it seems to me, they represent peculiarly British perspectives that continue to shape this country's education in ways that distinguish it from other, more successful, systems.

The first tradition is that British education is more prone to greater political interference than comparable systems. Politicians, irrespective of what they might say, frequently seem less concerned with the creation of a genuinely educated electorate than they are with the development of policies that appeal to, or appease, the middle-class voter. Consequently much educational policy derives from a myth of effective schooling which suggests that ability grouping, frequent testing, rigorously enforced school uniform and regular marking are all significant contributors to learning. The TIMSS study shows that this is simply not the case, but this seems not to have mattered to successive British policymakers. Research has further suggested the schools that adopt these mythically valuable practices are more likely to attract the middle-class parents than those that do not (Gewirtz *et al.* 1995). Since pupils from middle-class backgrounds are usually more successful in ways that schools value (for reasons that are described elsewhere in this volume – see the chapters by Barry Cooper, Paul Dowling and Robyn Zevenbergen for example), having a preponderance of pupils from middle class backgrounds usually results in an apparently successful school. This perpetuates the myth – schools that group pupils by ability, test regularly, enforce school uniform and insist on teachers' formally marking books, tautologically become successful because they attract those very students whom the school system is set up to favour. Those schools that do not attract such pupils are presented by the colluding inspection process as therefore being unsuccessful.

The second tradition concerns the anti-intellectual culture which permeates many aspects of British life and which tends to ridicule those who see purpose in, or take pleasure from, education. We see this in various TV programmes – soap operas, comedies, etc. We should be concerned also that the British press, unlike that elsewhere, is dominated by tabloids that wield considerable social and political influence. Their editorial stances, their vocabulary and tone, serve constantly to reinforce the perspective that educated people are somehow different, odd or at least a little eccentric.

The third tradition stems from this country's imperial past and a jingoistic sense that it has little to learn from others. For example, the National Curriculum

for English expects pupils to study English literature rather than English trans-
lations of foreign writers. In other words, rather than invite pupils to engage with
the ideas of great writers, British pupils are presented with a restricted cultural diet
and systematically denied the learning experiences of their overseas peers. The
history National Curriculum offers little more than a token acknowledgement that
British history is contextualised within the broader experiences of a world beyond
its shores. The British tradition in respect of the teaching of modern foreign
languages, coupled with an expectation that all foreigners speak English anyway,
leaves the vast majority of adults too inadequately prepared or too embarrassed to
attempt communication with anyone other than another speaker of English. In
short, the curriculum presented to British pupils perpetuates the myth that Britain
is a significant global player to whom others should defer. One outcome of this
traditional viewpoint is a form of xenophobia that undermines this country's
relationships with its European partners, can often present Britain as a figure of fun
to our overseas colleagues and militates against its pupils operating within a global
rather than a parochial context.

   In closing, I hope that this chapter has challenged your thinking about the
teaching and learning of mathematics. I am not suggesting that all (or indeed any)
of the ills of the British pedagogical tradition might be overcome merely by
mirroring the practice of other countries – partly because one cannot simply
transplant cultural practices from one setting to another. Also, as I have indicated
in the few paragraphs above, there are cultural and political barriers to the
development of an effective and worthwhile mathematics pedagogy. However, I
hope the chapter has offered something that will excite you as a teacher and your
pupils as learners to the extent that, at times, participants' roles may be re-
appraised.

Invitation to reflect

To help you to reflect on some of the underlying issues in this chapter, I invite you
to try some mathematical tasks for yourself. This may not work for everyone, but
one of the more effective ways of developing my own teaching is through an
engagement with mathematical problems. As you work through each problem try
to consider how you might introduce it into your own teaching. What are the
implications for the organisation of the classroom? What changes would you need
to make to your everyday practices? What skills would pupils need to demonstrate
or develop in order to solve the problems?

Problem 1

The first problem is a question I saw given to a class of grade 6 (year 7) pupils in
Budapest.

> An isosceles triangle has one vertex at the point (1,3). The other vertices are
> also on grid points. If the area of the triangle is 9 units squared, then how
> many such triangles can be found?

This is not a simple problem – it demands that you do some work to solve it – although the mathematics needed to solve it is simple. Importantly it forces you to engage with a range of mathematical ideas and skills. Once you have finished you might like to consider these questions:

- What topics did you use to solve the problem?
- What advantages do such problems have when compared with a routine exercise?
- How do such problems fit within the framework described above?
- How many of your year 7 pupils could access the problem?
- How would you help those who can't?
- Can you construct something similar?

I saw the above task presented as a homework following a lesson on area of plane shapes. The next lesson saw a productive ten minutes in which several pupils described their approaches and the mathematics used. Not all had arrived at the full thirty-six solutions, but my impression was that all went home understanding how they could be derived. My impression, also, was that the teacher had decided that it would be too difficult at this stage to expect his pupils to explore whether there might have been any possible triangles not aligned with a vertical or horizontal axis.

- Does it matter if not all pupils manage to achieve all the solutions?
- Is it important that they all understand the process by which the solution might be obtained?

Problem 2

The second problem is my adaptation of one seen in a Japanese lesson and follows from some lessons on angle sums of triangles and straight lines.

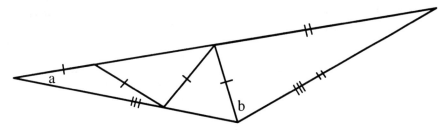

The picture shows one large isosceles triangle with four small ones inside it. If the angle at *a* is 21°, find the size of angle *b*.

Problem 3

The last problem came from the same lesson as the previous problem. It exemplifies a general result that, although not itself an object of study, provides a nice focus for a problem, which, I believe, embodies the principles outlined above.

The picture below is one large isosceles triangle comprising three smaller isosceles triangles. The task is to find the value of angle *a*.

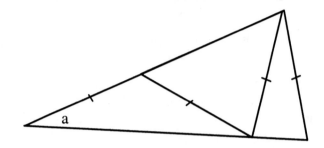

I offer no commentary on the last two problems. I leave you to decide what relevance or use they might have within your own teaching. It is my conjecture that they accord very well with the principles of the international framework and provide rich opportunities for all manner of mathematical thinking, development and consolidation.

In ending I invite you to take a straightforward question from an ordinary exercise and try to make it something more challenging, mathematically worthwhile and accessible to all.

Further suggested readings

I offer you three collections of edited papers that, in their totality, address a range of pertinent issues concerned with comparative studies in the teaching of mathematics. They are:

Kaiser, G., Luna, E. and Huntley, I. (eds) (1998) *International Comparisons in Mathematics Education*, London: Falmer Press. This book, which explores the teaching of mathematics in a variety of countries, also considers different aspects of the Third International Mathematics and Science Study (TIMSS). The TIMSS video study, for example, offers some fascinating insights into the teaching of mathematics in Japan, Germany and the United States. It is clear from the ideas presented that we can learn much from comparing the traditions and expectations of one country with those of another, although it is also clear that comparative studies are not beyond criticism and that generalities have to be carefully made and interpreted.

Hoyles, C., Morgan, C. and Woodhouse, G. (eds) (1999) *Rethinking the Mathematics Curriculum*, London: Falmer Press. This book looks at the mathematics curriculum from a variety of internationally informed perspectives. It reminds us not only that mathematics is conceived differently in different countries but also that respective national rationales for teaching it vary significantly. The book offers insights into the manner in which curricular decisions are justified and, significantly, warns that too many innovations in the past have failed because of their being too grounded in subjective accounts of individual teachers' lessons rather than sustained, systematic and generalisable research into the nature of effective teaching. Overall it offers the reader insights to challenge the view that mathematics is an international language – there may be partial agreements, but there are also substantial differences.

Jaworski, B. and Phillips, D. (eds) (1999) *Comparing Standards Internationally: Research and Practice in Mathematics and Beyond*, Oxford: Symposium Books. This book reminds us that comparative study is difficult and that the notion of standards itself is problematic. Despite the problems many of the chapters raise significant questions about the nature of effective mathematics teaching and show that what is effective in one context may not be in another. Significantly, there are chapters that offer particularly salient interpretations of the TIMSS findings and challenge any sense of complacency we may have as teachers of mathematics. In some regards the book is critical of British practices and offers some fundamental challenges to some of the long-held educational traditions. It is not always a comfortable read but it is worth it.

References

Andrews, P. (1995) 'Return to Budapest', *Mathematics Teaching* 151, 23–5.

Andrews, P. (1997) 'A Hungarian perspective on mathematics education: The results of a conversation with Sari Palfalvi, Eva Szeredi, Vera Sztrokay and Judit Torok', *Mathematics Teaching* 161, 14–17.

Andrews, P. (1999) 'Looking behind the rhetoric: some new insights from Hungary', *Mathematics Teaching* 167, 6–10.

Beaton, A., Mullis, I., Martin, M., Gonzalez, E., Kelly, D. and Smith, T. (1996) *Mathematics in the Middle School Years: IEA's Third International Mathematics and Science Study (TIMSS)*, Boston MA: Boston College.

Boaler, J. (1997) 'Setting, social class and the survival of the quickest', *British Educational Research Journal* 23(5), 575–95.

Boaler, J., Wiliam, D. and Brown, M. (1998) 'Students' experiences of ability grouping – dissatisfaction, polarisation and the construction of failure', paper presented to the *British Educational Research Association Annual Conference*, Queen's University, Belfast.

Cahan, S. and Linchevski, L. (1996) 'The cumulative effect of ability grouping on mathematical achievement: A longitudinal perspective', *Studies in Educational Evaluation* 22(1), 29–40.

Cogan, L. and Schmidt, W. (1999) 'An examination of instructional practices in six countries', in Kaiser, G., Luna, E. and Huntley, I. (eds), *International Comparisons in Mathematics Education*, London: Falmer Press, pp. 68–85.

DfEE (1997) *Excellence in Schools*, White Paper, London: Department for Education and Employment.

Gewirtz, S., Ball, S. and Bowe, R. (1995) *Markets, Choice and Equity in Education*, Buckingham: Open University Press.

Hallam, S. and Toutounji, I. (1996) 'What do we know about grouping pupils by ability?', *Education Review* 10(2), 62–70.

Harries, T. (1997) 'Reflections on a lesson in Kaposvar', *Mathematics Teaching* 161, 11–13.

Hatch, G. (1994) 'Coming up to Russian expectations', *Mathematics Teaching* 146, 29–32.

Hatch, G. (1999) 'It wouldn't be like that here!', *Mathematics Teaching* 168, 26–31.

Ireson, J. and Hallam, S. (1999) 'Raising standards: Is ability grouping the answer?', *Oxford Review of Education* 25(3), 343–58.

Jacobs, J., Makoto, Y., Stigler, J., and Fernandez, C. (1997) 'Japanese and American teachers' evaluations of mathematics lessons: A new technique for exploring beliefs', *Journal of Mathematical Behaviour* 16(1), 7–24.

Jennings, S. and Dunne, R. (1996) 'A critical appraisal of the National Curriculum by comparison with the French experience', *Teaching Mathematics and its Applications* 15(2), 49–55.

Kawanaka, T., Stigler, J. and Hiebert, J. (1999) 'Studying mathematics classrooms in Germany, Japan and the United States: Lessons from the TIMSS videotape study', in Kaiser, G., Luna, E. and Huntley, I. (eds), *International Comparisons in Mathematics Education*, London: Falmer Press, pp. 86–103.

Keitel, C. and Kilpatrick, J. (1999) 'The rationality and irrationality of international comparative studies', in Kaiser, G., Luna, E. and Huntley, I. (eds), *International Comparisons in Mathematics Education*, London: Falmer Press pp. 241–56.

Leung, F. (1995) 'The mathematics classroom in Beijing, Hong Kong and London', *Educational Studies in Mathematics* 29(3), 297–325.

Leung, F. (1999) 'The traditional Chinese views of mathematics and education: implications for mathematics education in the new millennium', in Hoyles, C., Morgan, C. and Woodhouse, G. (eds), *Rethinking the Mathematics Curriculum*, London: Falmer Press, pp. 240–7.

Lin, Fou-Lai (1988) 'Societal differences and their influence on children's mathematical understanding', *Educational Studies in Mathematics* 19, 471–97.

Lin, Fou-Lai and Tsao, Liang-Chi (1999) 'Exam maths re-examined', in Hoyles, C., Morgan, C. and Woodhouse, G. (eds) *Rethinking the Mathematics Curriculum*, London: Falmer Press, pp. 228–39.

Linchevski, L. and Kutscher, B. (1998) 'Tell me with whom you're learning, and I'll tell you how much you've learned: mixed-ability versus same-ability grouping in mathematics', *Journal for Research in Mathematics Education* 29(5), 533–54.

Monchablon, A. (1995) 'France', in Postlethwaite, N. (ed.), *International Encyclopaedia of National Systems of Education*, Oxford: Pergamon, pp. 331–9.

OFSTED (Office for Standards in Education) (1995) *The Annual Report of Her Majesty's Chief Inspector of Schools: Standards and Quality in Education 1993/94*, London: HMSO.

OFSTED (1996) *The Annual Report of Her Majesty's Chief Inspector of Schools: Standards and Quality in Education 1994/95*, London: HMSO.

OFSTED (1997) *The Annual Report of Her Majesty's Chief Inspector of Schools: Standards and Quality in Education 1995/96*, London: HMSO.

OFSTED (1998a) *The Annual Report of Her Majesty's Chief Inspector of Schools: Standards and Quality in Education 1996/97*, London: HMSO.

OFSTED (1998b) *Secondary Education 1993–97: A Review of Secondary Schools in England*, London: HMSO.

OFSTED (1998c) *Setting in Primary Schools*, London: OfSTED.

OFSTED (1999a) *The Annual Report of Her Majesty's Chief Inspector of Schools: Standards and Quality in Education 1997/98*, London: HMSO.

OFSTED (1999b) *Inspecting Subjects and Aspects 11–18: Mathematics*, London: OFSTED.

Pepin, B. (1996) 'An ethnographic study of mathematics teachers in England, France and Germany', paper presented to the British Educational Research Association Conference, Lancaster University.

Pepin, B. (1998) 'Curriculum, cultural traditions and pedagogy: Understanding the work of teachers in England, France and Germany', paper presented to the European Conference for Educational Research, Ljubljana, Slovenia.

Pepin, B. (1999) 'The influence of national cultural traditions on pedagogy: Classroom practices in England, France and Germany', in Leach, J. and Moon, B. (eds), *Learners and Pedagogy*, London: Paul Chapman, pp. 124–35.

Prais, S. (1999) 'How did English schools and pupils really perform in the 1995 international comparisons in mathematics?', in Jaworski, B. and Phillips, D. (eds), *Comparing Standards Internationally: Research and Practice in Mathematics and Beyond*, Oxford: Symposium Books, pp. 79–118.

Ruthven, K. (1987) 'Ability stereotyping in mathematics', *Educational Studies in Mathematics* 18, 243–53.

Ruthven, K. (1999) 'Reconstructing professional judgement in mathematics education: From good practice to warranted practice', in Hoyles, C., Morgan, C. and Woodhouse, G. (eds), *Rethinking the Mathematics Curriculum*, London: Falmer Press, pp. 203–16.

Schmidt, W. H., Jorde, D., Cogan, L. S., Barrier, E., Gonzalo, I., Moser, U., Shimizu, K., Sawada, T., Valverde, G. A., McKnight, C., Prawat, R. S., Wiley, D. E., Raizen, S. A., Britton, E. D. and Wolfe, R. (1996) *Characterizing Pedagogical Flow*, Dordrecht: Kluwer.

Slavin, R. (1990) 'Achievement effects of ability grouping in secondary schools: a best evidence synthesis', *Review of Educational Research* 60(3), 471–99.

Stevenson, H. (1999) 'The case study project of TIMSS', in Kaiser, G., Luna, E. and Huntley, I. (eds), *International Comparisons in Mathematics Education*, London: Falmer Press, pp. 104–20.

Stigler, J. and Hiebert, J. (1997) 'Understanding and improving classroom mathematics instruction: An overview of the TIMSS video study' *Phi Delta Kappan* 79(1), 14–21.

Stigler, J. and Perry, M. (1990) 'Mathematics learning in Japanese, Chinese and American classrooms', in Stigler, J., Shweder, R. and Herdt, G. (eds) *Cultural Psychology: Essays on Comparative Human Development*, Cambridge: Cambridge University Press, pp. 328–53.

Stigler, J., Fernandez, C. and Yoshida, M. (1996) 'Traditions of school mathematics in Japanese and American elementary classrooms', in Steffe, L., Nesher, P., Cobb, P., Goldin, G. and Greer, B. (eds), *Theories of Mathematical Learning*, Mahwah, NJ: Lawrence Erlbaum, pp. 149–75.

Stigler, J., Lee, Shin-Ying and Stevenson, H. (1987) 'Mathematics classrooms in Japan, Taiwan, and the United States', *Child Development* 58(5), 1272–85.

Sukhnandan, L. (1998) *Streaming, Setting and Grouping by Ability: A Review of the Literature*, Slough: NFER.

Whitman, N. and Lai, M. (1990) 'Similarities and differences in teachers' beliefs about effective teaching of mathematics: Japan and Hawaii', *Educational Studies in Mathematics* 21(1), 71–81.

Wiliam, D. (1998) 'Making international comparisons: The Third International Mathematics and Science Study', *British Journal of Curriculum and Assessment* 8(3), 33–7.

Subject Index

Since this entire book is about mathematics and mathematics education, the word 'mathematics' does not appear very much in this index. Almost all of the index entries could be considered as being "mathematics and ...". Italicised entries indicate entire chapters.

Author Index

This index contains those authors or institutions whose work is cited in the text. Where reference is made to a multiple authored work, an index entry is only made to the first named author. This index does not contain those sources listed in the Further Suggested Readings section of each chapter, unless their work have been specifically cited in the text. The philosophical and mathematical question of whether the index reference should be included in the index itself, has been overlooked and ignored!